THE HOMILIST:

A Series of Sermons for Preachers and Laymen.

ORIGINAL AND SELECTED.

BY ERWIN HOUSE, A.M.

New York:
PUBLISHED BY CARLTON & PORTER,
200 MULBERRY-STREET.
1860.

PREFACE.

Some five years since, through the agency of a London friend, I came into possession of a large number of English serial publications, chiefly of a theological type. It was suggested that, by a revision, and, in some cases, by a reuniting of certain discourses contained in these numbers, a volume of acceptable character could be prepared for American readers. The work was accordingly undertaken, and prosecuted at intervals during the five years referred to. The result is the present volume.

While the homilies or sermons furnished are not as long, averaging but about seven pages each, nor yet as elaborate as some modern printed discourses, they are not in the technical sense sketches or bony skeletons. It would be a violation of the principles of good taste to pass complimentary remarks on the few original specimens which occur in the body of the work; at the same time the reader must allow me to say of the greater number of edited homilies, that they possess the elements of *suggestiveness* in a degree quite above ordinary. It is scarcely possible for the mind to examine them without being quickened.

For the sake of presenting as great a number of homilies as possible, almost all anecdote and amplified illustration have been dropped. It is vastly easier, as the experience, I believe, of most ministers will bear witness, to find anecdotes than thoughts. A want of the age is *things*, not words—healthy saplings, just rising into light and "struggling into shape," not lifeless limbs, however exquisitely carved or brilliantly polished. The former *may* grow, the latter *must* rot.

My acknowledgments are specially due to Rev. D. Thomas, Rev. Joseph Parker, Rev. J. Page Pigg, Rev. Baldwin Brown, and others of England, for many valuable suggestions, and much of the matter of the volume. Persons who are familiar with the sermons of the late F. W. Robertson, A.M., will observe the transference of part of one of his discourses in the homily on the Prodigal and his Brother.

While the work is free from sectarian bias, care has been exercised to maintain a healthy evangelical tone. That the true-hearted, the hard-working, and the genuine Gospel teacher, as well as the earnest and thoughtful layman in all denominations, may find the volume worthy of attention and study, is my highest wish. E. H.

CINCINNATI, *April*, 1860.

CONTENTS.

THE HOMILIST.

HOMILY I.

WHAT HINDERS THE GOSPEL?—THE NEGATIVE ASPECT.

We . . . suffer all things, lest we should hinder the Gospel of Christ.
1 Corinthians ix, 12.

There are three thoughts in the text which it would be well briefly to notice before passing on to the general question, What hinders the Gospel?

First, *It is possible for man to hinder the Gospel:* "Lest we should hinder the Gospel." What an awful power is this with which we are endowed! The Gospel—the light and power of the world!—can we arrest its course, and prevent it from penetrating the homes and hearts of men? The Gospel—the river of life!—can we block up its channel, and stop its flow, and leave the world to droop and die of drought? Had the Almighty given us power to arrest the laws of nature, roll back the orbs of heaven, launch the thunderbolt, and kindle the lightning, would it have been equal in importance to this power of hindering the Gospel?

Secondly, *There is danger even of good men hindering*

the Gospel. It is no less an individual than Paul, a servant of Christ, an inspired apostle, that is afraid of being guilty of hindering the Gospel. He felt that there was a fearful liability, even in him. It is a solemn thought that sometimes good men and Churches can obstruct the progress of the Saviour's spiritual empire in the world.

Thirdly, *To hinder the Gospel is an immense evil:* "We suffer all things lest we should hinder the Gospel." What did the apostle suffer? He tells us in this very chapter that he forewent the enjoyments of domestic life: "Have we not power to lead about a sister, a wife, as well as other apostles?" As if he had said: "I have an undoubted right to take, *at your expense*, with me in my journeyings, a wife, whose delicate, gentle, and affectionate converse would cheer my spirit under my apostolic trials, and increase the comforts of my itinerant life. But this privilege I forego, lest I should hinder the Gospel." He forewent his claims to their support. "Who goeth a warfare at his own charges?" etc. "If we have sown unto you spiritual things, is it a great thing if we shall reap of your carnal things?" He had a divine right to claim ample support from the Churches, both for himself and family, if he chose to have a family; but he says: "Nevertheless, we have not used this power; but suffer all things, lest we should hinder the Gospel of Christ." What did he suffer? Thus he informs us, 2 Cor. xi, 23–31: "Are they ministers of Christ? (I speak as a fool) I am more; in labors more abundant, in stripes above measure, in prisons more frequent, in deaths oft. Of the Jews five times received I forty stripes save one. Thrice was I beaten with rods, once was I stoned, thrice I suffered shipwreck, a night and a day I have been in the deep; in journeyings often, in perils of waters, in perils of robbers, in perils by mine own countrymen, in perils by the heathen, in perils in the city, in perils in the wilderness, in perils in the sea, in perils among false brethren; in weariness and painfulness, in watchings often, in hunger and thirst, in fastings often, in cold and nakedness. Besides those things that are without, that which cometh upon me daily, the care of all the Churches. Who is weak, and I am not weak? who is offended, and I burn not? If I must needs glory, I will glory of the things which concern mine infirmities. The God and Father of our Lord Jesus Christ, which is blessed for evermore, knoweth that I lie not."

Here we learn that he suffered all things, all privations, persecutions, exposure to death in its most terrific forms, lest he should hinder the Gospel of Christ. He knew of no greater evil than this; he shrank from it more than from death, he deprecated it as the evil of evils.

The text assumes that *the Gospel is hindered*, and the assumption is a recognized fact in the Christian world. For eighteen long centuries Christianity has been here in its present form, and yet how few of the earth's population have heard the "glad tidings" of salvation, and how fewer still have heard, and are at this moment experiencing its saving power. "Darkness yet covers the earth, and gross darkness the people;" and "the dark places of the earth are full of the habitations of cruelty."

The population of the globe is estimated in round numbers at one thousand millions. Of these three hundred and thirty millions are the followers of Boodh, adherents of a system of utter atheism, which acknowledges no God, no Redeemer, no resurrection from the dead; one hundred millions are the worshipers of Brahma, Vishnu, and Siva, the most subtle and sophistical of all the religions of the heathen, and at the same time the most utterly obscene and licentious; one hundred and fifty millions are Mohammedans; one hundred millions are African idolaters, worshiping sticks, stones, or animals, as fetiches, and given up to the most debasing idolatry; ten millions are idolatrous inhabitants of the islands of the Pacific and Indian Oceans; sixty millions are connected with the Greek Church, and though versed in its corrupt creeds and image worship, know not the true God; one hundred and fifty millions are Roman Catholics, and though individuals among them may even through its mummeries have found Christ, yet the great masses are ignorant of him. Finally, one hundred millions are nominally Protestants, but how small a portion of these are really Christians!

Of the twenty-eight millions of the people of the United States, of the city of New York, of Boston, of Baltimore, of Cincinnati, of St. Louis, of Chicago, of San Francisco, how many are converted? One half, one fourth, one eighth, or one tenth? Men have been questioning of late whether Christianity has more genuine disciples now, in proportion to the population of the world, than she had in the apostolic age. Our own opinion would be an answer in the affirmative. We honestly think the world is growing better, not worse. It is better now than it was a hundred years ago, a great deal better. In the language of one of the purest and ablest men of America, Rev. Albert Barnes:

"The world is becoming better every year, every month, every day. In its progress society takes hold of all that is valuable, or that constitutes real improvement, and will not let it die. That which is worthless is superseded by that which is useful; that which is injurious and wrong is dropped by the way; that which goes permanently into the good order of the world alone is retained. There is more love of truth than there was sixty years ago, there is more science, there are more of the comforts of life, there is more freedom, there is more religion. There will be more in the next age than there is now, and so on to the end of time. Christianity never had so firm a hold on the intelligent faith of mankind as it has now. It will have a firmer hold on the next age, and will extend its triumphs till the world, the whole world, shall be converted to the Saviour. Old men often feel that the world is growing worse. I have not that feeling now; by the grace of God I shall never have it. I intend to hold on to the conviction which I now have at this mature period of my life, that the world is becoming better; I design to cherish this conviction when I die. I believe that the whole world will be converted to truth and righteous ness, and if I should be spared to that period when I should be willing to speak of myself as 'old and gray-headed,' I intend that there shall be at least one aged man who will take a cheerful and hopeful view of the world as he leaves it."

But while Christianity is making progress in the earth, and while its ultimate triumph is certain, is it not true that that progress might be greater? Is it not a fact that there are hindering causes at work, and ought we not to examine and see what these causes are, and how they are at work? So intimately related is the question to all that is deep and tender in Christian consciousness that we cannot pass it by unconsidered.

In order to clear away all misconceptions and to reach what we consider the *chief hinderance*, let us look first at the NEGATIVE side:

First, *The hinderance is not to be traced to the will or sovereignty of God.* It is sometimes said that the want of success in evangelical enterprises is owing to the decrees of heaven. If it can be made out that it is the sovereign WILL of God that Christianity should remain thus limited in its influence, and that millions of every age should pass into eternity without a saving knowledge of the truth; then it is for us assuredly to bow with reverent submission to his decrees, and remain content with the present state of things.

But is it God's will that men should perish? Is it his will that millions of men should glide down the stream of time and take the fatal plunge over the cataract into a miserable eternity? How shall we ascertain his will on this subject? Shall we *consult nature?* Do we find in nature any provision for any particular class of men to the exclusion of others? Are not his tender mercies over all the works of his hands? And is it likely that he who opens the treasures of his bountihood to all in nature, could by his decree exclude the great bulk of the race from the blessings of eternal life? Shall we consult the history of his *conduct with mankind?* When men began to multiply in the antediluvian age, and sink into the depths of ignorance and crime, did he not raise up Enoch and Noah to call their cotemporaries to repentance, and to invite them to mercy? When, after the deluge, men, as they grew in numbers, increased in crime and degenerated into the lowest impiety and vice, did he not call Abraham, as an evangelist, to preach the Gospel in the very darkest parts of the known world? Was not the Levitical institution, with its temple and priests and prophets and splendid ritualism, a kind of great *world lamp*, kindled and set up by Almighty God in the center of the race, and by him kept burning for long centuries in order to light up the earth with the beams of saving mercy?

Did not Jesus distinctly teach that he came to save, not any particular men, but universal man? What was the commission of the apostles? "Go ye into *all* the world, and preach the Gospel to *every* creature." Is not this race wide? Is not the language of both Testaments favorable to the salvation of all men, of all who are willing to be saved?

Isaiah xlv, 22; "Look unto me, and be ye saved, all the ends of the earth: for I am God, and there is none else."

Isaiah lv, 1: "Ho, every one that thirsteth, come ye to the waters, and he that hath no money, come ye, buy, and eat; yea, come, buy wine and milk without money and without price."

Matt. xi, 28: "Come unto me, all ye that labor, and are heavy laden, and I will give you rest."

John vii, 37: "In the last day, that great day of the feast, Jesus stood and cried, saying, If any man thirst, let him come unto me and drink."

Rev. xxii, 17: "And the Spirit and the bride say, Come. And let him that heareth say, Come. And let him that is athirst come. And whosoever will, let him take the water of life freely."

We call the whole history of God's conduct toward our kind to prove what, in words, he often declares: "*That he has no pleasure in the death of a sinner, but desires that he should turn unto him and live.*" Wherever then the impediment to the universal diffusion of the Gospel may be, it is not in the decrees of Heaven. The idea finds no sanction in the fair deductions of intellect, no sympathy in the genuine intuitions of the human soul, no record in the bright book of God. The scheme of salvation is offered as freely to the whole world as the light of heaven, or the rains that burst on the mountains, or the swellings of broad rivers and streams, or the bubblings of fountains in the deserts.

"But," says one, "if God wills the salvation of all mankind, is it not a proof of the weakness or impotence of his will that all are not instantaneously converted?" Our reply in brief is, that God deals not with mind as with matter. His power in the material universe is resistless. He wills the existence of worlds, and worlds spring into being. He wills the destruction of worlds, and worlds at once disappear. But in the moral department of his universe resistless force is an absurdity in idea, an impossibility in fact. A man pleases to swear; God can *compel* him not to swear, but in the act moral mind would be extinguished. It seems to us an impossibility to keep mind moral, and yet to act upon it resistlessly. Moral force alone, the force of truth and love, can act upon moral mind, and the characteristic and perfection of that force is *resistibility.*

Secondly, *The hinderance is not to be resolved into the restricted necessity for the Gospel.* If vast portions of the human family can be shown not really to require the Gospel; if they are found able to fulfill their obligations, rightly to serve their Maker, reach their destiny, and realize the perfect blessedness of their being without it, we may then find the hinderance in the feeling that the world will not have what it does not need, a superfluity; and we might thus justly content ourselves with the present position of the Gospel. But, alas! all evidence is against the supposition. That all mankind require Christianity as the most urgent necessity of their being, is incontrovertibly attested by two facts: (1.) That the happiness of mankind everywhere depends upon moral goodness; and, (2.) That moral goodness is nowhere found where Christianity is not. *These are facts,* ungainsayable facts. The philosophy of our nature confesses them, all history attests them, all credible travelers report their truth. Merchants read them in every market, sailors in every port, statesmen in every kingdom, missionaries in every district of the populated world.

The Bible, our ultimate authority, places the world's need of the Gospel beyond debate. It affirms that it is the only means of pardon, the only force to regenerate, the only balm to heal, the only power to enlighten, emancipate, elevate, and save.

Thirdly, *The hinderance is not to be found in the limited fitness of the Gospel.* If we should find that Christianity is only suitable to a small section of the race, and that for the great bulk it is entirely unfitted, there would be a sufficient reason to account for its present narrow influence. But is its adaptation restricted? If it does not suit all men it must be either because of some *natural* or *acquired* peculiarity of mind. Is there anything so *naturally* peculiar as to render that Gospel, which is suitable to some, unfit for others? Happily, modern missions yield a clear and decisive response to this question. They show, beyond doubt, that the Gospel is alike fitted to the intellectual and moral constitutions of all men; that the dreamy Hindoo, the lethargic Chinese, the obtuse Hottentot, and the savage Polynesian, are as susceptible of its influence as the native of America or England.

But is there any *acquired* peculiarity which would render the Gospel unfit to some? Are there men who become so intelligent and philosophic as to render the Gospel unsuited to them? Do men in the progress of intelligence outgrow it, as they have outgrown other systems that once had a hold upon mankind? Does the advance of intelligence tend to remove man from the fitness of the Gospel to him? We think not. While Christianity is suited to mind in its very lowest stage of culture, to the slave in his plantation hovel, it is also suited to mind in its very highest state of culture and knowledge—the philosopher in his study, the professor in the university. Let knowledge spread, let the mind of the world rise in breadth, clearness, and amount of its ideas; let schools multiply, let the streams of literature flow copiously into every dwelling; all this will but enhance the facilities for the diffusion of Christianity. Paul, in his evangelizing mission, seemed to recognize this. He went not to barbarous hordes, and to men without culture, but to Corinth, Ephesus, Rome, and Athens, the centers of civilization, the seats of literature and science. We cannot, therefore, find a cause for the limited influence of the Gospel in any supposed restriction of its fitness to all mankind, for no such restriction exists.

Fourthly, *The hinderance is not to be found exclusively in the depravity of the heathen world.* It is frequently in the pulpit and out of it that we hear the remark: Such are the mighty and terrible prejudices and darkness of heathens that the Gospel can progress but little among them. We grant, of course, that human depravity is an obstruction; but, as it is found in the unchristianized world, it is not by any means the only hinderance, nor yet so potent a one as at first sight would appear, and as is popularly supposed. At any rate there are two things that go very far toward showing that human depravity is not *sufficient* to account for its limited influence: (1.) *That Christianity is a system divinely constructed for the* VERY PURPOSE OF OVERCOMING *this depravity.* Christianity is a revelation neither made nor designed for innocent and holy beings, but for the corrupt and guilty; it is a reformative and purifying system. Had it been nothing but a system of natural religion, a simple theism, or a believing in the existence of a God, we might have been justified in referring its limited success to the depravity of the sinner. But, being a divinely organized system to grapple with and master this depravity, we can only refer its limited influence to the depravity of those to whom it is addressed in the same way as you refer the failure of a specific medicine to the particular disease for which it is intended.

Chemists tell us that common saleratus is an infallible antidote for corrosive sublimate. Suppose ten men to swallow the sublimate, and immediately on swallowing are presented with the remedy; six recover and four die. Why? Because the six take the remedy according to orders, and are at once relieved; while the four, incredulous as to the powers of the saleratus, simply taste it, or refuse it altogether. The Gospel is preached to ten men, and its character as a sovereign specific is fully described; six of the number embrace the truth in the love of it, and are saved; but the remaining four decline it through perverseness of will, or pride of heart, and in the end perish. Would any one affirm that Christianity was a failure in the case of the four because of its inherent defects? Rather would not the verdict be, the four men died because of their determination not to use the specific in the way the six did?

(2.) Another thing which would show that the depravity of this unconverted world is not sufficient to account for the limited influence of Christianity, is the fact *that this depravity did not prevent its wide diffusion in the first ages of the Church.* History tells us that before the close of the third century Christianity had penetrated every part of the then known world. The celebrated Origen declares that in all parts of the world, and throughout all Greece, and in all other nations, there were innumerable and immense multitudes who, having left the laws of their country and those whom they esteemed gods, had given themselves up to the law of Moses and the religion of Christ. Christianity about this time seemed to have had its hand upon the heart of the world; it "sat on thrones," was the sovereign power in society, the empress of states. Was the depravity that resisted it in every step to this wide-spread dominion weaker than the depravity of subsequent ages? Who that has read Suetonius Tranquillus will say that the world has seen a more depraved century than the first of the Christian era? Human nature, gorged with iniquity, was bloated and brutalized to the lowest depths. It seemed as if Pluto had emerged from the abyss of eternal night, escorted by all the vengeful spirits of the lower world, by all the furies of passion and insatiable cupidity, by the bloodthirsty demons of lust and murder to establish his visible empire and erect his throne forever on the earth. Going forth into the midst of this pollution, attacking the terrible idolatry, skepticism, bigotry, and sensuality that everywhere prevailed, it fell like an electric stroke on mankind, traversing all parts of the world with the rapidity of lightning, and triumphing in every struggle with the human heart. If the depravity of that first era did not hinder its progress, why should the depravity of the present times?

Fifthly, *The hinderance is not to be explained on the principle that Christianity is preliminary to the advent of another system which is to supersede this.* Some tell us that a *miraculous* economy is to succeed the present Gospel dispensation, by which the world is to be converted without much, if any, of human effort. But where is the authority for such a theory? Does the *universal law of human progress*, which is an ascending from the material to the spiritual, from the particular to the general, from the local and evanescent to the universal and eternal, and which Paul describes first as natural, and afterward that which is spiritual, sanction such an hypothesis? It is superfluous to write the *no.* Does the theory provide *a more effective system of means for regenerating men?* Nay! it gives us no means suitable to effect a reformation at all. It gives us its miracles, but what converting power is there in them? Miracles have tried and failed. If miracles could convert, how came the millions, led forth by Moses from Egypt, to die infidels? "They could not enter into the promised land because of their unbelief." And why, too, were not the population of Judea made Christians by the miraculous ministry of Christ? Judea was the theater of stupendous miracles for ages, and yet its inhabitants through successive ages were *moral infidels.*

HOMILY II.

WHAT HINDERS THE GOSPEL—THE POSITIVE ASPECT.

Thus much for the negative side of the question. If neither the sovereignty of God, nor the limited necessity or fitness of the Gospel, nor yet the depravity of the heathen world, can be alleged as the real hindering causes of Christianity in the world, what is the *real* hinderance? We think we can find the chief if not the whole obstruction in one word, a WRONG REPRESENTATION of the Gospel, a holding of "the truth of God in unrighteousness."

In Judges i, 19, we learn the following: "And the Lord was with Judah; and he drove out the inhabitants of the mountains; but could not drive out the inhabitants of the valley, because they had chariots of iron." Here we have stated God's general plan of procedure with man, which is, that *he frequently makes human agency the condition of his own action; and that so entirely does the Almighty abide by this plan that if the required human agency is not put forth he will not work.* The statement is emphatic that God *could not* drive out the inhabitants of the valley, because they, the inhabitants of the valley, "had chariots of iron." We are not to suppose that these chariots of iron were too strong for Almighty God. He could have shattered them and the mountains around them by a simple act of his will. But these "chariots of iron" were objects of terrible fear to the Israelites; they so discouraged and frightened them that they would not do the part which God designed them to do; and because God would not violate his own plan he "*could not* drive them out." God's plan is the best, and he cannot deviate from the best. Now, the plan by which he promotes the circulation of the Gospel among men is most clearly revealed in the Bible, and it is simply this: *A proper representation, not a simple profession, of it by man.* The divine idea is to be reflected on man through man. Good men are the orbs which God holds in his right hand in order to reflect the sun-rays of his redemptive love upon the world. This treasure he has "put in earthen vessels." The God-man, Jesus Christ, brought the Gospel idea into the world at the first. Human nature, in the life of Jesus, gave a true expression of it to the race.

"Touched with a sympathy within,
He knows our feeble frame;
He knows what sore temptations mean,
For he hath felt the same."

Before he left the world Christ intrusted the representation of the Gospel to his disciples, and charged them to be faithful. Had they not manifested it the world would have lost it; or had they *mis*represented it the world would have suffered by it. But they were men who not only made a profession of religion; they showed forth the fruit, and thousands felt its life-giving and transforming power. The disciples in their turn, before they left the world, charged their successors, "in the sight of God," to commit "to faithful men," who would be able to teach others also, "the things which they had heard of them." Thus through man the Gospel came into the world at first, and through man it has ever since been sustained; and this is manifestly the plan of God for its propagation.

Why the great Author of the Gospel should proceed on such a plan, should leave the promotion of the Gospel to depend upon man's representation of it, is a question which, if it were proper, it is not necessary for you or me to settle. I do not know why it is that the grass in the valleys and the trees on the mountain are made to depend on the sunlight and the falling rain for their beauty and development. I suppose that God *could* have so arranged the material universe, or at least that portion of it which we occupy, as to cause a tree even to grow without the shower. He *could* make a perfect tree in an hour, in a moment, by a volition; but he does not, and it is not proper that I should concern myself about the question, Why is the growth of the vegetable world such as it is? Nor is it proper for either you or myself to spend time in discussing the question, Why has the progress of the Gospel in the earth been made to depend on the efforts and the agency of man? It is enough for us to know, as the reasons of his procedure in any case, that as his nature is LOVE, the ultimate reason of every act is some benevolent idea. LOVE is the planning genius of the universe; it frames and fashions all. It is the contriver of all divine contrivances, the inventive faculty of God. Nor is it difficult to see love in the plan which he has furnished of extending Christianity in the earth. What an honor does it confer on human nature to make it the reflector and exponent of divine ideas! You, having felt the blessed effects of the Gospel in your own spirit, are intrusted with its representation and recommendation to others, and how now are your liveliest and kindliest sympathies kindled for their welfare! The language of your heart, in its gushing fullness, is:

"O that the world might taste and see
The riches of his grace;
The arms of love that compass me
Would all mankind embrace."

And how full, on the other hand, of thankfulness and love are the hearts of those whom you have been instrumental in saving! Thus the greatest social harmony among men is promoted, and thus the source of human happiness is increased.

Three general remarks may suffice to show that there has

been enough of *wrong* representation of the Gospel to account for its present limited influence.

Observe, then:

I. THAT THE GOSPEL REGARDS THE CEREMONIAL AS SUBORDINATE TO THE DOCTRINAL. If this is so, a *mere ritualistic* manifestation of the Gospel is a wrong representation. Though the Old Testament had many rites, the New Testament has only two—baptism and the Lord's Supper. But the rites of both the Old and New Testaments were intended to answer the same thing in the economy of revelation, namely, to shadow forth doctrines. This is evident from three considerations. First. That the great design of the Bible is to improve the moral character of man. In the language of the Old Testament, it is "to take away the heart of stone, and to give a heart of flesh;" and in the language of the New, it is "to create him anew in Christ Jesus, unto good works." It is to direct the sympathies into new channels, the will to new purposes, the faculties to new engagements; to inspire the whole soul with a new life, and turn its every sentiment and energy God-ward. Secondly. In the nature of the case this can only be accomplished by the presentation of reformative ideas—ideas adapted to effect the desired change. No priestly manipulations, no burning of incense, no incantations, nothing apart from *ideas* can effect a change in man's moral character. All reformations grow out of thoughts. He who changes his course of conduct simply because he is told to do it, acts contrary to his rational nature. "Whatsoever is not of faith is of sin"—sin against our make as men. As the soul glides along the warm and swelling sea of feeling, it can only be turned to new points of the moral compass by them. Thirdly. That the rites of revelation are exquisitely fitted to convey reformative ideas. All the purifications and sacrifices under the law, as well as the two "ordinances," as they are called in the Gospel, are a kind of pictorial, and therefore popularly impressive, representation of two great reformative doctrines; namely, that man's nature is so thoroughly corrupt as to require the application of an extraneous agency in order to renovate it; and his sinfulness against his Maker is so heinous as to require the death of another for its expiation. The ritualism of the Bible, which in its first period was multiform and gorgeous, is like a series of pictures, some highly elaborated, and some more sketchy; but the subjects of them all are too palpable to be mistaken; they are these reformative doctrines. Every stroke and shade is designed to bring them out in their bold and majestic proportions.

If, then, the ceremonies of the Bible are nothing but the *symbols* of its doctrines, a ritualistic or a *sensuous* manifestation of the Gospel is a wrong or *mal*-representation of it. By the word ritualistic we mean the representing of ceremonies as doing that which doctrines cannot accomplish; representing them not as vehicles through which to convey divine thoughts, but as vehicles through which to convey some *mystic grace*. We mean the exalting of ceremonies above truths; attaching more importance to the form than the substance, the painting than the subject, the means than the end. We mean the appealing more to the sensuous than to the spiritual part of human nature; lodging religion in the eye and the ear, rather than in the heart; ministering to the senses rather than the soul.

But has such an improper representation of the Gospel ever been made as this? Ask history. For nine long centuries this was almost the only representation the Gospel had in Europe. Rites were multiplied and magnified until almost every ray of doctrinal truth was obscured. The middle ages are called the "dark ages;" and properly so, for the cloud of ceremonies became too dense for the pure light of Christianity to penetrate. Nor did the Reformation terminate this state of things; it only swept, as it were, some small clouds from the religious sky. In the Roman Church and the Greek Church, and in even some Protestant Churches, how much ritualism we still have! Well may we exclaim, "The light shineth in darkness, and the darkness comprehendeth it not!" Under the sable shades of forms and ceremonies "the light of life" is hid.

Observe again:

II. That the Gospel regards the doctrinal as subservient or ministering to the promotion of the ethical. We use the word ethical in the broadest and fullest sense of moral philosophy, as meaning *all that pertains to human conduct and duty.* And if the proposition be true, a simple *theological* manifestation of the Gospel is a wrong representation. Christianity consists mainly of two elements—*doctrines* and *precepts*, subjects for faith and rules for life—theology and morality. In instituting a comparison between these two elements, we would not be understood as intending to depreciate in the least the importance of true doctrine. *True doctrine is vital to all true morality.* Doctrines and precepts are rays from the same eternal sun of truth; the former, however, throwing their radiance upward, revealing the vast heavens that encircle us, and impressing us with ideas of infinitude; the latter flowing down upon our earthly path, and guiding our feet into the way of life. Of what use would the sun be to us if all its rays streamed *upward*, unfolding the boundless blue, and none reached our earthly sphere to show us how to act? The theology of the Bible is useless to a man *unless it changes his heart and molds his life anew.*

Now that the doctrinal is made subservient to the moral or practical is clear from the following considerations:

First. From the teachings of the New Testament, Christ's preaching was pre-eminently practical. Read his sermon upon the mount, and observe from the beginning to the close what special prominence he gives to the life and conduct. The apostles in this respect closely followed the example of their Master. Paul is the only one who seems to give himself to doctrinal discussion to any great extent, but even he is ever careful to make his doctrines bear on practical life. He exhorts Timothy to the "holding of faith and a good conscience." He would not have doctrines merely intellectually held, but held always with "a good conscience." He looked upon doctrines as a means to originate and "maintain good works."

Secondly. From the relations of Christian doctrine to the springs of human life. There are doctrines in science, like the axioms of mathematics, that have little or no relation to human feelings and impulses, the springs of human conduct.

You believe that two and two make four, that four multiplied by four makes sixteen, but neither makes any impression on your heart. Such truths have no power whatever to affect the moral character of your every-day life. Not so with the doctrines of the Gospel; they have a relation to every sentiment of your spiritual nature. The doctrines concerning God, and Christ, and man touch you at every point. The sense of advantage, the sense of right, the sense of God, the sense of an after life are the mightest impulses of the soul; and upon all these do the doctrines of the Gospel bear. They are heart-chords which doctrines can either set to music or wake to thunder. You bury a friend, perhaps your wife or your first-born child. Blinded with tears you stand by the grave's mouth, and as the clods fall on the coffin below, your faith looks up, and a voice falls on your ear, "I am the resurrection and the life." As you turn away to mingle in the conflicts of life, does not the belief in your heart that you and your loved ones shall meet again, shape, and modify, and change your life? Observe further, in proof that the doctrinal is made subservient to the practical, that,

Thirdly. Doctrines are useless to any man unless they do *promote a holy life.* Let a man be thoroughly acquainted with every part of the Bible, let him understand every principle in its relation to the whole circle of truth, let his theology be as correct and comprehensive as that of the highest angel student in the universe, yet if his life remains unreformed and unsanctified by his knowledge, his theological attainments would only swell his responsibility, and aggravate his misery at last.

Fourthly. From the declarations of the Bible. The Bible teaches that it is not he who "heareth" the word that shall be saved, but he that "doeth it;" that it is not a hearer of the word that is blessed, but a doer of the work.

Fifthly. From the fact that even the doctrinal cannot be fully understood without the practice of that which concerns the heart and life. Christianity is only thoroughly understood by the heart. Its doctrines must be transmuted into feelings to be properly understood. The "little book" must be eaten, the system must be tried to be known. Intellect is not the only knowing faculty either in the highest or the lowest department of being. The knowledge of sizes, and forms, and colors, of odors and sounds, came not to us through reason; it was the sensuous faculty that conveyed them to our consciousness. To a boy who had never tasted an apple, or an orange, or other fruit, you might talk forever about their flavor, and he would comprehend no more at the end than at the beginning. The knowledge of God and of light and love comes not to us through the intellect, the understanding, but through the spiritual faculty, the heart. The things of the heart can only be understood by the heart. Who knows "the things of the Spirit" but the Spirit? "If any man will do the will of my Father he shall know of the doctrine whether it be of God, or whether I speak of myself." And again: "He that saith I know him, and keepeth not his commandments is a liar, and the truth is not in him." The doctrines of Christ are not learned like the doctrines of Newton or Euclid, by mere intellectual study; they are learned by the heart and the life. Action alone translates Christian doctrines into meaning.

Now, the doctrinal being thus subservient to the moral, is not a merely theological manifestation of the Gospel an imperfect and wrong one? By a *mere* theological manifestation we mean a manifestation where the theological has been exalted above the ethical and practical, the theory above the practice; where Christianity has been made a metaphysical minister to the brain, rather than a loving prompter to the heart and guide to the life; where "the letter that killeth" has been exalted above "the spirit that giveth life."

Please bear in mind that we do not depreciate the doctrinal; our aim is to condemn the practice which makes the doctrinal more than all else. In how many Churches have ministers contended for the creed of their Church as being the only true creed, and how zealously have they studied to show that salvation out of the pale of their particular belief is a very uncertain matter. And mark this, too, that certain Churches claiming to ignore all creeds have yet from the pulpit and the press denounced and trampled in the dust all doctrines except the ones held by themselves! They have indulged the secret and the open sneer; they have in public assemblies ridiculed the tenets of other denominations, and have shown in all their movements and motives a spirit more becoming the pit than Christ. They have spent more time tenfold in enforcing correctness of head-belief than in talking of heart-belief and heart-life and purity. And in such an exhibition of the Gospel, is it hard to see how that Gospel has been hindered in its course?

Observe,

III. That the Gospel regards the true ethical—the principles that regulate the conduct and the life, as embodied in the life of Christ. And if this is so, is not a mere dry *legal* manifestation of the Gospel, a formal, professional exhibition only of it, a wrong representation? Christ is not only the decalogue, but the whole of Heaven's code. All the eternal principles of moral law and order he reduced to life, he translated into human actions. "He fulfilled all righteousness." Our whole duty is summed up in his command: "Follow me." Assimilation to Christ is the perfection of man.

From this it follows that every manifestation of the Gospel not thoroughly in keeping with the *spirit* and *life* of Christ is a wrong representation. Whatever in the Church gives the world a wrong idea of Christ misrepresents the Gospel. And how much has there ever been, and still is, which is thoroughly inconsistent with his ever blessed life!

All *lordliness* in the Church misrepresents the Gospel; for Christ "made himself of no reputation, took on him the form of a servant," was "meek and lowly in heart," identified himself with the poorest of the poor, and became the minister of all. How often have the high in the world's esteem, the rich and the presumptuous, acted as lords over God's heritage! thus by system misrepresenting the profoundly humble and self-denying spirit of Him "who went about doing good," and who, when exhausted, had no place whereon to lay his head!

Everything like *severity* in the Church misrepresents the Gospel; for it is opposed to the spirit of Him who did not cause his "voice to be heard in the street," and who would not "break the bruised reed nor quench the smoking flax." And what severity has the professed Christian Church shown? How it has impaled and imprisoned, gibbeted and burned heretics! How it has in innumerable cases lent its arm to war! The remark has too often been made that Christian nations have been the great leaders in battle, and that ministers of the Gospel have been anxious to consecrate banners and help on the work of carnage.

Everything like *formalism* in the Church misrepresents the Gospel, for it is opposed to the Spirit of Him who taught that "God is a spirit, and they that worship him must worship him in spirit and in truth." In Christ religion was a life, not an office or a form; but how strangely different the religion of multitudes of Church members! Their names are on the class-book, or Church register, and that said, all is said. They go out on the Sabbath to the morning service, and then returning home their hearts are at ease till the next Sabbath at eleven o'clock. They may live within a stone's cast of the church, but you seldom or never see them at Sabbath night preaching, nor in the afternoon at class or Sabbath school, nor yet ever at the Wednesday or Friday night prayer-meeting. Intelligent and careful men say that not more than *one fifth* of all who bear the name of Protestant Christians add anything of *perceptible* importance to the efficiency of the Church in the work of the world's conversion. A gigantic moral incubus are these formal professors to the car of Christ, and no wonder that men of the world looking on them conclude that religion, after all, is only a matter of opinion, or a matter of convenience, or a good cloak for hypocrites.

Any *unloving* manifestation of the Gospel is a wrong representation, and therefore a great hinderance. The Gospel is a history of divine love. Its one great central truth is that "God is love," and that he loves man though a sinner. The Gospel is love, divine love incarnate, reasoning, toiling, praying, and suffering for man. The severe aspects of God in the Bible are only to his love what the shadows are to the sun. Shadows imply that the sun is still shining on, but some object obstructs its benignant rays. It is human sin that at times obstructs the bright rays of divine love, and flings the shadow of apparent anger on our path; but divine love still shines behind the obstructive object, and lights up the universe with bliss. The Gospel being thus full of love, any cold or unkind manifestation of it is a wrong representation, and operates as a hindering cause. Does the Church represent *love?* warm, self-denying, world-wide love? Look around and see. Alas! that there are so many Churches rent by the evil spirit of discord! But yesterday a minister told us that his great trouble was with his people, not with sinners. Two prominent men had been pitted against each other for years. They spoke not to each other, but shunned each other's presence and glance. The other members knew of the feud, and the town and neighborhood people knew of it too, and the work of the Lord was stayed. It was impossible to awaken sinners to danger when they saw men professing to have the love of Christ in their hearts thus at open war. How many members of the Church there are in whose breasts burns the lurid fire of sin, rather than the bright and glorious blaze of heavenly love! They tell you that some one has offended or maltreated them, and that they will not listen to an explanation or reconciliation. When such things happen how the body of Christ bleeds, and how Zion goes mourning among men!

All *selfishness* is a misrepresentation of the Gospel, for it is opposed to the Spirit of Christ, who, though he was rich, yet for our sakes became poor, that we through his poverty might be made rich. How *rich he was!* how rich in honor, and glory, and dominion, and bliss, and power; and yet how poor did he become for your sake, for my sake! Yet how little we suffer for him, how unwilling to contribute to the extension of his cause in the earth; how we hold to the present and grasp at the future, and covet earnestly worldly honor and riches!

In illustration of our want of self-denial, let us descend to some transactions of every-day pertinency. Mr. A. is a member of the Church, lives well, professes to love the Gospel, and is regular in his attendance on the ministry. He has a fine dwelling, and everything in and about it comfortable. His wife and children love him and are loved in return. His income is enough to furnish full meals as the hours come round, and there is no lack of funds for the article of dress. For *really* superfluous dresses and new bonnets the sum paid each year amounts to two hundred dollars. How much does he give for the support of the ministry? Ten or fifteen dollars, and hard wrung at that. How much to the missionary cause? Possibly five dollars; most likely, however, three dollars. The sum total contributed in the twelve months for all religious and benevolent purposes does not reach fifty dollars.

Over the way yonder is Mr. B.; he has abundance of real estate, but is forever complaining of the taxes. He is called on for a contribution to the cause of missions, but the words are scarcely out of your mouth before his voice cries out in dolorous accents, "We are so poor, so very poor, we *do* not know what to do." Observe, his lands, and cattle, and crops are worth $10,000 or $20,000; and observe further, that whatever his children want in the way of finery they obtain. Mr. B. chews and smokes to the extent of fifty cents a week by his own confession; but he puts the missionary cause off with a subscription of half a dollar, to be paid at or before the session of the next annual conference!

You may call these extreme cases, but you know, and we know scores and hundreds of others which are more extreme. A man in a certain Western state is worth over $100,000. By one single transaction in pork he made, a short time since, a clear profit of $47,000, and yet when applied to for a subscription to build a church in his native place he gave $10. To his minister he pays in cash each year $15, and thinks himself doing nobly. There are men by scores and hundreds in Indiana and Ohio, and, in fact, in any of the states you may mention, worth from $3,000 to $5,000 and $10,000 each, who do not give to the support of religion each year so much absolutely as $2 apiece. We happen to know three farmers, Methodists, in a certain township of a certain county in Ohio. One of them, by the county recorder's book, is assessed at $12,000, the second at $20,000, and the third at $28,000, and yet not one gives so much as $6 a year to benevolent or religious purposes. The love of money has acted on them differently from love of any other kind, covering and casing them with an armor that sets at defiance all appeals.

Now turn your attention to the congregation where you worship. Who are doing their duty? A few, a very few mechanics and widows are giving all they ought; but what are the men who have the dollars doing? Some are thanking God for a free Gospel; others are calculating what to do with the interest accruing on their bank, railroad, or funded stocks; other some are bargaining for a fine corner lot, or a hundred acres of land, and all are forgetting the case of the four fishermen first called by Christ, who, making nothing of the treasures of this life except as they pointed to the treasures uncorrupted in heaven, rejoiced not only "that they were counted worthy to suffer shame for his name," but were also willing "to die for the name of the Lord Jesus." Do not such cases as these show why the Gospel is hindered? Do they not show that the disposition in the Church is to make self first, and religion second or last?

"But," interposes one, "while these cases may be plain enough and true enough, it is not fair to use them as representing the average contributions to the Church." For a moment, then, let us look at some one Church, the Methodist Episcopal, for instance. According to the General Minutes for 1859 the membership was 956,555, and the total contributions to the Missionary, Bible, Tract, and Sunday-school causes, $315,140, being an average per member of about thirty-three cents. If we add to this sum the expenses of their traveling ministry, church repairs, and some other things, we have a grand total of $2,115,140, or about two dollars and twenty cents per year per member. At a low valuation, the amount of real and personal estate subject to taxation in the United States is $9,500,000,000; of which amount $5,000,000,000 are in the hands of Church members, and probably of this latter sum $1,500,000,000 in the hands of the members of the Methodist Episcopal Church. Now, suppose for every dollar owned each member should annually give to the cause of God and benevolence one half a cent, which does not vary much from the amount paid as state and federal taxes, what would the sum be? Over seven millions of dollars instead of two, as now, to benevolence. Is the amount large? is it more than ought to be given? is it more than can be given? The statistics in regard to perfumery, jewelry, and tobacco show that Church members in this country spend more for these articles than they do for religion. We do not here argue the necessity of spending less for, or dispensing with them, but simply inquire whether pious men and women should give less to God than to themselves in the way of self-decoration and gratification?

When we compare the sums used by nations for armies and navies, with the sums spent by Christians for extending God's cause, we discover how little of religious self-denial there is in the world. In the last *twenty* years the total sum spent by the various religious and benevolent societies of the United States, exclusive of Roman Catholic, has a little exceeded thirty millions of dollars, which is about one third as much as the army and navy of this country cost for the year 1859. Including the repairs on ships, arsenals, etc., the money annually spent by the nations of

Europe for naval and military purposes does not fall short of $800,000,000, a sum at least one hundred times greater than the amount spent by the Christians of the United States for the support of the ministry and all other religious purposes.

"But to pay for religion as we pay for war would require great sacrifices." True, but where in the New Testament Scriptures, or the Old, is it written that the kingdom is to prevail without severe self-denial? In the days of the primitive disciples the *love* of money was unknown. In charity, "their deep poverty abounded to the riches of their liberality;" and the question was not, as in our day, "How much shall I give?" but "How much may I withhold?" Indeed, they gave the *whole* of what they gained; and never was the utterance made, "I give, or I shall give as much as I can *conveniently*." We may expect nothing but a permanent and perpetual hinderance of the Gospel in the earth so long as *convenience* is the ruling law of giving. If a son is lost, or imprisoned, in some distant country, or cast upon some lonely island, the father and mother do not debate day after day as to how much they can conveniently give for his recovery. Or if he is sick and threatened with speedy death, money is not thought of, personal comfort is not taken into the account, nor health, nor in some cases life itself, if the loved one may recover. And if Christian men had as much love for the cause of their Saviour, as they have for the welfare of their children, what self-denials would they not practice!

From these and kindred suggestions, is it difficult to see that the Gospel has had such a representation among men as to account for its present limited influence in the world? Indeed, when we think that man is the chosen instrumentality of God to extend his kingdom in the earth, and that he will not work unless man works, is it not strange that Christianity has prevailed as it has? In how many instances have men professed religion for the sake of some selfish, worldly end, how often they have caricatured the Gospel, how often played the hypocrite, and how often concealed the living, loving Christ, the friend, brother, and Saviour of universal man, under the repulsive forms of ceremonies, polemics, assumptions, and formalities?

It is time the Church should feel its duty and its responsibility; high time that its members should live as they profess. The Church is God's spiritual army, and his ministers are to marshal the hosts "against the mighty." But what are generals without the rank and file? Success depends scarcely less upon the valor of the individual soldiers than upon the wisdom of the officers. The conqueror of the world caused to be inscribed upon the spoils taken on one occasion from the enemy, "*Alexander, son of Philip,* WITH THE GREEKS *(the Lacedemonians excepted) gained these spoils from the barbarians who inhabit Asia.*" Captains only and generals cannot conquer; the individual soldiers must be right; *all* must be right, and all ready to fight; not some in their tents, and some at home, and some asleep, and some off on furlough, but every one armed and equipped in his place.

Is it any wonder that Voltaire and his infidel companions, who figured in the French Revolution, judging of Christianity, as they foolishly did, as it appeared in the Papal Church, should hate it, and swear to throw it off as a foul incubus on the heart of their nation? Is it any wonder in later times that that great man of science, Humboldt, seeing Christianity only as it appeared in the Prussian state clergy or the Romish priests of Germany, should treat its claims with indifference and contempt, and should say of the clergy as he did of the eyes of the chameleon, One eye is on the earth, and one on heaven, but the preference is for the earth wholly? Is it any wonder that other men of our own day and country should stand aloof from the claims of religion when they see such distorted exhibitions of it in professors?

For the same reason that, of old, God "could not drive out the inhabitants of the valley," he cannot now convert the world, because there is a want of the proper agency, a right representation of the Gospel by men. In his "Philosophy of History," Dr. Schlegel states, in explanation of the rapid extension of Christianity in the first century, that its professors saw and felt the presence of their invisible King and Lord, and that they "valued earthly existence only as it contributed to the one end, the diffusion of the principles of Christ among men." Elsewhere he remarks, that having conquered the world by their principles the Christians could have so held it, but that ceasing to practice self-denial, and having "let in discord among themselves" by the indulgence of improper tempers respecting unimportant points, the victories of the cross began to wane.

Let the Church learn a lesson from the experience of the primitive disciples. The logic of a holy life is the power which sinners cannot resist. With the Holy Ghost animating the heart, victory must attend the toil of every Christian man and woman.

O come the day when the living, personal Christ, with a brother's warm heart, overflowing with love, and a father's kindly sentiments of affection streaming from his lips, he who of old trod the hills of Capernaum and the shores of Galilee, the "friend of sinners," shall appear again in his Church, the spirit of every act, the meaning of every service, the sovereign of every heart!

HOMILY III.

THE PROSPEROUS FOOL.

The ground of a certain rich man brought forth plentifully: and he thought within himself, saying, What shall I do, because I have no room where to bestow my fruits? And he said, This will I do: I will pull down my barns, and build greater. LUKE xii, 16–18.

The parables of Christ strike us as particularly illustrating and sustaining the expression: "Never man spake like this man." When we consider the circumstances under which many of them were delivered—that they were unpremeditated, grew up out of the occasion and on the spur of the moment, and yet that they combined unity of purpose with comprehensiveness and beauty in minutest details, we may well come to the conclusion that he who uttered them was indeed divine!

The Church too, we may remark, while confessing its infinite obligation to the Son of God for these parables, is also indirectly indebted for some of them to the opposition and contradiction of the world. Out of the murmurings of the

Scribes and Pharisees arose the three consecutive parables of the "Lost Sheep," the "Lost Money," and the "Lost Son;" so here, out of an incident, a mere interruption to the sermon, arose this one of the "Prosperous Fool." Our Lord is discoursing to his disciples upon the trials of life and the Providence that overrules them all; upon the persecutions of the righteous, and the Holy Ghost who shall sustain them in these trials, when, just as he has arrived at the most solemn part of the discourse, one of the company breaks in with the unseemly interruption: "Master, speak to my brother, that he divide the inheritance with me!" You are shocked at the frivolity and profanity of the man. What has the Holy Ghost, speaking to a disciple at the hour of extreme peril, to do with a dispute about "dividing the inheritance?" Yet in condemning him shall we not condemn ourselves? What strange incongruous thoughts are present in every congregation in the midst of the most solemn and pointed appeals! If by a spiritual photography the thoughts of all men could be brought out plain as the features of their various faces, what a startling revelation! Indeed, without wishing to plead excuse for wandering thoughts, I may say (if the seeming paradox can be endured for a moment) that with some minds the closer their attention the more are they tempted to wander amid the various branchings of the subject, according to the laws of association and suggestion; and each man differently, according to his circumstances, mental constitution, and spiritual experience. Some allusion or passing word is enough to set in motion so powerful a train of thought as to lead the subject of it to the mistaken belief that the speaker had actually uttered what has passed only through his own mind. Let us not be hasty in our condemnation of this man. Perhaps after all there was not so much frivolity or profanity about him.

But look for a moment at the Saviour's reply. He refuses to give judgment in this worldly matter, but offers counsel, which if received will be found of more value than the whole of the "inheritance." "He said unto *them*," (not the disciples generally, but the two brothers,) "Take heed and beware of covetousness;" or, as it should be, "every kind of covetousness;" covetousness in seeking what we are entitled to; covetousness in withholding what is another's; "for," and this is the text of which the parable is the subject, "a man's life consisteth not in the abundance of the things which he possesseth." From the lowest point of view, clearly, the mere animal life stands not in the abundance *possessed* over and above what is used and appropriated, but in sufficiency; in what actually needs to be absorbed in the functions and economy of life. In competency a man's life may stand; but there is a point of affluence to which the sustaining, or lengthening out of life, stands in, at least, no direct relation. That gold which the miser hoards might as well, in relation to his life, be so much shingle from the ocean shore! But, in a higher sense, emphatically "*life*," "A MAN'S life," consists not in his possessions. A man's life in its ideal, after the great Head and pattern of humanity, is a spiritual life dependent on the bread of heaven.

But, passing from this pregnant text, let us look at the subject. Here is a man well to do, calculating, painstaking, and prosperous, but he is a fool!

There are four aspects under which his folly presents itself:

1. In his realized prosperity and plans for the future he forgets or ignores God. "The fool hath said in his heart, There is no God."

There is no evidence that this man belonged to the class thus indicated, but he is a practical atheist, "a secularist." Not one word of Him who gives us "fruitful seasons:" he speaks of "*my* fruits" and "*my* goods" as though he stood absolutely independent of the great Giver. And for this there seems the less excuse considering that the occupation of the man was that of a farmer, not a manufacturer. For the sons of Tubal Cain, the artificers in brass and iron, something of palliation may perhaps be urged. There are so many second causes between them and the great First Cause, so many links in the chain between earth and heaven, that if they see not that its upper end is grasped in the hand of the Eternal their blindness may be extenuated if not excused. The mason has perhaps never seen the quarry from whence the marble block was hewn; the carpenter has never stood in the shadows of that forest where the timber grew; the cunning workman in gold and silver and precious stones has never gone down into the mine from whence those treasures were brought; but this man, by his contact with nature, lives, shall we say, in the more immediate presence of the all-quickening Spirit, by whom nature's womb is made pregnant and fertile? His "grounds brought forth plentifully." He himself is a child of nature, nursed in her lap, fed by her hand, soothed by her songs.

The roar of the blast-furnace he hears not, nor the din of whirring wheels; the smoke-laden atmosphere of the great city has never confused his brain nor saddened his heart; but in quiet waiting he has looked for the "early and the latter rain," knowing that with all his husbandry he cannot make a single blade of grass. At length the harvest came; the corn bowed in its ruddy ripeness to the reaper's hand; the fig-tree blossomed, the almond-tree flourished, the vine hung out its purple clusters; the date yielded its sweetness, and the olive its fragrant oil: "God crowned the year with his goodness;" but the man in the atheism of his heart talked only of "*my* fruits" and "*my* goods." No homage, no gratitude! We learn, after all, that this matter of practical atheism depends not so much upon the circumstances of the man as the man himself. You tell us that the temple in which you best can worship is the universal one whose dome is the great firmament, that the only book of revelation is the great book of nature, that the only sermons you would hear are those preached by her perpetual ministers; you tell us there is "divinity in a moss, theology in a beetle, and in the changing seasons the veritable creed of the apostles;" but how is it that where these advantages are greatest, apart from the revelation of the Bible, men are commonly most degraded and sensual? "Where every prospect pleases" *there* naught but "man is vile!"

Let the man indeed listen to the voice of the Divine Spirit within him, and then truly he is in harmony with universal nature; her symbols, prophecies, and promises are dear to him—the very words of God; to him she shows herself perchance in meanest garb and coldest mood, and yet he reverently bows down and worships, if he may but touch the hem of her garment; to another, on whose soul the ineffable light has never streamed, she appears in all her gorgeous beauty and her glittering jewelry; but he looks on unmoved, as upon a painted sign-board!

> "Earth's crammed with heaven,
> And every common bush afire with God;
> But only he who sees takes off his shoes:
> The rest sit round it and pluck blackberries."

Another element in the folly of this man is found,

II. In his utter selfishness. The brotherhood of men depends on the fatherhood of God. No schemes of philanthropy will prosper that do not rest on a divine basis. This man not only talks of "*my* fruits" and "*my* goods" as though he had no Father in heaven, but also as if he had not a brother on the earth. And observe too that this intense selfishness, while it is in part his folly, is his misery also; his wealth is a source of disquietude, burdens him with cares and labors: "What shall I do, because I have no room!" etc. Not that I mean to preach the nonsense that riches are as great a trouble as poverty—as great a *trial* in one way I doubt not they are; but as to the trouble, let the shorter lives of the indigent, as compared with the affluent, answer that. Besides, the rich man *may* rid himself of the burden of his riches; but the poor man, how can he be rid of his poverty? Still riches do bring cares along with them, especially to the man who has no heart to use them for God and for his fellow-man. This poor simpleton in his blind selfishness does not see that he has already barns and storehouses enough; abundant room ready to his hand if he did but know it; room in the homes of the destitute, in the hearts of the sorrowful, in the mouths of the hungry. Heavenly garners these, where, if he will but deposit his fruits and his goods, he shall receive in return at last more abundant fruit gathered from the tree of life. Alas, he knows it not! and, fool that he is, he is asking in the perplexity of his heart, "What shall I do because I have no room?"

"What shall I do?" A question sometimes asked now in the same selfish spirit, but under different circumstances, and in a lower moral tone. "What shall I do?" Not because "I have no room for my goods," but because I have no goods and no fruits. "This is what I will do; I will *seem* to have; I will enter on large commercial speculations, I will set up my country house, I will pride myself in the best horses, the best wines, the best pictures; the philanthropist, the scholar, the antiquarian, shall sit at my table; at the head of subscription lists, benevolent and religious, my name shall appear; and if by this daring scheme I do not become rich, at least for a time men will think me so." "This is what I will do." And so the commercial history of this country has its speculators, and when the crisis comes there are desolated homes, and broken hearts, and sudden deaths, and suicides!

But this man is not of such; not a railway speculator, not a bank director, not a shareholder in mines; he is a well-to-do, industrious, *prudent* man, and yet he is a FOOL! and wherefore? Because, living in a world with God about him everywhere, and with the bitter wail of suffering humanity in his ears, he is living for himself alone.

His folly is seen in this, that he proposes,

III. To SATISFY SPIRITUAL CRAVING WITH MATERIAL FOOD. "I will say to my *soul*, Thou hast much goods," etc. You may object to this that the man never really thought about his soul at all; that with him the "soul" is simply the sentient life, not the immortal spirit. Be it so; yet he has a soul, and it is the moving of this within him that will not let him rest satisfied with what he has, that makes him ever reaching out after a good not yet attained; a future on which in some way the hopes of all men center. This longing after a rest and joy, as yet unknown to him, is the inarticulate crying of the soul within him for the true rest and the true joy. Fool that he is, he is still a man, and the man's spirit cannot live by bread alone. He may "*fill his belly* with husks that the swine do eat," but he can never *feed* upon them. Not to discern this is his folly and his sin. Are there not many among us who, like him, are seeking their highest good, their most anticipated future, in mere worldly ease, mere carnal provisions? You will never so find this ease; you will never so realize this festival and holiday of the soul.

There is indeed rest for you if you will have it; but it is only to be found in Him who said, "Come unto *me* all ye that labor and are heavy laden, and I will give you rest." There is food for the soul—it is "the bread that cometh down from heaven;" there is drink for the soul—it is "the water of life proceeding from the throne of God and of the

Lamb;" there is a merry-making for the soul when, cleansed from its sins in the precious blood of Christ, and clothed in his righteousness, the father says to his child, "Go now thy way; eat thy bread, and drink thy wine with a merry heart, for God accepteth thy works."

The crowning element of his folly is in the fact,

IV. THAT HE OVERLOOKS DEATH. The theories men hold may be right or wrong, but death is certainly a fact! a fact that none but a fool will dare to disregard. Supposing the purpose of this man to be ever so feasible, yet he might at least have reflected that death was also probable. But this formed no part of his calculation. As the day closed he would congratulate himself on the prudent resolve he had come to, and ere he retired to his homestead he would see that the sheep were penned, that the cattle were housed, and that the implements of husbandry stood ready for the morrow's work. As the setting sun withdrew its light from barn and storehouse, and shocks of corn, and stubble fields, and vintage fruits, and the stars came "faltering out," how little did he think that sun, and star, and landscape should be seen by him no more!

> "'Tis a stern and startling thing to think
> How often mortality stands on the brink
> Of its grave, without any misgiving;
> And yet in this slippery world of strife,
> In the stir of human bustle so rife,
> There are daily sounds to tell us that life
> Is dying, and death is living!"

"This night thy soul is required," or, "*they* require thy soul." *They*—the ministers of divine justice, stern, inexorable—"*require* thy soul." Not so God speaks to his faithful servants when he calls them home to their reward. Touched by his gentle hand, soothed by his kindest word, they fall asleep in Jesus, and wake to the soft music of the harps of heaven! And yet it is a solemn thing to die so suddenly! "From battle, and from murder, and from sudden death, good Lord, deliver us!"

Wherefore "from sudden death?" Live, live to God, my brother, and be not careful about death; it is a part of your inheritance, for all things through Christ are yours. You may die suddenly sitting at your desk, or at the social board, or playing with your children; it matters not as to time or mode of death *if the life be Christian.* But let each one who is not a Christian pause and tremble even at death!

"Lo! on a narrow neck of land,
'Twixt two unbounded seas, I stand,
Secure, insensible:
A point of time, a moment's space,
Removes me to that heavenly place,
Or shuts me up in hell!"

HOMILY IV.

THE FIERY FURNACE; OR, TRUE PRINCIPLE EXEMPLIFIED.

"Shadrach, Meshach, and Abednego, answered and said to the king, O Nebuchadnezzar, we are not careful to answer thee in this matter. If it be so, our God whom we serve is able to deliver us from the burning fiery furnace, and he will deliver us out of thine hand, O king. But if not, be it known unto thee, O king, that we will not serve thy gods, nor worship the golden image which thou hast set up." DANIEL iii, 16, 18–25.

MAN is a worshiper. If there were no God before whose shrine he could bend his knees, he would make himself an object of worship. We have a remarkable instance of this in the narrative before us. Though the gorgeous temples at Babylon were crowded with all kinds of images, Nebuchadnezzar caused another of immense size and splendor to be added to their number. Here we have an account of the inauguration of that costly idol; especially of an incident of great importance which occurred on that occasion, namely, the avowed nonconformity of three young and pious Hebrews.

What was the design of the Babylonian despot in the erection of this colossal image? Two different answers might be given to this question. It was intended either as an expression of his gratitude to the deity whom he imagined had so greatly prospered him on the battle-field, or as a representation of himself under the title of the long expected "Divine Son," or universal sovereign of the world. We adopt the latter idea. The fact that he summoned all the great officers of the empire to be present at its inauguration is a clear proof that this was not an ordinary idol. It is not probable that he would thus have ordered all the officers from their labors and posts of duty merely to add to the magnificence and splendor of an ordinary scene. The proud monarch had something of far greater importance in view; he wished to secure for himself the homage of his chief officers, and through them that of his numerous subjects.

Then the terrible punishment threatened upon disobedience to the royal mandate is a further proof of the great importance the Babylonian despot attached to this ceremony. Though accustomed to receive implicit obedience, it is evident that on this occasion he expected that some of his people might dare resist his orders and decline to bow the knee to his "golden image." This threat was in perfect keeping with the despotism of Chaldea and the spirit of that benighted age. It was an impious attempt at enforcing uniformity in religion by the strong arm of the civil power. It contained the very essence of all religious persecution. But in spite of the severity of the threat the three Hebrews were found true to their principles, and dared to oppose the king's impiety. How could they pay homage to an idol? Every principle of their religion, every feeling of their heart revolted against the very thought. The honor due to their God they will not lavish on their monarch. Their choice being thus made, the terrible threat was soon executed. The strongest men in the army were ordered to bind and cast them into the awful furnace. But O the mighty power of their religion! Though the heat was so intense as to melt their iron chains it had no injurious effect upon themselves. In the fiery furnace they were safe; they could stand upright, they could walk, they could converse with one another, and above all they had the presence and fellowship of the God whom they so faithfully served and worshiped. The enraged monarch, who had anxiously watched all this, at last, trembling with excitement, cried out: "Did not we cast three men bound into the midst of the fire?" "True, O king." "Lo, I see four men loose, walking in the midst of the fire, and they have no hurt; and the form of the fourth is like the Son of God."

What idea did Nebuchadnezzar attach to this FOURTH person? We believe he viewed him as the long expected "Divine Son" of the ancients, whose very title he had that day impiously assumed. The upright conduct of Shadrach, Meshach, and Abednego became instrumental in defeating the tyrant's blasphemous plan; and he is thus forced to acknowledge another as the "Son of God."

Here we see *true principle exemplified;* here we behold true principle severely tested, nobly maintained, and ultimately triumphant.

I. TRUE PRINCIPLE SEVERELY TESTED. Every principle will sooner or later be tried. There is a fiery furnace that will test the principles and motives of every heart. The test in the case of the young Hebrews was peculiarly severe:

First. *They had to oppose the will of a powerful benefactor.* Though a cruel despot, Nebuchadnezzar had generously befriended these three exiled Hebrews. Though virtually slaves he had raised them into important offices in the realm, he had placed them "over the affairs of the province of Babylon." They of all men ought to show him their deep gratitude. Did they not owe everything—their position, their influence, yea, their very lives—to his generosity; they deeply felt this; they knew they would be considered ungrateful; the thought pained their hearts. But a feeling of gratitude must give way to a sense of duty; they would have been glad to please their sovereign, but they dare not displease their God. In too many instances man and not God, the world and not religion, receives the first consideration; expediency and not principle governs the heart and shapes the conduct. It requires courage to say NO to the behest of a benefactor.

Secondly. *They had to incur the odium of an excited public.* It is not pleasant to be an object of scorn and ridicule; we naturally look for approbation and sympathy. But none in that vast and gorgeous assemblage sympathized with the sentiments of the young Hebrews. No one had a conscience too tender to worship the huge image. No sooner was the signal given than all that vast crowd of courtiers, princes, and governors of provinces, fell down and paid the commanded homage. These three young men alone stood erect. What a position to be in! Every eye was fixed upon them; they were jeered, ridiculed, and treated with the bitterest scorn. It required some courage to withstand all this. It is not an easy thing to stand erect in the hour of danger, and "to assert the rights of conscience and of God in the midst of a rabble carried away by excitement and by sin." But it is not impossible. The enlightened and earnest Christian has courage to appear, like Elijah, *alone*, the advocate of true principles.

Thirdly. *They had to forfeit the honors and emoluments of office.* Worldly policy would have stepped forward and reasoned thus: "Why relinquish such lucrative situations? Why forfeit your exalted positions? Why not for this once conform to the new religion of your sovereign? While you bow the knee to the image you may *curse* it in your hearts, and you know that on the *heart* God looks." Such reasoning as this would have laid many prostrate before the idol, but it had no weight with Shadrach, Meshach, and Abednego. Their minds were made up; their principles they would not betray; their God they would not offend. "The reproach of Christ is greater riches than the treasures in Egypt."

Fourthly. *They had to meet death in one of its most terrible forms.* Death in itself is never pleasant; but a violent death is peculiarly terrible. Such death stared these young men in the face. Either idolatry or the terrible fiery furnace was now to be their choice. Which will they choose? The test is awfully severe. Human nature trembles at the very thought of it. "O Shadrach, Meshach, and Abednego, think what you are doing. If you do not value the smiles of royalty, the applause of the public, and the wealth and honor of your worldly position, think of the terribly heated furnace, have mercy on yourselves!" But even this ghastly form of death fills them with no terror; the red circling flames are to them objects of no alarm; nothing can induce them to sacrifice their principle and offend their God.

Here we observe,

II. TRUE PRINCIPLE NOBLY MAINTAINED. What answer did they give to the enraged monarch? "Shadrach, Meshach, and Abednego answered and said to the king, O Nebuchadnezzar, we are not careful to answer thee in this matter." In all matters relating to the welfare of the state they would have cheerfully complied with his wishes; but in the matter of the golden image he was wrong, and they *could* not obey his command. We notice,

First. *Their calm demeanor.* Though the tyrant raged, they maintained perfect calmness. Do we not see here a mark of true greatness? How calm and courteous was their reply to the king! "We are not careful to answer thee in this matter." They were ready to obey all his *just* demands, but they could not give him the homage due to their Maker. Yet their disobedience was not the result of a blind, impulsive zeal, but of calm, prayerful deliberation. They had carefully examined the royal mandate, they understood its terrible meaning, and when summoned to the tyrant's presence they betrayed no fear: serene calmness filled their bosoms and lighted up their countenances. True godliness possesses sweet sustaining power.

Secondly. *Their strong faith.* Their language was the language of faith, the language of a pious heart firmly confiding in the faithfulness of Heaven. Their faith took hold of two things: The *power* of God—"Our God is *able* to deliver us from the burning fiery furnace." And also his *willingness*—"And he *will* deliver us out of thine hand, O king." These two elements form the basis of true faith. You confide in that person because you believe him to be both able and willing to befriend you. The want of either of these elements would impair your trust. Our glorious Redeemer is mighty to save: "He saves to the uttermost;" and no trusting soul has ever been disappointed in him. "He *will* deliver us."

Thirdly. *Their inflexible determination.* "But if not, we will not serve thy gods, nor worship the golden image." "If in his infinite wisdom our merciful God should not interpose on our behalf in this hour of trial, yet our confidence in him will be none the less: if we are not permitted to honor him by our lives, we are resolved to honor him by our death." This was a noble resolve, and it is ever of vital importance in religion. Its possession will enable you to meet with calmness the stern realities of life, to say "NO" to every sinful suggestion, and to rejoice in your Saviour even in the prospect of death. Here we observe:

III. TRUE PRINCIPLE ULTIMATELY TRIUMPHANT. Several very important points were gained by this glorious triumph of true principle:

First. *The impious ambition of the monarch was checked.* Nebuchadnezzar was resolved to be esteemed as the long-expected "Divine Son," and to receive as such divine homage; but when his highest ambition was on the eve of being realized, he was bitterly disappointed, the cup of glory was dashed from his lips, and he was forced to acknowledge the friend and protector of the Hebrews as the "Divine Son." "And the form of the fourth is like the Son of God."

Secondly. *The living personality of the "Divine Son" was established.* The deities of the Gentiles were the creations of their own fancy. Nebuchadnezzar had probably no faith in them. But the person whom he saw in the "fiery furnace was not a *myth*, but a real living person. The king observed his form, saw the living expressions of his visage, and witnessed him walking backward and forward in the furnace. The God of Shadrach and his companions was a living person, not an imaginary object. We worship not an idea, but a God who has a heart to love us and an arm to save us.

Thirdly. *The faith of the weak and the wavering was confirmed.* Had their bitter affliction almost driven the poor Hebrew captives into despair? The occurrence on the plain of Dura would revive their hope, and fill them with wonder and gratitude. Many a disconsolate exile would be greatly encouraged, his faith strengthened, and the expiring embers of his religious love fanned into a flame. Yes! they could after this trust in God. The merciful dealings of Heaven toward a brother in distress fill us with hope and gladness.

Fourthly. *The welfare of the captive Jews was effectually promoted.* The great officers of the provinces could not soon forget the "fiery furnace." On their return to their respective homes they would tell, not of the size and splendor of the image, the glory and pomp of the scene, and the honor and greatness of their monarch, but of the conduct of the three Hebrews, the mysterious vision, and the miraculous deliverance. Their treatment of the exiles would be more humane and generous, and they would naturally infer that the people whose God would thus interpose on their behalf were not to be despised.

Fifthly. *The honor of the true God was greatly enhanced.* Dark in the extreme were the prospects of true religion on that memorable morning. The powerful despot of Babylon sets himself up as an object of worship. He assumes the priority among the Gods: "Who is that god that shall deliver you out of my hands?" He has all the empire with him; three young strangers only dare resist his impiety. But this midnight gloom ushered a glorious morning; the Son of God descends into the flames; the furious element is instantly curbed; the furnace becomes the scene of miraculous interposition; the faithful are saved, and the wonderful event is officially proclaimed. The true God is greatly honored.

How valuable is vital godliness! It possesses a sustaining power. It brings down upon the soul the richest blessing of God. Be faithful to it; let its living principles be exemplified in your life.

HOMILY V.

LOOKING FOR A MAN; OR, THE DIVINE IDEAL OF MAN UNREALIZED.

Run ye to and fro through the streets of Jerusalem, and see now, and know, and seek in the broad places thereof, if ye can find a man, if there be any that executeth judgment, that seeketh the truth; and I will pardon it. JEREMIAH v, 1.

THE Hebrew word *eesh*, here translated man, is, by Dr. Lee, rendered, "a man of the higher and better sort," which authorizes us to do what the text itself suggests—

emphasize the word MAN in the passage before us. The human family is vast and ever multiplying, but *true* men have ever been rare. The prophet now, when the black tide of depravity in Jerusalem was at a high mark, was commissioned to make a speedy and earnest search among the teeming population for a *man*, a true man.

The passage suggests three thoughts concerning a *man:*

I. THE DIVINE IDEA OF A MAN. This is given in God's own language in the text. A *man* in his sense is one "*that executeth judgment, that seeketh the truth.*" This language comprehends all virtue, complete excellence of character. It involves (1.) a righteous working out of the divine will so far as it is apprehended, and (2.) an earnest endeavor for a further knowledge of the divine will. In these two things—getting new ideas, every moment, of the divine will, and translating them into practical life as they occur—the moral perfection of a creature consists. This is the divine idea of a *man;* it involves the harmonious action of the intellect, the heart, and all the active powers. How different is the divine ideal of a *man* to that which popularly prevails. Compare it (1.) with the ideal of the muscular, which is *force;* (2.) with the ideal of the secular, which is *wealth;* (3.) with the ideal of the intellectual, which is *knowledge;* (4.) with the ideal of the vain, which is *show.* In relation to the last, the modern youth of our country are painful illustrations. They conceive that the cigar, the cane, the ring, the garb, and the gait, have something to do in making a *man.* Fools! it is not the physical structure, the muscular force, the intellectual accomplishments, the secular opulence, nor the splendid dress, that constitute a *man*. The divine idea of man has only once been perfectly realized on the earth since the fall, and that in the life of Christ.

II. The lamentable rarity of a MAN. The prophet was commanded "to run to and fro through the streets of Jerusalem, and to search the broad places," the market-places, in order to find a *man*. The city at this time had not been desolated by war, nor had its inhabitants, so far as we know, been thinned by any circumstance or catastrophe; its streets resounded with the tread of a crowded population, its broad market-places were thronged with those who bought and sold in order to get gain; but amid this dense concourse of human animals, feeding, thinking, bartering, all acting with more or less energy, and some flaunting in the attire of fashion, to find a *man* was a difficult work. A man among a teeming population of human animals was a rare object! This sad state of things may be regarded in two aspects:

First, *As a sad revelation of the moral condition of Jerusalem in the days of the prophet.* It would seem that the religious reformation wrought by Josiah had expended all its beneficent results, and that idolatry and general corruption had set in and was surging high. Such corruption among a people who had such religious privileges, and in the very scene where the Temple stood, shows the wonderful forbearance of God and the terrible perversity of the human heart! This sad state of things may also be regarded,

Secondly, *As representing too truthfully the condition of our own age.* The great search of a true prophet now in our country would be for *men*—a search not in the cynical spirit of Diogenes, but in the loving spirit of a weeping seer. Where among the millions in your crowded towns and cities do you find, to any considerable extent, the divine idea of man actualized? Verily we are a fallen people. Pampered animals, sordid grubs, literary pedants, hollow pretenders, painted butterflies, lie about you on all hands; but a *man*, Where? "Go through the streets and search the broad places for a *man*."

III. THE SOCIAL VALUE OF A MAN. "And I will pardon it." For the sake of a *man*, God promises to pardon Jerusalem. The value of a man to society, to the race, is everywhere represented in the Bible. First. *A* MAN *is a condition on which God favors the race.* Sodom and Gomorrah would have been spared had there been but ten righteous persons, *men*, there. For Job's sake, Heaven pardoned his three erring friends. Job xlii, 7. The principle receives its full illustration in the mediation of Christ. For his sake men are pardoned. Secondly. *A* MAN *is an agent by which God improves the condition of the race.* His law is to bless man by man. He educates, enfranchises, purifies, saves man by man. He made Moses the deliverer of Israel, Elijah "the chariots of fire and the horses" to his country, Paul the messenger of his Gospel to the heathen, Luther the liberator of his religion, etc. The true man is the only veritable patriot, philanthropist, preacher, priest. Be not deceived! it is not the boasted prowess of your fleets and your armies, not the genius and the wisdom of your statesmen, not the commerce of your merchants, not the discoveries of your sages, not the amazing skill of your artists and engineers, nor even the industry of your population, which confer the greatest benefits on your country and your race; but the moral virtues, the righteous activities, the heavenly spirit, the reverent devotions, of a *man*.

Brother, learn from this to appreciate the sublime object of Christ's mission to our earth, and rightly to use his blessed system. Why came he into the world? It was to remold men after the divine ideal. It was to make true men. It was to give the human creature a "new heart," a "new spirit;" to regenerate the character and transform man *after the image of him that created him;* in one word, to actualize in the millions of the race the divine ideal of *man*. Blessed work! No one but Christ can accomplish it. He has done so, and is doing so. Industry may make the human animal a millionaire; education a soldier, an artist, a statesman, a sage; but Christianity alone can make him a MAN.

HOMILY VI.

THE SUFFERINGS, DEATH, AND RESURRECTION OF CHRIST FORETOLD AND VINDICATED BY HIMSELF.

From that time forth began Jesus to show unto his disciples, how that he must go unto Jerusalem, and suffer many things of the elders and chief priests and scribes, and be killed, and be raised again the third day. Then Peter took him, and began to rebuke him, saying, Be it far from thee, Lord: this shall not be unto thee. But he turned, and said unto Peter, Get thee behind me, Satan: thou art an offense unto me; for thou savorest not the things that be of God, but those that be of men. Matt. xvi, 21–23.

The events which Christ here predicts as about to occur in his personal history are events not only of vital moment to man, but of profound interest to the universe. They are things into which "the angels desire to look;" they are the foundation facts of that Gospel which makes known "the manifold wisdom of God" unto "the principalities and powers in heavenly places;" that Gospel which to man is "the power of God unto salvation unto every one that believeth."

I. These events are here foretold by himself to his disciples. The fact that Jesus should thus lay so distinctly before the minds of his disciples the stupendous events about transpiring in his history is suggestive of at least three things:

First. *It is suggestive of his superhumanity.* Christ

gives here a specimen of his thorough knowledge of his own futurity. The scene of his sufferings, "Jerusalem;" the multiplicity of his suffering, "many things;" the instigators of his sufferings, "the elders, the chief priests, and the scribes;" and the mortal termination of his sufferings, his being "killed," were all distinct objects in his horizon, and were all now fully laid under the notice of his disciples.

> "O suffering friend of human kind!
>   How, as the fatal hour drew near,
> Came thronging on thy holy mind
>   The images of holy fear!
> Gethsemane's sad midnight scene,
>   The faithless friends, the exulting foes,
> The thorny crown, the insult keen,
>   The scourge, the cross! before thee rose."

Yes, and what is more wonderful still, even the *fact* and *period* of his resurrection were clear to his vision. Surely such knowledge of the future of our individual life does not belong to our simple-humanity. As men, an impervious vail conceals our future. We know not what shall be even on the morrow. All beyond the present, so far as our *individual* life is concerned, is black as midnight. We can see nothing. No ray falls to light the next approaching hour. But it is not the mere knowledge of his future that suggests to us the idea of his superhumanity, but the calm magnanimity with which he looked upon the stupendous events which were approaching him. With the nameless indignities which awaited him at Jerusalem, the mysterious horrors that would roll their blackest clouds over his heart in Gethsemane, and the infernal assaults and tortures that would come upon him as he hung upon the cross, spread out in all their immensity of anguish before his eye, he was sublimely equanimous in spirit. The gathering tempest, with its sky-blackening clouds, and its wild boding winds howling about his soul, ruffled him not. What mere man could stand calmly in the presence of such a future? I would not have my coming year, nay, my coming week revealed; I fear its revelation would paralyze my reason, disorganize my frame, and entirely unfit me for the duties of life.

Secondly. *It is suggestive of his voluntariness in suffering.* With such a knowledge of what awaited him some months on in the future, could not he whose word had just hushed the storm upon the Galilean lake have escaped them? Undoubtedly. His sufferings were not accidental; he was not the victim of iron necessity, of resistless fate. He was free. "I have power to lay down my life and to take it again: no man taketh it from me."

Thirdly. *It is suggestive of his considerate kindness toward his disciples.* Why did Christ thus foretell his sufferings to his disciples? Not as some do, for the sake of parading his sorrows and his trials. Far from it. Great sorrows like great loves court silence rather than speech. Why then? Evidently for their good. They required to have their minds disabused of certain wrong impressions which they had entertained concerning his mission. They clung to the hope that he would assume the pomp and power of worldly dominion; that as a triumphant conqueror he would take his sword, slay the Romans, and make Jerusalem the mistress of the world. He here disabuses their minds of these material notions. He brushes away these illusions from their brain. Still more they required to be prepared for those wonderful events in his history, so that when they came, instead of having their faith in him shaken by them, they would have it established by regarding them as the fulfillment of his prediction. It was for their good that he thus foretold his future.

II. THESE EVENTS ARE HERE INDICATED BY HIMSELF TO PETER. "Then Peter took him, and began to rebuke him, saying, Be it far from thee, Lord: this shall not be unto thee. But he turned and said unto Peter, Get thee behind me, Satan: thou art an offense unto me: for thou savorest not the things that be of God, but those that be of men."

In this conduct of Peter and our Saviour's address to him, four things strike our attention:

First. *The rapidity with which good men can pass from a proper to an improper mental mood.* In the preceding verses (16–19) Peter appears in a glorious attitude of soul. He confesses Christ to be "the Son of the living God;" for which Christ pronounces him blessed, inasmuch as he had been instructed by the Father, had grasped the foundation truth on which the true Church was to be built, and was now invested with the key to unlock the great kingdom of grace and truth. But here this same Peter passes almost at once into a spiritual mood in which Christ denounces him as an adversary. Now it is true that Peter had a peculiarly impulsive nature; his transitions were rapid and extreme; in a moment he could pass from the equator to the pole in feeling. Albeit, to such changes we are all more or less exposed in this life; we are now on the mount of hope, and now in the vale of despondency; now glowing with affection, now cold in indifference; now valiant, and now timid. Yet inasmuch as these improper mental states are not cherished, they are rather as bubbles raised on the stream by the outward breeze than plants growing naturally out of the soil.

Another thing which strikes our attention in Christ's conduct with Peter is,

Secondly. *The equal readiness of Christ to mark both the proper and improper in the conduct of his people.* The voice which blessed Peter when in the proper mood denounced him now. It is mercy in both. To chastise the wrong in us is as useful as to commend the right. But what was there in Peter's conduct to call forth this apparently severe reprehension? 1. *There was an arrogant irreverence.* Peter took him, probably, by the hand,* and began to "rebuke him." It would seem as if Peter had been so elated with the benediction which Christ had pronounced upon him, and the commission he had intrusted to him in the preceding verses that he had forgotten himself, forgotten the position he really occupied. He rebuked Christ! What arrogancy! The torch advising or censuring the sun. 2. *There was a culpable ignorance.* "That be far from thee." Far from him, Peter! Why for this he came into the world. If these things are not to occur to him hell forthwith must open her fiery jaws and swallow thee up, yea, thy race as well! "O fools, and slow of heart to

* *προσλαβόωενος αὐτὸν*. This controverted passage is best interpreted, "Taking him by the hand," an action naturally accompanying advice, remonstrance, or censure.—*Bloomfield.*

believe," etc. 3. *There was false sympathy.* We must do Peter the justice of supposing that something like compassion for Christ prompted this. But Christ is no object of compassion. He does not suffer against his will. Whether the cross is on his shoulders or he is on the cross, he is not an object for pity. Sentimental tears of compassion he repudiates as out of place, not required, and even offensive. "Weep not for me," etc. In his deepest agony he is an object for praise, not pity; commendation, not commiseration. He suffered not as a helpless victim, but as a free and an almighty champion.

Another thing which strikes our attention in Christ's conduct to Peter is,

Thirdly. *The character we should regard as acting a Satan to the soul.* "But he turned, and said unto Peter, Get thee behind me, Satan, thou art an offense unto me; for thou savorest not the things that be of God, but those that be of men." Mark says that he "turned about and looked at his disciples." What a look! What mingled feelings were in that flashing glance! What unutterable meaning and mystic force that *look* threw into those words of withering rebuke: "*Get thee behind me, Satan.*"

Satanas signifies an evil adviser, an adversary; and as such Peter now acted, and Christ with characteristic honesty denounces his conduct as offensive and satanic. Mark well the moral of this. He who gives us advice to tempt us from the path of duty, however attached to us and however friendly his motives, is a *Satan to us in that act.* Nay, his satanic power over us is in proportion to his love. The ill advice of an enemy is the devil without power.

"'Tis love that makes the tempter strong,
And wings his thoughts into the heart."

The devil is never so strong as when he works through the affections of a tender mother, a noble father, a brave brother, a beautiful sister, a generous lover. Let us learn to say even to the most loving and the most loved, when they seek from a false affection to turn us from a noble path of usefulness and duty, because it taxes so much our energies and demands from us such sacrifices, "Get thee behind me, Satan." Brother, keep Satan in the rear, and leave him further and further behind, until the impassable gulf of eternity shall lie between!

Another thing which strikes our attention in Christ's conduct with Peter is,

Fourthly. *The supreme work of human life.* What is it? Devotedness to "the things of God." "Thou savorest not the things that be of God, but those that be of men." The views of Peter savored of selfish ease and power. Such were not the things of God, which are self-sacrificing love, unswerving truthfulness, and supreme sympathy with the infinitely good. What are the things of God? "Whatsoever things are true, whatsoever things are honest, whatsoever things are just, whatsoever things are pure, whatsoever things are lovely, whatsoever things are of good report:" *such are the things that be of God*, and he is our Satan who seeks to turn us from them.

HOMILY VII.

THE HONEST SKEPTIC, AND HOW TO TREAT HIM.

But Thomas, one of the twelve, called Didymus, was not with them when Jesus came. The other disciples therefore said unto him, We have seen the Lord. But he said unto them, Except I shall see in his hands the print of the nails, and put my finger into the print of the nails, and thrust my hand into his side, I will not believe. And after eight days again his disciples were within, and Thomas with them: then came Jesus, the doors being shut, and stood in the midst, and said, Peace be unto you. Then said he to Thomas, Reach hither thy finger, and behold my hands; and reach hither thy hand, and thrust it into my side; and be not faithless, but believing. And Thomas answered and said unto him, My Lord and my God. Jesus saith unto him, Thomas, because thou hast seen me, etc. John xx, 24–29.

Wonderful day was that on which the Great Mediator rose from the dead as the conqueror of death and the Captain of human salvation. In it all past and future eras in the annals of redeemed man meet as in a central epoch. It is a bright orb in the sky of earth's moral history, throwing its radiance on all events, however distant and minute.

On the evening of this ever memorable day, the disciples, drawn by a common interest in the wonderful facts of Christ's history, assembled together, probably for conference and devotion. "The doors were shut," for they were afraid of the Jews. They knew that the men who had imbrued their hands in their Master's blood, would not hesitate to inflict agony and death on them. While in this room Jesus appears to them. No iron doors, no granite walls, no massive bolts can exclude him from his people. "He stood in the midst, and said, Peace be unto you." To assure them that he was not a specter, but the same veritable Jesus that two days before was nailed to the accursed tree, he shows to them the hands through which the rugged nails were driven, and the side into which the heartless soldier plunged the spear. The fear of the disciples departed, their faith was established, and they "were glad when they saw the Lord." Christ repeats his benediction, gives to them their commission, and qualifies them to discharge it by breathing on them the inspiring influences of heaven.

There were two disciples absent from this remarkable meeting, Judas and Thomas. Poor Judas could not be there; he had gone "to his own place" of retribution; he had done with such meetings forever; he was somewhere in eternity in the iron grasp of avenging justice. Alas, Judas, no more Christian conferences and godly devotions for thee!

But where was Thomas? Was he unacquainted with the hour or place of meeting? Did he flee too far off at the crucifixion to be able to attend? Or had he other engagements which precluded the possibility of his joining his brethren on this occasion? It is idle to speculate about the causes; all we know is that he was not present. Whether his absence was unavoidable or otherwise is not stated.

Some time in the course of that week, perhaps immediately after the meeting had broken up, the disciples met Thomas and told him that they had "seen the Lord." But he could not believe their statement, and he candidly told them so. "Except," said he, "I shall see in his hands the print of the nails, and put my finger into the print of the nails, and thrust my hand into his side, I will not believe." While there is an energy in this man's skepticism rather startling, there is a manly outspokenness about it which one is disposed to admire.

Eight days roll by, the second "Lord's day" dawns, and the disciples meet again. Thomas is present now. The doors are shut as before; Christ appears; after pronouncing his benediction he singles out Thomas and says to him: "Reach hither thy finger, and behold my hands; and reach hither thy hand, and thrust it into my side; and be not faithless, but believing." Such is the wonderfully suggestive incident before us.

An *interesting religious skeptic*, an *exemplary religious guide*, and a *supereminent religious faith*, are the three prominent objects in this narrative. They stand out in bold relief and commanding attitude on the canvass of this fragment of evangelical history. They are not characters foreign to our times and spheres, at which we have to gaze with a little curiosity and then pass on; in them we, the men of this age, and of these United States, have a vital interest; they demand, and will repay our deepest and devoutest study. Let us then bestow some earnest attention on each separately. We have here:

I. An interesting religious skeptic. There are certain features in this skepticism of Thomas that mark it off from the conventional and common skepticism of mankind.

First. *The skepticism of Thomas was negative, not positive.* Thomas did not put himself in antagonism to the fact announced, and meet it with a dogmatic and positive denial. He did not echo the everlasting NO that thunders evermore in the infidel world; all he said was, I cannot believe it without more evidence. He did not manifest any affinity of feeling with that presumptuous herd of mortals who arrogantly proclaim Gospel facts impossibilities, Gospel doctrines absurdities, and Gospel believers brainless fanatics or cunning knaves. Had he fully expressed his feelings he might have said: I do not deny its possibility, this would be to arrogate to myself infinite intelligence; nor do I impeach the veracity of you, my brother disciples; all that I say is, that such is the character of my intellect that I cannot believe such a strange and unheard-of fact on your unsupported testimony.

Secondly. *The skepticism of Thomas was intellectual, not moral.* The wish is often the father to the thought, the creed the offspring of the heart; but it was not so here. There is evidence that his love to Christ was fervid and forceful. About three months before this, when Lazarus lay dead, Christ said to his disciples: "I go, that I may awake him out of his sleep." Thomas being present, said: "Let us go that we may die with him." A noble burst of generous feeling this, indicative of his strong attachment to Christ. His heart then, we may presume, was in favor of the fact. Only too glad, we may suppose, would he be to welcome the beloved dead to life again. The difficulty was purely intellectual. The circumstance of a dead man coming to life, rising from a grave on which a large stone had been placed and firmly sealed—a grave sedulously guarded, too, by the Roman soldiers—was altogether so stupendous and unique that his intellect could not yield it credence without extraordinary evidence. In this, too, his skepticism differed widely from the general skepticism of mankind. Men's difficulties in believing now are not so much intellectual as moral.

Thirdly. *The skepticism of Thomas was frank, not underhanded.* To whom did Thomas now avow his unbelief? To the sordid worldlings who felt no interest in these things; to the sneering infidel who would readily nurse his doubts into atheism; or to scribes and Pharisees who would be only too delighted at the indications of his apostasy from this new and odious faith? No; to the ten men who told the fact he avowed his unbelief; like an honest man he expressed his disbelief in the face of the believers. Let modern skeptics imitate his example in this. Let them be ingenuous and manly in their deportment; let them, instead of appealing to the thoughtless crowd and seeking to work insidiously their infidel notions by jeers and jokes, innuendoes and tales, into the minds of the unreflecting multitude, go at once to the Church, to the men that believe, and say openly and respectfully, as did Thomas: We cannot believe in the doctrines you offer unless you give us more evidence. This would be manly and honest, and this might serve the common cause of truth and the common interest of our race.

Fourthly. *The skepticism of Thomas was convincible, not obstinate.* There are some men so inveterate in their prejudices that no amount of evidence will modify their opinions. You may as well argue with granite as with them; as well endeavor to remove Mount Washington from its rocky foundations as to uproot old notions from their brain. Such was not Thomas. After he first avowed his unbelief, did he seek, as is generally the case with skeptics, every possible means to establish himself in his infidel view? Nay, did he even avoid opportunities for obtaining evidence that should shake him in his foregone conclusions? The reverse of all this is the fact. He remained open to conviction, he sought new evidence. "Eight days" after he declared his skepticism we find him with the disciples, no doubt in search of sufficient proof to convince him that Christ had risen from the dead. It is not improbable that he spent the whole of the intervening week in the same earnest endeavor. He was an honest doubter; and honest doubt is active—active, because it is a law of mind to seek certitude.

Such then was the skepticism of Thomas; it was negative, not positive; intellectual, not moral; ingenuous, not mean; convincible, not obstinate. Such skepticism stands in striking contrast to that impertinent dogmatism, moral grossness, underhanded obliqueness, and stolid obstinacy which mark too many of the skeptics of this age. I confess to a kind of sympathy with the skepticism of Thomas's type. It indicates intellect of the higher species, honesty of heart, activity of thought, and often an agony of feeling. I have more faith in the virtue, more hope in the destiny of such skepticism than I have faith in the virtue or hope in the destiny of mere traditional faith. Honest skepticism is better than dead technical sainthood.

Another far more interesting object which we have in this narrative is,

II. AN EXEMPLARY RELIGIOUS GUIDE. We have here detailed the method in which Jesus, the heavenly guide of mortals, dealt with this poor skeptic. How does he act toward him? Does he denounce him as a heretic and expel him from the circle of his disciples? Does he treat him even with cold indifference, which to sensitive natures would even be worse than actual severity? No. How then? Let the ministers who fulminate from the pulpit denunciations against all who cannot subscribe to their tenets; let the sectarians who, with self-complacency, consign to perdition all beyond the pale of their little Church, mark well the conduct of Christ toward this Thomas. Eight days after Thomas had avowed his skepticism Christ finds him out, enters the room where he was with his brother disciples, fastens his loving looks upon him, singles him out, and says: "Thomas, reach hither thy finger, and behold my hands; and reach hither thy hand and thrust it into my side: and be not faithless, but believing." Three things are observable here:

First. *The direct speciality of his merciful treatment.* He dealt with Thomas personally. He did not address some general remarks bearing on the subject of doubt to the whole company, leaving Thomas to apply them if he would to his own individual case. He deals directly with him. He knew the highly critical state of his mind; he saw that the man was on the margin of the cold, dark, chaotic world of infidelity, and that he required prompt and special attention, or he would be irrevocably gone.

Secondly. *The exquisite considerateness of his merciful treatment.* The request of Thomas was objectionable on many grounds: there was an indelicacy of feeling, and a presumptuous extravagance about it, more or less revolting to our finer sensibilities. Nor can we see that the request went for anything like rational and conclusive evidence. He might touch the wounds, and the fact of Christ's identity would remain open to debate. Still, though the request is thus open to objection, Christ with exquisite considerateness condescends to grant it. He might have reproved him with severity for venturing such a demand; but instead of allowing a word of reproach to escape his lips, he at once, and lovingly, accedes: "Reach hither thy finger, and behold my hands; and reach hither thy hand, and thrust it into my side: and be not faithless, but believing."

Thirdly. *The moral influence of his merciful treatment.* What was the effect thus produced upon the heart of Thomas? He answered and said, "My Lord and my God;" or, The Lord of me and the God of me. As if he had said, I am more than convinced, more than satisfied; I am subdued by thy merciful condescension, I am won by the majesty of thy love. It was not, I trow, the mere touch of the wounds that produced this sublime effect upon his soul; it was the moral royalty of his merciful treatment. It is the spirit not the letter of your argument that will overcome skepticism. Far enough am I from disparaging the efforts of your Paleys, your Butlers, and your Lardners; but I believe that he whose life and words are inspired with the benign spirit of Christianity, though he may have no logic and no learning, will do more to subdue skepticism than your most cogent argumentations or your most eloquent appeals.

Mark well then, my brothers, Christ's method of treating skepticism, and take heed to the fact that in this respect he has left us an example that we should follow in his steps. But how has the Church acted toward sceptics? Has it treated them with tender consideration, singled them out, as Christ did Thomas, for special acts of kindness suited to touch their hearts, the seat of the disease? The volumes of history that lie about me unite in one emphatic NO. History tells us, that for many years the Church branded honest doubters as heretics, delivered them to the bloody inquisitors, and consigned them to the fiendish horrors of martyrdom.

The other interesting object in this narrative is,

III. A SUPEREMINENT RELIGIOUS FAITH. "Jesus saith unto him, Thomas, because thou hast seen me, thou hast believed: blessed are they that have not seen, and yet have believed." These words imply two facts:

First. *That it is possible for those who have never seen Christ to believe in him.* Wherever his Gospel goes, there goes evidence sufficient to produce faith without any personal manifestation of Christ whatever. There is, 1. The testimony of competent witnesses. A competent witness is one who has sufficient knowledge of the fact whereof he affirms, and a truthfulness of principle that would guard from any temptation to deceive. The declaration of such a witness I cannot but receive. Society could not go on, could not exist, were men to repudiate such testimony. Now, are not the Gospel witnesses pre-eminently of this class? Had not the apostles every opportunity of thoroughly knowing those facts of Christ's history which they propounded? Had they any possible motive to deceive? On the contrary, were not their inducements to deny the facts far stronger than those to declare them? There is, 2. The testimony of our consciousness. There is such a congruity between the doctrines of the Gospel and the intuitive beliefs of mankind, between the provisions of the Gospel and the deep-felt wants of mankind, that it comes with a self-evidencing power. It commends itself to "every man's conscience" in the sight of God. On this ground, rather than any other, I imagine it is generally believed. Consult the great body of believers on the question, and they would say what the Samaritans of old avowed: "Now we believe not because of thy saying, but because we have *heard him ourselves.*"

Thank God! it is possible to believe without seeing. In ordinary matters we are doing so every day. "Faith is the evidence of things not seen." The illustrious believers whom Paul celebrates in the eleventh chapter of the Hebrews, believed without seeing. Abraham believed in a city he never saw; Noah in a deluge long years before the windows of heaven were opened and the floodgates of the great deep broken up. Ever since the departure of Christ from this material sphere of being, the language of the Church has been: "Whom having not seen, we love; in whom, though we see him not, yet believing, we rejoice with joy unspeakable and full of glory."

The other fact implied in these words is,

Secondly. *That those who believe in him without seeing are peculiarly blessed.* "Blessed are they that have not seen, and yet have believed." We are apt to think that the cotemporaries of Christ, that the apostles who saw him, heard him, touched him, were privileged above all the rest of the human family. This is a delusion. The unseeing believer is the most signally blessed. Why? For the following reasons: Faith *without sight is more praiseworthy than faith by sight.* There are some, I know, who deny all moral character to faith; they say that man is no more accountable for his belief than he is for the color of his skin. This I admit to be true of a certain kind of faith. There are two very different kinds of belief: the one *voluntary*, the other *involuntary*. The one comes by a proper inquiry into evidence, and the other springs up irresistibly whenever a fact is visible to the senses, or a proposition is feelingly truthful to the mind. The evidence both of the bodily senses and the mental intuitions renders faith involuntary, and takes away from it therefore all moral merit. For such faith, we say, man is not responsible. But the *voluntary* is a very different thing. This depends upon a man's agency. There is a universe of facts that lies beyond the realm of my senses and that transcends all my *a priori* ideas. Belief in those facts—and it may be shown that the belief is indispensable to our well-being—requires evidence, and the evidence requires careful, honest, and earnest investigation. Man may examine evidence or he may not; he may examine it in a right or a wrong way. Here then is the responsibility. This voluntary faith has a moral character. Why do men not believe in Christ? It cannot be said for the want of evidence, for as a fact there is evidence that has satisfied millions, and will satisfy millions more;

but because that evidence is either entirely neglected, or, if examined, examined improperly. Now the faith of Thomas sprang from the sense, and had in itself but little if any moral merit. "Blessed therefore are they that have not seen, and yet have believed."

Faith *without sight is frequently more accurate than faith by sight.* The senses are deceptive, the eye especially makes great mistakes; "things are not what they seem;" nature is not what it seems; men are not what they seem. The eye would have us believe that the heavenly bodies are but lamps of various sizes hung up in the heavens; that the earth beneath our feet is the largest object brought within our notice, and that it sits like a queen in the midst of the system, serene and motionless, while all the heavenly luminaries like attendant angels pass round it, ministering evermore to the requirements of its life, and to the brightness and beauty of its forms. In all this the eye deceives, and in a thousand other minor matters it is busy with its delusions. Reason collects evidence and corrects these mistakes; it weighs the heavenly bodies and tells their density to a grain; it measures them and tells their dimensions to an inch. It calculates their velocity with the utmost accuracy. Reason has evidences on which to build a faith of unquestionable truthfulness.

Faith *without sight is more ennobling than faith by sight.* It involves a higher exercise of mind. Whatever tends to stimulate and work the mental faculties is good. Faith founded on rational evidence implies and demands this mental action. Sensuous faith does not require this: the mind may sleep while it comes and remains. The history of the apostles furnishes a striking illustration of this. How morally weak, because mentally inactive, were their minds during their personal connexion with Christ! Their faith in him was more or less the faith of *sight.* Hence how weak and timid they were. Peter had not power to avow him, none of his disciples had force enough to stand by him in his dying hour. "They forsook him and fled." But after his ascension, when they were thrown upon themselves and upon rational evidence, how giantly strong they become in a few days. They make the Sanhedrim tremble, they brave the most terrible powers of opposition, they turn the world upside down. It insures a higher mode of life. Were our faith in Christ to be merely built upon the senses, I can scarcely see how it could raise the mind from its present earthly and material state. Indeed, faith founded on the senses must confine the soul more or less to the sensuous department of life. Hence, as a fact, the disciples, so long as their faith rested on this ground, had the most material notions of the Saviour. On the contrary the faith that comes without seeing, that depends upon evidence requiring an examination that brings us in contact often with the most stirring facts, the most glorious principles, and the most quickening spirits, transports us beyond the realm of sense and introduces us into the world of spiritual forces—the things not seen and not temporal, but unseen and eternal. Moreover, it gives a wider sphere of being. The man whose faith is bounded by the evidence of his senses must have but a very narrow world. With the places he has not actually seen he will have no interest, no connection. The stupendous systems that roll away in the boundless districts of space, and the mighty principalities of spirits that populate those systems, will be nothing to him. Nay, life which is invisible, mind which is invisible, God who is invisible, will be nothing to him if he believes only what he sees.

From all this it is clear that especially "blessed are they that have not seen, and yet have believed."

In conclusion, the subject serves several important purposes:

First. *It suggests an incidental argument in favor of Christianity.* The fact that there was such a man as Thomas among the disciples, who could not believe without extraordinary evidence, and who manfully avowed his belief before the whole, plainly shows that there was no *collusion* between these witnesses of Christ, and that they were not a body of superstitious and credulous men.

Secondly. *The superiority of our advantages over those of the cotemporaries of Christ.* In certain sentimental moods we are disposed to say: Would that we had lived in the days of Christ, and enjoyed the privileges of his disciples. Would that we had gone with him on some of his journeys! walked with him the shores of Galilee, sailed with him over the sea of Tiberias, sat down with him on the mountain brow, entered with him the villages and cities which he visited! Would that we had heard him preach, and witnessed the wonderful things he suffered and wrought! Ah! this is not only useless wishing but unwise. It is *better* to be where you are. "We have a more sure word of testimony, unto which ye do well to take heed."

Thirdly. *The duty of the Church in relation to doubters.*

Who are the men in the Church that are most severe with doubters? Not the men who have the most intelligent, earnest, practical faith in Christ; but the men whose faith is either traditional, and therefore arrogant and blustering; or superstitious, and therefore moody, whining, and shaken with every breeze of doctrine. These in every age have been the fierce denouncers and the heartless persecutors of souls struggling with doubt. If we would be true to our profession as disciples of Christ, we must imitate his example in his conduct with doubters. "If a man be overtaken in a fault, ye which are spiritual, restore such an one in the spirit of meekness; considering thyself, lest thou also be tempted."

> "Let not this weak unknowing hand
>   Presume thy bolts to throw,
> And deal damnation round the land
>   On each I judge thy foe.
> If I am right, thy grace impart,
>   Still in the right to stay:
> If I am wrong, O teach my heart
>   To find the better way."

Fourthly. *The relation to Christ, which it is the supreme interest of humanity to seek.* It is that which Thomas expressed when he exclaimed, "My Lord, and my God." This man's faith reached the highest point. It was more than a satisfaction with the fact of Christ's resurrection, more than a trust in his divine person, more even than a confidence in his personal relation to him: it was a loving and loyal surrender of his being to him. "My Lord, and my God!" I am entirely thine: my intellect, my affections, my powers, my energy, my all, are thine. Thou art mine: mine to guide me in difficulties, guard me in dangers, supply me with all I need through all the coming ages of being.

This is the blessed transcendentalism: a loving self-abandonment to Christ, a moral absorption in him.

HOMILY VIII.

NO NEUTRALITY IN RELIGION.

He that is not with me is against me; and he that gathereth not with me scattereth abroad. MATTHEW xii, 30.

THE earliest, bitterest, and most constant of Christ's enemies were the Pharisees. Religiously proud, formal, and hypocritical to the last degree, it is not surprising that they were the unrelenting persecutors of him who taught the truth in its simplicity, exemplified it in its beauty, proclaimed the spiritual kingdom of God, and openly denounced them as "blind guides and hypocrites." They watched him with eyes full of malice, spake against him with tongues full of venom, and at last reddened their hands with his innocent blood. Now they who are in antagonism to truth are in a false position. "*Magna est veritas, et prevalebit*"—the truth is mighty, and must prevail; and the day of its triumph is that of their downfall. This is in some measure illustrated by the context. There was brought to Jesus "one possessed with a devil, blind and dumb: and he healed him, insomuch that the blind and dumb both spake and saw." This indubitable miracle amazed "all the people," and with one earnest voice they asked, "Is not this the Son of David?" What will the Pharisees do now? Speak they must, or silence gives consent. Unable to deny that supernatural power had been exerted, and resolved not to allow Christ's royalty, they coin and issue a diabolical lie: "They said, This fellow doth not cast out devils, but by Beelzebub the prince of the devils." With two irresistible arguments, Jesus repels their blasphemy. He reasons thus: If I cast out devils by the power of *the* devil, he is contending against himself, which is inconceivable; besides, my disciples, who are in a sense your children, cast out devils; ask them if they are leagued with Satan, and their indignant NO shall judge you. Having crushed the Pharisees with the sheer weight of their own objection, our Lord affirms that, with regard to the stupendous conflict waged between truth and error, holiness and sin, heaven and hell, no man can be neutral; that we all are inevitably identified with one or other of these interests; with Christ and against Satan, or with Satan and against Christ. Viewing the miracle in question in these two lights—first, as a sign of that mighty spiritual war on which Immanuel has entered; and second, as a pledge of the complete victory which he will ultimately achieve over all his enemies—how well-timed is this solemn word: "He that is not with me," etc.

Two lines of thought open before us. I shall show:

I. Who are allied with Christ. There is a fearfully large class of persons who are manifestly and avowedly *not* with him; their attitude is unequivocally hostile. Probably they would not relish being pushed with the inevitable consequence that they are therefore with Satan; but they do not hesitate to say that a religious life is not to their taste, that they are unprepared to renounce "the pleasures of sin" and to bow their necks to the yoke of God's Anointed. Alas, their name is legion!

Turning from these, the professed enemies of the Son of God, we confront another class, equally large, and whose position is yet more dangerous. Orthodox, according to best authorities, in their beliefs, scrupulous in their observance of religious ordinances, conscientious in the practice of a secular morality, and favorable to the enterprises of Christian zeal, they imagine that nothing more is required at their hands, and would bitterly resent being accused of enmity against the Cross. Behold the true Pharisee! Religious formalism is slaying its ten thousands. Men are mistaking the chaff for the wheat; because of "blind guides and hypocrites," they are forgetting that "the kingdom of God is not meat and drink, but righteousness and peace and joy in the Holy Ghost." There may be very much in a man's character that is estimable and lovable while yet he lacks the one essential thing, without which "he is nothing."

Then let the formalist stand aside, for he is not with Christ. I will now make two remarks in positive delineation of the character of those who are with him.

First. *They are delivered from the power of Satan.* There is a certain dominion which he has acquired over humanity. What an appalling proof of this was furnished by those miserable beings whose very bodies were afflicted with Satanic influence? In this chapter Christ admits that

Satan has a "kingdom," and likens him to a "strong man armed," in possession of a house and its goods; he is elsewhere pronounced to be "the god of this world," "the prince of the power of the air," and "the spirit that now worketh in the children of disobedience." All this is strongly declarative of the ascendancy which he has obtained over the human soul. The teachings of Scripture and the facts of the case are as one; every man not emancipated by the glorious Gospel is led captive by the devil at his will. I do not say that he rules over men in the exercise of an irresistible objective power; no, he cannot compel the worst sinner to commit a single sin; he can tempt only; but, inasmuch as the heart is corrupt, he does not tempt in vain. Human depravity is the fulcrum of Satan's power, and the strength of sin is the measure of his dominion. But God's love is mightier than the devil's malice. "The seed of the woman has bruised the serpent's head." "For this purpose was the Son of God manifested," etc. 1 John iii, 8. His death was a death-blow to "the power of darkness," for it atoned for man's sin, and procured the gift of the omnipotent Spirit.

Still, we are not saved as a necessary consequence of mediation. Salvation is a subjective work, and one in which the human will is concerned. How well the whole process is described in the commission received by Saul of Tarsus as he stood up, blind and penitent, amid the insufferable glory of the Damascus road! "I send thee to open their eyes," etc. Acts xxvi, 17, 18. Wondrous change! The ransomed sons of God. We give "thanks unto the Father, who hath made us meet to be partakers of the inheritance of the saints in light; who hath delivered us from the power of darkness," etc. Col. i, 12, 13.

Secondly. *They are in co-operation with Christ.* This thought is expressed in the last clause of the text, which alludes to the harvest-field, where he who does not help unavoidably hinders. The field is the world; of the harvest Christ is Lord; all his servants are laborers therein; "and he that reapeth receiveth wages," etc. John iv, 36. Now the work of Christ is the destruction of sin out of men's souls, and therefore this co-operation relates, (1.) *To the accomplishment of our personal salvation.* The deliverance from Satan's dominion, already considered, does not comprehend the complete purification of the heart; and yet that is the great purpose of the Gospel. The Redeemer gave himself for us that he might "redeem us from all iniquity;" and if we thoroughly sympathize with him, we shall not be at ease so long as the foul "prince of this world" hath anything in us. Goodness is the measure of usefulness. To do good we must *be* good. The holiest binds the heaviest sheaf and takes the largest wages. (2.) *To the salvation of our fellows.* Experimental Christianity is irrepressibly communicative; it charges the heart with unmingled benevolence toward all men; it is that charity of God "which seeketh not her own," but is ever outgoing in holy activities for the good of others. Christ finds Andrew and Philip; forthwith Andrew finds Simon, and Philip finds Nathaniel. One conversion is, or ought to be, the first of a series. Do you seek a proof of alliance with Christ? Tell me, What are you *doing?* What is the aim of your life? Is it the acquisition of knowledge? the accumulation of wealth? the gratification of your affections? To be his, and be worldly, selfish, or indolent, is impossible. If our hearts beat for him our hands will gather with him. And he that cannot ply the sickle will bind the sheaves, and he who cannot bind the sheaves will glean the stray ears; but none may stand "idle all the day."

In passing, it is proper to allude to those who are, as it were, *in transitu*. Not yet in the enjoyment of "the glorious liberty of the children of God;" their hearts are gone from Satan; they abhor his service and loathe his wages. One act of faith, and they are clean escaped out of the snare of the devil! Believe, my contrite brother, and thou art free, and joined to the blood-sprinkled host who uplift the standard of the cross! Leap up, thy bands are sundered; go forth, the prison doors are open wide; grasp sword and shield; hurl defiance at thy foes, and henceforth fight the battles of the Lord!

II. All not thus with Christ are of necessity against him. In proof of this position I observe:

First. *That man's natural state is one of antagonism to God.* Do we enter the world with neutral characters? Are the tablets of the soul blanks, whereon we may write what we will of good or evil? Could we read the heart in the earliest stages of responsible life we should trace these fearful words: "Enmity against God." "We go astray from the womb speaking lies." Sin is not simply a negation, the mere absence of goodness; for a real substantive existence must be assignable to a principle which can war, and that successfully, against its opposite. The sinful are not only without God; they also fight against him; and this inevitably. Shall it then be said, Wherein is the sinner culpable? In reply, it is enough to point to the cross. "As by one man's disobedience," etc. Rom. v, 19. "God was in Christ," etc. 2 Cor. v, 20, 21. Sinner! it is your worst offense, your most intense expression of antagonism to God, your loudest protestation of friendship with Satan, that you "resist the Holy Ghost," and live in sight of the cross, without loving Him who bleeds for thee thereon.

Secondly. *That it is a necessity of man's nature to influence for good or evil all with whom he may associate.* Man is social. The Creator has implanted in us a desire for the society of our kind, and from the gratification of this instinct flows much of human happiness. But we are *impressible* as well as social beings; and we cannot come into contact with each other without exercising a mutual influence, morally beneficial or injurious. Now the character of a person's influence will correspond with the state of his heart; for as is the heart so is the life. "A good man out of the good treasure," etc. Matt. xii, 35. Hence the righteous are "the salt of the earth;" "but one sinner destroyeth much good." We cannot limit the effects of our conduct to ourselves. It is easy to cast the seed into the furrows that lie open on either hand, but who can say whereunto it will grow? O the influence of the strong in mind, the large of heart, the high in rank, the wealthy in estate; of pastors, of parents, of friends, and I will add, with emphasis, of authors! We see many and great effects now, but we shall be astounded by the revelations of eternity. The good man shall hear of his good influence in the heavenly world; and the bad man of his bad influence amid the scenes of retribution. How awfully suggestive is the last request of the rich man: "Send Lazarus to my father's house, for I have five brethren, lest they also come into this place of torment." Brothers! we are blessing or cursing the world; we are heaven-lighted stars piercing the "gross darkness" that covers men's souls, and indicating the central source of bliss; or dark clouds, big with curse, shutting out the sweet light of life, and causing men to wander into error, to fall into sin, and, it may be, to stumble headlong into everlasting ruin. Then well might Christ say, "He that is not with me," etc.

Thirdly. *That our allegiance is Christ's righteous and inalienable due.* He is of royal dignity, and therefore sustains to us relations out of which come vast, solemn, and eternal claims. He is the Creator and Sustainer of our being; above all, he is our Redeemer, and by the shedding of his blood has acquired a new right to all we are and have. "Ye are not your own," etc. 1 Cor. vi, 19. Who among us can stand aloof from a suffering Christ and the great work which he has undertaken, and be guiltless? Neutrality, so called, is robbery; it is foulest rebellion, it is basest ingratitude, it is the damning sin. "Curse ye Meroz," said the angel of the Lord, "Curse ye bitterly the inhabitants thereof, because they came not up to the help of the Lord, to the help of the Lord against the mighty."

Friends of Jesus! be of good courage. True, principalities and powers are against you; but God, and truth, and the holy universe are for you. The issue is not uncertain; the victory of Christ has made victory sure to every faithful soul. Then up to the high places of the battle-field; urge ye where the strife is hottest; strike where the foe is strongest, and, dying, live forever!

Enemies of Jesus, beware! In vain you fight against him; "for he must reign until all enemies are put under his feet." Be wise betimes; have done with sin; break with Satan; put up your swords; is it not enough that they have pierced the heart of Infinite Love? The hour of retribution is stealing on apace, and then . . . ! who shall speak of such things? The battle is hot, but in the midst of the strife mercy pleads with you. "Now, then, we are ambassadors for Christ, as though God did beseech you by us; we pray you in Christ's stead, be ye reconciled to God."

HOMILY IX.

MAN'S RELIGIONS AND THEIR TESTING DAY.

Not every one that saith unto me, Lord, Lord, shall enter into the kingdom of heaven; but he that doeth the will of my Father which is in heaven. Many will say unto me in that day, Lord, Lord, etc. MATT. vii, 21–27.

THIS passage teaches,

I. THAT MEN ARE NOW RELYING ON VERY DIFFERENT KINDS OF RELIGION. Most men have some kind of religion. Man has been called "a religious animal." He has at once worshiping instincts and capacities. However destitute of knowledge and civilization he may be, he is generally found in possession of a creed, a shrine, and a God.

We have suggested to us in the text no less than four kinds of religion:

First. *The religion of profession.* "Not every one that saith unto me, Lord, Lord, shall enter into the kingdom of heaven." These words imply that many of the human family would call him "Lord, Lord." And in the course of ages has it not thus happened in the case of millions? As a nation we call Jesus "Lord." We build temples for his worship; we recognize the Bible in our laws; but as a nation does our conduct agree with our profession? Are his laws held everywhere supreme? rather, are they anything more than speculative ideas to us? His words, perhaps, are a vague creed to us, but certainly they are no supreme, ruling code. He has commanded us not to lay up treasures on earth; not to labor exclusively for the meat that perisheth; not to take anxious thought for the morrow; not to return evil for evil, but to do good to our enemies, and thus imitate Him, "who when he was reviled, reviled not again." These are his laws, written as with a sunbeam, in his own word; but is not our conduct in direct opposition to these injunctions?

Another form of religion suggested by this passage is:

Secondly. *The religion of merit:* "Many will say to me in that day, Lord, Lord, have we not prophesied in thy name? And in thy name cast out devils, and in thy name done many wonderful works?" The spirit of this is, Have we not merited thy favor by what we have done? There is a fearful tendency in man to attach the idea of merit to his religious conduct. How many there are who imagine that by their social integrity, their benevolent deeds, their devotional observances, they will procure the favor of their Maker? But he who has this idea has not learned the alphabet of Christianity. Were I as holy as an angel, as devoted as a seraph, could I ever do aught that would merit a single favor from my Maker? No! for the power with which I should work would be his, and the instrumentality by which I acted would be his, and the time I employed would be his, and the influence which incited me would be his: what merit, then, could attach to my operations? How absurd, therefore, for a sinner to attach the idea of *merit* to the best of his labors!

Another form of religion suggested by this passage is,

Thirdly. *The religion of hearing:* "Whosoever heareth these sayings of mine," etc. This also has ever been a very popular form of religion. Great numbers were now hanging on the lips of Christ, and feeling probably an interest in the wonderful things he uttered. Never, perhaps, was the religion of hearing so general as now. But hearing the Gospel is not true religion. There are many things which give men an interest in hearing the Gospel, altogether apart from the true religious feeling. There is, 1. *Man's native desire for excitement.* Every man has an instinctive desire for excitement; the mind pants for it as the "hart for the water-brook." The poetry, the narrative, the discussion, the speech, the scene that will kindle the most emotion, the oratory that will move and melt, will ever be the most welcome to the human heart. And within the widest sweep of creature thought are there any subjects so suited to stir the human passions and move the human heart to its center as those with which the preacher has to do? There is, 2. *A native desire for knowledge.* Deeply seated in the intellect is the craving after truth, a craving which no amount of information can gratify. Supplies only serve to quicken it; allay it they cannot. The Gospel ministry meets this desire also. The Bible contains an exhaustless mine of truth, and it is the province and duty of the minister ever to bring out things new as well as old.

The fact that the Gospel ministry serves to gratify these two instincts in human nature is sufficient to show that no man has a right to infer that he is religious because he feels an interest in *hearing* the word. It serves, moreover, to explain the fact that there are two widely distinct classes of Gospel hearers, the morbid sentimentalists and the theoretical intellectualists. The former are never gratified in the sanctuary unless their passions are stirred and their animal sympathies awakened. They wish gunpowder and mercury mixed with every sentence, and nothing is so pleasant to their ears as a sudden and terrible detonation, as of a magazine explosion. And the latter, the theoretical intellectualists, esteem nothing as Gospel but certain doctrinal views. They feed on the polemic, the deeply metaphysical, the ultra mundane, and their creed is often dust.

Another form of religion suggested by this passage is,

II. THAT A CRISIS WILL DAWN WHEN ALL THE VARIOUS KINDS OF RELIGION SHALL BE TESTED: "*That day.*" The universal forebodings of humanity, man's moral reasonings on providence, and analogy concur with the Bible in teaching that such a day will come. It is not the frenzy of poetic numbers, but it is the irrepressible instinct of the individual heart that cries out:

> "That awful day will surely come,
> The appointed hour makes haste,
> When I must stand before my Judge
> And pass the solemn test."

Christ says, "*that day*," as if his hearers were thoroughly convinced of its coming, and were assured of its pre-eminent importance; "*that day*," when all the purposes of mercy shall be realized, when the mediatorial economy shall be closed and Christ deliver up the kingdom to God, even the Father; "*that day*," when earth's "marble tomb" shall burst asunder and the graves send forth their mighty dead; when all the men who have ever breathed this air or trod this earth shall stand forth in the full consciousness of their personal identity in the presence of their Maker and their Judge; "*that day*," when the despised Galilean, the wearied traveler at Jacob's well, the malefactor on the cross shall appear on that great white throne, before whose refulgent brightness the heavens and the earth shall melt away; "*that day*," when every providential mystery shall be explained, every complaint silenced, every murmur hushed forever; "*that day*," to which all other days have pointed, to which the events of all other days have flown, whose sun shall never set, and whose transactions will never be reversed or forgotten; "*that day*," when an everlasting separation shall be made between the righteous and the wicked; when the redeemed universe, shaken by the storms of centuries, shall settle into a peace that no sin shall break again; "*that day*," when all the bright epochs of time, which, like stars, have been glimmering out their pale and chilly rays from the benighted firmament of the race, shall be lost in the brightness of a sun that shall rise to set no more.

The other general truth contained in this passage is,

III. THAT ON THAT DAY THE TRUE AND FALSE RELIGIONISTS WILL BE MOST SIGNALLY DISTINGUISHED. First. *The false religionists will be filled with intense anxiety; the true will not:* "Many will say to me in that day, Lord, Lord," etc. How agitated the false in that day, how calm the true!

Secondly. *The false religionists will be rejected, the true will not.* "And then will I profess unto you I never knew you," etc. How ineffably dreadful will it be to be disowned by Him whose smile is heaven, but whose frown is hell! "I never knew you;" never approved of you; though you heard with interest my Gospel, though you wrought great things in my name, yet I never approved of you.

Thirdly. *The false religionists will meet with destruction, the true will not.* "Therefore whosoever heareth these sayings of mine, and doeth them, I will liken him unto a wise man, which built his house upon a rock: and the rain descended, and the floods came, and the winds blew, and beat upon that house; and it fell not: for it was founded upon a rock. And every one that heareth these sayings of mine, and doeth them not, shall be likened unto a foolish man, which built his house upon the sand: and the rain descended, and the floods came, and the winds blew, and beat upon that house; and it fell: and great was the fall of it." In Judea there are periodical rains which often continue for successive days; these rains often fill the glens of the mountains to their overflow, and the accumulated waters rush forth and roll in foaming torrents down the hills, bearing everything before them. The house that was built above them would be secure, but that at the base would be exposed to the utmost danger. Picture the scene of the house thus built on the sand. It is just finished, and the owner has taken possession of it as his home. There he hoped to enjoy comforts which would amply repay his labor and cost. For a season all is fair. It is girded by the hills, the valleys bloom around, the genial air breathes softly by. It seems a beautiful residence, a well-chosen home. The traveler admires it on his journey. But the summer months roll away, autumn succeeds, and now the dreary winter comes. There are indications of a storm; the clouds gather, blacken, and spread; the winds howl in threatening notes, rains commence, torrents fall on the earth day after day without abatement, the glens of the mountains are full to overflow, they come rushing down the hills with an ever-increasing force, they dash against the sides of the house, they accumulate around it, they penetrate and loosen the foundation; meanwhile the winds are raised to a hurricane, and are beating all their force upon the building. At length the foundation gives way; not a stone, a timber, escapes; it is utter ruin. "Great was the fall!" Such is the image which Christ employs to describe the terrible condition of the false religionists in "*that day*."

How miserable the circumstances of this man! Think of the *amount* of his loss. All the money, anxiety, and labor which its erection cost him sacrificed forever. Think of the *time* of his loss; the house is destroyed just at the period when *most required*, in the tempest; think of the *irremediableness* of his loss. The materials are probably borne away by the flood, and a re-erection is impossible.

In sublime contrast with this, behold the stately and stable dwelling of the "doer of the word" up upon the rock yonder. It stands unmoved amid the severest tempests of *that* day, and, with a full consciousness of security, the tenant looks calmly out, and enjoys the wild sublimity of the scene.

HOMILY X.

THE PENITENT THIEF.

And he said unto Jesus, Lord, remember me when thou comest into thy kingdom. And Jesus said unto him, Verily, I say unto thee, To-day shalt thou be with me in paradise. LUKE xxiii, 42, 43.

THERE is this difference between these words of Christ and any of the other utterances on the cross, that here we have a dialogue, and consequently we cannot enter fully and fairly into the meaning of this holy saying without examining the words of the other party with whom the conference was carried on.

I. THIS MAN WAS A HARDENED SINNER—A TRANSGRESSOR OF THE LAWS OF HIS COUNTRY, AS WELL AS OF THE LAWS OF HIS GOD. (1.) He had gone so far in the way of crime that he allowed the justice of the sentence of death under which he was then suffering. (2.) When he was placed in this dreadful position he was so lost to everything which was religious and rational as to unite with the other criminal to revile the Saviour. "The thieves also which were crucified with him cast the same in his teeth." (3.) These two men were of the lowest class of criminals, doubtless of the party of Barabbas, who were guilty of depredation and murder. The heartless enmity of the priests and Pharisees was seen in all its virulence, in ordering that Christ should be crucified between such criminals; but their wrath was overruled to the praise of God. The hardened sinner was melted into penitence, and in the hour of his agony saved by Christ.

II. What were the means that became effectual to awaken in him a concern for the salvation of his soul? The two criminals were equally near to the Saviour. What one heard and saw the other heard and saw; and yet one continued in his hardened, impenitent, and guilty state; the other, subdued and penitent, earnestly prayed for mercy. *The same Gospel is a savor of life unto life*, etc. The same hour witnesses one soul passing from death to life, and another sinking beyond the reach of salvation. The early education and religious advantages of these two men might have been widely different, though they had come to the same miserable end. The penitent thief might have had pious parents, who had well instructed him in the principles of religion. It might have flashed across his mind that even then, with broken hearts and sorrowful breasts, they were praying for him. Or perhaps he had heard the words of the kingdom during the public ministry of the Lord, and that this scene now recalled them. Or it might have been that the words of Christ, so tender and filial, which he had just uttered about his mother, or the still more wonderful prayer that he had offered for his enemies, had come home to his conscience and penetrated his heart. Or perhaps this man had not had so many advantages as the other in early life, that sinning against more light had made the other more insensible to his destiny. Whatever were the means used, the result was as rapid in its progress as it was glorious in its form and permanent in its duration. He stepped on the threshold of death destitute of any hope; but ere he had entered within its dark and dreary borders light dawned upon his mind. He felt, thought, prayed, and was blessed.

III. The change was wrought by the power of the Holy Ghost. Whatever might have been the means, through them came to his heart the current of life. Such a marvelous change could be the workmanship of no power but that of God.

IV. The dying malefactor exercised faith in Christ under the most discouraging circumstances. He believed that he who was suffering at his side was the Messiah. He appealed to him as a *king*. "*Remember me when thou comest into thy kingdom.*" This was done, not when the winds and waves were yielding submission to the potent charm of his words; not when the grave was giving up its prisoners in obedience to his command; not when the tumultuous throngs were loud in their shouts of hosannah; not when he was permitting the inherent glory of his nature to gleam forth through the mortal body which concealed it; not when he was uplifting his arm to defend his followers, and defeat his foes; but when he was in the depth of his humiliation —dishonored, forsaken, helpless in the hands of his enemies, stretched as a malefactor on the cross. The faith of the dying thief shrinks not from comparison with the highest examples in the annals of the immortal heroes of God. Abraham's faith was great, but it fastened itself on God when he revealed himself as the Eternal Creator, and the Almighty Ruler of all things. Moses's faith was strong, when, with meek confidence, he went into the presence of the mightiest monarch of the age to demand the freedom of the oppressed people; but the "I AM" had revealed himself in the burning bush, and promised his presence to succor and to bless. The ancient prophets believed; but impressive scenes, special revelations, and displays of resistless power had been manifested to them. The disciples of Christ believed, because *they saw his miracles.* But the thief placed confidence and trust when he was apparently impotent in the hands of his triumphant foes. He witnessed no other tokens of royalty around the cross than the crown of thorns, the mock robe, the scepter of reed; and even that had dropped from his bleeding hands. His faith in the Saviour was great, if we consider (1.) *He believed in him as the Messiah;* (2.) *He believed in him as one whose dominion and sovereignty would survive the shock of death;* and (3.) *He believed in him as one that would show mercy to the unworthy.* The salvation of the thief was extraordinary, but his faith was also extraordinary. In presenting this as an encouragement to death-bed salvation, it should be solemnly considered, and faithfully represented, that the faith which secured the salvation has seldom been equaled, and never surpassed.

V. WE SEE THAT, DURING THE SHORT TIME THAT ELAPSED BETWEEN THE EXERCISE OF THIS EXTRAORDINARY FAITH AND THE DEATH OF THE MALEFACTOR, THE VARIED EVIDENCES OF CONVERSION AND THE RICH FRUIT OF GENUINE FAITH WERE FULLY DISPLAYED. (1.) *Contrition and confession of sin.* "We indeed suffer justly; for we receive the due reward of our deeds." (2.) *He expressed his admiration of Christ, and boldly defended his name and character from the accusations and aspersions of those who condemned him.* "This man hath done nothing amiss." Another fruit of faith seen in the dying thief was, (3.) *That he employed his expiring energies, and spent his last moments in endeavoring to convince and convert his fellow-criminal.* "Dost thou not fear God, seeing that thou art under the same condemnation?" (4.) *Then it might have been said of him, as it has been said of every converted man, "Behold, he prayeth."* His prayer was addressed through the one Mediator—the High Priest who alone can present our supplications acceptably to God in the right spirit—as an unworthy sinner, for the right blessing, to be remembered by Christ. That implied all he needed to enrich him forever.

We now proceed to contemplate,

VI. THE WORDS OF OUR BLESSED REDEEMER TO THE THIEF, IN ANSWER TO THE APPEAL WHICH WE HAVE GLANCED AT. "Verily, I say unto thee, To-day shalt thou be with me in paradise."

First. *The words imply that Christ was in the conscious possession of supreme authority, even at that hour of his sufferings and humiliation.* Without any equivocation or hesitancy, he claims to himself the right and the power of admitting whom he will into the paradise of God. He gives the condemned malefactor a title to enter there.

Secondly. *We see in these words the principle on which prayer is answered.* The blessings that are asked for may not be given, but the blessings that are adapted to the real wants of the suppliant. "To-day thou shalt be with me in heaven." This was far more, vastly greater, than the prayer implied, but it was just the gracious favor that suited his wants. He was dying. Of what use would it be to him to say that he should have temporal honors, earthly riches, or even office, in the kingdom of grace on earth? All such things, valuable in their place, would be an incumbrance and burdensome then. But to be assured that he should be admitted into the realms of everlasting glory, was a balm that soothed and healed the suffering, agonizing soul.

Thirdly. *In this answer we see that Christ, in his dealings with sinners, confirms his promises by utterances to correspond with the mental and moral hinderances of belief.* It would have been most natural for a man of the dying malefactor's character to doubt the promise that he should be admitted into paradise. Therefore Christ confirms his promise with a solemn asseveration: "*Verily* I say unto thee."

Fourthly. *These words solve the important and interesting question of the immediate existence of the soul after death.* "*To-day* shalt thou be with me in paradise." The good pass, without entering any intermediate state, to their destined felicity; the wicked and impenitent go, without lapse of time, into their own place. There is no change of character, or of principles, in death.

Two remarks:

First. *The different views which persons entertain relative to Jesus Christ mold their moral nature to tenderness and penitence, or to hardness and guilt.* There were equally near to the Saviour two individuals—the one passing into heaven, the other sinking into perdition; both in similar circumstances, and both dying. But one believed in Christ, loved him, sought his help; the other nursed in his breast irreconcilable enmity toward him.

Secondly. *The danger of delaying turning to God is most impressively set before us here.*

If we should see a man who went over the Falls of Niagara in a boat and was saved, should it encourage us to venture in the rapids? What a risk this thief ran; how near he came to losing that heaven which he has now secured; one hour's delay would have placed this man beyond the reach of mercy. *Here is the only case in the Bible of repentance at the close of life. One instance is given that none may despair; and only one, that none may presume.*

HOMILY XI.

THE MORALITY OF LANGUAGE.

But I say unto you, That every idle word that men shall speak, they shall give account thereof in the day of judgment. For by thy words thou shalt be justified, and by thy words thou shalt be condemned. MATT. xii, 36, 37.

HUMAN language is looked upon in different aspects by different men. Some look upon it *grammatically*, trace its etymology, and arrange its words and sentences according to the conventional rules of speech. Some look at it *logically;* study it in its relation to the laws of human reasoning. Some look upon it *philosophically;* view it in its relation to the nature of the things it is intended to represent. And some look upon it *morally;* contemplate it in its relation to the laws of conscience and God. *Grammatical* language is mere conformity to acknowledged rules of speech; *logical* language is conformity to recognized principles of reason ing; *philosophical* language is conformity with the order of nature; *moral* language is conformity with the laws of God. There is a regular gradation in the importance of these aspects of language. The first is of the least importance, the second next, and the third next, and the last the most important of all. It is strange and sad to see that the amount of attention which men pay to these aspects is in the inverse ratio of their importance. The first, the least important, is the most attended to; the second next, the third next; and the last, the most important of all, almost entirely neglected. In the department of speech we have more grammarians than logicians, more logicians than philosophers, more philosophers than honest saints. It is to this moral aspect of language that Jesus calls our attention. *We have here the heinous enormity of some language, the true function of all language, the only method for reforming corrupt language*, and the *responsibility* associated with even the most *trifling language.*

I. THE HEINOUS ENORMITY OF SOME LANGUAGE. Some "speak against the Son of God," and "some against the Holy Ghost." Such language involves,

First. *The grossest injustice.* The language of strong invective and denunciation against some men may be, to some extent, justified by their unrighteous principles and unworthy conduct. But not so here. What fault can any find in the Son of God or in the Holy Ghost?

Secondly. *The foulest ingratitude.* What have the Son of God and the Holy Ghost done for us in our salvation? The suggestion of the question is enough.

Thirdly. *The greatest profanity.* Against whom are they speaking? To speak against a human sovereign is sometimes a capital offense. But this is against the Eternal Prince of the universe.

Fourthly. *The maddest hostility.* When you hear a man speak against another you may be sure that there is strong feeling of malignity at the root. We deal tenderly with the characters of those we love. We speak *for* them when accused to the utmost of our power. When men, therefore, are found "speaking against the Son," and "against the Holy Ghost," you may be sure that there is a profound feeling of hostility at the root. But how mad, how irrational is the feeling! There is no *reason* for such enmity; on the contrary, there is every conceivable reason against it. *Right* and *expediency* are equally against it.

How heinous then is language when thus used against God! And yet, alas! it is not uncommon. You have it from the pen of the infidel in treatises, poems, orations, and from the blasphemous lips of the scoffer and profane.

II. The true function of all language. "Either make the tree good, and his fruit good, or else make the tree corrupt, and his fruit corrupt: for the tree is known by his fruit." The idea suggested is, that language is to be to the real heart of man what fruit is to the tree, *the exact expression of itself.* The fruit embodies and represents the very essence and heart of the tree. Even so should language. The function of words is faithfully to represent the soul; they should be to man's inner being what the beam is to the sun, the fragrance to the flower, the stream to the fountain, the fruit to the tree: faithful exponents of itself.

If this is the true function of language, there are two sad and general perversions of it.

First. *When words are used without meaning.* "Words are but air" is a current expression, and too often is truthfully applicable to the utterances of men. In the idle chat of gossip, the formal expressions of etiquette, the vapid compliments of society, you have words that do not stand for any real sentiments in the soul. As a rule, perhaps, where you have the most talk you have the least soul, the most profession the least principle, the most loquacity the least spiritual property and power. Language is perverted,

Secondly. *When words are used to misrepresent.* They are frequently so used. They are employed not to reveal, but to conceal what is within; they are masks to misrepresent the face of the heart. Such words as dishonest tradesmen use in striking their bargains, the seducer in rifling the virtue of his victim, the ambitious candidate in winning the suffrages of the people. The world truly is full of such perversion.

The fact is, that so depraved is society that it cannot afford to be sincere, cannot afford to show its real heart in its language. It feels compelled to use the divine faculty of speech, one of the choicest gifts of Heaven, to misrepresent the true state of its mind. What a change would come over society at once were no words used but what were "the fruit" of the heart! Let every man in America to-morrow begin to show his real sentiments and feelings in his language, let every word be the true mirror of the soul, and American society would be shaken to its foundation. What contracts founded in deception would dissolve! What friendships based upon false professions would be ruptured! Souls which had mingled together in social intercourse, when they came by faithful speech to see each other face to face, would start asunder with mutual repulsion, and rush away with instinctive horror and indignation.

How great then is the depravity of our world that we are bound to throw over it the drapery of falsehood! We have reached such a state that there seems to be a felt necessity for lying; we are either afraid or ashamed to use our words as the sun uses its beams, to show its nature.

III. The only method of reforming corrupt language. "O generation of vipers, how can ye, being evil, speak good things? for out of the abundance of the heart the mouth speaketh. A good man out of the good treasure of his heart bringeth forth good things; and an evil man out of the evil treasure of his heart bringeth forth evil things." What treasures are in the heart! What unbounded productiveness of thought, feeling, and action! The inference of Jesus from this is, "make the tree good and his fruit good." The scribes and Pharisees spoke blasphemously, because their hearts were bad. They were true to their hearts: if they had spoken otherwise they would have spoken hypocritically. Therefore, reformation of language must be preceded by reformation of heart.

This will appear further evident if we consider the elements of correct moral language. These elements we deem to be *sincerity* and *purity*. By *sincerity* we mean the strict correspondence of the language with the sentiments of the heart; and by *purity* we mean the strict correspondence of those sentiments with the principles of everlasting right. Sincerity without purity, were it possible, would be of no moral worth. But sincerity of expression without purity of sentiment seems to us, as we have already intimated, all but socially impossible. A corrupt man is both ashamed and afraid to expose the real state of his heart to his fellow-men. But let the sentiments be pure, let the passions be chaste, let the thoughts be generous, let the intentions be honorable, let the principles be righteous, and then, instead of there being any motive to insincerity of language, there will be all the incentives to the utmost faithfulness of expression.

The condition then required for correct moral language is what Jesus here teaches, purity of heart. For "how can ye being evil speak good things?" Unless the fountain is purified the stream will ever be tainted; unless the tree be made good the sap that lies in the root will give a tinge to the foliage and a taste to the fruit. Would we then have a correct language? Would we have the kind of language among men which the Bible enjoins? speech "seasoned with salt, ministering grace unto the hearers;" "pleasant words which are as a honey-comb, sweet to the soul and health to the bones;" a tongue among the people which shall be as "choice silver" and "a tree of life?" Would we have this blessed state of speech? we must struggle to produce that moral regeneration which Jesus so constantly and earnestly enforces. The "cup" and "platter" must be cleansed "within;" the people must have "a new heart and a right spirit;" they must be "renewed in the spirit of their minds;" sinners must "cleanse their hands" and the "double-minded" must "purify their hearts;" the heart of humanity must be "cleansed by the washing of regeneration and the renewing of the Holy Ghost."

IV. The responsibility associated even with the most trifling language. "I say unto you that every idle word that men shall speak they shall give account thereof in the day of judgment." The Pharisees might have imagined that as they had but spoken, and had perpetrated no real act of enormity, no guilt was contracted. Christ disabuses them of such an impression by assuring them, "That every idle word," etc. Every idle word: not merely the profane and impious language of the scoffer and blasphemer, but every *idle* word, words that have little or no meaning; the most airy words of wit and humor spoke in jest, not to delude or pain, but simply to please. "Every idle word," etc. "For by thy words thou shalt be justified and by thy words shalt thou be condemned."

There are three considerations which may serve to show us the responsibility that attaches to idle words: their *reactive force*, their *social influence*, their *divine recognition.*

First: *Their reactive force.* So constituted are we that our expressions, every one of them, must have a reflex influence. "Those things which proceed out of the mouth come forth from the heart, and *they defile the man.*" The man who indulges in idle and frivolous talk damages his own mental faculties and moral sense thereby. In such speech there is no demand for the reflective powers, and they become impotent; there is no development of the sentiments of truth, benevolence, and religion, the very stamina of our moral nature, and they become more and more inoperative and dead. In idle talk the soul in every way is impaired; its rich soil, capable of producing trees of knowledge and of life, is wasted in flowery but noxious weeds. Whatever we do that is unworthy of our nature damages our own powers and interests.

Secondly: *Their social influence.* Science affirms that every movement in the material creation propagates an influence to the remotest planet in the universe. Be this as it may, it seems morally certain that every word spoken on the ear will have an influence lasting as eternity. The words we address to men are written not on parchment, marble, or brass, which time can efface, but on the indestructible pages of the soul. Everything written on the imperishable soul is imperishable. All the words that have ever been addressed to you by men long since departed are written on the book of your memory, and will be unsealed at the day of judgment and spread out in the full beams of eternal knowledge.

Thirdly: *Their divine recognition.* The great Judge knows every word we have spoken. Not only "the hard speeches" which ungodly men have spoken against him will he bring into judgment, but also "every secret thing." "Out of thine own mouth will I judge thee."

HOMILY XII.

PAUL AND SILAS; OR, THE TRANSCENDENT POWER OF CHRISTIAN PIETY.

And at midnight Paul and Silas, etc. ACTS xvi, 25–40.

THIS fragment of apostolic history sets forth in the most striking and inspiring aspects the surpassing power of personal Christianity,

I. WE SEE HERE CHRISTIAN PIETY ELEVATING THE SPIRIT ABOVE THE GREATEST TRIALS. "At midnight Paul and Silas prayed and sang praises unto God." Where were they in these midnight hours, and what was their physical condition? The preceding verses inform us that they were in the inner prison, the darkest part of the dungeon, their bodies lacerated with the stripes of the lictors, and their feet made fast in the stocks. At "midnight," kind nature's season for sleep, they were sleepless. They could not sleep; their bleeding wounds drove sleep away. Yet instead of spending those midnight hours of physical torture in bitter imprecations on their enemies, or rebellious murmurings against heaven, they "prayed" and "sang." Those old prison walls, which were accustomed to echo groans and sighs, resounded now with unearthly strains of joy and praise. There was midnight without, but sunshine within; their bodies were in chains, but their souls were free. Their religion bore them aloft to regions of unrestricted liberty and unclouded light.

What gives religion this power to raise the soul above such torturing and terrible trials? First. *Its faith in the divine superintendence of man's entire history.* The apostles knew that they were not in their present wretched condition by accident or chance, but that the whole was under the wise and kind control of the eternal Father. This is consoling. Job felt this. "He knoweth the way that I take." Secondly. *Consciousness of God's approval.* Had their consciences accused them of having acted contrary to the will of God, there would have been darker midnight and a severer suffering within than without. But the reverse was the consciousness. The "well done" of heaven echoed within, and set all to music. "If God be for us, who can be against us?" "Being justified by faith, we have peace with God," etc. Thirdly. *Memories of Christ's trials.* The religion of man is vitally connected with Christ. His intellect is filled with memories, and his heart with the spirit of Christ. He compares his trials with those which Christ endured, and he experiences a support by the comparison. Fourthly. *Assurance of a glorious deliverance.* "Our light afflictions which are but for a moment," etc. "I reckon that the sufferings of this present time are not worthy to be compared with the glory which shall hereafter be revealed in us."

These things explain, to some extent at least, the soul-elevating force of religion. He who has this religion has a well-spring of joy within himself. He can glory in tribulation, and find a paradise in a dungeon.

II. We see here Christian piety insuring the interposition of the Greatest Being. "And suddenly there was a great earthquake, so that the foundations of the prison were shaken, and immediately all the doors were opened, and every man's bands were loosed." This was an undoubted miracle, and demonstrated in the most impressive manner the fact *that God takes special care of the good.* The Great One observes all, sustains all, directs all, owns all, but has a special regard for pious souls.

First. *Reason would suggest this.* Would not reason suggest that the eternal Spirit would feel a greater interest in mind than in matter? that the eternal Father would feel a greater interest in his offspring than in his mere workmanship? that the source of all love and holiness would feel a greater interest in those who participate in his own moral attributes than in those who do not?

Secondly. *The Bible teaches this.* (1.) In explicit declarations. "To that man," says the Almighty, "will I look, even to him that is poor and of a contrite spirit and trembleth at my word." "As a father pitieth his children, so the Lord pitieth them that fear him." "Wherefore if God so clothe the grass of the field," etc. (2.) In the biography of the good. Did he not specially interpose on behalf of the patriarchs, prophets, and apostles? God will ever interpose for the good. If necessary he will make the heavens rain bread, and the rock outpour refreshing streams. He will divide the sea, and stop the mouth of lions.

III. We see here Christian piety capacitating the soul for the highest usefulness.

First. *The Philippian jailor was prevented from self-destruction.* "The keeper of the prison awaking out of his sleep, and seeing the prison doors open, he drew out his sword, and would have killed himself, supposing the prisoners had fled." Imagining the wondrous escape of the prisoners, and being held by the Roman government responsible for the safe custody of the prisoners, he was overwhelmed at the fearful penalties to which he was exposed. He determined to kill himself. Instead of regarding such an act as a crime, he would perhaps attach a virtue and nobleness to it. He would only be following the example of Brutus and Cassius, who, after their defeat by Antony and Augustus, fell on their swords, with many of their friends, in this very Philippi. But Paul prevented this. "Do thyself no harm; we are all here." The voice of Christianity to man is, "Do thyself no harm;" no harm of any kind. The good are ever useful in preventing evil.

Secondly. *The Philippian jailor was directed to true safety.* "Sirs, What shall I do to be saved?" This question indicates, we think, a complex state of mind. He had regard not only to material and civil deliverance, but to spiritual and eternal. The question implies a *sense of peril* and a sense of the *necessity of individual effort.* What shall I do? Something must be done. Paul without circumlocution and delay, in the fewest possible words, and at once, answers, "Believe on the Lord Jesus Christ and thou shalt be saved." Some paraphrase it, "Heartily embrace the Christian religion and thou shalt be saved." Believe on him as the representative of God's love for the sinner, as the atonement to God's law for the sinner, as a guide to God's heaven for the sinner.

Thirdly. *The Philippian jailor experienced a delightful change of heart and of mind.* "And he took them the same hour of the night and washed their stripes, and was baptized, he and all his straightway. And when he had brought them into his house he set meat before them and rejoiced, believing in God with all his house." What a change! The ruffian, who "thrust them into the inner prison, and made their feet fast in the stocks," and who felt perhaps not one single pang of sympathy for their intense suffering, now tenderly washes their "stripes," and entertains them with pious hospitality. The terror-struck soul who "called for a light and sprang in, and came trembling, and fell down" in utmost horror before Paul and Silas, is now full of joy and faith. "He rejoiced, believing in God."

IV. WE SEE HERE CHRISTIAN PIETY INVESTING THE SOUL WITH THE TRUEST INDEPENDENCY. "And when it was day the magistrates sent the sergeants, saying, Let those men go."

First. *Here you see their independency of soul in their superiority to their fear of man.* As soon as they were miraculously delivered from prison they might have hurried away from such a scene of enemies; but they remained, although the magistrates gave them liberty to depart. They were not afraid. They could chant the forty-sixth Psalm: "God is our refuge and strength," etc.

Secondly. *Here you see their independency in refusing great benefits, because offered on improper grounds.* Paul said unto them, the messengers of the magistrates: "They have beaten us openly uncondemned, being Romans, and have cast us into prison, and now do they thrust us out privily? Nay, let them come themselves, and fetch us out." Glorious independency! As if Paul had said, These Roman magistrates, as they are called, in beating us openly uncondemned, and thrusting us secretly into prison, have violated the laws of Rome, and trampled on our rights as citizens; politically we have not deserved this treatment, and we will not accept, as a favor, that which we demand as a right. Let these magistrates come themselves and fetch us out; and this will be a practical confession that they were wrong, and a practical vindication of our conduct as citizens. A great soul will repudiate favors offered on mean, unjust, or unworthy grounds. A good man will refuse liberty, social influence, wealth, unless they can be honorably and righteously obtained.

Thirdly. *Here you see their independency triumphing over their enemies.* The magistrates, feeling they had done wrong, "came and besought them, and brought them out, and desired them to depart out of the city." These tyrants became fawning suppliants at the feet of their prisoners.

Such is Christian piety as first displayed in Europe, and displayed in Europe in a prison. Piety is not that weak simpering thing which often passed for it, and still too often passes for it. It is the mightiest force on earth. It lifts the soul into rapture, light, and grandeur, amid the most terrible physical suffering, darkness, and thraldom. It insures divine interposition on its behalf, and moves the arm of Omnipotence in its favor. It qualifies for the highest usefulness, checks the progress of evil, directs souls to the true means of salvation, and works out a glorious transformation in the character of man. It invests the soul with the loftiest independency; an independency which defies antagonism, repudiates benefits unless righteously and honorably presented, and makes governments do it homage. True Christians have not received "the spirit of fear, but of love, power, and of a sound mind."

HOMILY XIII.

JUDAS; OR, ASPECTS OF A GUILTY CONSCIENCE.

Then Judas, which had betrayed him, when he saw that he was condemned, repented himself, and brought again the thirty pieces of silver to the chief priests and elders, saying, I have sinned in that I have betrayed the innocent blood. And they said, What is that to us? See thou to that. And he cast down the pieces of silver in the temple, and departed, and went and hanged himself." MATTHEW xxvii, 3–5.

THE history of Judas teaches us three things. First. *The power of one sinful feeling to counteract the influence of the best society.* Judas was "one of the twelve." For nearly three years he associated with the pure, loving-hearted John, the ardent and honest Peter, the truthful and upright James. Above all, with Jesus. What doctrines and prayers he heard! What dispositions and deeds he witnessed! But notwithstanding this all went for nothing with him. Like showers on rocks and sands. Why was this? The corrupt feeling of *avarice* was within, and this perverted all. It rotted all the good seeds that were thrown into him.

Secondly. *The power of man to conceal his sinful feelings from others.* When Jesus, at the last supper, said, "One of you shall betray me," each began to say, "Lord, is it I?" They did not know who. We know not what is going on in the breast of others. Each is a world to himself.

Thirdly. *The power of conscience to inflict merited punishment.* This is seen in the text.

Here you have a guilty conscience in four aspects:

I. Waking into anguish at the accession of new light: "When he *saw* that he was condemned repented himself." First. *The nature of the anguish which he now experienced:* he "repented himself." Who shall estimate the misery represented by these words? This anguish was not the fear of punishment. He knew that he had done a popular act, and that his countrymen, perhaps, would make him a hero for ridding them of such a public disturber as Christ. It was the *essential wrongness*, not the *personal consequences* of the act that pained him now. It is self-crimination, self-loathing, self-reprobation. "A wounded spirit who can bear?"

Secondly. *The accession of the new light which produced it:* "When he saw that he was condemned." He did not expect this result when he perpetrated the deed. He had no unkind feeling, perhaps, toward Christ. Probably he thought his act would bring on the crisis in his history which he, in common with the other disciples, anticipated—his ascension to universal empire. But when "he saw" the opposite result, then his conscience bounded into fury. Let Heaven cast *new* light upon the sinner's deeds, and then conscience will start. This new light must come.

II. Ineffectually struggling to obtain relief. He makes two useless efforts. First. *Restitution in a wrong spirit:* "He brought again the thirty pieces of silver," etc.

To his avaricious nature they were once very valuable, but now he felt they were curses. Conscience reverses our estimates. These silver pieces now seemed red with blood and hot with fire. He could not retain them. But the restitution was in a wrong spirit; it was from a *selfish* desire for relief, and not from a *self-sacrificing* desire to make satisfaction for the injury.

He makes, secondly, *confession to the wrong party.* To the chief priests and elders, not to God, he says, "I have sinned," etc. The confession I take as a powerful testimony to two things: 1. *To the moral freedom of human nature.* Logically, we debate as to whether internal impulses and external circumstances do not coerce men, destroy their liberty of action, and make them slaves. An awakened conscience despises such logic, and makes short work with it. It impels the man to say with all the emphasis of his nature, "I have sinned; I am the author of the act; not my propensities or circumstances, but I." This confession is a powerful testimony, 2. *To the moral purity of Christ's life:* "Innocent blood." Judas, being admitted into the inner circle of our Saviour's social life, in common with other disciples, had every opportunity of judging of his real character; and now, therefore, his testimony to the purity of his life is far more powerful than the testimony of any other could possibly be. Far more so, for example, than Pilate's. Pilate only saw the outward, Judas the inward.

III. Heartlessly repulsed by guilty associates. "What is that to us? See thou to that." "The ungodly," says Bengel, "though associating in the commission of a crime, desert their associates when it has been accomplished." The godly, though not taking part in the crime, endeavor, after its commission, to save the sinner's soul. I submit three remarks on the conduct of these men.

First. *It was cruel.* They were the tempters: they offered the bribe; and in doing so, no doubt they were genial and bland.

Secondly. *It was unavoidable.* They had guilty consciences as well as Judas, and in this very matter too. Perhaps their consciences began to trouble them a little now. The guilty *cannot*, if they would, comfort the guilty.

Thirdly. *It was representative.* It was a specimen of conduct that must ever take place under similar circumstances. It is so in hell. Every appeal of the tempted to his tempter will meet with the response, "What is that to us? See thou to that." The infidel to his disciples, the debauchee to his victims, etc. The heartless response of every seducer in hell, to the agonizing entreaties of his victim is, "WHAT IS THAT TO US? SEE THOU TO THAT." Your bland tempters must become your tormenting devils.

IV. PLUNGING INTO ETERNITY IN DESPERATION. He "went and hanged himself." Two things here:

First. *The intolerableness of his existence.* Life itself became an unbearable burden.

Secondly. *The irrationality of his existence.* Conscience threw reason off its balance. If he had reasoned a moment he would have known that suicide could destroy neither *existence, conscience, sin, or misery;* but on the other hand would make all these more terribly real.

From this subject we infer, 1. *That there is a moral government over man in this world.* A guilty conscience proves this. 2. *That compunction is not conversion.* 3. *That a guilty conscience must find either hell or pardon.*

HOMILY XIV.

THE FEEDING OF THE FIVE THOUSAND; OR, THE COMPANION OF CHRIST.

And they that had eaten were about five thousand, besides women and children. MATT. xiv, 21.

"WHEN Jesus heard of it he departed thence by ship into a desert place apart." The expression, "heard of it," does not refer to what John's disciples told him; nor, we think, to the statement of Herod, in the second and third verses of this chapter, where the narrative dropped, in order parenthetically to relate the murder and burial of John; but to what his own disciples had told him, on their return from the mission on which he had sent them. From Mark's account, and also from Luke's, it appears almost certain that this was the case. Mark says: "And the apostles gathered themselves together unto Jesus, and told him all things, both what they had done, and what they had taught." The words of Luke are: "And the apostles, when they were returned, told him all that they had done. And he took them, and went aside privately into a desert place belonging to the city of Bethsaida."

Indeed, perhaps the two communications, the one from

the disciples of John, concerning the tragical end of their Master, and the other from his own disciples about their ministries, were all but coincident. As the bereaved and sorrowing deputation withdrew, probably the other appeared flushed with the memory of their moral victories, though physically fatigued with their arduous campaign. "When Jesus heard it, he departed thence by ship into a desert place apart." Various reasons may be assigned for the withdrawal of Jesus into this desert place. Bloomfield, who supposes that ἀκούσας refers to John's death, and Herod's opinion of himself, says that "it was on both accounts, as well as to avoid the imputation of blame for any disturbance which might be expected to follow."

Let us now attend to some particulars of that compassion of Christ which are displayed in this narrative.

We infer from this narrative,

I. That his compassion extends to all the diversified infirmities of our nature.

First. *Here are the sufferings of the afflicted which engage his compassion.* "And Jesus went forth and saw a great multitude, and was moved with compassion toward them, and healed the sick." The "multitude," we are informed in the preceding verse, were the people that followed him on foot out of the cities. Mark says, "ran afoot." The word is not used in contrast with riding, as would at first appear, but in contrast with going by sea on ship. Jesus sailed across the lake, while the people went round by land to the place where he went ashore. Here in crowds they stood around him. Many of them were afflicted with diseases more or less distressing. He saw in the deep sunk eye, in the withered cheek, in the tottering frame, of many in that multitude great suffering, and his heart was touched with sympathy, and "he healed the sick." Christ feels for human suffering.

Secondly. *Here is the fatigue of his disciples which engages his compassion.* He looks at his disciples, worn and jaded with their labors, and he says to them: "Come ye yourselves apart into a desert place, and rest awhile: for there were many coming and going and they had no leisure so much as to eat." "He," says Stier, "speaks not of his own, but of the disciples' rest;" and because they were somewhat too full of all the things that they had done and had taught, he kindly leads them into the solitude where is the true rest. They are not to create such a sensation or make such a noise among the people on their return to them. "Come *ye* also now into retirement, as I am wont to do, and even now have need of it for myself; rest yourselves from your journey, because ye too have labored." But when Christ permits or commands rest, he yet significantly adds, a little. More is at present not yet granted them; labor soon again sought out him and them. "He knoweth our frame, he remembereth that we are dust." He knows that we require rest even from our honest labors. He is no hard master. His "yoke is easy and his burden is light."

Thirdly. *Here is the spiritual destitution of the people which engages his compassion.* Mark says: "And Jesus, when he came out, saw much people, and was moved with compassion toward them, because they were as sheep not having a shepherd; and he began to teach them many things." It was the state of their souls that stirred his heart the most. Spiritually they were without *food* and without *protection*, as "sheep without a shepherd."

Fourthly. *Here is the physical hunger of the multitude which engages his compassion.* "And when it was evening, his disciples came to him, saying, This is a desert place, and the time is now spent; send the multitude away, that they may go into the villages and buy themselves victuals." These words would give us the impression that the benevolent desire to prepare food for the hungry thousands arose first in the minds of the disciples. But such impression would be manifestly false. John, in his account of the case, gives an incident which the other evangelist omitted, and which shows that the desire arose in the merciful mind of Christ. "When Jesus then," says John, "lifted up his eyes and saw a great company come unto him, he saith unto Philip, Whence shall we buy bread that these may eat?" Christ puts the question, not of course because he did not know what to do, but that he might "prove" to the apostle himself, and prepare the minds of all to appreciate, the magnitude of the miracle he was to perform. And he addressed the interrogation perhaps to Philip rather than to the rest, either because, as some suppose, that Philip was the disciple who took charge of the food; or, which is more probable, his somewhat materialistic temperament (John xiv, 8) rendered it specially desirable. True to his sensuous tendencies, Philip began to calculate how much money would be required to procure such a quantity of food. "Two hundred pennyworth of bread is not sufficient for them," said he. Now, after the appeal had been thus made to Philip, and he had spent perhaps some time in his calculation, "and when the day was now far spent," or as Luke has it, "began to wear away," the other disciples began to feel anxious. "And they came to him, saying, this is a desert place and the time is now past, send the multitude away that they may go into the villages and buy themselves victuals." What a soul-bracing thought it is, that there is ONE who feels for earth's woes, and is "mighty to save!"

We infer from this narrative,

II. THAT HIS COMPASSION IS ASSOCIATED WITH AMPLE CAPABILITY TO RELIEVE. The incident shows,

First. *That his capability to relieve transcends their conception.* Perhaps he allowed his disciples to tax their invention to the utmost to find out how the vast hungry multitude could be fed; and after they had failed he says: "They need not depart. Bring them [the five barley loaves and two fishes] hither to me. And he commanded the multitude to sit down upon the grass." Mark says: "He commanded them to sit down by companies upon the green grass. So they sat in ranks by hundreds and by fifties." Behold the wondrous scene! Five thousand men, besides women and children, seated on the *green grass.* There is none of the confusion generally attendant on crowds in this scene. There is no jostling, no intermingling, no noise. All is exquisitely arranged by the Master; they sit down *in ranks by hundreds and fifties.* All eyes are centered on Jesus; a silent wonder reigns through the crowd. He takes the five barley loaves and the two fishes; he looks up to heaven, blesses these simple articles of food, and then divides them among all, and "they all eat and are filled." "Few miracles," says Livermore, "could be less exposed to cavil than this, which not only addressed the eye, but which satisfied the appetite of thousands." What could have been more morally sublime, or a higher proof of divine authority than the creation, so suddenly, of an immense quantity of food to relieve the famishing crowd? The incident shows,

Secondly. *That his capability to relieve transcends their necessities.* They only required food for the occasion, but they had much more. "They took up the fragments that remained, twelve baskets full." His gifts are never exhausted; there always remains something over. He gives nothing with a niggardly hand. To show the immeasurable depths of his love and the amplitude of his power, he always gives more than is required. In nature it is ever so. Less light would illumine the world, less water fertilize the earth, less air would feed the world's great lamp of life. Nature, which has fed the generations that are gone, has as much if not more for the generations that are to come. The fragments that remain are always greater than the stock that has been used. In the Gospel it is so. In the Gospel he has supplied the need of millions, but he has "unsearchable riches" in it still. Nay, his blessings seem to increase by consumption. The more they are used, the more they multiply and grow. Thus God's great universe grows richer every day.

We infer from this narrative,

III. That Christ's compassion is never exercised to encourage wastefulness. "Gather up the fragments that nothing be lost." Although he miraculously creates a wondrous profusion of food, he inculcates the lesson of frugal use. "Let nothing be lost." Use all, abuse none. In one sense nothing can be lost, not an atom of matter, not a thought of mind; nature, both in the material and spiritual realm, allows nothing that once comes within its grasp to escape. In a moral sense, however, a thing is lost when it is not rightly used. Food is lost when it is allowed to rot; truth is lost when it lies dead in the soul; the soul is lost when it does not serve its God. The lesson is: do not let heaven's blessings run to waste; appropriate them to the right purpose: those that rightly use them shall have more, those that abuse them shall lose what they have.

We infer from the narrative,

IV. That Christ, in the exercise of his compassion, would direct men to the infinite source of all good. "And looking up to heaven, he blessed and brake and gave the bread to his disciples." He blessed God for the food. This was a custom among the Jews. "Blessed be thou, O Lord our God, the King of the world, who has produced this food from the earth!" That was the form. But it was not from custom that Christ did it. It was heart with him. His spirit rose in gratitude to the infinite Father. And he assumed this heaven-turned attitude, and used words in order to impress the minds of the multitude that they must turn their hearts to heaven as the source of all good.

This is a wonderful narrative. Every part demands a thoughtful pause. It is instinct with divinity; it heaves with suggestions about suffering man and the redeeming God. It is a little mirror reflecting the world and its heavenly Helper. Let us ever look at them both together. I know the world is burdened with woes. Deep throes of anguish rise from the heart of humanity every day:

> "Each new morn
> New widows howl, new orphans cry, new sorrows
> Strike heaven in the face that it resounds!"

But, thank God! I know too that there is one come from heaven to heal the broken-hearted.

HOMILY XV.

THE PUBLICAN IN THE TEMPLE.

And the publican, standing afar off, would not lift up so much as his eyes unto heaven, but smote upon his breast, saying, God be merciful to me a sinner. I tell you, this man went down to his house justified rather than the other. LUKE xviii, 13, 14.

IN these well-known words we have,

I. A CONVICTION OF PERSONAL GUILT. "God be merciful to *me a sinner*." We are not confounded into a mass of persons by "Him with whom we have to do." Each stands alone and isolated from his fellows. "Every man must give an account of himself," etc. "Every soul must bear his own burden." The convicting agency of "the Spirit of truth" gives us a solemn sense of individuality and personal accountability to God; like the hand of a detective policeman, seizing and dragging us out of the crowd.

II. Passionate grief on account of sin. He "*smote* upon his breast," the seat of grief; "godly sorrow" surged in waves of distress over "his broken and contrite heart." Grief is not uncommon among men, but how rarely witnessed is such grief as this! This feeling is produced by reflection on,

First. *The deep offense we have offered to God.* This is the chief element in true penitence: "Against *thee*, thee only, have I sinned." "I have sinned *against heaven*, and in thy sight." This is "repentance *towards God*."

Secondly. *The awful injury we have inflicted on ourselves.* Every sinner is like the Gadarene demoniac who cut himself with stones. In sinning against God, the true penitent sees that he has sinned awfully against his own soul.

Thirdly. *The hurtful influence we have exerted on others.* "Every corrupt tree bringeth forth evil fruit," and this fruit is not "for the healing" but destruction of men's souls; "one sinner destroyeth much good."

III. Deep humility mingled with shame before God. This is seen,

First. *In his standing afar off*, that is, from the oracle, denoting that he felt unworthy to appear within the sacred precincts, as if he felt that his presence would pollute the place of the holy!

Secondly. *In his not lifting up so much as his eyes unto heaven*, (or so much as lifting up his eyes,) identical with the Psalmist, "My sins have taken hold upon me so that I am not able to look up," etc. What produces this "shame and confusion of face?" The perception of the divine purity. "I have heard of thee by the hearing of the ear, but now mine eye seeth thee, wherefore I abhor myself and repent in dust and ashes." The holiest of men feel this in the view of God. Hence Isaiah: "Woe is me for I am undone, because I am a man of unclean lips, and dwell in the midst of a people of unclean lips, for mine eyes have seen the King, the Lord of Hosts."

IV. Earnest prayer to Heaven. Observe:

First. *The object of the prayer: "mercy."* From justice nothing to expect but punishment. Mercy is well called "the sinner's only plea." Observe:

Secondly. *The character of the prayer.* 1. It is *simple* and *brief*, denoting *sincerity* and *earnestness*. Few are the words, but the whole soul of the suppliant is in them. 2. *It is presented in the way of God's appointment.* "He went up to the temple to pray," most probably at the time of the offering of the daily sacrifice. Hence the rendering given to these words—*ἱλάσθητί μοι.* "Be propitious to me through sacrifice; "or, Let an atonement be made for me." Like "righteous Abel," he seemed to know that "without shedding of blood there is no remission."

V. A happy result. "I tell you this man went down to his house justified rather than the other." "This man," so confused and humbled before God; "this man," on whom his self-complacent fellow-worshipers poured so much disdain; "this poor man," who "cried unto the Lord," and sought mercy in the way of the divine appointment; "this man rather than (or not) the other," went down to his house approved of God and relieved of his distress. "Thus saith the high and Holy One that inhabiteth eternity, whose name is holy, I dwell in the high and holy place; with him also that is of a contrite and humble spirit, to revive the spirit of the humble, and to revive the heart of the contrite ones."

HOMILY XVI.

RIGHT ESTIMATE OF LIFE.

So teach us to number our days, that we may apply our hearts unto wisdom. PSALM xc, 12.

THE prayer implies,

I. THAT THERE IS A CERTAIN JUDGMENT TO BE FORMED AS TO THE DURATION OF AN EARTHLY LIFE. What is it? Not the exact *hour*, *scene*, or *circumstances* of our end. We thank Heaven for concealing all this. Ignorance of this is, First. *Essential to our practical watchfulness.* Secondly. *To our personal enjoyment.* And, Thirdly. *To our social usefulness.* It means that we should have a practical impression that life here is *temporary* and *preparative.* The prayer implies,

II. THAT THERE IS A TENDENCY IN MAN TO NEGLECT THE FORMATION OF SUCH A JUDGMENT. Why this tendency? 1. Not from the want of circumstances to suggest it. History, observation, experience, all remind us every day of our end. 2. Not from any doubt that we have about the importance of realizing it. All acknowledge the importance. But, First. *From the secularity of one controlling purpose.* Secondly. *From the instinctive repugnance that we have to death.* Thirdly. *From the moral dread of future retribution.* And, Fourthly. *From the delusive suggestions of the tempter.* He says now as ever: "Ye shall not surely die." This passage implies,

III. THAT THE FORMATION OF A CORRECT JUDGMENT IS ESSENTIAL TO PRACTICAL WISDOM: "That we may apply our hearts unto wisdom." First. *Such judgment would serve to impress us with the connection between this life and the future.* Secondly. *It would serve to moderate our affections in relation to this earth.* Thirdly. *It would serve to reconcile us to the arrangements of Providence.* We are pilgrims, voyagers, scholars. Fourthly. *It would serve to stimulate us to render all the circumstances of this life subservient to a higher.* Time is bearing us and all away.

"The eternal surge
Of time and tide rolls on, and bears afar
Our bubbles; as the old burst, new emerge,
Lashed from the foam of ages, while the graves
Of empires heave but like some passing waves."

HOMILY XVII.

THE SPIRIT OF A HAPPY LIFE.

Giving thanks unto the Father, which hath made us meet, etc. COL. i, 12.

THERE are four classes of men in relation to life:

First. *Those whose life has no purpose.* The millions seem to have no worthy object in view; they act with purposeless souls. Secondly. *Those whose purpose is limited to the world.* They aim at knowledge, wealth, fame. Thirdly. *Those whose life has a purpose in relation to the future.* These look at the present in relation to the future, and endeavor to make it subserve its interest. And, Fourthly. *Those who feel that their purpose in relation to the future is already realized.* This is the state of mind in the text. The state of mind here is not a mere hope that all is right, or even an assurance. It is more; it is a *thanksgiving* that all is right. The lamp is trimmed and burning, the vessel has unfurled her sails, and is sure of reaching the harbor. Now there is no man, I think, however infidel he may be, who would not desire to possess this state of mind; to look to the future with such a heart. This state of mind implies three things:

I. A BELIEF IN A SCENE OF FUTURE BLESSEDNESS. Thankfulness for a preparation for it evidently implies this. There are two things suggested here about this scene. First. *Its physical character.* It is called an "inheritance." Heaven is a locality. It is sometimes called "paradise," a "house," "Jerusalem." Secondly. *Its spiritual character:* "Inheritance of the saints in light." Light is the emblem of intelligence, purity, happiness. The state of mind in the text implies,

II. A BELIEF IN THE NEED OF A PERSONAL PREPAREDNESS FOR IT. Why feel thankful for that which is a superfluity? Heaven requires training. The training is not *intellectual* or *mechanical*, but MORAL. To see the necessity of this, compare the spirit and conduct of all in heaven with that of depraved man on earth. First. *All in heaven have a consciousness of God's approbation; depraved men are not so.* Secondly. *All in heaven are actuated by devout disinterestedness; depraved men are not so.* Thirdly. *All in heaven feel the highest delight in spiritual exercises; depraved men do not so.* Fourthly. *All in heaven feel an intense interest in Christ; depraved man does not.* Fifthly. *All in heaven joyously abandon their own will to God's; depraved man does not.* From all this it follows that there must be a wonderful change to fit for heaven. The state of moral mind in the text implies,

III. A BELIEF IN THE PREPAREDNESS BEING EFFECTED BY THE AGENCY OF GOD. There could be no thankfulness without this conviction. The gratitude implies: First. *That the work is transcendently valuable to us.* We could not feel thankful for that which was of no service. What is to be compared with this in value! Secondly. *That the work is accomplished with the design for our good.* A party may do a service for us, but if we feel that he did not intend to serve us, we could not feel thankful. Thirdly. *That the work is accomplished in perfect sovereignty.* If we felt that he was bound to do it, we could not feel thankful.

This subject does three important things: First. *Presents our early life in an important aspect.* It is a scene of moral culture. He who regards it as a divan, a mart, or laboratory, mistakes. Secondly. *Presents the Creator in an attractive aspect.* A FATHER: a Father by means of nature, providence, the Gospel, and the Church, training his children for glory. Thirdly. *Presents Christianity in a sublime light.* What a glorious state of mind is this! Some are *dead* to the future, some *dread* the future, some *feebly* hope in the future. But the Christian *thanks* God for a preparedness to meet it. Gratitude is bliss. Blessed state of mind this to have in such a world as *ours.*

HOMILY XVIII.

THE UNREASONABLENESS OF PEOPLE IN REGARD TO THE PULPIT.

That we may be delivered from unreasonable men, etc.—2 THESSALONIANS iii, 2.

FROM the verse preceding the text we learn the Gospel idea of a *true* preacher: "Finally, brethren, pray for us, that the word of the Lord may have free course, and be glorified, even as it is with you." Observe,

First, *That a* TRUE *Gospel preacher has always one great master theme.* What is that theme? the doctrines of science, the theories of philosophy, the passing questions of the day? No! "THE WORD OF THE LORD." Words are not always mere empty sounds, that die away upon the air; they are often the mightiest forces in the world. They are not only the symbols by which mind shows itself to mind, but they are the weapons by which mind achieves its conquests over mind. A skeptic was once assisting an aged Christian lady from a train of cars, when she, thanking him for the kindness, said: "Do you know Jesus Christ, the Saviour of men?" The words fell with strange suddenness and power on the man's heart, and no reply was made. He went home, but the words of the veteran disciple rang in his ears, and in less than a week he was bowing at the foot of the cross seeking Jesus the Saviour of men, whom he soon found in the pardon of his sins. That aged woman probably had no idea that her nine words would work so great a change.

A word is always powerful in proportion to the power of the mind it represents. The words of Shakspeare and Milton have proved mighty; they woke up the thoughts of generations and heaved the minds of ages as tides heave the ocean. When the words of Demosthenes fell upon his countrymen they became a trumpet blast, at whose sound every man was ready for war. Why? Because his mind was mighty. But of all words "the word of the Lord" is the most mighty, for the Lord is the most mighty in mind. His word is at once *the expression* and the *weapon* of almighty energy. The sword by which he wins his victories over error and wrong, and establishes his empire of truth and righteousness in the world, is "the word of his mouth." The Gospel is *the* word of the Lord. The Lord has spoken many words. He has given revelations to other intelligences according to their exigencies and faculties; but this is *the* word: "God manifested in the flesh."

This word is the master theme of *true* Gospel preaching. Is it a narrow and barren topic of discussion, think you? a something only suited to a certain class of mind, such as the unreasoning, credulous mind of childhood, or the feeble intellect of the ignorant old woman? No! it is a theme suited to the loftiest as well as the lowliest intellect; it is the center and spirit of all true science, the root and sap of that majestic tree of knowledge which grows in the paradise of God, upon whose delicious fruits the profoundest intellects do ever feed and feast.

From the preceding verse we learn,

Secondly, *That a* TRUE *Gospel preacher has ever one glorious* AIM. What is the aim of the *true* preacher in his dealing with this word? Is it to make a display of self, is it for purposes of controversy, is it to construct it into some theological system or enginery that may favor certain theological views, or that may serve as a ladder for self-aggrandizement? Alas! it *has* been thus treated, and it is still so treated. There are some men who are preachers because it is, all things considered, the easiest way by which they can obtain their living, and by which they can be counted respectable. "I have been preaching fifteen years," said a professed minister to us once, "and had I a convenient way now, either by clerking or merchandising, of securing bread and butter for myself and wife and children, I should quit preaching." Who can calculate the extent of the mischief which such a conscienceless preacher must work? No man has any business in the ministry who has not distinctly, and fully, and unqualifiedly renounced self and the world in every form. Never was a truer thing said than that said by Dr. Samuel Johnson when urged to accept a pastoral charge on the ground that the remuneration was considerable and the *duties very easy:* "*No man, sir, has any right to make those duties easy.*"

The *aim* of the true preacher in all his discourses is that the word "may have free course and be glorified;" that it may run swiftly, and realize its end as it runs. He is anxious that it should run *swiftly*, for it bears pardon to a condemned, health to a sick, comfort to a sorrowful, life to a dying world. He would have it run swiftly from soul to soul, family to family, nation to nation, as the racer runs to win his prize, as the messenger of the king's pardon runs to the criminal who is about to be dragged to the scaffold, as the physician runs to the man who has just taken poison into his system.

But as it runs he would have the word realize its heavenly design, "be glorified." The glory of a divine thing is in the answering of its divine intent; whatever answers the end of its being is glorified. The sun is glorified in its light and heat; the seed is glorified in the harvest. Christ, in his parable of the sower, seems to teach that the human mind is as truly made to receive into it the divine word, ripen it into life and fruitfulness, as the soil is the seed of the husbandman. When this is the case the word is glorified, and God is glorified in it; a realized plan of wisdom is the brightest mirror of its author's mind. This is, then, the aim of the true preacher. He repudiates forever the discourse which, merely in a rhetorical or technical sense, is perfect. His constant inquiry is, Will my sermon instruct, and arouse, and save men? And his maxim, slightly modified from the maxim of the first Napoleon, is: "*The only text worth considering is* SUCCESS!" You know some men who have been reading or reciting discourses for ten or twenty years. Their sentences are properly rounded, their quotations are apposite and correct, their doctrines orthodox, their conclusions logical, but they accomplish nothing; you never hear of men being turned to God through their instrumentality. If you could read the language of their hearts as from Sabbath to Sabbath they stand up before their congregations, would their words not be some such as these? "Well, dearly beloved brethren, I have come into your pulpit to-day because I have agreed to come. It is in the terms of an old contract between us; a contract that was formed, to be sure, when I was disposed to take a somewhat more fanatical view of the matter than I am at present. But I respect the bargain; worship is a social decency, and a graceful adjunct to civilization. Established usage looks in this direction, and religious institutions are a politic kind of constabulary. I am here in my place as the bell rings, and I take occasion to remark to you, as I think I have done before, that it is proper you should be saved. The Bible is pronounced authentic by competent antiquarians, and has uncommon literary merits. The laws of good breeding have settled it that virtue is a desirable accomplishment, besides being a safe protection against unpleasant penalties invented by magistrates; and Christian faith I will recommend as a prudent specific against disagreeable consequences, generally reported to follow wicked courses. Amen."

But the true preacher, when he handles the word, does it with an eye looking into eternity as well as on time, and his one, all-absorbing object is that it "may have free course and be glorified;" that its beneficent influences, like a river, may increase in volume and speed, bear down all obstructions, and roll its crystal waves of life through every home and through every soul.

From the preceding verse we learn,

Thirdly, *That a* TRUE *Gospel preacher seeks the intercessorship of the good:* "Brethren, pray for us." Intercession is an established principle in God's method of governing and blessing his spiritual universe. As in the physical system he lights one world by another, and sustains one life by another, so he in the moral blesses one spirit by another. Spirits are made to pray for spirits; intercession is an instinct of soul. The boy of the widow embarks on a vessel for distant seas, and as his form fades on the deck her heart goes up in prayer to God: "Protect, O Father, my wandering boy! When the night and the tempest come down on the waters, and when the waves beat madly around the vessel's side, do thou keep him as in the hollow of thy hand, and return him to home and me in safety." In yonder dwelling lies a loved child "sick nigh unto death." How patiently the mother and father have watched! how forgetful of their own pains and weariness! But listen, and you will hear their hearts' prayer:

"Send down thy winged angel, God!
  Amid this night so wild;
And bid him come where now we watch,
  And breathe upon our child!

"She lies upon her pillow, pale,
  And moans within her sleep,
Or wakeneth with a patient smile,
  And striveth not to weep.

"We love—we watch throughout the night
  To aid, when need may be;
We hope—and have despaired at times;
  But now we turn to thee!

"Send down thy sweet-souled angel, God!
  Amid the darkness wild;
And bid him soothe our souls to-night,
  And heal our gentle child!"

Intercession is the *highest* function of prayer; it is the devoutest breath of benevolence; it is the soul losing itself in the interest of others, as the soaring eagle loses her eyry in the sun. The true preacher will ever realize the necessity of the intercession of the good. Ever conscious will he be that all success in his holy work depends upon the blessing of God, and that it is his sovereign ordination to vouchsafe that blessing in answer to the trustful, filial, and importunate prayer of holy souls. "I can always preach best," said Fletcher, "when I know that there is a man in the assembly who is from his heart praying for my success." If Paul, a man of capacious intellect, lofty genius, high culture, and withal divine inspiration, felt the need of the prayers of the good to help him on his work, how much more should preachers who have no such distinguished qualifications! There is too much dependence on talents and intellectual resources and elocutionary skill, and too little of a disposition to throw ourselves, as preachers, on God, through the prayers of the good.

From the preceding verse we learn,

Fourthly, *That a* TRUE *Gospel preacher frequently meets with opposition from those whom he seeks to benefit.* Paul prays to be "delivered from unreasonable and wicked men." The unreasonable men were, probably, the pagan philosophers, who were constantly raising objections to the new religion. And the wicked or perverse men were, perhaps, those Jewish zealots, whom no argument could convince, and no kindness conciliate. The more thoughtful, conscientious, earnest, and plain, and the more true to the genius and aim of his vocation a preacher is, the more opposition, as a general thing, he will have from "unreasonable and wicked men." You preach to a congregation in which the leading men are known to be engaged in the liquor traffic, and at once you have an organized and bitter set of opposers arrayed against you. Men who know they are in the wrong become very much excited at an allusion simply to their sin; and in how many a Church has some leading man of "unreasonable" character sown trouble and sorrow for his pastor—such sorrow and trouble as have driven him, with an aching heart, to some new field.

Having thus obtained from the preceding verse our idea of a TRUE PREACHER, we shall proceed to fasten our attention on one point, namely, *the unreasonableness of people in regard to him.* We have nothing to do with their conduct in relation to false and worthless preachers—men who sometimes parade the village streets with cigars in their mouths, or who can be seen at noon or eventide mounted on a corner store box, whittling pine sticks and cracking jokes with loafers—we have no word of defense to utter on behalf of such.

I. The men are unreasonable in relation to their minister who expect from him perfection of character. Far be it from us to lower, in the slightest degree, the high standard of excellence at which every minister is especially bound to aim. We would not relax the obligation to cultivate distinguished holiness, or offer a word of apology for ministerial sins. But there are men who expect too much from them. There is a generation belonging to most Churches, "pure in their own eyes," who display far more anxiety about their minister's piety than their own. They are ever suspecting his virtue, and ever ready to detect his faults. He must be perfect. Defects which are overlooked in others are heinous in him. Things, in fact, which are not evil at all—a burst of indignation, a hearty laugh, a witty expression, a genial, natural, unprofessional manner and talk—are regarded as unbecoming, and even morally faulty. Hence he who has strong natural impulses in him, and striking angularities of mind, must either hypocritically conceal all these under the garb of professional seriousness and sanctity, or else his piety will be questioned, and even denied, by these people.

Now we say nothing of the uncharitableness and inconsistency of all this; for it is generally the hearer that has the "beam" in his own eye that sees most readily the mote in his minister's; but we have to do with its *unreasonableness.* We say, that the men who look for perfection in the minister are "unreasonable men." Are not ministers, like all men, the children of the fall? Do they not inherit passions common to their race? Were they not, like others, born of imperfect parents, and brought up under the influences of corrupt society? Have they not the inward tendencies and outward temptations to sin which belong to all? Is it so clear that a pastor's life is more favorable to high piety than the life of the farmer, the merchant, and the mechanic?

Moreover, were the apostles perfect? Were they not ever fighting against the corruptions of their nature, and pressing after that which they had not attained—the prize of perfection? It is "unreasonable," then, to expect perfection in ministers. Reason would tell you to thank God for the excellences which you discover in them, to expect the development of imperfections, to throw over them the mantle of charity when they appear, and to invoke the Holy One to make them "perfect in every good word and work."

"It is expected," said John Wesley once, "that the preachers be men of one work and noted for piety; at the same time I see no reason why they should not be the most vivacious and cheerful men in the world." A bishop of the Methodist Episcopal Church, now dead, was noted for his almost hilarious disposition in conversation, and yet no man was more pious at heart or successful in his ministrations.

II. Those Church members are unreasonable who expect their minister to be always presenting those

SUBJECTS WHICH ARE AGREEABLE TO THEIR OWN NOTIONS, AND SUITABLE TO THEIR PARTICULAR STATE OF MIND. There is a class who expect their minister to echo in every sermon their own thoughts, and upon every question that comes up to pronounce their views. Every discourse, too, must have something to meet their peculiar circumstances, and to gratify their individual taste. Unless this is the case they instantly display a spirit of dissatisfaction. They will return from the sanctuary, not with hearts bounding with gratitude for the opportunity afforded of blending their thoughts, sympathies, and souls in the worship of the great congregation, but with uncomfortable and almost angry feelings toward their preacher, because he did not exactly utter things according to their tastes and wishes. These people know the entire circle of truth. Although, perhaps, they have spent the whole of their time in tilling the earth, vending their goods in the shop, or keeping books in the counting-house, and never devoted a whole week in their life to an earnest endeavor to get a connected and harmonious view of the system of divine truth, yet they, forsooth, know all! They speak as if every particle of divine thought had been weighed in their little balance; as if their little plummet had sounded the depths of metaphysical divinity. Hence, whenever the minister pronounces an idea not exactly in accordance with their view, they have no hesitation in criticizing or wholly denouncing it.

We call the men who thus act unreasonable men,

First, *Because their notions do not constitute the Gospel.* As astronomy is not the stars, and geology is not the earth, religious creeds are not the Gospel; they are only a few imperfect human ideas about a grand and glorious system of infinite wisdom and love. The most comprehensive system of theology ever wrought out by the human intellect is only, when compared with the Gospel, as one poor acre of land cut off from the mighty continents of the globe. Is it not unreasonable to suppose that the minister who has consecrated his being to the exploration of the whole—to walk every road and scale every hill, to dig into every mine, to gather flowers and fruit from every zone, is to be shut up within the few square yards that your little logic has hedged off from this immeasurable territory of wealth and beauty? Is it reasonable to suppose that he whose work it is to study and sound out all the notes in redemption's scale of music, should be everlastingly ringing the few imperfect notes that you have acquired? notes, too, whose blendings as yet make no melody that can charm the world?

It is unreasonable,

Secondly, *Because the duty of the minister is to lead from "first principles."* His office is to bring out "things new" as well as old. He has to teach, and teaching implies the presentation of things not known before. The honest preacher therefore is not the one who, parrot-like, is always going over the same subjects in the same old phraseology, but is one who presents new lessons of heavenly wisdom to his people. From the lower he advances to the higher branches, and none but the unreasonable will complain of him because he leaves the primer and first reader for the higher readers in the great Bible school. There is an infinitude for him to learn in the Gospel.

> " Were man to live coeval with the sun,
> The patriarch pupil would be learning still,
> And dying, leave his lesson half unlearned."

It is unreasonable,

Thirdly, *Because, though his ministry suit not some of the Church members it may suit others.* Such are the diversities in our mental make, circumstances, and experiences, that though the sermon suit not that old saint, it may be just the thing for that young convert; though it may have no particular fitness for the Christian well grounded in the faith, it may be beautifully adapted to the inquiries of him who is exceedingly anxious to be rightly directed. The diseases of the mind are various, and the prescriptions adapted to some would have no value for others.

Sometimes we think the sermon poorly adapted to the comprehension of the more illiterate of the congregation; but here, as in other cases, the mistake is our own. The celebrated Dr. Bellamy was once preaching on the divine character and government when he had among his auditors a pious old negro man. At the close of the service a deacon of the Church, who thought the sermon utterly beyond the reach of the old man, and therefore of no profit to him, inquired with some anxiety, " Well, my old friend, I fear you have not had much food for your soul to-day?" " O yes! my poor soul has been fed eber so much; Massa Bellamy make God *so big* to poor negro's soul, so BIG."

III. THE MEN ARE UNREASONABLE TOWARD THEIR MINISTER WHO SUPPOSE THAT HE WILL BE EQUALLY ACCEPTABLE TO ALL CLASSES OF HEARERS. It happens not unfrequently when people hear that Hon. Mr. Brown, or some other titled dignitary, has been to hear their preacher and has expressed his dissatisfaction, called him too superficial, or too full of argument, or too full of anecdote and story, or too crude, or too speculative, or too something else, that their own confidence in him is shaken, and they begin to have fears that he is not the man he used to be or, at least, is not the man for their charge. This is general. A spirit of dissatisfaction with the preacher has often crept into a congregation through the prejudiced and unfavorable judgment expressed by some one, or a few, possessing perhaps a little moneyed or other influence in the town. This we pronounce unreasonable:

First, *Because of the diversity of mental organization that exists among men.* No two human faces are alike, and no two human minds are alike on all points; they differ in the kind and measure of leading faculties. Some are more distinguished for imagination than others; they like the truth done up with the roses of poetry; others have a predominance of the logical faculty, and they pride themselves in being called common-sense, plain, blunt men: tropes, figures, roses, and flights of fancy are a loathing to them. Then there are others of a philosophic turn of mind; you can satisfy them neither by poetry nor logic; they are disposed to accept nothing except that which discusses "the reason of things." Then, again, there are hearers strongly characterized by the intuitional propensities and powers; they want none of your figures, your logic, nor your philosophy; but the clear, manly, and devout statement of divine things that meets their sense of the true, the beautiful, and the good. We know a gentleman, a member of the

Church, who, the very moment the logical field is entered by his pastor, drops his eyelids and plants his elbow or forehead in calm repose on the back of his forward neighbor's pew. He says he does not like *metaphysics:* meaning by this word everything except that which suits his state of mind. When, however, the field of logic is left, and an allusion is made to the auroral blush of morn, or the vermilion dyes of the sinking charioteer of day, or the bannered clouds that go careering through the infinite depths of the summer's blue sky, he is himself again; his eyes burst forth in full power, and he is all aglow with the fervor of the preacher's description of his favorite topics.

Secondly. *Because of the diversity of experience that prevails among mankind.* Minds which are thus diverse in their make are as diverse in the experience through which they have passed. No two occupy exactly the same point of vision in relation to truth, and therefore they can never take the same view; one will see an angle where another sees a curve, one a hollow where another sees a protuberance. These different points of vision, too, they have reached by different routes. No intellects have traveled exactly the same road; and intellect often, if not always, looks at truth through the medium of the past, or through the coloring of one's vocation or profession. Two men witness a battle, one from a hill-top, the other from a valley. One is an army tailor, the other a professional letter-writer. The impression made on the two minds will be very dissimilar, as also will be their descriptions of the battle. A shoemaker was once shown a portrait by Apelles, the prince of Grecian painters. He had not a word to say about the faultless figure and the noble countenance, that seemed instinct with life and intelligence, but remarked that *the shoes were not a neat fit.* The criticism was perfectly natural, because he looked through the coloring or experience of his trade as he made it. A gentleman who once spent a night in a lumber-camp in Maine, says that he found the conversation of the woodmen was about nothing but the felling of timber. With them it was literally true that "a man was famous according as he had lifted up axes upon the thick trees." A preacher who would make his remarks specially effective with these men would have to allude to axes and trees.

If, then, men are different in mental constitution, and different in professional tastes, how, in the nature of things, is it possible for one preacher to be equally acceptable to all? Why, Peter did not see clearly some of the glorious objects that came within the sweep of Paul's vision. "Every man in his own order." The stars that gem the coronal of night shine with a different and an unequal luster. The plants that variegate the earth are not all exactly the same size, or form, or color. No two human intellects shine alike, or think alike; and the impossibility of being alike is a glorious impossibility. Let each seed as now, from the woodland violet, hiding its modest face in the crevice of the rock, to the mammoth pines of Oregon and California, produce a form peculiar to itself, and thus preserve forever the infinite variety of the landscape. Let " one star differ " forevermore "from another star in glory," and thus preserve the power of the nightly firmament to inspire us by the boundless variety of its lustrous dome.

Let not all minds think alike. Uniformity in human thought would be an anomaly in the universe and a curse to the race: it would reduce our world to mental stagnation and death. Let us not, then, be so foolish as to expect that he who is a minister to one must be a minister to all. It cannot be. A man is only truly a minister to the grade of mind next below him, and between whom and himself there is some degree of similitude and sympathy. You may have a lamp that is big enough for your little cottage room, but it is not big enough for the City Hall yonder.

It is said by astronomers that the sun which lights up our system would be lost in midnight amid the boundless amplitudes of another. If ALL preachers are not fitted to preach before the great men of the earth, there are SOME that can; but do not say that those who fail here are unfitted to minister to many, aye, to any almost of the great number of other congregations.

IV. THE MEN ARE UNREASONABLE TOWARD THEIR MINISTER WHO IMAGINE THAT THEY CAN DERIVE GOOD FROM HIS PREACHING IRRESPECTIVE OF THEIR OWN EFFORT. There are not a few men and women in congregations who expect to get good, and even to be made good, by the minister; and that in a way, too, almost entirely independent of anything being done on their own part. They come to church, and they listen and are orderly and respectful; but this is about all they do. And yet they expect to receive great spiritual benefit, and cry out against the dryness and unprofitableness of the ministry if their expectations are not realized. They say, We do not feel ourselves benefited by the preaching of our minister—we are not being fed at all. But are you doing your part? Acting as you do, you are "unreasonable men" if you expect any good. In the nature of the case, no preacher can benefit you unless you do *three* things:

First. *You must prepare your mind to receive good from his sermons.* Such is our mental constitution that ideas can only deeply affect and permanently influence us as we single them out, and get each separately to occupy and possess the mind entirely for the time. We must sweep for the moment every other idea from the soul, and get the one we wish to influence us to fill the whole horizon. A student in developing a theorem, or working out a difficult equation in algebra, cannot at the same time be occupying his mind with a land trade or a sugar speculation. He must have but the one thing present with him if he expects to master his equation, or, having mastered, to remember the steps by which he reached the result.

In this age of stir and speculation men must spend some time, before entering God's house, in clearing their minds of worldly rubbish if they expect to receive good. It will not do to carry with them their houses and barns, their stocks and their farms, their city lots and their abundant merchandise; for it is not *possible* for any sermon properly to influence men who thus act. You, whose moral sensibilities are incrusted by the drying heat and bustling tread of six days' commercial life—whose whole spiritual being, in fact, is overlaid with business memories and business hopes, you must spend some time in your closet with God and your own souls, endeavoring to break up this hard crust that overlays your spirit; you must tear up the weeds, cut down the briars and brush, and clear the soil, if you expect with benefit to receive the "engrafted word." "How did you like the sermon?" said a gentleman once to an elderly member of the Methodist Church where we reside. The discourse was by a young man, and by many pronounced discursive and lame. "Like it," said the member in reply, "well, sir, I like all sermons. I was praying before I went to church, and all the time I was at church, and my soul was greatly blessed."

Secondly. *You must reflect upon the subjects which he presents to your notice.* A preacher may preach ever so instructively; he may develop doctrine after doctrine, and establish truth after truth; but what of all this if the hearer is with his heart, like the fool's eyes, in the ends of the earth? or what if he is sound asleep in his seat? A pupil at school, no matter who his teacher may be, must study his lesson. Let the greatest of mathematicians or astronomers attempt to teach a class the principles of descriptive geometry, or the integral calculus, or the methods of calculating an eclipse; of what use will be his vast acquirements if the members of his class will not reflect on what he says? We hear often of stupid sermons, but is not the stupidity too often in the hearer rather than in the speaker? No being can help a hearer independent of his own personal reflection. A preacher may bring to you the divine materials out of which the temple of a holy character is to be formed, and he may point out to you the plan of the building and the best way to accomplish the object, but he cannot build for you; no man, no angel can build for you.

If the edifice is ever to be reared your own hand must do it; you must "build up yourselves in the most holy faith."

Thirdly. *You must reduce to practice the doctrines he preaches.* When does truth become incorporated in our nature, and therefore do us good? Not merely when it has made an impression on the feelings; if that is all it will evaporate in real life, as dew in the sun. Not merely when by reflection it has taken the form of an intelligible idea in the intellect, for then it may merely shine with a cold moon-beam influence upon the understanding, and have no power to penetrate and vivify the heart. But when it has been taken up in an act, when it has been embodied in a deed, then it has become part of ourselves.

You may hear the most eloquent sermon ever preached by mortal tongue on benevolence and prayer, and it may make a deep impression on your mind at the time; but, unless you suitably embody the feelings awakened by some act of mercy and devotion, the discourse will prove no real and permanent boon to you. Old divines used to speak of meditation as that digestive and appropriating power of the mind by which sermons were turned into nutrition and became part of the man. We would not disparage meditation; but our impression is that it is *action* that does this. Character is made up of habits, and habits are made of acts; and it is only when the idea or impression is translated into an earnest act that it becomes a real power. Religious truth, if left to remain in the form of ideas in the mind, is only to the man like the rain-drop upon the leaf; it may glisten like a diamond in the sun and add a moment's brilliance to the object, but it is of no service to the tree; but when ideas are translated into deeds, they are like the rain-drops penetrating the roots, and bearing new energy into every branch.

The want of action is the reason why so many people in our day are not fed by sermons. Hence, who are the men in congregations who complain of the want of food in sermons? They are the do-nothings, the sentimental loungers, who are forever studying their "frames and feelings," or else are in hot pursuit of some new notions or new preacher. Men of religious action, the benevolent visitors of the poor, the tried and self-denying instructors of the ignorant, they are always fed by the sermon; they live for something besides verbal and literary criticism.

You who complain of not deriving good from the sermons of your preacher neglect each of the *three* necessary conditions on which alone any good can *possibly* come to you. You expect good when you come to the sanctuary with a mind unprepared to receive the good seed; when you make no effort to study thoroughly to understand and appreciate the statements that are addressed to you, and when you never attempt to reduce to action the doctrines that are proclaimed. Unreasonable men! would you expect a boy at school to advance who never studied, but who slept half the time, or had his eyes and thoughts on things outside the school-room? Would such a boy, introduced into a gymnasium, ever have his chest expanded, or his muscles developed by simply listening to lectures on parallel bars, dumb bells, and spring boards? Could a man reasonably expect to become a great painter who should spend his whole time in listening to lectures on the art, instead of taking up the pencil and the brush in order to embody the ideas on canvass? Well might ministers say: Deliver us from such unreasonable men!

"I heard a sermon once," said a brother to us, "from a venerable itinerant preacher, on benevolence. I thought the effort very lean, but one thing impressed me a little. 'Go,' said he, 'and do something after I have done preaching. Have it to say when I come back, four weeks hence, that you *have* done something, and my word and God's word for it, you will be a better and a happier man.' I knew a poor widow living on the edge of some woods about a mile from my home. Her husband had been dead two or three years, and with three helpless little girls she had a hard conflict with poverty. I had often spoken kindly to her, and thought my duty ended when the words were uttered; but when the sermon of the old white-headed preacher was done the resolution was formed to go and do something. Next day I visited the cellar and measured out a bushel of potatoes, a bushel of apples, and a variety of other things, and having put them into a wagon, started for the cottage of the widow. A load of wood, for which I paid three dollars, preceded me. An hour's drive brought both loads in front of the house; and when my explanation was given there were wet eyes and warmer hearts in both parties. The widow wept for joy, and the children joined suits while I, finding my feelings too much for my strength, had to give way also to tears. The act was one that gave me a new spiritual start; and when the preacher, at the end of the four weeks, came back, I thought his discourse one of the most eloquent I had ever listened to. The change was in myself, not in him or his preaching."

V. THE MEN ARE UNREASONABLE TOWARD THEIR MINISTER WHO RECEIVE HIS SPIRITUAL SERVICES WITHOUT A PROPER SECULAR ACKNOWLEDGEMENT. No true preacher will ever preach with an eye to the dollar. All mercenary considerations will be borne down and engulfed by his ever-deepening concern to win souls. Still, in common with other men, he will have his potatoes and flour to buy, and his grocery and meat bills to settle, and according to the present arrangements of society he will generally have to adjust these matters with money. Whence is he to receive this? As a general rule it comes only as the reward of labor. He labors not, it is true, with a carpenter's plane, nor with the hammer of the blacksmith, nor with the plow of the farmer; but nevertheless he labors. The office of a true preacher is no sinecure, no lounger's berth; there is no work so arduous as his. It is the labor not of limbs, but of brain and heart; it is a constant draw upon the very fountains of nervous energy. Five hours of hard study is a greater tax on the body than ten hours of ordinary manual labor. "All persons who have been accustomed to close study," says Dr. George Moore, "will remember the utter and indescribable confusion that comes over the mind, and the strange failure of physical strength when the will has wearied the brain. The hand-workers live long lives if they work in the open air; but the head-workers too often exhaust the nervous system and have miserable health or early graves."

Nor is there any work so useful to society as the work of preachers. The ministry of the United States are a great police force to society. Where is the business man in community who would be willing to abolish the ministry? Where is the man who would favor the sale of all our churches, with the intention of converting them into money and putting the money out at ten per cent. for some other than religious purposes? The truth is, the preachers of our own country are not only the best but the cheapest policemen the country has. Is there any worker, therefore, who is entitled to more respect than the minister? If the labor is the most arduous and the most useful, ought it not to secure the most ample secular return? Paul recognizes and enforces this common-sense claim: "Who goeth a warfare any time at his own charges? Who planteth a vineyard, and eateth not of the fruit thereof? Or who feedeth a flock, and eateth not of the milk of the flock? For it is written in the law of Moses, Thou shalt not muzzle the mouth of the ox that treadeth out the corn. Doth God take care of oxen? If we have sown unto you spiritual things, is it a great matter if we shall reap your carnal things? *Even so hath the Lord ordained that they which preach the Gospel shall live of the Gospel.*"

In the light of these words, how unreasonable does the conduct of some people appear in relation to their minister. There are men who receive and expect large services from him, and who make little or no return. They pay or *promise* to pay fifty cents or one dollar a quarter, making from two to four dollars a year, and for this paltry sum they expect preaching every Sabbath, and a pastoral visit once in every two or three weeks, or else they set up complaints against him and seek to spread a spirit of dissatisfaction through the neighborhood. There are families in almost every congregation all over the country who spend more for candies and toys for their children, or who, to keep up with the newest styles, give more to the milliner for new bonnets than they give to their preacher. If it is the oyster season, and they are residents of the city, there is money in their pocket for the oysters, but a slim supply of funds for the preacher. If a farm in the neighborhood is to be sold cheap they have money, or borrow it, for the first payment, and then having put themselves in debt, they cannot of course give anything more for the balance of the year! You pay one dollar and a half or two dollars a week for hired help in your house: the act is well enough, but how much do you give the preacher? In all honesty ought you not to give him twenty-five dollars a year, this being one quarter only of what you pay your kitchen girl? ought you not to give fifty dollars? But you do not; you screw and squirm, and threaten to go to some other cheaper charge every time an allusion is made to the preacher's support. "It is nothing," say you, "but *money*, *money*, *money* all the time!" But then don't you know that you are the man that complains the most, and yet the one that gives the least? Does not every man know, who knows anything about the financial matters of a Church, that the members who send up the most piteous lamentations about money are always and invariably the men that subscribe but never pay their subscriptions, or else subscribe so little that the poorest widow equals them? You can obtain some interesting statistics on this point by early application to the stewards of the charge where you belong. Call at some of their official meetings and make inquiries. You will find them both agreeable and communicative.

The officers of the navy and army of the government receive three thousand, four thousand, six thousand, and ten thousand dollars a year; the superintendents, presidents, secretaries, and general ticket agents of our railroads receive from eighteen hundred to fifteen thousand dollars a year; book-keepers and salesmen receive from six hundred to four thousand dollars a year; mechanics and tradesmen make from four hundred to fifteen hundred dollars a year. But what are the salaries of preachers in this country? The Wesleyans of Great Britain receive an average of near fifteen hundred dollars a year; while the average of Methodist preachers of America, including house-rent, does not reach four hundred dollars a year. The Presbyterian and Congregational Churches in the large cities pay more, but take the country through, the average paid their ministry is only about three hundred and sixty dollars a year; the Episcopal Church pays still less; the Baptist Church about three hundred and twenty dollars, and the Methodist Protestant Church scarcely three hundred. Now is it not unreasonable for Church members to expect their preachers to live on such allowances, to preach good sermons, and to do full pastoral work?

Their children have to eat like other children, and if they cannot get bread from the congregations whom they serve, they must work with their own hands for it. And if the attention of a preacher is thus divided his services inevitably become imperfect and of but little profit. Can a man who has just lost a child or a wife preach while suffering his great sorrow? Can a man who is racked with distress as to where the money for the next pair of shoes, or the next barrel of flour, or the next anything needed shall come from; we say, can a preacher thus harassed be in a state of heart and mind for active service? We think not. Anxiety, above almost every other thing, affects the functions of the body, and especially of the stomach, and then follows nervous disease in all its various forms, and then again comes general lassitude and ineffectiveness out and in the pulpit on the part of your preacher. When a merchant employs a young man as clerk he is careful to tell him to make as his *one* business that of selling well and rapidly. Every other thing must be dismissed, every occupation that would divide the attention must be ignored, and he must give himself wholly to his work. Ought not men to place their preachers in such a position as to allow a similar free, full, and undivided attention to the one thing in hand?

VI. THE MEN ARE UNREASONABLE TOWARD THEIR MINISTER WHO EXPECT HIM TO BE VERY USEFUL, WHILE THEY ARE PRACTICALLY COUNTERACTING HIS INFLUENCE. There are men in most congregations who are more than ready to complain of the want of their preacher's success—"croakers." They talk of the dull times, the few that are being added to the Church, the little increase made to the congregation, and the small amount of influence exerted upon the neighborhood; and they refer all this to the ineffectiveness or the want of a popular element in the preacher, when, at the same time, much of the cause is in themselves. They not only do not encourage him with their sympathies and prayers, and aid him by their hearty co-operation, but, practically, they hinder him. The power of a minister upon his neighborhood depends greatly on his people. They are his witnesses; the force of his statements on the minds of others depends not half so much on the potency either of his logic or eloquence as upon the testimony furnished by the every-day life of his people. They are his "epistle known and read" of all the men in his charge. Suppose now that his members are narrow in their conceptions, gross in their sympathies, false in their dealings, and hypocritical in their lives, what will be the effect on the community where they reside? Will they not be like the man whom a lawyer brought into court as a witness to confirm the statements of his client, but who, the moment he was placed in the witness-box, swore the opposite of what he before professed, thus stripping the counsel of all his power over the jury? The ministry of many a faithful, toiling preacher has been neutralized and destroyed by the conduct of those who are known as his people. Like Achan in the camp, they prevent all victorious deeds being wrought for the truth and God.

We know several congregations where the people stand side by side and shoulder to shoulder with the preacher. They do not use dissecting knives on his sermons, but pray for him, and defend his character, and assist him in his pastoral work, and the consequence is that these congregations are growing congregations, sinners are converted, and the cords of Zion are lengthened and made strong. If all congregations were as the few, what a work of evangelism the country would witness!

There is much talk about *the ministry for the times.* We would not for a moment defend the loafing preacher, the man who does as little as he can, studies none, and delights chiefly in gossip and street-corner debate. But is there not quite as much need of *a church for the times* as a ministry for the times? Are there not too many Jerry Larkum's in the Church, men who luxuriate in the prospect of a millennium, but who do everything in their power to keep it back; men who hear a sermon for the sake of telling their wives and children how poor it was, and who delight in nothing so much as when their preacher becomes embarrassed or makes a bad failure.

Of professional censors and dyspeptic Christians there are all too many. We want, for the world's good and reformation, those who will make Christianity the sovereign, predominating purpose of the soul. "Go a little deeper," said a wounded guardsman of Napoleon to the surgeon who was probing a wound just above his heart, "and you will find the emperor." So the real Christian may say: "Go a little deeper, go to the core of my heart, and you will find the Saviour. Other affections may lie on the surface, but this master feeling, this all-burning passion for Christ's cause and Christ's ministers, lives and lurks in the inmost depths. Other feelings I am possessed of, but this one possesses me: 'For me to live is Christ. For this *one thing* I do, forgetting those things which are behind, and reaching forth unto those things which are before, I press toward the mark for the prize of the high calling of God in Christ Jesus!'"

HOMILY XIX.

THE MEMORY OF FORGIVEN SINS.

Who was before a blasphemer, and a persecutor, and injurious.
1 TIMOTHY i, 13.

GOD'S forgiveness is full, free, and thorough. Yet forgiving, he does not forget. God remembers forgiven sins, but he does NOT, will not, remember them *against us*. "Thou wilt cast all their sins into the depths of the sea." *We* should remember them. Let us think of the forgiven past, not with self-condemnation, for that were to do what God will not do, and so far to undo what he has done, but with a view to self-improvement and the divine glory.

Four benefits may be derived from a proper recollection of our forgiven sins:

I. THE MEMORY OF FORGIVEN SINS IS FAVORABLE TO HUMILITY. Spiritual pride is a sin to which the eminently holy, gifted, and useful Christian is liable. Let the first remember how he formerly defiled himself; the second, to what unworthy objects he directed his noble faculties; the third, that his pardoned sins may be, probably are, working fatal mischief in the world. Years ago he may have said a word that wrongly influenced some soul, and that soul in consequence may have gone far astray, and may now be a wanderer on the "barren mountains of sin;" and where is there room for pride? Why did Paul describe himself as "less than the least of all saints?"

II. The memory of forgiven sins is conducive to watchfulness. Forgiveness has not destroyed our liability to sin. Forgiven sins have left *weak places* in our souls. Remember your old habits, your "besetting sins." Those weak places will be the principal points of attack by our spiritual foes, and the strongest fort is no stronger than its weakest part.

"Angels our march oppose,
Who still in strength excel,
Our secret, sworn, eternal foes,
Countless, invisible;
From thrones of glory driven,
By flaming vengeance hurled,
They throng the air, and darken heaven,
And rule this lower world."

It becomes us therefore to watch vigilantly the return of "unclean spirits," who, as night besiegers, are ever anxious to make the attack on the citadel of our hearts, and in the weakest places.

III. The memory of forgiven sins is productive of compassion. We pity sinners. We have no inclination to call fire from heaven to consume them. Pardon has made our hearts tender toward "all men." "For we ourselves also were sometimes foolish, disobedient, deceived," etc. The unforgiven are the unforgiving, the unmerciful, and stony-hearted.

IV. The memory of forgiven sins awakens gratitude. We are in danger of forgetting "all" the Lord's "benefits," but we cannot if we remember our sins. To the enlightened, the sanctified, heavenly mind, God's mercy in the forgiveness of sins will stand out in bold relief against the background of such thoughts as these: The iniquity of those sins: *their number, their miseries, actual and prospective.* O the depth of that mercy! The sight of it made David cry aloud: "Bless the Lord, O my soul, and all that is within me, bless his holy name. Bless the Lord, O my soul, and forget not all his benefits." Feed the flame of gratitude with thoughts of forgiven sins. See what Paul says in the context.

Thoughts of forgiven sin give never-ceasing impulse to the song of the redeemed in heaven: "Unto him that loved us, and washed us from our sins in his own blood, and hath made us kings and priests unto God and his Father; to him *be* glory and dominion for ever and ever."

But O the memory of unforgiven sins in the dark scenes of retribution!

HOMILY XX.

THE GREAT CALAMITY.

Although the fig tree shall not blossom, neither shall fruit be in the vines; the labor of the olive shall fail, and the fields shall yield no meat; the flock shall be cut off from the fold, and there shall be no herd in the stalls: yet I will rejoice in the Lord, I will joy in the God of my salvation. HABAKKUK iii, 17, 18.

HABAKKUK was receiving communications from God when he wrote the text. The condition of the Jews called forth the sympathy of this good man. He exemplifies that sympathy by appealing to the Most High on their behalf, and he receives attention from the mighty God of Israel. How little he was influenced by the material, and how much by the spiritual, our text abundantly proves.

I. THE DIVINE RULE IS TO MAKE AN ABUNDANT PROVISION FOR MAN'S PHYSICAL WANTS. The great Creator gives him the fig tree, the vine, the olive, the fields, the flock, and the herd. Observe, 1. *The vastness of God's wealth.* 2. *His supreme regard for man's comfort.*

II. THE GOOD MAN RECOGNIZES THE POSSIBILITY OF A TOTAL FAILURE IN THIS PROVISION. "Although the fig tree," etc.

First. *Such a failure is fearful to contemplate.*

Secondly. *Such a failure must occur through one or both the following causes:* 1. *Man's neglect.* "The sluggard that will not plow by reason of the cold shall beg in harvest and have nothing." It is a fixed law in God's universe that "the man who will not work shall not eat." 2. *A direct visitation from God.* One fiery blast from Jehovah's nostrils would burn up the material and animal kingdoms. At his presence the mountains melt away, and the earth smokes.

III. THAT IN THE VERY FACE OF THIS CALAMITY THE GOOD MAN TRIUMPHANTLY CONFIDES IN GOD. "Yet will I rejoice in the Lord." The wisdom of this conduct is seen in two things:

First. *In the divine immutability.*

Secondly. *Great calamities afford scope for the development of great principles.* Trials, if very heavy, kill little men but make great ones. Just as an Atlantic billow bears the reeling ship aloft, so does the mighty wave of trouble lift to notice a true son of God. *Trials strengthen and develop love and faith.*

IV. THAT THIS SUBLIME CONFIDENCE IS EXERCISED BY THE GOOD MAN BECAUSE HE HAS EXPERIENCED A GREAT DELIVERANCE. "I will joy in the God of my salvation."

First. *This is a deliverance from the greatest evil.*

Secondly. *This is a deliverance to the possession of the greatest good.* This man has in him the elements of immortality. He is a king's son and an heir of heaven. Heaven is his future residence and the universe his estate.

HOMILY XXI.

ONE IN TEN.

And Jesus answering, said, Were there not ten cleansed? but where are the nine? These are not found that returned to give glory to God, save this stranger. LUKE xvii, 17, 18.

THIS is the language of disappointed love; and the narrative teaches:

I. THAT MOST MEN UNDER GREAT TRIAL WILL APPLY TO HEAVEN FOR RELIEF. The leprosy was a great affliction. It was *painful*, *infectious*, *hereditary*, and *incurable* by ordinary means. In times of great commotion and trial all men believe in the existence and ability of God.

II. THAT GOD SOMETIMES ATTENDS TO THE PRAYERS EVEN OF UNGODLY MEN. All of the ten lepers were healed. There are some prayers which God binds himself to answer. "Call upon me in the day of trouble; I will deliver thee, and thou shalt glorify me." "Call unto me, and I will answer thee, and show thee great and mighty things which thou knowest not." There are prayers again that God may answer or not.

III. THAT WHILE MOST PRAY IN DISTRESS, ONLY THE GOOD WILL FEEL TRUE GRATITUDE FOR DELIVERANCE. Only one returned. Gratitude was expected from all—was the obligation of all.

IV. THAT WHERE TRUE GRATITUDE EXISTS IT WILL SHOW ITSELF. This one came and gave thanks. Gratitude will show itself: First, *Voluntarily;* Secondly, *Humbly;* Thirdly, *Independentlv—alone.*

HOMILY XXII.

THE TWO PATHWAYS.

Enter ye in at the strait gate: for wide is the gate, and broad is the way, that leadeth to destruction, and many there be which go in thereat: because strait is the gate, and narrow is the way, which leadeth unto life, and few there be that find it. MATT. vii, 13, 14.

These words teach:

I. THAT HUMAN LIFE HAS TWO, AND BUT TWO MORAL PATHWAYS: the "broad and the narrow way." The diversities which obtain among mankind, in their circumstances, constitution, attainments, forms, spheres of action, and lines of pursuit, are well-nigh endless. On certain classifying principles it would be easy to arrange them into very numerous and distinct divisions. To the eye of Jesus, however, all appeared in two great journeying classes. He saw all souls flowing in one of two directions. In the march of moral mind, to any conceivable point of business or pleasure, to the most ephemeral thought or transient feeling, there are but two lines, the RIGHT and THE WRONG; there is *no middle way for souls* to anything, however trivial. Every thing felt, thought, done, endured, or enjoyed by a moral being is moral, and is morally good or bad. This fact (1.) makes human life very solemn, and (2.) renders the ascertainment of our true character very easy.

We learn from the passage:

II. That all on both these pathways are progressing to diverse but appropriate ends.

First. *All are progressing.* In neither the broad nor the narrow way did Christ see anything standing or sitting—all were *going.* There is nothing stationary: the whole universe, mental and material, like an ever-moving machine, has every wheel in action, even the small dust. Nor is anything stationary about moral character; it is ever passing from stage to stage. There are two features in the progress of moral character, whether in goodness or evil, worthy of note. First. *It is individually optional.* The stars, the winds, the waves, can neither modify nor stop their progress. They have no control over the forces which urge them on. Nor can we stay or modify the progress of our bodies to dissolution. We cannot pause a moment in our march to the grave; both asleep and awake we are going. But, morally, the progress of the soul is with us; we move or stop it as we please. We can pause in our moral pathway, or retrace our steps, or go faster on. The other feature in the progress of the soul worthy of note is, Secondly, *That it is ever accelerative.* By this I mean that the longer it continues to move in the line, either of goodness or evil, the more momentum it gathers and the faster it proceeds. Its progress is not like the progress of the planets or the ocean. The stars do not seem to move quicker now than they did in the days of Adam, nor does the ocean ebb or flow with greater speed. But the progress of the soul in character is something like the progress of the cascade, it gathers fresh momentum every moment. Hence a bad man will perpetuate deeds of iniquity to-day, the bare idea of which would have overwhelmed him a short time ago; and hence, too, a good man will perform now, with ease and happiness, deeds of self-sacrifice which at the outset of his religious life he would not venture to attempt.

Secondly. *All are progressing to diverse but appropriate ends.* The broad way "leadeth to destruction." The word destruction does not mean annihilation, but perdition; not the termination of existence, but the termination of the blessings of existence; the destruction of everything which makes existence worth having, or even tolerable. The narrow way "leadeth unto life." Life here is the opposite or antithesis of destruction. It means not mere existence, but *blessed* existence. The one course, therefore, leads to *ill*-being, and the other course to *well*being. Now both these ends, though so *diverse*, are *appropriate* to the cause. A life of sin leads naturally to this destruction. In every sin there is a throwing away of some portion of the blessings of existence, and man has only to keep on sinning in order to strip himself of everything but *sheer being*. And so of holiness; holiness *leads* to life—*is* life. "To be carnally-minded *is* death, but to be spiritually-minded *is* life and peace." "Be not deceived; God is not mocked; whatsoever a man soweth, that shall he also reap; he that soweth to the flesh, shall of the flesh reap corruption; he that soweth to the spirit, shall reap everlasting life."

From this passage it appears:

III. That the avoidance of the one pathway, and the adoption of the other, are the imperative obligation and interest of all. Here is the command: "Enter ye in at the strait gate."

Two things are here suggested:

First. *That the duty involves great difficulty.* It is a "strait gate." There is no difficulty in entering on the broad road. The gate is wide; you can step easily through. One cause of the difficulty we have here suggested in the *number* pursuing each course; there were many entering the "wide gate," and walking the "broad road," but only "a few" passed through the "strait gate" into the narrow way. Man is a social being, is wonderfully influenced by *numbers;* he will follow the multitudes as the tides follow the moon. This mighty social force has ever been against holiness in the world. It was especially so in the days of Christ. All the classes in Judea were against the new religion of rectitude and love. He, therefore, who would adopt a religious life has to extricate himself from the ten thousand ties with which society binds him to itself. He must be *singular;* he must leave the multitude and walk with the few.

But however difficult, it *must* be done. God commands it, and our eternal wellbeing depends on it. No man has a right to be in the broad road; every moment he is trampling on the eternal principles of law and order, battling with the moral influences of heaven, violating all the high intuitions of his own nature, and walking under the darkening shadows of that ever-blackening and expanding thunder-cloud of retribution, whose elements, if it burst, will

"Beat upon his naked soul
In one eternal storm."

HOMILY XXIII.

ONE AND ONLY ONE PROBATION, A BENEVOLENT ARRANGEMENT.

I shall behold man no more with the inhabitants of the world. ISAIAH xxxviii, 11.

Neither can they pass to us, that would come from thence. LUKE xvi, 26.

THERE are two facts that give death a profound solemnity:

First. *That it separates a man forever from his connections in this world.* Hezekiah felt this now: "I shall behold man no more," etc. Job felt this: "When a few years are come, then I shall go the way whence I shall not return." What living man has not been impressed with this idea? the idea that when he dies he shall return to his house no more. The old scene of his first impressions, the brown school-house and the hill behind, with the old play-ground, and the comrades with whom he roamed the woods and valleys and fields; and farther on in life, his anxious labors, his tender friendships, and his dear associations, are all left, and left forever. However trying this world may be, it contains much, very much that is dear to us. Here we felt the first sensations of life; here the first trains of thought arose; here we have received the elements of our character; here all our joys have been experienced, our trials endured, and our labors prosecuted. Here sleep the dust of our parents and friends. To leave all this forever is a sad thought. To "return no more" forever to the field we have cultivated, to the shop where we have transacted our business, to the study where we have striven after knowledge; to return "no more" to our dwelling and to the dear circle of the heart—how solemn all this!

The other fact that gives death profound solemnity is,

Secondly. *That it separates a man forever from all probationary means of improvement.* Abraham gave this idea to the rich man in the world of perdition: he assured him there was an *impassable "gulf" fixed between him and all remedial means.* After death character seems stereotyped. He that is unjust remains unjust forever. This is a more solemn fact than the other, though perhaps not so deeply or generally felt. To be cut forever, if we are wicked, from Bibles, sanctuaries, and all mediatorial influences and helps; to have an impassable gulf between all that is bright and fair in the universe and one's self—how solemn this!

Now the point to which attention should be fastened is, *That this fact, which is profoundly solemn, is neither cruel nor unjust, but, on the contrary, highly benevolent.* Skeptics ask the question, Why should this be? Why should there not be a plurality of probations? Why should not man have more chances than one? Where is the goodness of God in making man's destiny through eternal ages to depend on his conduct during the few passing years of this earthly life? Now we are prepared to maintain that there is much more divine goodness displayed in his giving man only *one* probation than in giving him *two* or any number more.

I. THERE IS MORE GOODNESS IN THIS ARRANGEMENT TO THE INDIVIDUAL HIMSELF Three facts will illustrate this:

First. *That in case a man had a second probation, and it failed, his guilt and misery would be considerably enhanced by it.* (1.) *Punishment will be in a great measure proportioned by the privileges and opportunities abused.* "He that knoweth his master's will, and doeth it not," etc. "If I had not spoken to them," said Christ, "they had not had sin." What is the guilt of a heathen compared with a man living in Christian lands? (2.) *That the privileges and opportunities connected with his first probation are such as to impose incalculable responsibility.* "If he that despised Moses's law died without mercy," etc., what then would be the guilt of a man who had not only lived through a first probation but a second? What wrath would he be treasuring up? etc.

Secondly. *That the man who abused the first probation would be most likely to abuse the second.* If a man pass through all the remedial influences of the first probation—nature, sacred literature, sanctuaries, the counsels and admonitions of the pious, the Gospel ministry—and not be saved but hardened by all, would there not be a *certainty* that if he entered upon a second probation the second would also fail? (1.) *Because he would enter upon the second with hardened sensibilities.* He did not so the first. We began our existence here with *tender consciences.* At the first we shrank from the false and the vile. Our whole moral nature revolted at the first sin. You remember the day and the place where you uttered the first profane word or the first falsehood. You thought then, so horrified were you with your own conduct, never again will I do either. But how was it in subsequent years, and how is it now? (2.) *He would enter upon the second with confirmed habits.* His thoughts and actions would be bound to forms. It was not so with the first. We argue now that the longer a man remains unconverted the less likely is it that he will ever be. Every day's delay makes the work harder and harder, and diminishes the probabilities in favor of a man's becoming religious. "Can the Ethiopian change his skin, or the leopard his spots? then may ye also do good that are *accustomed* to do evil." If it be asked, May not some new influences be brought to bear upon the soul in the second probation that did not act upon him in the first? We ask, What new influences are possible? We can only conceive of two kinds: the *penal* and the *merciful.* Will *penal* sufferings convert? Does the father awaken love in the child by the rod? Will ages of misery in hell awaken love to the Creator? Purgatorial fire is a philosophical absurdity; love to God is virtue, and can the GREAT ONE ever make a creature love him by tormenting him with suffering? And as to *merciful* influences, Can there be any more merciful power brought to bear upon the soul than now? Can God give a more moving and mighty expression of his love than sending his only begotten Son?

Thirdly. *That man's knowledge of a second probation would tend to counteract upon his mind the saving influence of the first.* (1.) It would strengthen that *procrastinating principle* in his nature which leads him now to postpone the question of salvation. If now, when he knows he may have only a single day to live, or even a single hour, he postpones the question of religion to "a more convenient season," (Felix did this even after the mighty force of Paul's appeal to his conscience,) how much more would man, if he were assured that when these few years of his earthly existence had run out, there would come another season in the great future enabling him to do there what he had neglected to do here. (2.) *It would strengthen that presuming tendency in his nature which induces him to run the risk of the future.* There is a tendency in man to rely on precedents, to argue from the past to the future. Because it has not been so it will not be so, it *must* not be so. "Because sentence against an evil work is not executed speedily, therefore the heart of the sons of men is fully set in them to do evil." On the whole, then, we say it is *good* to the man *himself* that there should be but one probation: *plurality* of probations would be a curse to the race.

II. There is more goodness in this arrangement to the universe. First. *Because it puts a greater restraint upon evil.* How would evil spread by the multiplication of probations! Who does not feel that it is a mercy that such men as Nero, Napoleon, etc., have only to live a short time? Depraved as men are, it is a blessing that the period of human life has been abbreviated, that they do not live to their nine hundred years, as in antediluvian times. Secondly. *It heightens the motives to virtue.*

In conclusion: First. *This subject teaches the great solemnity of life.* Why are we here? To gratify the senses, to amass a fortune, or to gain a little influence in the world? No! but to prepare characters for eternity. Secondly.

This subject explains the earnestness of God in his appeals to man for reformation now. How earnest is God! "As I live, saith the Lord God, I have no pleasure in the death of him that dieth; but rather that he should return from his ways and live." Great beings are never earnest about little things. "To-day," says God; he knows that

"The sun of grace once set,
Shall rise no more."

HOMILY XXIV.

THE SUPPLIANT ENCOURAGED.

"If any man lack wisdom, let him ask of God, that giveth to all men liberally, and upbraideth not. JAMES i, 5.

THERE are at least six circumstances which are likely to induce men to upbraid those who seek of them a favor:

I. WHEN THE SUPPLIANT HAS BROUGHT DISTRESS ON HIMSELF. In this case the party applied to is likely to upbraid and say, It is your own fault that you are in this condition; had you acted otherwise you would have been well enough off. But although the sinner has brought his wretchedness upon himself God will not upbraid.

II. WHEN THE SUPPLIANT HAS ENDEAVORED TO INJURE THE PARTY OF WHOM HE SEEKS THE FAVOR. In such cases he is likely to meet with severe reproofs. How can you think of asking a favor of me whom you sought so much to injure? But although the sinner has sought to injure God, he will not upbraid him when he asks a favor.

III. WHEN THE SUPPLIANT BECOMES TOO FREQUENT IN HIS APPLICATION. If he has been relieved frequently before he is all but certain of being upbraided. Not so with God; the more frequent the more welcome. "In *everything* by prayer and supplication let your requests be made known unto God."

IV. WHEN THE SUPPLIANT IS AN UTTER STRANGER TO THE PARTY APPEALED TO. There is then suspicion, and the plea is that acquaintances and neighbors have the first claim. There is upbraiding; but not so with God; none are strangers to him.

V. WHEN THE SUPPLIANT HAPPENS TO APPEAL AT AN INCONVENIENT HOUR. Too early in the morning, or too late at night, or in the midst of engagements with friends, clients, or customers. Then there will be upbraiding; but not so with God.

VI. WHEN THE SUPPLIANT APPLIES TO ONE IN WHOSE HEART THERE IS NO TRUE BENEVOLENCE. This is the cause of all upbraidings. But not so with God; he is "LOVE."

HOMILY XXV.

THE FINAL HOME OF THE CHRISTIAN NOT ON EARTH BUT IN HEAVEN.

For here we have no continuing city, but we seek one to come.
HEBREWS xiii, 14.

THE context is pervaded by this thought: that he is a true believer who thoroughly identifies himself with Jesus, trusting in his atonement alone for acceptance with God and eternal life.

The text presents three truths for consideration:

I. THAT MAN HAS NO PERMANENT HOME ON EARTH; he is emphatically a pilgrim and a stranger. First. *The inconstancy of human life.* Secondly. *The inevitable event of death.* Thirdly. *The doom which awaits the earth.*

II. THAT THE PERMANENT HOME OF THE CHRISTIAN IS IN HEAVEN. Heaven is frequently spoken of in Scripture under the notion of a city. Of it true believers are citizens. (Phil. iii, 20.) The use of the figure teaches,

First. *That heaven is a place.* Secondly. *That heaven is a permanent place.* Thirdly. *That heaven is sure to the faithful believer.* The words literally are: "*The city which is to come.*"

III. THAT TO ATTAIN HEAVEN IS THE CHRISTIAN'S SUPREME CONCERN. The text is intensive. Literally: "*We earnestly seek*," etc. Who does not love *home?* Our *hearts* are there.

First. *Heaven is secured to the believer conditionally.* Secondly. *That condition must be fulfilled on earth.* Thirdly. *Its fulfillment requires the vigorous application of the whole mind.* Finally. *The hope of heaven inspires Christian courage.* "Let us also go, *that we may die with him.*"

HOMILY XXVI.

THE END BETTER THAN THE BEGINNING.

Better is the end of a thing than the beginning. ECCLESIASTES vii, 8.

CONCERNING some things, we may say the end is not better than the beginning.

First. *There is sin.* Sin is better, if the word better can be applied to that which is essentially bad, in its beginning than in its end. In its first stages sin is a comparatively pleasant thing. The fruit to Eve was delicious; the thirty pieces of silver in the hands of Judas at first were prized; but the *end*, how sad! "Lust, when it has conceived, bringeth forth sin: sin, when it is finished, bringeth forth death." Sin begins sometimes in pleasure, but ends in pain; begins in music, but ends in groans. The days of a sinner's childhood are often bright and genial; he often excites high hopes in the bosom of fond parents; his teachers predict great things from his genial tendencies and fine talents; but as he yields to pleasure, silences the voice of conscience, follows the desires of the flesh, his heart grows obdurate, his habits are confirmed, age comes on, and he dies without repentance and without hope.

Secondly. *There are unwise enterprises*, concerning which the end is not better than the beginning. The first stages of a mercantile or national enterprise, to the projector, who believes in its importance and feasibility, are interesting and pleasant. The soul is interested, its energies are brought into full play, and its hope soars high. But if the methods of action are unwise, the enterprise will soon prove to be a house built upon the sand, which must totter and fall before the storm. The end of all unwise plans is worse than the beginning.

Thirdly. *There are partial reformations.* A thoughtless sinner is aroused to a sense of his sin and danger. He resolves on reformation, he renounces his old practices, he severs himself from his old associates, he feels himself impressed with the truths of religion, he joins himself to the pious and faithful. For a time he takes delight in his new work; but after a while there comes a change; he ceases "running well," and goes back to the beggarly elements of the world, and "the last end of that man is worse than the first."

The subject has a positive aspect. There are things whose end is better than the beginning:

Firstly. *There is an honest and a persevering search after truth.* At the outset of all investigations the mind is often tasked with the arbitrary, harassed with doubt, and perplexed with difficulties; but as it proceeds things appear more reasonable, obstacles are removed, and the mist gradually rolls off the scene. The mind, in commencing its search for truth, is like a traveler in a strange land in the dim dawn of the morning. Every object is indistinct. Step by step he moves, amid all the anxieties of doubt, on his untrodden path; but as he advances the light increases, the horizon expands; at length the sun strikes the meridian; he reaches an eminence from which he can look backward and onward, from which he can see things in all their distinctness, realize their proportions and beauty; his end is better than his beginning.

Secondly. *There is the history of Christianity.* Its beginning, to all appearance, was bad. It came from despised Nazareth; its founder was the son of a carpenter, who died as a malefactor; its first preachers were fishermen of a humble grade. Systems, institutions, kings and peoples, civilized and savage, were against it; "it was despised and rejected of men." But its end will be better; its path is becoming clearer and clearer every day; it is fast moving on to universal dominion; it will one day be the empress of the world. The little stone shall grow into a mountain.

Thirdly. *There are true friendships.* Most true friendships at their outsets have trials. Misunderstandings, shaking confidence, wounding love, and giving rise to painful suspicions, are not uncommon at the commencement of true friendship. But as it proceeds mutual knowledge, mutual excellence, mutual love increases, and the twain become one.

Fourthly. *There is the life of a good man,* whose end is better than the beginning. To this, we think, Solomon particularly refers: "Better is the day of one's death than the day of one's birth." Birth and death! What words, what events are these! The one is the medium of admission to this world, the other the medium of dismission from it. Our world is a great thoroughfare of souls; through birth thousands come into the world every day, and through death thousands pass away. Here is an analogy between these two events, birth and death: (1.) Both introduce to a new mode of existence. The change of the mode of existence which occurs when we first come into this world is not greater than the change which death will effect.

(2.) Both introduce into a sphere for which there has been an antecedent preparation. The child has organs fitted to this planet; it is made for it; the elements, laws, and provisions are suited to its organization. So it is with death. Death introduces the soul into a state for which it is fitted by this world; some by the life lived have characters morally organized for hell, some for heaven.

Now the statement that the end of life is better than the beginning is not in accordance with the general sentiments of mankind. The birthday is generally considered to be a season of gratitude and joy; and death, whether it occur in the spring-time of youth, or the decrepitude of age, is a season of sorrow and mourning. Humanity enters the world with joy and leaves it amid tears.

That the end of a good man's life is better than the beginning may be further illustrated:

I. At the end of his life he is introduced into a better state. First. *He begins his life amid impurity.* The first air he breathes, the first word he hears, the first impression he receives are tainted with sin; but at its end he is introduced to purity, saints, angels, Christ, God!

Secondly. *He begins his life on trial.* It is a moral battle;

shall he conquer? It is a race; shall he win? It is a voyage; shall he reach the haven? The *end* determines all.

Thirdly. *He begins his life amid suffering.* "Man is born to trouble," etc. "In this tabernacle we groan, earnestly," etc.

> "The air is full of farewells to the dying
> And mournings for the dead;
> The heart of Rachel, for her children crying,
> Will not be comforted."

If the parent knew how much the child would have to suffer during his life; if he could pierce the vail that hides the future, and see the temptations, the trials, the persecutions, the sorrows, the departures to evil, the moral falls he would make, would he not rather tremble than rejoice at his birth?

II. At the end of his life he is introduced into better occupations. Our occupations here are threefold, *physical, intellectual, moral.* All these are more or less of a painful kind. In the first we are toiling for bread; in the second grappling in the dark with the mere rudiments of knowledge; in the third we are mortifying "the flesh with its corruptions and lusts." But in the state into which death introduces us, the engagements will be congenial to the tastes, invigorating to the frame, delightful to the soul, and honoring to God.

III. At the end of his life he is introduced into better society. We are made for society. There is, strictly speaking, no such thing as an anchorite or a misanthrope; all men in a normal state desire the companionship of fellows. How often have we felt that our days would be filled and run over with unspeakable peace and satisfaction if we could but realize, in our mingling with society, as complete a friendship as we have dreamed of in the reveries of the heart, and languished for when listening, afloat, in the wizard sphere of music. But society here is frequently *insincere*, *non-intelligent*, *unaffectionate*. There is much to pain in its duplicities, its treacheries, its hypocrisies, in its ignorance, and in its cold-heartedness. The harshest draught in the cup of human life is wrung from misplaced affections. Byron, speaking of one who had been betrayed by a friend, says with great justness:

> "It is as though the dead could feel
> The icy worm about them steal,
> Without the power to scare away
> The cold consumers of their clay."

But how delightful the society into which heaven will introduce us! We shall mingle with enlightened, genuine, warm-hearted souls, rising in teeming numbers, grade above grade, up to the eternal God himself. "There the wicked cease from troubling, and there the weary be at rest; there the prisoners rest together; they hear not the voice of the oppressor. The small and great are there, and the servant is free from his master."

HOMILY XXVII.

THE PHILIPPIAN JAILOR; OR, CONVERSION.

Then he called for a light, and sprang in, and came trembling, and fell down before Paul and Silas, and brought them out, and said, Sirs, what must I do to be saved? And they said, Believe on the Lord Jesus Christ and thou shalt be saved, and thy house. ACTS, xvi, 29–31.

HERE we have,

I. THE INITIATIVE STAGES TO CONVERSION. First. *A terrible sense of danger.* The earthquake and the strange and sublime conduct of the prisoners roused his guilty conscience. Secondly. *An earnest spirit of inquiry.* "What must I do to be saved?" Thirdly. *A readiness to do whatever is required.* This is implied in the question. Something must be done by me; I'll do whatever it is.

Here you have,

II. THE EXCLUSIVE MEANS OF CONVERSION. "Believe on the Lord Jesus Christ." Faith in Christ is indispensable to produce this moral change. First. *A change of character requires a change in beliefs.* We are controlled and moulded by motives; motives are beliefs. Secondly. *The new beliefs necessary to produce the true change must be directed to Christ.* Christ alone gives us *the true ideal of character, the true way of reaching it, and the true aids to enable us to do so.*

Here you have,

III. THE GLORIOUS ISSUE OF CONVERSION. "Thou shalt be saved." What is salvation? It is not in any measure a *physical* change, not merely an *intellectual* change, not necessarily a *local* change. It is a *moral* revolution. It is the soul rising from sensualism to spirituality, from selfishness to benevolence, from the world to God. First. *This conversion will insure the salvation of our own souls.* "*Thou* shalt be saved." Secondly. *Will lead to the conversion of others.* "And thy house." It does not mean, of course, that his beliefs would save his family independent of their own belief; but that it would prompt him to use such efforts as would, under God, lead his family to a faith unto salvation.

HOMILY XXVIII.

THE CHRISTIAN RUNNER IN RELATION TO HIS SPECTATORS.

Wherefore, seeing we also are compassed about with so great a crowd of witnesses, let us lay aside every weight, and the sin which doth so easily beset us, and let us run with patience the race that is set before us, looking unto Jesus the author and finisher of our faith; who for the joy that was set before him endured the cross, despising the shame, and is set down at the right hand of the throne of God. HEBREWS xii, 1, 2.

THE Christian life is often represented by a race. Many passages afford proof of this: 1 Cor. ix, 24–26; Gal. v, 7; Phil. ii, 16; iii, 12–14. There are those who may be regarded as spectators. *Angels, ancient worthies, the Church, and even the world* may be looked upon as parts of that company.

This passage teaches:

I. That the Christian runner is an object of deep interest to his spectators. This is evident from two things:

First. *The position of the spectators.* They surround the Christian runner. He is said in the text to be "compassed" by them. They see how he *begins, progresses, and finishes.* He cannot throw aside a single glance, relax a single effort, or violate a single condition of the race, without being observed and detected.

Secondly. *The number of the spectators.* That is vast. "So great a cloud of witnesses." The number of angels, ancient worthies, and pious people that take an interest in the believer's course cannot be computed.

This passage teaches:

II. That the Christian runner should put forth great efforts because of his spectators. "Wherefore seeing," etc, "let us lay aside every weight," etc.

First. *He should divest himself of every encumbrance.* "Lay aside every weight." There are many things that will always act as encumbrances on the Christian racecourse. *Ceremonialism, religious errors, business perplexities, fear of man, inveterate prejudices, sinful propensities;* all these are so many dead weights."

Secondly. *He should avoid the sin to which he is most peculiarly prone.* "And the sin which doth so easily beset." *Unbelief* was the besetting sin of the Jews. Against that they were exhorted to guard. It was their most formidable antagonist. We all experience a greater proneness to some sins than to others. *Pride* is a sin to which one is peculiarly prone. It may arise from a constitutional tendency, or from gross ignorance. Wherever it exists it is an evil, and should be checked. It hinders improvement, renders the character unlovely, gives a facility, to temptation, and is ever a source of great unhappiness. *Covetousness* is the besetting sin of another. He lives to accumulate, not to distribute; to get, and not give. *Intemperance* of a third. The wine-cup exercises upon him a bewitching influence. He is convinced of the sinfulness and ruin attending his course, but finds it difficult to resist. *Evil speaking* is the besetting sin of a fourth. There is a great proneness to talk, and without extraordinary care to state what is calculated to injure rather than benefit the party spoken of. Hence the exhortation, "Speak not evil one of another, brethren." *Anger* is the besetting sin of a fifth. How difficult for some to restrain this feeling! How easily aroused! On what a slight provocation it will light up the eye and mantle the cheek!

Thirdly. *He should maintain great self-possession.* "Run with patience the race that is set before us." There are many exhortations to patience. "Let patience have her perfect work." "And to temperance patience." There is great need for patience in the study of God's word and government, in watching for the results of Christian enterprise, in contending against the prejudices of ungodly men, and in the endurance of the varied ills and vexations of human life.

This passage teaches,

III. That the Christian runner has an object before him from which his thoughts should not be diverted by his spectators. "Looking unto Jesus," etc. Jesus is the object. In looking to Jesus he has to consider three things:

First. *The work of Jesus.* "The author and finisher of our faith."

Secondly. *The history of Jesus.* "Who for the joy that was set before him endured the cross, despising the shame." Jesus was once in toil and suffering. He then endured great agony, and despised the shame associated with its instrument. He was sustained in this by the reward he had in prospect. Think upon these facts in his history. Emulate his manliness, and draw inspiration, as he did, from the prize before you.

Thirdly. *The exaltation of Jesus.* "And is set down at the right hand of the throne of God." He is now greatly honored. God, for his patience, perseverance, and sufferings has exalted him. Even so ye shall be rewarded if ye "run with patience the race that is set before you."

HOMILY XXIX.

RELATION OF CHRIST TO THE HUMAN SOUL.

Behold, I stand at the door and knock; if any man hear my voice, and open the door, I will come in to him, and will sup with him, and he with me. REV. iii, 20.

IN these words we have three things: Christ's attitude toward the soul, his action upon it, and his aim in reference to it.

I. HIS ATTITUDE TOWARD THE SOUL. "I stand at the door." He is *constantly* in contact with the soul. He does not come occasionally and then depart; he *stands.* This shows, first, *His deep concern.* In the eye of Christ the soul is no trifling object. He knows its *capabilities, relations, power, influence, interminable history.* This shows, secondly, *His infinite condescension.* Frail man, who stands at thy door? The Creator of the universe, etc. This shows, thirdly, *His wonderful patience.* Day after day, year after year, he *stands* there, "waiting to be gracious."

II. HIS ACTION UPON THE SOUL. He does not stand there as a statue doing nothing. He *knocks.* He knocks at the door of intellect with his philosophical truths; at the door of *conscience* with his ethical principles; at the door of *love* with his transcendent charms; at the door of *hope* with his heavenly glories; at the door of *fear* with the terrors of his law. He knocks by providences and by preaching, by men and events, by books and Bibles. This is his action. The fact that he thus stands and knocks and the door does not open, shows three things: First. *The moral power of the sinner.* The soul has the power to shut out Christ. It can bolt itself against its Creator. This it does by *directing* its thoughts to other subjects, by *deadening* its convictions, by *procrastinations.* This shows, secondly, *The consummate folly of the sinner.* Who is shut out? Not a foe or thief; but a friend, a physician, a deliverer. This shows, thirdly, *The awful guiltiness of the sinner.* It shuts out its proprietor, its rightful Lord.

III. His aim in reference to the soul. It is not to destroy it; but to come into it and identify himself with all its feelings, aspirations, and interests. "I will come into him, and will sup with him, and he with me." This is figurative language, but easily understood. It means,

First, *Inhabitation.* "I will come into him." We are perpetually letting people into our hearts. How pleased we are if some illustrious personage will enter our humble homes, and sit down with us, etc. It means,

Secondly, *Identification.* "Sup with him, and he with me." I will be at home with him, be one with him. A conventionally great man deems it a condescension to enter the house of an inferior; he never thinks of *identifying* himself with the humble inmate. Christ does this with the soul that lets him in. He makes its cares his own.

Open the door, then, sinner; let in the genial ray and the salubrious breeze upon thy benighted and withered heart; open the door, let in the Physician, and he will heal thee of all thy maladies; open the door, let in the Emancipator, he will break all thy bonds and set thee free;

open the door, let in the King to thy wretched cell, thou criminal, he has pardon to bestow. Open the door; reason, conscience, all true voices in all worlds say, "OPEN THE DOOR."

"In the silent midnight watches
  List—thy bosom door
How it knocketh, knocketh, knocketh,
  Knocketh evermore!
Say not 'tis thy pulse is beating:
  'Tis thy heart of sin;
'Tis thy Saviour knocks and crieth,
  'Rise and let me in.'

"Death comes on, with reckless footsteps,
  To the hall and hut:
Think you, Death will tarry knocking
  Where the door is shut?
Jesus waiteth, waiteth, waiteth,
  But the door is fast;
Grieved, away the Saviour goeth;
  Death breaks in at last.

"Then 'tis time to stand entreating
  Christ to let thee in;
At the gate of heaven beating,
  Waiting for thy sin.
Nay—alas, thou guilty creature!
  Hast thou then forgot?
Jesus waited long to know thee,
  Now he knows thee not."

HOMILY XXX.

THE DEVIL AND THE SWINE; OR, THE POWER OF EVIL OVER HUMANITY, AND THE POWER OF CHRIST OVER EVIL.

And when he was come to the other side into the country of the Gergesenes, there met him two possessed with devils, coming out of the tombs, exceeding fierce, so that no man might pass by that way, etc. MATT. viii, 28–34.

THIS is one of the strangest incidents in the history of the marvelous, the life of Christ. It naturally starts at once two questions: first, Whether these two men were actually possessed with devils, or the subjects of some species of mental insanity, such as hypochondria, epilepsy, or lunacy. This is a question of no practical moment, though it has originated a large amount of controversy, and is capable of originating a great deal more. The second question is, Of what spiritual service can the record of such incidents as these be to us, the men of this age? As it is inscribed in this world-book, it is natural to suppose it bears in it something of value for humanity. What use is it intended to serve? To gratify the sense of the marvelous within us? or to start abstruse discussions, either as to the influence of certain conditions of the atmosphere upon the brain, or the influence of disembodied spirits upon mankind in the world? It does these two things assuredly. But we scarcely think either or both uses are of sufficient importance to account for its being recorded in a book intended for humanity. It is, I think, charged with a lesson which urgently requires the earnest study of every man that is, or ever shall be. What is that? *The baneful power of moral evil over human nature, and the blessed power of Christ over moral evil.* Whether these men were literally possessed, or were the mere subjects of a mental disease, it matters not to this lesson; the great lesson in either case comes out with equal prominence and force. It is independent of all controversies that have ever been raised on this subject.

I. The baneful power of moral evil over human nature. Whichever hypothesis be correct, possession or disease, *moral evil* is the cause of all the sad and terrible feelings of these two men. If they were *possessed*, the devils entered them because they were sinners; evil spirits find no dwelling-place in holy natures: or if it were mere *disease*, diseases of all kinds spring from sin. Misery never springs from holiness. All natural evils grow out of moral, as the branches of the oak out of the acorn. Looking upon the incident as expressing the baneful power of sin upon man, we have four of its baneful tendencies developed:

First. *Its deranging tendency.* They were "coming out of the tombs." The tombs of the Jews were very frequently excavations in the rocks, and were sometimes very spacious, containing different compartments for the dead. They were sometimes the haunts of robbers, and sometimes places of refuge, whither the frightened resorted in times of war. These men were so mentally deranged, that instead of dwelling in the ordinary habitations of their class and attending to the duties of life, they tenanted those tombs, and filled, perhaps, their imagination with ghastly images of the dead. Supposing that they were diseased, rather than possessed, they fancied that there was within them a "legion," a mighty multitude of the spirits of those men whose bodies crowded those tombs. What aberration!

Now, although this is a very wonderful and extreme case of deception, it may fairly be regarded as indicating the tendency of moral evil, or sin, to deceive. Sin is deceptive. The apostle speaks of the "deceivableness of unrighteousness." What delusive ideas it gives men about life and happiness, and glory, and God! Souls under its influence are everywhere living among the tombs. Instead of being out in the bright and happy universe of true life, filling their right place, and discharging the high duties of being, they are down in the tombs of dead souls. There is one class of persons which these two men especially represented, and that is those who, in religious matters, are constantly living in the sepulchral region of ideas, dogmas, and ceremonies which belong to other ages. There is a large number of men whose thoughts are so antique, and whose minds are so gloomy, that you may say, almost without figure, that they are living "among the tombs."

Secondly. *Its malicious tendency.* "They were exceeding fierce, so that no man might pass by that way." All the kind instincts of their nature had become extinct. Their whole soul was in flames of wrath. The sight of suffering would delight them, the throes of agony would fall as music on their malignant ears. The tendency of sin is to make men malicious, to destroy "natural affection," to eradicate all the kindly sympathies of the heart, to set man against his fellow as well as against his Creator. The apostle, in sketching the character of sinners, says: "The poison of asps is under their lips; their mouth is full of cursing and bitterness; their feet are swift to shed blood; destruction and misery are in their way; and the way of peace have they not known." Does not the history of the world show this to be true? What is the history of man on earth but a history of oppression, cruelty, bloodshed, and slaughter? You see the malicious, fiendish spirit not merely in the men who are actually engaged in slaughtering each other, but in a form as bad—and for many reasons worse, because of the mean cowardice associated with it—in those who heartlessly advocate the enterprise of destruction, while they lounge at home on the couch of ease. Sin and benevolence are eternal opposites.

Thirdly. *Its foreboding tendency.* "What have we to do with thee, Jesus, thou Son of God? Art thou come hither to torment us before the time?" Whether this be the utterance of infernal spirits which had possession of these men, or that of their own insane and aberrated minds, you have in both suppositions the idea that sin is connected with terrible forebodings of the future. The Bible gives us to understand that devils are looking forward with awful terror to some future; they are "reserved in chains of darkness unto the judgment of the great day." The judgment will make their chains more firm and galling, their midnight sky more black; raise their tempestuous storm of wrath to higher degrees of fury and anguish. In the case of men and devils sin imparts a dread of the future. "Art thou come to torment us before the time?" As if they had said, We know that there is a time of torment before us, we have no doubt of that; we have no hope of escaping that. "Art thou come to torment us before the time?" Sin is cowardice. It unmans the soul. It makes it afraid; afraid of death, afraid of God, afraid of the future, afraid of its own visions, and of its own self. It makes it the miserable victim of fear.

Fourthly. *Its degrading tendency.* "And there was a good way off from them a herd of swine feeding. So the devils besought him, saying, If thou cast us out, suffer us to go away into the herd of swine." The tendency of sin is not to ascend from the lower to the higher, but to descend from the higher to the lower; it does not aspire to rise from the man to the angel, but inclines from the man to the brute, the swine. The request of these maniacs, or demoniacs if you will, strange though it sounds, *is only an expression of the general downward tendency of sin.* Sin brutalizes. Sin gives the soul an appetency for the *unclean*, a swineward direction. It is by no means uncommon to see human souls running into a low animalism. Through the *media* of worldliness, sensuality, and voluptuousness, the moral metempsychosis takes place every day, and souls transmigrate brute-ward. A. has made his fortune in the city, and has retired into the aristocratic suburbs to pamper appetite and to live in luxury. He has passed the noon of life and is gaining animalism every day. Thirty years ago he had an active intellect, fine susceptibilities; there was something like genius beaming in his looks and playing on his brow. But where in him do you see any of these mind-traits? He is dull, coarse, plethoric. Whither is his soul gone? It has run swineward. Is not this A. the type of a numerous and growing class that populate the suburbs of large cities and towns? The first chapter of Paul's letter to the Romans is an illustration of the swineward tendency of souls under sin.

Here you have, then, a picture of the ruinous influence of moral evil, or sin, upon humanity. It makes it morally mad; it puts out its kindly sentiments, and inspires it with the malignant; it fills it with forebodings of the future and degrades it into the brutal forms of life. *Sin is ruin.*

II. The blessed power of Christ over moral evil. The passage suggests two thoughts in relation to Christ's power over evil:

First. *He has power to eradicate evil from man, and by so doing restore him.* "And he said unto them, Go." And they went. The evil, whether it was *principle* or *person*, was expelled. Mark gives the history of one of these men after the expulsion of the evil, and probably what he says of one was true of both—that "he sat at the feet of Jesus, clothed, and in his right mind;" sat as a studious listener and devout worshiper. He tells us, also, that he began to publish what Christ had done for him through Decapolis. We rejoice that Christ has power to eradicate the evil, and to expel the devil from man. He does it now as truly as he did in the case of these men; not, it is true, by miracle, but by his regenerating and sanctifying truth. And where this is done we find a wonderful change in the individual's history. Like the prodigal, he comes to himself, to his right mind; he listens to Christ, and publishes his fame abroad.

Secondly. *He has power not only to eradicate evil from human nature, but to destroy its very existence.* "And behold the whole herd of swine ran violently down a steep place into the sea, and perished in the waters." Perhaps this was intended to symbolize the fact that Christ will one day destroy evil itself; that he will destroy entirely the works of the devil; that error and wrong, that selfishness and impiety, and every unholy principle to which man is now subject, will one day be utterly destroyed—will be buried forever in the great swelling sea of intelligence, rectitude, and truth.

Two remarks are here suggested in relation to Christ's way of destroying evil: (1.) *That his method of doing it sometimes involves the sacrifice of human property.* These people lost their swine. But what was the sacrifice to the good effected? The delivering of one soul from the devil is worth all the cattle upon a thousand hills. Much secular property must always be sacrificed in the process of destroying moral evil in this world. (2.) *That through this destruction of property Christ's work will meet with opposition from interested parties.* "And they that kept them fled, and went their ways into the city, and told everything, and what was befallen to the possessed of the devils. And behold, the whole city came out to meet Jesus; and when they saw him, they besought him that he would depart out of their coasts." Why did they beseech him to depart from their coast? One might have thought that, seeing he could rid humanity of such tremendous evils, they would entreat him to dwell among them in order to relieve others of their afflicted neighbors. They were, most probably, afraid of losing more of their property; *they cared more for their swine than for their species.* It has ever been so. The true spiritual reformer, if his teaching in any way interfere with secular interests, though he may bless hundreds of devil-ridden souls, is earnestly desired, if not compelled, to leave the coast. Paul must leave Ephesus because the "craft is in danger;" and Christ must leave Decapolis because the inhabitants value their swine. When will the time come that men shall say, Let our craft and cattle, our property and position go, so long as men are being delivered from devils.

HOMILY XXXI.

THE PRE-EMINENCE OF GOD'S WORK.

I am doing a great work, so that I cannot come down. NEHEMIAH vi, 3.

NEHEMIAH was doing a great work. He had been cupbearer to Artaxerxes Longimanus, the Persian monarch. When he heard of the distressed state of the Jews in Jerusalem he was deeply affected, and sought permission from his royal master to visit them, that he might render them seasonable succor. Ezra had preceded him ten years before, and occupied himself chiefly in collecting the sacred writings and in restoring the worship of God; but Nehemiah's heart was set upon the restoration of the civil polity and the proper security of the city, and to these points he directed his ardent powers upon his arrival. This is the great work to which he alludes. He was a pious man, and influenced in all this by a religious and patriotic zeal. He succeeded, and well he might, for he had just the requisite qualities of energy, faith, intelligence, and perseverance for a great work.

I. God's work is still a great work. What is it? It resolves itself into two parts: 1. Work in relation to one's self: faith in the Redeemer, progressive holiness, and final glory. 2. Work in relation to others: there are the poor to relieve, the ignorant to instruct, the miserable to console, the sick and dying to visit, the Church of Christ to build up, and the world to save.

II. God's work must be done first. Nehemiah received a complimentary note from Sanballat and several other great personages, who wished to have a conference with him about the work he had in hand. This attention would have turned the brain of some weak ones and induced them instantly to desert the work; but this ardent young Hebrew had a profound conviction of the importance of his work, and a lurking suspicion of the honest intentions of those who addressed him, hence this terse and pertinent reply. He knew too well the value of such compliments to be diverted from a business which involved such important interests. The language of his conduct was this: God's work first, compliments next.

Even so now. The pleasures, customs, amusements, and courtesies of life must not be allowed to come between us and the great work of God. Is there anything more important than the salvation of our soul? and must not that be first? Is there any work more dignifying to ourselves, more honorable to God, more momentous to our fellow-men than God's work? and must that be set aside for worldly compliments and pleasures? No; God's work must be first, and that man's religion is to be suspected who makes it second.

III. God's work preserves from mischief and misery. What had been the consequence had Nehemiah met Sanballat and the rest of the magnates as they requested? Perhaps they had imprisoned him or murdered him; and then the great work had been stayed and Jerusalem left in mourning. The disobedient prophet went out of his way, and a lion met him and killed him. The path of duty is the path of safety. Her ways are pleasantness and peace. Fill thy hands and thy heart, my brother, with God's great work, and it will save thee from the snare of the devil, from the stratagems of a delusive world, and from the degenerative forces of thy own heart.

IV. God's work should be loved for its own sake. There must be a deep and all-commanding sympathy with it. This feeling had taken possession of Nehemiah's heart. It absorbed and engrossed him. His whole soul was there. Work of all sorts is well done under such impulses. One likes to see a poet with the soul of a poet, a painter with the soul of a painter, etc.; but above all, a Christian doing God's great work, with his whole mind and strength consecrated to it.

V. God's work should be begun, continued, and ended with prayer. This was the spirit of Nehemiah. See his prayer at the beginning, chapter i. Again in the midst of these conflicting times, vi, 14, and chapter ix.

It is a great work we have to do, and of ourselves we are unequal to it. But let us look up and press on; strength shall be given according to the day. "Lo, I am with you always," etc. What precedents have we! Paul, the glorious army of martyrs, the brave old Puritans, and above all, our divine Master, who wrought all day and prayed all night.

But some, nay, many, have not yet entered upon the Lord's great work; self, the devil, the world have had dominion over them. Sad work, and sad pay! Let those who are in this work already buckle on the harness afresh, etc.

HOMILY XXXII.

THE HEART OF STONE; OR, THE SOUL WITHOUT RELIGION.

A new heart also will I give you, and a new spirit will I put within you: and I will take away the stony heart out of your flesh, and I will give you a heart of flesh. Ezekiel xxxvi, 26.

The analogies which exist between the soul generally, and the unregenerated soul particularly, and the stone, are both numerous and important.

I. The soul of man is, like the stone, a mystery. Here is a stone: but what is it? I see it, weigh it, and feel it. But what is it? Color, weight, and tangibility are not entities. By these qualities we may recognize the entities and form an opinion respecting them. In this sense the stone itself is a mystery, and may be looked on as a type or picture of every soul, saved or unsaved. Every soul feels, reasons, and thinks; and yet the soul is neither feeling, reason, nor thought; these are mere qualities which belong to the soul in every state, but form no part of its essence. By these we recognize the spiritual entity, and form an opinion respecting it. In itself it is a mystery.

II. The soul of the unregenerate, however, is, like the stone, very hard. All stones are not equally hard: though hardness is a characteristic of each. Neither are all souls equally without feeling or moral susceptibility, though all are sadly deficient in this respect. This is illustrated, (1.) By the cruel practices of Pagan nations, infanticides, parricides, self-torture, human sacrifices, sutteeism, etc. (2.) By the indifference of those who are not Pagans, even Christians, to the welfare of others. There is a world of selfishness in the Church. Many have entered the Church for selfish purposes; to secure secular advantages on earth, and heaven at last. As they take up religion to get to heaven themselves merely—for gain, they care little or nothing for the condition of others. (3.) By the difficulty invariably found of awakening the soul to an earnest inquiry for its own personal and highest interest.

III. The soul of the unregenerate is, like the stone, not what it originally was. The stone is hard; but it was not always so. From the form of its elemental parts, the minute particles that form it, I see it has not been always as hard as it is now. Here in this part of it you see a fossil, the track of a reptile, the scales of a fish, the shell of a mollusk, the bark of a tree, or the leaf of a flowerless plant. This stone must have been soft when the reptile crawled upon it, when the fish swam in the water above it, leaving its scales upon the mud beneath, when the aquatic snail left behind it its silicious home, and when the tree fell or the leaves were scattered. Every pebble or grain of sand was once a part of a great rock, and that rock itself a soft material; but heat, pressure, and time combined, made it *hard*. Even the flint existed in a soft and pulpy form. It is composed for the most part of the debris of animals, minute but mighty, which once lived and formed calcareous shells from the ocean waters. They all perished in their turn, and were buried in the sponges which then lived on our shores. In process of time they were hardened into flints. Similar is the history of your soul, my unregenerated brother. It was once soft, tender, and full of feeling, though now it is hard. This is proved, (1.) From the universal traditions of men. All nations have their notions of a golden age that is past. (2.) From man's intuitive ideas of the moral nature of God. We cannot conceive it possible that such an unfinished mass of heterogeneous elements as man is proved to be, combining the highest intellectual glory with the lowest animal degradation, should come from the hand of God just as he is. (3.) From the infallible testimony of the Scripture: "God made man upright," but they have sought out many inventions."

IV. The unregenerated soul has, like the stone, been gradually hardened. Whatever tendencies to evil are bound up in the heart of a child, this I venture to affirm, no man is born a monster. Even Nero, who assassinated his mother, set fire to the Roman capital, and brought to an untimely grave, in misery, thousands of men, women, and innocent children, had once a tender heart like others. It was *gradually* hardened. "Would to God I could not write!" was his feeling exclamation once when a death warrant was presented to him for signature.

V. The unregenerated soul, like the stone, bears in itself a faithful record of all the powers which have helped to make it what it is. In the stone some of its particles are spherical, showing that once, after having been broken from the mother rock, they were for centuries under the action of flowing water; others are crystalized, showing that once they were in a state of solution; others are organic, showing that they were once the seat of vegetable or animal life. In the form and composition of these particles we find a record of the various changes through which the stone has passed, as well as the numerous influences which have been at work in the effecting of those changes. Could we only understand the mute language eloquently uttered, a history of the world for ages, chemically, botanically, and zoologically, might be constructed from a single stone. The soul of man is similar. In eternity it may be possible to trace distinctly in every soul in heaven or hell a faithful record of all the influences which on earth have ever tended to elevate or degrade it. Our own power of vision may be sufficiently strengthened in the future to conduct with ease such a wonderful analysis. The influence we now exert, great or small, good or evil, will *never* cease to act. The fluttering of the insect's wing, in the calm of summer or in the winter storm, alters the atmospheric current and the relative position of every material particle in the universe as truly, and in proportion to the moving force, as the peal of a thousand thunders, the shock of the earthquake which covers continents with ruins, or the rupture into a million of fragments of a planet in its course. Our actions also make indelible impressions by means of air, light, heat, electricity, and moral and intellectual laws, upon others both near us and afar off. We may yet trace our own words and deeds in souls, like fossils in the stone, in souls eternally ruined or made for ever blessed. As every scene we witness makes an indelible impression on the retina of the eye, so that, when it is mentally reproduced by the imagination, a faint outline is visible in the eye itself; and as the last scene the dying man beholds remains imprinted on the retina until the very remembrance on which the scene is drawn be disintegrated and dissolved by the process of decay, so the various powers which have acted on the soul and aided its upward or downward motion, will remain for ever, and may be yet legible on its very structure.

VI. The unregenerated soul, like the stone, may be softened by the application of appropriate means. The flint may be reduced to pulp by chemical reagents, and molded like the clay to any form. The hardest metals may be dissolved; so may also the hardest heart. *The love of Christ* is the dissolving element for souls. If your heart is hard, my friend, go to the bleeding Saviour. Let his dying love but touch its hard material and in a moment it will become soft and tender, and may be molded by the grace of God into the image of that Saviour himself.

HOMILY XXXIII.

HUMANITY LOST, SOUGHT, AND FOUND.

What man of you, having a hundred sheep, if he lose one of them, doth not leave the ninety and nine in the wilderness, and go after that which is lost, until he find it? And when he hath found it, he layeth it on his shoulders, rejoicing. And when he cometh home, he calleth together his friends and neighbors, saying unto them, Rejoice with me: for I have found my sheep which was lost. LUKE xv, 4–6.

THE language is highly figurative, but very expressive. It gives us humanity in three aspects, as *lost*, *sought*, and *found.*

I. As LOST. Man is likened to a sheep that has wandered from its fold, left its associates and its shepherd, is lost in the intricacies of the wilderness, and is unable to find its way back. It is lost. Man is lost *physically*, *intellectually*, *socially*, *religiously*. Three things are suggested concerning his sad condition:

First. *It involves a forfeiture of great privileges.* The lost sheep is deprived of the fellowship of its companions, the provision of the fold, and the guardianship of the shepherd. The other thing suggested concerning this sad condition is,

Secondly, *That it is a state in which the owner still holds his claim.* Into whatever district the sheep went, it was still the property of the man from whom it departed. So it is with man. We are still his and bound to serve him. We can never destroy the claim. We have humanity here,

II. As SOUGHT. The owner leaves "the ninety and nine," and "goes after that which is lost."

First. *Here is special effort.* He leaves his own sphere and "goes," etc. Jesus is a special messenger, the Gospel is a special message, the Spirit is a special agent. God has gone out of his way to restore us.

Secondly. *Here is persevering effort.* "Until he find it." God perseveres with individuals, families, nations. We have humanity here,

III. As FOUND. "When he hath found it he layeth it on his shoulders rejoicing," etc.

First. *The restoration is the result of divine seeking.* The lost sheep did not find its way back and never would.

Secondly. *Is the source of immense joy.* The owner rejoices and calleth upon all his neighbors to rejoice. God and his angels rejoice. Blessed be God! millions of fallen men have been restored. All the saints on earth and in heaven were once "as sheep going astray, but are now returned unto the shepherd and bishop of souls."

HOMILY XXXIV.

THE INNER MAN, OR SOUL-GROWTH.

For which cause we faint not; but though our outward man perish, yet the inward man is renewed day by day. 2 Cor. iv, 16.

First. *Man has two natures.* He has an "inner" and an "outer" man. Consciousness, science, and the Bible unite in teaching us this wonderful fact in our existence. Within this bodily organization there is a *being* which observes, reasons, feels, resolves, and acts. This is the "inner" man, the self of our existence, the *man* of the man. It is the mover and manager of this machine, the tenant of this house, the ruler of this temple.

Secondly. *The outward nature is subject to the law of decay.* The law of dissolution is operating on the body every moment. Particle after particle departs with every pulsation. Up to a certain period of life it is true, where there is no disease, this law is to some extent counteracted in its operation; but the period arrives when it comes fully into force, and reduces the frame to its primitive elements. Decay is written on the outward man. We may struggle against this law, but it must go on, and one day it will master us.

Thirdly. *That while the outward man decays, the inner man may grow in strength.* We would not depreciate the assistance which "the inner" derives from "the outer," which the soul derives from the body. Through the bodily organs we receive those impressions which rouse alike our intuitional sentiments and intellectual powers. Like the atmosphere to the seed, the body is the medium which conveys to the soul those sunbeams and showers which quicken it into life and nourish its powers. We do not maintain that a feeble and an unhealthy body is as favorable to the moral growth of the soul as a hale and vigorous one; far from it. All that is taught is, that the soul can grow even while the body is decaying. So long as the brain will act the soul can grow. "These light afflictions, which are but for a moment," etc.

Thus, while decay is the law to which the outer man is subject, progressive power is the law to which the inner is subject. While the body exhausts its energy by labor and becomes feeble with years, the soul grows strong by labor and young with age; while the body is passing every day to the dust, the soul soars toward the boundless and everlasting.

Our subject is the growth of the "inner man."

I. THE CONDITIONS OF THIS SOUL-GROWTH. There are at least three things necessary to growth: healthful life, wholesome nutriment, and proper exercise. *There can be no growth, of course, without life.* All plants and animals, however young, cease to grow the moment life departs. But the life must be healthful. Diseased life will never have a vigorous growth. What is the healthful life of a soul? Supreme sympathy with God: the inner man is dead where this is not. There is no daily renewal of life in the soul of a sinner. *There must be wholesome nutriment.* No life can live upon *itself;* all vegetable and animal life requires the support of outward elements. The soul cannot live upon itself: whatever may be its innate sentiments and powers, it must have the outward. *There must be proper exercise* also. Even plants seem to require exercise, although they have no power of self-motion; the air bends their fibers, and thus strengthens them. The body requires exercise. It is so with the soul. It must exercise its powers of thought, affection, and will. Have you got these conditions of *growth?* Have you *life*, *nourishment*, and *exercise?* If you have not, you may have them. Christianity has a power to impart the life, supply the nourishment, and stimulate the exercise.

II. The characteristics of this soul-growth.

First. *Beautifulness.* There is nothing so beautiful as the growth of a soul. The growth of a flower rising from the earth is beautiful, multiplying its leaves, budding into beauty, and blossoming into perfection; so is the growth of a child, passing from stage to stage, unfolding new powers every year, until it stands upon the platform of a perfect man; so is the growth of an empire rising from a barbarous horde, widening its territory, and progressing in civilization, until it takes its place among the nations of the earth. But the growth of a soul in virtue, in usefulness, in assimilation to God, is a more beautiful object than these. That flower will wither, that man will return to dust, that empire will pass away like the dynasties that are no more; but the soul will advance forever, rise from "glory unto glory."

Secondly. *Constancy.* Growth is not a thing of fits and starts. The plant grows every day, the child advances every hour: it does not grow one day of the week and pause on the others. If our souls are growing the process is constant. If we are not religious *always* we are *never* religious. If we are not religious in the market we are not religious in the temple.

Thirdly. *Blessedness.* A *growing* state is a *happy* state. See the lambs gamboling on the sunny hills; see the little bird when first it leaves its nest, chirping gladsome notes; see the child, freed from the leading-strings of the nursery and running on the greensward alone, what ecstacies gleam from that little face and sparkle in those eyes! the infusion of new energy, the expansion of limbs, and the invigoration of muscle, are all connected with happiness. If you are growing in soul you are happy. "They that wait upon the Lord shall renew their strength." Everything grows about us if the soul grows. If the soul grows in beauty, everything becomes more beautiful; if the soul grows in harmony, everything becomes more harmonious. If the soul grows in knowledge of the universe, the universe grows greater and brighter.

Fourthly. *Endlessness.* The soul's capacity of growth seems to me immeasurable. The capacity for growth in all other life under the sun is limited. The tree that grows a thousand years finds a point at which it stops and decays; not so with the soul. "It doth not yet appear what we shall be." John said that eighteen hundred years ago; and though perhaps his soul has been growing ever since, he would say so with greater emphasis now.

Fifthly. *Responsibleness.* Man may not be responsible always for the growth of his body, but he is for the growth of his soul; if he has a dwarfish body he cannot help it, but if he has a dwarfish soul he himself is to blame.

We learn from this subject,

First, *The necessary condition of man's well-being.* What is it? It is that the inner man grow. It is not that your wealth should increase, that your influence extend, that your social circle widen; for your body decays, and with the decay of the body all these things lose their worth; but it is the growth of the soul. Secondly. *The absolute necessity of the Gospel.* You cannot grow without spiritual *life*, spiritual *nourishment*, and spiritual *incentives* to action. And nothing but the Gospel can give you these. Thirdly. *The true method of using the world.* It is to make it promote the growth of the soul. Do not murmur under trying dispensations; these may be conducive to the growth of the soul. Do not envy the prosperity of the ungodly; all their worldly splendor is but the adornment of a corpse. Fourthly. *The Christian's view of death.* Death! What is it? It is not the extinction of your being, it is not the suspension of your powers, it is not even the interruption of your progress; *the soul is renewed day by day.* It is nothing but a change in the mere costume of our being. The tree in its progress changes its foliage, and the bird its plumage; and we in our progress must change our garments. "This mortal must put on immortality!"

Brother, take care of thy soul; thy body is decaying day by day.

> "While man is growing, life is in decrease;
> And cradles rock us nearer to the tomb;
> Our birth is nothing but our death begun,
> As tapers that instant they take fire."

HOMILY XXXV.

MISTAKEN NOTIONS RESPECTING MAN'S INABILITY.

Why stand ye here all the day idle? MATT. xx, 6.

THE parable indicates some of the causes of spiritual idleness. It is an old proverb, "There is a right way and a wrong way of doing everything." Also a right and wrong way in preaching the doctrines of the Gospel. A right way where people are stirred up to diligence and activity; a wrong way where the hearers of the word are rendered more slothful and careless. This is often the case where human inability is preached. Against all pleas for doing nothing let the text ever sound in the ears of the slothful: "Why stand ye here all the day idle?" One *great cause* of spiritual indolence—*Mistaken notions respecting man's inability.*

First. *The Bible represents God as angry with people for pleading weakness and inability.* Moses did. "And Moses said unto the Lord, O my Lord, I am not eloquent, neither heretofore, nor since thou hast spoken to thy servant; but I am slow of speech, and of a slow tongue." Exodus iv, 10–13. Jeremiah pleads inability to execute a commission he had received from the Lord. "Then said I, Ah Lord God, behold I cannot speak, for I am a child. But the Lord said unto me, Say not I am a child." The pleading of inability in these cases the Lord would not receive.

Secondly. *There is no occasion for being weak, since there is a remedy.* Seek the Lord and his strength. Isaiah was weak, but the Lord having strengthened him he offered his services: "Here am I, send me." Ezekiel was weak both in soul and in body, but the spirit entered into him and set him on his feet. You who have talked for years respecting your weakness, are you really desirous of obtaining power and strength, so as to be able with Paul to say, "I can do all things?"

Thirdly. *Weak people are not qualified to do the Lord's work.* David was surrounded by mighty men: his three mighties, and others "not so mighty as the first three." The Son of David must have mighty men around him. Mephibosheths lame in their feet won't do. Look to the mighties mentioned in the Acts: Peter, Paul, Barnabas; to the mighties in Hebrews xi; the Reformers: Calvin, Knox, Zwingle, Luther, Wesley. Christ gives his people not the spirit of weakness, but "the spirit of power and a sound mind," and thus qualifies to do his work. Christ must have strong men in his Church, not weak ones. "And there was sore war against the Philistines all the days of Saul: and when Saul saw any strong man or any valiant man he took him unto him." Let our motto be, TRUST, TRY. Weak people, or people who are resolved to be always weak, *are obstructions;* reminding us of the inhabitants of Meroz who refused to come forward to the help of the Lord; of the Tekoites who put not their necks to the work of the Lord, (pleading inability, of course;) or perhaps more closely resembling Sanballat the Horonite, Tobiah the Ammonite, and Geshem the Arabian. Nehemiah ii, 17–20.

Fourthly. *Weak people nurse their weakness; and this promotes indolence.* Where a person is relieved from fever, the medical man is anxious that his patient should rise from bed, get out of doors, and take a little gentle exercise. "But I am so weak I cannot rise." "You must rise; you are only nursing your weakness."

And we have many analogous cases in the Church. To these it is said in vain, "Rise up, take exercise; exercise thyself in faith, in prayer, in the Sunday-school, in going about doing good. All these exercises will strengthen thee and impart good health to thy soul."

Fifthly. *Weak people won't do anything either in their own name or in the name of Christ.* Indolence is so agreeable to their nature. If sensible of weakness, ask for power. Thousands, millions, have got power from on high. Every man that goes to heaven is a man of faith, of love, and power. "He that overcometh shall inherit all things." God's witnesses in all ages have not been weak, but powerful. Under sloth's influence you say you are weak. This in few cases is the language of humility. "When I am weak," says Paul, "then I am strong." "I can do all things."

HOMILY XXXVI.

ON THE USE OF EXTERNALS IN RELIGION.

And behold, there was a man named Zaccheus, which was the chief among the publicans, and he was rich," etc. LUKE xix, 2–10.

A RICH man, and no doubt accustomed to gratify curiosity, Zaccheus climbed up into a tree that he might not lose the great sight, the marvelous man whom all the people followed. He "sought to see Jesus who he was"—the outer man only. We are not told he had any desire to learn of the Great Teacher the laws of God, or the nature of his kingdom, or to beseech forgiveness. Yet Christ approved of his curiosity. He called him down and went to his house. Zaccheus received Christ joyfully, and "salvation came to his house that very day."

The principle involved is, that the use of the mere externals of religion is sometimes blessed by God to a spiritual end, even when that has not been the object in view. Here this principle is shown in its application to *knowledge;* but it is equally applicable to the emotions and the will as to the intellect.

There are things connected with religion which a man may possess or employ without a truly religious aim, which may be the means of spiritual life, but are not that life; not even positive signs of it.

I. SOME OF THESE THINGS ARE NECESSARY. The Holy Spirit does not supersede perception and reason. A man is not converted, nor made to grow in grace, by an immediate act of omnipotence, independent of the natural modes of reaching his perception, emotions, and will. He is not conveyed in vision into the presence of Christ, but must, like Zaccheus, climb up into a tree, or in some other ordinary way first get a sight of the Son of man. Hearing must go before believing, acquaintance precede love. So that a certain amount of *biblical knowledge* is indispensable. Church *organization* is necessary. It has been abused, made to usurp altogether the place of individual action, but it cannot be totally dispensed with. Without it some methods of spreading Christianity would be impossible, others inefficient. Were there no visible Church there would be no public worship, no union with the brethren, no stirring up to love and good works, and one great demonstration of the existence and vitality of Christianity would be lost. Christianity has a social object no less essential than its personal object; and were each Christian to isolate himself, all the manifold benefits ordained to result from the action and reaction of Christians on each other's hearts and minds would be rejected.

II. Some of these things are useful. Our spiritual stature is but short, and if by "climbing up into a tree" we can supplement its deficiencies, the aid, though humble, is not to be despised. Spirit is cramped by matter, circumscribed by weakness, crippled by sin. The body and the world have just claims, and they pertinaciously urge unjust ones. It is of importance then to enlist on the spiritual side of our nature whatever can afford it help, strengthen it, or fortify it against attack. *Preaching* is useful in obvious ways to almost all—to the unstudious more than to others. Its benefits, when not immediate, often become apparent at a subsequent period in the facts and impressions it has conveyed. *Painting*. Let not the idolatrous abuse blind us to its use in religion. Have you never read a grand and touching sermon on canvas? felt tears spring to your eyes, a prayer to your lips, at the sight of matchless love and sorrow beaming from some picture of your Saviour? The religious artist and the preacher alike endeavor to form vivid conceptions of what Christ on earth must have expressed in looks and actions, and of the remarkable incidents of his career, and then strive to convey their ideas to us by pencil and by words. Both help to place us, in thought, in the position of those who saw our Lord. Some great fact in his life may be more clearly and firmly impressed on the mind by one sight of a picture than by years of occasional listless reading of the Gospels; and who shall estimate the arresting and quickening power of one such fact?

III. The use of externals is often blessed by God. Christ approves the attempt to get even a superficial view of him. The unconverted man is not told it will be useless to hear or read until he knows that the Spirit is touching him. Curiosity is not only permitted, it is a duty. The mere æsthetic thirst is sometimes made the means of bringing to the feet of Jesus to "learn of him," and to true spiritual communion with him. The character of Christ, if only in its human aspect, is powerfully attractive, it appeals to our noblest instincts. Drawn into his presence, a man is in a position to receive that influence of the Holy Spirit which shall lead him to "receive him joyfully" into his heart. When the motive is to increase knowledge, love, or good works, much more may the blessing be expected. God does not demand a more purely ethereal religion than our mixed nature is capable of. "We have not an high priest which," etc. He grants us material aids to spiritual service. Let then no man judge another.

IV. WE MUST NOT STOP AT THE EXTERNAL. Zaccheus had to come down and go closer. Many a man has stopped in the tree into which he has climbed, until Jesus has passed by, never to return. Of what good is it to find a point of vantage, from which you may see Christ, heaven, and hell, or trace out the path of duty, if, resting there, you make no effort to go to your Lord, to walk in the narrow path, to reach heaven? Had you a fulcrum through which you might move the world, what gain if you put not forth your strength to the lever?

HOMILY XXXVII.

THE TRANSCENDENT WORTH OF CHRISTIANITY.

Then said Jesus unto the twelve, Will ye also go away? Then Simon Peter answered him, Lord, to whom shall we go? Thou hast the words of eternal life. JOHN vi, 67, 68.

WE take these words to illustrate the transcendent excellence of Christianity. There are three facts here suggested which indicate this:

I. It provides for the totality of human wants. "Eternal life." This means not merely eternal existence; endless existence may be an endless curse. It means *eternal well-being.* It means eternal existence apart from evil, and in possession of all good. All the wants, all the desires of humanity may be summed up in these two words: *eternal well-being.* Man's deepest struggle is to preserve life, to make it as *long* and as *happy* as possible. He shudders at the idea of any termination; the happier he, the more awful the idea of an end. In his deepest soul he feels that an "eternity of bliss is bliss."

Now this Christianity provides for; it has "the words of eternal life."

First. *Its "words" revoke that legal sentence of eternal death to which humanity is subject.* The Bible teaches, (1.) That men are doomed to eternal death. (2.) That through the Gospel this doom may be averted.

Secondly. *Its "words" remove that moral disease insuring eternal death, to which humanity is subject.* The Bible teaches, (1.) That men are infected with the mortal malady; and, (2.) That the Gospel removes it and implants the seeds of eternal life.

Another fact here indicating the transcendent value of Christianity is:

II. It respects the freedom of human nature: "Will ye also go away?" Christ uses no coercion. He treats men according to their nature; men are made to act freely, and they never can act as men only as they are free. Hence Christ says, "Will ye?" First. *Christ does not want our service.* He can do without us. He could destroy the old creation and create a new universe. Do not stay with me from the idea that I want you. Secondly. *Christ will not accept forced service.* (1.) Because there could be no moral virtue in such service. He requires us to serve him because by doing so we grow morally good. (2.) Because there could be no happiness in such service. He wishes our happiness. The gloomy looks and the sepulchral tones of religious serfs are an abomination to him. Be free then.

Another fact here indicating the transcendent value of Christianity is:

III. It takes the strongest moral hold upon human life: "To whom can we go?" Though free we are bound. What are its binding forces? First. *The gratitude it inspires.* Gratitude ever binds to the benefactor. Secondly. *The love it enkindles.* Love always binds the heart to its object; and the more excellences the object displays the stronger the tie becomes. Thirdly. *The hope it awakens.* Hope binds the heart to the object promised. Christ makes wonderful promises. Fourthly. *The congeniality which it produces.* Christianity suits man in every respect, heart, conscience, intellect, all.

To whom then can the man go who has really secured Christianity? How can he extricate himself? To whom can you go? Will you go to *rationalism*, to *Romanism*, to *Paganism*, to *secularism?* There is nowhere else you *can* go to if you would.

HOMILY XXXVIII.

MORAL REMEDIALISM.

He hath sent me to heal the broken-hearted. LUKE iv, 18.

THREE things are manifestly implied in these words:

First. *That there is misery in our world.* Amid all the beautifying influences of nature, and under all the gay and mirthful forms in which society appears, there is much suffering. There are broken hearts. There are some hearts broken by tyranny, some by slander, some by disappointment, some by bereavement, some by conviction of sin. What sighs of human anguish are breathed to Heaven, what showers of tears fall to the earth, what billows of distress surge through human souls every day! There is but ONE that knows. Another thing manifestly implied here is:

Secondly. *That this misery is not here by divine appointment.* This is suggested by the fact that he has sent Jesus to remove it. Whence comes this misery? Does it, like fire from the volcano, or springs from the mountain, rise by the constitution of nature? No. The benevolence of the Creator and the structure of the universe forbid the thought. God did not create man with a broken heart, nor did he create the thing which has broken the heart. Misery is of the creature, not of the Creator. "O Israel, thou hast destroyed thyself." So uncongenial is human misery with the heart of God, that he sent Christ to remove it. The other thing manifestly implied in these words is:

Thirdly. *That there is a high probability that this misery will one day be entirely removed from the world.* He has sent a Healer into the world equal to the work. He knew the nature and extent of the disease, the qualifications necessary to remove it, and we may feel assured that he never would have commissioned a being to a work which he had not the qualifications to fulfill. There is suffering in the world; but there is a Physician too who "can save to the uttermost," etc.

A moral healer should be in possession of two things: *Suitable remedial elements*, and *power effectually to apply them.*

I. He should possess suitable remedial elements. The employment of instrumentalities is a principle in all God's dealings with man. He acts invariably through secondary causes; he produces, rears, sustains, educates, and saves man in this way.

What are the elements necessary to heal broken hearts?

First. *Forgiveness.* (1.) Whenever man feels conscious that he has offended his Maker he is and must be miserable. The idea that he has incurred his Creator's displeasure, will blacken the firmament of his soul, fill it with thunders and with fiends. This idea made the heathen world one of darkness, superstition, and woe. The deepest groan of humanity is this: "O wretched man that I am!" (2.) This consciousness he is bound to feel some time or other. He can no more prevent it rising in his nature than he can bind the influence of Pleiades or loose the bands of Orion. It must come, and when it comes it bites like a serpent and stings like an adder. Now there is nothing can relieve the soul in this state but forgiveness. This Christ gives. "He has power on earth to forgive." He comes to the soul and says, "I, even I, am he that blotteth out thy transgressions for mine own sake, and will not remember thy sins. I have blotted out as a thick cloud thy transgressions, and as a cloud thy sins." When the soul feels that this is done, it can chant this psalm: "Blessed is he whose transgression is forgiven, whose sin is covered. Blessed is the man unto whom the Lord imputeth not iniquity, and in whose spirit there is no guile."

Another necessary remedial element is:

Secondly. *Harmony.* Conscience and selfishness, moral desire and animal preferences, are ever battling within. "The wicked are like the troubled sea." What can harmonize? There is but one thing, and that is *supreme sympathy with the supremely good.* Love to God in the soul is as necessary to bind all its impulses and powers together in harmony, as attraction is in the material world to unite all the atoms, globes, and systems together. Christ generates this in the heart. He reveals God in all his lovable attributes.

Another necessary element is:

Thirdly. *Divine sympathy.* Sympathy is a healing element. "As iron sharpeneth iron, so doth the countenance of man his friend." A sufferer instinctively seeks for sympathy, and suffering instinctively awakens it. It is a healing element. A word, a look, an act of sympathy, how soothing! It acts upon the dark and troubled soul as the sun of a serene morning upon the dome of heaven when chasing away the battling clouds. In proportion to the felt excellence and greatness of the being who expresses sympathy is its heart-healing value. Christ, the Son of God, assures us of his sympathy. "He is made in all parts like unto us." "In all our afflictions he was afflicted." His sympathy has a heart-healing power.

Another heart-healing element is:

Fourthly. *Hope.* Awake hope of future success in the heart of the man crushed by disappointment, hope of forgiveness in the soul of the sin convicted, hope of recovery in the mind of the diseased, of liberty in the captive, of forgiveness in the condemned, of a renewed friendship in the heart of the bereaved; and in all these cases you will do much to heal. Hope is indeed a heart-healing element. This hope Jesus brings to the world. He is in it as the "hope of glory." "Blessed be the God and Father," etc.

The other qualification necessary to the healing of broken hearts is:

II. Power of effectually applying the proper remedial elements. The possession of remedial elements is not enough. Medicine adapted to remove the disease of the patient may be so applied as to render the disease more malignant. Proper application is fundamental. Three things seem necessary to a proper application of remedial elements to broken hearts:

First. *Adequate knowledge.* The moral physician should know the laws of the moral constitution, and the exact nature of the disease. The man who attempts to heal bodily diseases must, to succeed, make himself acquainted with the varied parts and laws of the human organization. No one can heal the soul without understanding it. Christ thoroughly understands it. "He trieth the reins." "He knows what is in man." He knows too the source of the disease. He knows everything about every suffering soul. Men must study souls to restore them.

Another thing which seems necessary to a proper application of these remedial elements is:

Secondly. *Thorough happiness.* No one can heal souls who is not happy himself. Can darkness ever dispel darkness? No more can sorrow banish sorrow. If I am in distress of heart, and one comes to comfort me who has himself a gloomy heart, he will fail. His intentions may be good, his conversation of a consolatory character, but the darkness of his own heart will chill and cloud the whole. But if he is truly happy in spirit he has only to speak to give some relief. Happiness overcomes sorrow as light overcomes darkness. It must be so. Happiness is an infinite and necessary element; it is the mood and expression of God; misery is infinite and contingent, and the product of the creature. The more true happiness a man has in him, the more of God he has in him, and the more powerful is he for good. He who in the name of Christ goes forth with a gloomy heart, a downcast countenance, speaking in sepulchral tones to relieve the woe of the world, misrepresents Jesus, and augments rather than diminishes the world's misery. Sadness is like darkness in its influence. Go out to the fields when the stars of God are hid, and the heavens are robed in blackness, and you will feel a depressive influence upon the heart. Such is the influence of a gloomy heart upon your own. Happiness, on the other hand, is like the broad bright day pouring forth a genial influence on all, making all life to have new energy and shout for joy. Christ is happy. He is the "God of peace;" "the ever-blessed God;" the bright Sun of righteousness, that hath "healing in his wings."

Another thing which seems necessary in order to the proper application of these remedial elements is:

Thirdly. *Exquisite tenderness.* A physician may effect a bodily cure without this. Indeed, it seems sometimes desirable that he should be utterly insensible to the sufferings of his patient. But not so with souls. They, in suffering, require in their consolation exquisite sensibility. A coarse-minded, hard-hearted man can never heal broken hearts. The sorrowing soul would shrink and recoil at the utterances of the unfeeling and the coarse, as the tenderest plants at the rough blasts of heaven. Man in sorrow requires the most delicate treatment. Jesus is qualified on this ground. He is tender. He does not cause his voice to be heard in the street. "A bruised reed does he not break, the smoking flax shall he not quench."

From this subject it may be inferred,

First, *That Christianity is the hope of the world.* The world abounds with broken hearts. Christianity alone presents the suitable balm and the physician.

Secondly. *That true Christians are the real benefactors.* They have the balm to offer, the physician to recommend.

Thirdly. *That the restoration of the world may be anticipated.* He who has undertaken the work will accomplish it. Our world is a moral hospital; it is tenanted with sufferers; it resounds with groans. But it will not always be so.

——— "The time will come
When he shall wipe away all tears from off
All faces. Ye revolving seasons
Haste, then, and wheel away a shattered world."

HOMILY XXXIX.

THE CREATOR AND THE SIN OF HIS CREATURE, MAN.

"These things hast thou done, and I kept silence; thou thoughtest that I was altogether such an one as thyself: but I will reprove thee, and set them in order before thine eyes. PSALM i, 21.

THESE words led us at once to consider certain facts in the divine conduct in relation to the sins of men.

We learn from the passage,

I. THAT HE FULLY OBSERVES THE DEVELOPMENT OF HUMAN SIN. "These things," the evils indicated in the previous verses, "hast thou done." He *knew* that these sins had been committed. That he does observe sin is clear. (1.) *From his nature.* He is the ALL-PRESENT and the ALL-SEEING. Psa. cxxxix. (2.) *From the declaration of the Bible.* "He that planteth the ear shall he not hear?" etc. Psa. xciv, 9–11. (3.) *From the universal consciousness of sinners.* All sinners *feel* that God knows their sins. Their remorse, their confessions, their forebodings, all indicating that this is their feeling. (4.) *From the retribution that has overtaken sinners even in this world.* Achan, Ananias, etc. "I know thy works." Though sin may be committed in the darkest midnight in profoundest secret, God observes it; and "the hidden things of darkness will one day be brought to light."

We learn from the passage,

II. THAT HE FOR A TIME FORBEARS WITH THE ENORMITY OF HUMAN SIN. "I kept silence;" I did not launch my thunders, etc. Full retribution does not follow sin at once on this earth. Judgment is delayed. (1.) *The spiritual improvement of humanity requires this.* If adequate retribution followed at once every sin, not a human being would have one moment to "repent and believe the Gospel." The first moral act being sinful would hurl to hell. The reason he forbears is, that he is "not willing that any should perish," etc. (2.) *The mediation of Christ explains this.* Why, under the government of a righteous God, does not punishment follow sin at once? Did it not do so among the angels in the first great rebellion? The interposition of Christ explains it. Mediation is but one short mighty prayer, which is, "Spare it a little longer." The divine government of our world is mediatorial. Men here are dealt with not on the ground of their own character, but on that of Christ's mediation. The continuation of man's existence on this planet, the scene of so much beauty, goodness, and pleasure, is to be referred to the mediation of Christ. But this form of government will not always continue. The "kingdom will be delivered up," etc.

We learn from the passage,

III. THAT HE THOROUGHLY UNDERSTANDS THE REASON OF HUMAN SIN. "Thou thoughtest that I was altogether such an one as thyself." In some respects we are like God; we could form no conception of him unless there were some points of resemblance. But the evil of man is, that he should act as if God was "*altogether*" like himself. *Sinners act as if they thought that because they can conceal their sins from others they can from God.* Men can and do hide their sins from others. They can so adorn their corrupt natures with pious professions and external moralities as to pass for great saints among men. Sinners act as if they could thus impose upon Omniscience. (2.) *Sinners act as if they thought that because they have no deep impression of the enormity of sin God has not.* To the sinning millions sin is a trifle, a thing to be sported with. "Fools make a mock at sin." Because they think lightly of it they are prone to think the great God does so. But to him it is a terrible enormity. It is the "abominable" thing he hates. The doom of fallen angels, the judgments that have fallen on humanity through all ages, and above all, the crucifixion of Christ, show that sin is an awful thing in his sight. (3.) *Sinners act as if they thought that because they overlook the little in the great that God does so. Sinful* men are influenced by their ideas of great and small; they overlook small matters in concerns of greater importance; they consider the poor pauper nothing to a mighty empire; and they foolishly ascribe this feeling to God. (4.) *Sinners act as if they thought that because their tardiness in carrying out a purpose often arises from the want of a greater interest in it, it is so with God.* "Because sentence against an evil work," etc. (5.) *Sinners act as if they thought because they become indifferent in the course of time to those who have offended them, that God will do so.* Toward men who have done us an injury we may at first feel indignation, but in the course of years that indignation settles down into perfect indifference. It is not so with God. The sins of years do not destroy his intense interest in us. "Turn ye, turn ye. Why will ye die?"

We learn from the passage,

IV. THAT HE WILL ASSUREDLY AWARD PUNISHMENT FOR HUMAN SIN. "I will reprove thee, and set them in order before thine eyes." God will not always keep silence. "Though a sinner live a hundred years and his days be prolonged," etc. Ecc. viii, 11–13. There is a day of judgment coming. "The Son of man will come in his glory," etc. Then "we must all stand at the judgment-seat of Christ," etc. "In that day God shall bring every work into judgment, with every secret thing, whether it be good or evil." In this very Psalm we have a magnificent description of this terrible day. "Our God shall come and shall not keep silence," etc. (3–7.) In this day God will set their sins in order. (1.) *In order as to their real character.* Every sin will be seen in its true enormity. (2.) *In order as to their terrible influence.* The evil of each sin will be seen in the ruin it has brought upon souls. (3.) *In order as to their true desert.* Every sin shall find its adequate punishment.

Brother, the conclusion of the matter is this: Sin must be *punished* or *pardoned.* There is no alternative. If pardoned it must be on *this earth* and *through Christ.* There is no alternative. The Son of man hath "power on earth," and only on earth, "to forgive sins." "Through this man is preached unto you forgiveness of sins," etc. Here then is pardon:

> Pardon for infinite offense! and pardon
> Through means that speak its value infinite!
> A pardon bought with blood, with blood divine,
> With blood divine of him I made my foe!
> Persisted to provoke! though wooed and awed,
> Blessed and chastised, a flagrant rebel still!
> A rebel, 'midst the thunders of his throne!
>   "Bound, every heart! and every bosom burn!
> O what a scale of miracles is here!"

HOMILY XL.

MAN'S MORAL POSITION IN THE UNIVERSE.

Who is on the Lord's side? Exodus xxxii, 26.

This is the solemn question which Moses addressed to the children of Israel immediately after he descended from the mount, and discovered that they had worshiped the golden calf which Aaron had set up.

Among other things taught in this chapter, there are five worthy of note:

First. *The strength of the religious instinct.* For forty days Moses had been upon the mount, and the people had not been visited by any palpable manifestation from the one true and living God. Their religious natures were restless. They said to Aaron, "Up, make us gods," etc. Man must have a god. If he loses the true one he will create a false one. So strong is this instinct in human nature that the arguments of infidelity cannot destroy it; the darkness of heathenism cannot quench it.

Secondly. *An unrighteous compliance with a popular demand.* The people cry out for gods, and Aaron, the professed minister of the true God, panders to the popular taste. He knew that there was but one God, the true and living One; that idolatry was irrational and impious; and yet he yields to their cry. The sin of Aaron was in ministering to the prejudices of the people; a sin, it is to be feared, too prevalent even in the Christian Church. The minister who preaches to meet the prejudices and tastes of his people, commits the same sin as Aaron did when he made the "golden calf." He who would get the thousands to listen to him has only to set up "the golden calf" of vulgar sentiment.

Thirdly. *The marvelous efficacy of prayer.* The righteous indignation of God was kindled against these idolaters, and he seemed determined to destroy them, when Moses prays, and it is said, "The Lord repented him of the evil which he thought to do unto his people." I cannot explain this. The Bible teaches that "the effectual fervent prayer of a righteous man availeth much," and gives us many instances of this; but *how* it affects God I know not. Let us grasp the fact and live accordingly.

Fourthly. *The importance of determining our true moral position in relation to God.* "Who is on the Lord's side?" Of all the questions the inquisitive nature of man is capable of raising, none more important than this, and that for the following reasons: (1.) Because there is a danger of deception upon the point. There are thousands on the side of Satan who entertain the idea that they are on the side of God, and some, perhaps, who are on the side of God who have doubts and fears. The scribes and Pharisees thought they were on the Lord's side; and so did Saul when he was persecuting the Church of God. (2.) Because deception on this question is fraught with immense evil. A man who is on the side of Satan, and yet fancies he is on the side of God, is in a perilous position. He is beyond the appeals addressed to the sinner; he rejects them from the idea that they are inapplicable. " He sins in the name of God," etc. (3.) Because this life is the only opportunity which we have of correcting mistakes upon this question. A man if he finds out that he is on the side of the devil may, by the help of grace, change his position now, and step to the other side; but in the other world there is a great gulf fixed, and all change is impossible.

The question which we would now raise is, What are the criteria by which we can ascertain our true moral position? In order to avoid mistake, I shall notice the *negative* and *positive* side of the question.

I. The negative side.

First. *That we are not conscious of any positive dislike to God is no evidence that we are on the Lord's side.* Few men, perhaps, however depraved, are conscious of a positive dislike to God. The reason of this is obvious, namely, the blessings which here crown man's earthly existence. Nature smiles on him and so does Providence. Were Jehovah to be crossing his plans, to be constantly breaking his purposes, blasting his hopes, then his anger would rise into consciousness. Pharaoh, perhaps, before the mission of Moses, had no conscious hatred to God. There, on his imperial throne, he had every desire of his heart; but when he had one purpose after another broken, he said, "Who is the Lord?" etc.

Secondly. *That pleasure in meditating on God's moral character is no evidence that we are on the Lord's side.* God has so constituted the human mind that it is bound to admire excellence in the abstract, to delight in "the law of God after the inner man." There is not a conscience in the universe that does not approve of benevolence, honesty, truth. "The consciences of hell are with God," etc.

Thirdly. *Unexceptionableness in the fulfillment of our social religious duties.* A man may have a high reputation in the world for honesty and honor; he may be lauded, too, for the regularity and decency with which he attends to religious ordinances, and yet not be on the Lord's side. The young man in the Gospel is a case in point.

Fourthly. *That an interest in the services of the sanctuary is not in itself conclusive evidence that we are on the Lord's side.* An individual may take a lively interest in the services of God's house, the psalmody, the discourse, the prayers, and yet not be on the Lord's side. The fact is there is a natural love in the human soul for excitement, and so long as the services of the house of the Lord can minister to this excitement even an irreligious man may feel an interest in them. "Herod heard John gladly."

Fifthly. *That contrition for sin is not in itself a proof that we are on the Lord's side.* Few sinners, perhaps, can be found who have not at times had some deep compunctions of soul. Agrippa, Felix, etc.

Sixthly. *Strong desires for heaven are in themselves no proof that we are on the Lord's side.* It is natural to desire happiness. All the trials and toils of life tend to heighten this desire. Preach rest to the weary, health to the diseased, plenty to the poor, and will you not awaken their desires? There is no virtue in desiring heaven.

Seventhly. *That zeal in propagating our religious views is in itself no proof that we are on the Lord's side.* It is natural for a man who has an opinion to desire to propagate it. The Hindoo, the Mussulman, the Mormonite, all wish their opinions to spread. The Pharisees compass sea and land to spread their views, etc.

Eighthly. *That success in our endeavors to propagate our religious opinions is in itself no evidence that we are on the Lord's side.* It would seem that an individual may be useful, in a spiritual sense, to others, and yet be destitute of true godliness. In the last day we shall hear of men who will knock at the door, saying, "Lord, Lord," etc.

Ninthly. *That the fact of being regarded by others as Christians is in itself no proof.* Philetus was regarded as a Christian. What then is the evidence?

II. THE POSITIVE SIDE. There is a test laid down by the apostle, (Rom. viii:) "He that hath not the spirit of Christ is none of his." But what is the spirit of Christ? What are the characteristics of that spirit? I may mention three:

First. *The spirit of Christ was a spirit of religious supremacy.* Religion in Christ was not an occasional sentiment, or attitude, or service. It was the very soul of his soul; the heart of all his experience. God was the central thought of his intellect, the paramount object of his heart, the one great reality of being. Everything else to him was form and shadow. He was the life of all lives, the law of all laws, the very soul of universal being. "His meat and his drink was to do his will." In the profoundest solitude he felt that he was with him. Worlds and systems were to him nothing compared with the approbation of his Father. Now, he that has not this Spirit, he that makes religion a subordinate thing, has not the spirit of Christ. He that makes religion a branch thing, that is, one of the parts of human duty; he that makes it secondary to something higher, rather than the highest end of being, the all in all, is not on his side.

Secondly. *The Spirit of Christ is a spirit of religious individualism.* By this I mean that he religiously realized his own individuality, and acted accordingly. He had his own convictions and principles, and he acted them out from himself. The sentiments of his age did not crush or check his own individuality. Although of "the people there was none with him," he still pursued his way. "He trod the wine-press alone." He was not deterred by what others thought or felt. It was his to be faithful to his own soul and to the eternal Father. Now, he that has not this *religious individuality* is none of his. He that sells his individuality, as a priest to a Church, as a soldier to a government, as a statesman, author, or preacher to popularity, and acts from forces without, rather than from his own moral convictions, "has not the spirit of Christ," etc.

Thirdly. *The spirit of Christ is a spirit of religious philanthropy.* I say *religious* philanthropy, for there is a philanthropy that has no connection with religion; a mere natural sympathy with the race, nothing more. Christ's love for man arose from his love for God. He saw man in the light of his love for the infinite Father, and man became precious in his view. The philanthropy of Christ was not destroyed by enmity. He loved his enemies. What is the spirit of Christ in relation to enemies? Read Matthew v. Has the man who is wreaking vengeance on his enemy the spirit of Christ? Has he the spirit of Him who on the cross prayed, "Father, forgive them, for they know not what they do?" Has the man who is systematically engaged in destroying men's lives the spirit of Him who came into the world, not to destroy men's lives, but to save them? Has the man who acts either from anger, from avarice, or ambition, the spirit of Him who, although "he was rich, for our sakes became poor, that we through his poverty might be made rich?"

You will say this is a severe test; I cannot help it; it is not mine. If men are to be tried by this test you will say, how few are Christians! It is better to find it out now. The spirit of Christ *is* Christianity; the life of Christ *is* Christianity. He, indeed, who lives not that life, who has not that spirit, "is none of his." The question for us to ascertain is, Have we the spirit of Christ? If not, to get it is our work, of all works the most urgent.

HOMILY XLI.

LAST HOURS OF AN OLD SAINT.

By faith Jacob, when he was a dying, blessed both the sons of Joseph; and worshiped, leaning on the top of his staff. HEB. xi, 21.

THIS is a brief, simple, and touching record of the death of a man who, notwithstanding his many signal imperfections, developed virtues, entered into spiritual relationships, and enunciated predictions which invest his biography with a race-wide and imperishable interest.

The text gives us two things:

I. AN INTERESTING DYING POSTURE. Jacob was "leaning on the top of his staff." From the account which we have in Genesis he seems to have passed through the immediate article of death on the bed. We must therefore picture him just before he lays himself on the bed for the last time, sitting down leaning on his staff with the cold hand of death upon him, and passing through its first stages. This staff had a twofold function, *material* and *spiritual.*

First. *The staff served to support his tottering body.* He was an old man. Time had stolen strength from his frame; he was a dying man, shivering on the dark borders of the grave, and he used the staff for his support. Few scenes are more saddening and humiliating than that of an old man, doubled by the weight of years, creeping along the road or sitting by the side of a hedge, staff in hand, supporting that tottering frame in whose agility, strength, and beauty he once prided himself. Yet to such infirmity age reduces all. How touchingly are those infirmities delineated by Solomon. Eccles. xii.

Secondly. *The staff served to refresh his soul with delightful memories.* A staff sometimes is a helpmeet to the soul, a kind of companion in solitude, giving a mute response to our lonely thoughts and aspirations; yes, more than a companion, a memorial, a history. An old staff has the power to revive past impressions. There is a mysterious and solemn power in the mind to invest the simplest objects with which we have been in conscious contact—a flower, a stone, a tree—with an energy to wake up in our souls the remembrance of things that have past. Visit the scenes of your childhood, and almost everything about you will speak some old impression to life again. The hearth on which you played. the trees before the door "the old arm chair" on which a departed mother sat and pressed you to her bosom, all have a mystic power of evoking thoughts and impressions long buried in forgetfulness. The spirits of departed impressions start to the soul in successive crowds as you tread the scenes of your young life. The "staff" on which the patriarch now leaned his dying frame had, we suppose, a power of this kind. It seems to have been long his companion. He bore it probably away from his father's house when a boy. Perhaps it was his grandfather Abraham's; for with it he crossed the Jordan when a youth. It had been with him during many years of servitude. It lay perhaps by his side as he slept at Bethel; it was with him when he wrested with the angel. That his memory did act now is clear from what he said, chap. xlviii, 3–7.

O what memories would that old staff evoke! There is nothing unimportant to man. All that impresses him now will act on him again. We impart something of ourselves to every object with which we are brought into *conscious* contact, something that will speak to our memories forever, a kind of archangel's trump to wake the buried thoughts.

II. A GLORIOUS DYING EXERCISE. "He blessed both the sons," etc. Sometimes you see old men dying with a heart withered and dry as leather, all sensibilities gone. Sometimes with a misanthropic disgust of life: tired of the world and sick of the race; sometimes filled with terrible forebodings about the future. Not so with our patriarch. He "blessed" both the sons of Joseph. The exercise was twofold: *social* and *religious*. It was *social*. He blessed the two sons of Joseph. It is beautiful to find this old man, with a body trembling beneath the weight of years, and the cold hand of death upon him, having his heart expanded in warm sympathies for posterity: his own personal infirmities and interest lost in the concerns of his grandchildren and his race. It was *religious*. "He worshiped." "He adored the top of his rod," says the Catholic, quoting the Douay Bible. Nonsense! He worshiped the God whose mercy the old staff brought to memory. He remembered the God of his fathers, and felt the inspiration of gratitude, reverence, and adoration.

Jacob's dying attitude and action,

First. *Shows that the dependence of man upon small things must increase with his years.* Jacob was now depending upon a "staff." Men labor for independence, but time makes them more and more dependent every day. Affliction, infirmities, age, cause us to feel what we are prone to forget, that we are dependent not only for our comforts, but for our very existence, on the smallest things: a word of sympathy, a breath of air, a drop of water, an old "staff," etc.

Secondly. *Suggests the unextinguishableness of our spiritual instincts.* Can it be that the social instincts which were now so strong in the patriarch on the very eve of his dissolution were to go out at death? Was he, who displayed this interest in future ages, to be quenched for ever in a few hours? Can it be that he whose soul now went forth in the worship of the Everlasting One, was now himself to go out of being? No, no, it cannot be! The fact that Jacob, when dying, felt this interest in others suggests to me that he was destined for everlasting companionship. The fact that he worshiped when dying, suggests to me that he was about entering into the immediate presence of the Ever-adorable One.

Thirdly. *Explains the philosophy of a happy death.* Such is the influence of the soul upon the body that it can, by passing into certain moods, destroy the consciousness of the greatest physical tortures. Hence martyrs have felt the stake a bed of roses. Let the soul be absorbed with the concerns of God and the universe, and then pain and death are but shadows and sounds. It was thus with Paul. "I am now ready to be offered, and the time of my departure is at hand." If you would be happy in death you must go out of self; become self-oblivious; be lost in the interests of the creation and the glory of God.

HOMILY XLII.

THE GUARDIAN OF SOULS.

Bishop of your souls. 1 PETER ii, 25.

Three facts are implied in these words:

I. THAT MEN HAVE SOULS. How trite such an utterance! The greatest facts in the universe are trite.

First. *The fact is the most demonstrable fact to man.* (1.) All the evidence that we have both for the existence of matter and mind is derived from phenomena. The *essence* of both is hidden. (2.) The essence whose phenomena come most powerfully under consciousness is most demonstrated. (3.) The phenomena of mind come far more powerfully under consciousness than those of matter. We are not conscious of the qualities of matter, only of the impressions which they make upon us; but we are conscious of the phenomena of mind. Thought, feeling, volition—we are conscious of these.

Secondly. *The fact is the most important fact to man.* Consider the capacities, relations, influence, deathlessness of a soul.

Thirdly. *The fact is the most practically disbelieved fact by man.* Most men profess to believe it, but few men really do so. The popular ideas of pleasure, respectability, beauty, prosperity, glory, all of which are *material,* show that there is no general faith in the existence of the soul.

The body reigns everywhere · its charms are everywhere recognized as supreme.

II. That men's souls require a guardian: an ἐπίσκοπος, an overseer. This is clear from three things:

First. *From the natural fallibility of souls.* No finite intelligence, however holy and exalted, can do without a guardian.

Secondly. *From the fallen condition of souls.* They "have gone astray." They are "lost." Look at the mistakes they make about the chief good, worship, etc.

Thirdly. *From the natural instincts of souls.* Souls through all ages have been crying out for guardians. Hence the popularity of priests and prophets, bishops and religious leaders; hence too the readiness to follow almost any one who will profess to guide the soul. The human soul wants a guardian. It is in a shadowy maze, it wants a guide; it is on a perilous sea, it wants a pilot.

III. That Christ is the one guardian of human souls. He is *the* Bishop. What should be the qualification of him who can take care of human souls? Perhaps there is no work in the universe so momentous and difficult as that of rightly directing and guarding souls. He that would do so should have at least four things:

First. *Immense knowledge.* He should know the nature of souls, the moral situation of souls, the right way of influencing souls. He should know what they have been, what they are, what they may become. He should have,

Secondly, *Unbounded love and forbearance.* The waywardness, the insults, the rebellion of souls would soon exhaust any finite amount of love and patience. He should have,

Thirdly, *Ever increasing charms.* Souls are to be drawn, not driven; and none but the morally attractive can really and rightly draw. He should have,

Fourthly, *Inexhaustible power.* Power to extricate from present difficulties, to guard against future, and to lead on through interminable ages. Christ has all these qualifications, and more. No one else has.

Let him then be my overseer. I trust no sage, nor ecclesiastic: I look to him. "Into thine hands I commit my spirit." CHRIST IS THE BISHOP OF SOULS.

HOMILY XLIII.

THE MEANING OF HOPE AS AN INSTINCT OF THE SOUL.

Thou didst make me hope when I was upon my mother's breasts.
PSALM xxii, 9.

THE text is a strong figure, intended to express the idea that hope is an inbred sentiment of the soul, a power original and not derived, as truly a part of the complete soul as the eye, or any other member, is a part of the complete body. The body, it is true, may exist without the eye, but in a very imperfect state; and the soul may exist without hope, but in a very incomplete state. There are emaciated souls, souls with deadened senses and broken faculties, as well as emaciated bodies. Notwithstanding, this hope is an instinct, an instinct which keeps the face of the soul ever toward the future, nay, which bears it ever into the future, and gives it there a happy and beatified life.

I want to inquire into the meaning of this instinct. It suggests much important truth: truth about God and Christianity, our duty and our destiny; truth which deserves and demands our devotional attention.

I. This instinct implies the distinguishing goodness of God in the constitution of our nature. The principle of hope is one of the chief blessings of humanity. We do not say that the action of hope is always conducive to our wellbeing. The fact is this power of the soul, like every other of our depraved nature, is frequently abused. Men long after things which are beneath their nature, and thus degrade their souls; and hope for things which they have no good reason to expect, and thus subject themselves to all the inconveniences and anguish of disappointment. A large amount of the world's misery arises from a wrong direction of the instinct of hope, ending in vexation and disappointment. But the principle itself is, nevertheless, an incalculable boon. First. *It is one of the most powerful impulses to action.* Man advances in dignity and blessedness as he grows in intellectual and moral strength; and he thus grows only as the faculties and powers of his soul are kept in healthful exercise. Hope is one of its chief incentives. Like the tide in the ocean, it throbs through every part and keeps the whole in motion. Nearly all the labor of the world consists in preparation for the future. Destroy hope, and every wheel in the agricultural, maritime, manufacturing, commercial, literary, and religious world would become still, and the whole would sink into quiescence. Secondly. *Hope is one of the chief elements of support under the trials of life.* Hope buoys us up beneath the load, gives us a steady anchorage under the fiercest surge and gales. Hope sees some light fringing the darkest cloud, hears some sweet promises articulating amid the din of distress. Thirdly. *Hope is a source of joy.* Joys of memory and the pleasures of the passing hour are not to be compared with the joys that men derive from anticipation and hope.

"Man never is, but always to be blessed."

By this instinct he has always a beautiful and blessed realm, into which he enters. There, in seas of imaginary delight, he bathes his weary soul.

Now have you not a proof of God's distinguishing kindness to you in giving you such an instinct as this? He might have given you a nature that would unfit you for taking any interest in the future, and left you with an instinct that would chain you to painful memories of the dreary past. Or he might have given you, instead of this, some power that would compel you to make the future a terrible thing, a thing every idea of which would strike daggers into your soul. What reason, therefore, have we, when we contemplate our nature, to adopt the language of the Psalmist, and say: "Bless the Lord, O my soul, and all that is *within me*, bless his holy name!"

II. THIS INSTINCT OF HOPE SUGGESTS A FUTURE STATE OF EXISTANCE. Hope is an instinct that always refers to the future; it is a *prospective sentiment.* The fact that there is such an instinct in our nature, and which continues to the *last* stage of our mortal life, does certainly suggest, if not prove a future state. It is suggested, first, *On the ground of analogy.* In the constitution of the body we find that for every sense and appetite there is external provision. There is light for the eye, there is sound for the ear, sweet odors and fruits, all suited to our senses and appetites. In our social relations we find objects suited to our social instincts, objects to love, and to reciprocate our affection. As the eye implies light, and as the social instinct implies existences kindred with our own, is it not reasonable to suppose that there is provision for this instinct of hope? Has God provided for every other and neglected this? Has he opened no fountain where the soul can slake its thirst for future good? The supposition is scarcely admissible. It is suggested, secondly, *On the ground of the divine goodness.* Is it consonant with the goodness of the Eternal to suppose that he gave craving appetites to creatures for which he has made no provision? Has he made man to thirst for future good, and is there no future good? *If in this life only we have hope, we are of all creatures most miserable.* This instinct prophesies of a future.

III. This instinct means that progress in blessedness is the original law of our being. Hope is not only a sentiment pointing to a future, but to *good* in the future. Were man so satisfied with present good as to have no instinct of longing for higher joys, we should have no evidence from his nature that he was intended for progress in blessedness. But finding that, whatever he has, he seeks after more, that the getting of one truth increases his desire for another, that the possessing of one virtue impels him to aspire after another, the inference is that progress in blessedness is the great original law of our being. Our nature shows that our Maker never designed for us a final resting-place in our career, never appointed for us an ultimate terminus where we should pause and have no more interest in the future; but on the contrary that the point reached to-day should be the starting-place of to-morrow. Why then are men so often miserable? *It is because they sin against this fundamental law of their natures.* They are made for progression in happiness, but they have forsaken the fountain of living waters. Misery is the creation of the creature, not of the Creator. It springs from the breaking of laws, not the obeying of them. "He that sinneth against me wrongeth his own soul."

IV. THIS INSTINCT OF THE SOUL SHOWS THE FITNESS OF CHRISTIANITY TO HUMAN NATURE. Christianity does two things: First. *It reveals future scenes of unending progress in blessedness.* It comes to this instinct of hope to give the most glowing and glorious visions of the future. It presents to the mind heaven in its most enchanting aspects, etc. Secondly. *Christianity not only reveals future scenes of unending progress in blessedness, but supplies man with the means by which it is to be obtained.* Christianity may hold these beautiful things before you, and you may desire them; but you cannot *hope* for them unless you know they are obtainable. Hell may know of these scenes of blessedness, and may desire them, but there are no means for it to obtain them. Christianity, however, not only unfolds them to the human mind, but supplies the means. What are the means? First. *They are conscience-pacifying.* There is such a sense of guilt resting on the human conscience, such an impression that God is offended, that the instinct of hope is frequently overcome by the feelings of dread and alarm as to the future. Man will never have a firm hope of heaven till this consciousness of guilt be removed, until conscience get the assurance that past sins are forgiven, and that it is reconciled to God. Now Christianity is meant for this. It points him to the propitiation of Christ, and it assures him that by faith in his sacrifice all past sins are forgiven. Secondly. *It supplies him with soul-purifying means.* The soul is corrupt, the affections are polluted, and there is required some power to rectify all the inner errors, to correct all the wrong.

Christianity is the want of your nature. Light, and air, and water are not more fitted to the constitution of your bodies than Christianity is fitted to the instincts of your soul. Believe me, there is nothing else can meet your nature but this. Education, philosophy, science, none of these can do it. Christianity is the only suitable minister to this instinct of hope.

V. THIS INSTINCT OF HOPE INDICATES THE CONGRUITY OF THE RELIGIOUS LIFE WITH OUR NATURE. Religion is a progressive principle. It is a "following on to know the Lord;" a forgetting of "the things that are behind," "a pressing on to the things that are before;" it is "an abounding hope through the power of the Holy Ghost." A religious life centers the soul in the "God of hope," and causes it to abound in hope through the power of the Holy Ghost.

In conclusion, remark, first, *That the greatest calamity that can happen to your nature is the extinction of this hope.* This is the lamp of the soul that shines on it in its greatest gloom. Quench this, and all is midnight within. It seemed to go out for a time with Job when he fell down and exclaimed, "I have heard of thee," etc. It went out with Judas, and his existence became intolerable. It goes out forever with the lost. There is no hope in hell. There is eternal despair there.

Secondly. *Let me remind you that the tendency of sin is to destroy this instinct.* "The hope of the hypocrite shall perish." Every sin is the putting out of some star in the heavens of your future. Go on sinning, and one by one will go out, until there will be nothing but "blackness and darkness forever."

Let me urge you, then, to put your nature under the influence of that system of Gospel truth which unfolds to you such a glorious future, and supplies to you the means by which to realize its blessedness. Resolve that your hope shall lay hold, not upon the trifles of an hour, the foolish vanities of the world, but on eternal life.

HOMILY XLIV.

DUTY SACRIFICED TO CONVENIENCE.

The sluggard will not plow by reason of the cold; therefore shall he beg in harvest, and have nothing, etc. PROVERBS xx, 4.

THE text suggests three general introductory observations:

First. *That there are two powers constantly pressing their claims upon man: those of duty and convenience.* It was so with the sluggard. There was the field before him to cultivate; it was his duty to do so. There was the love of ease and comfort. "By reason of the cold," etc. Secondly. *That these two generally come into collision here.* The feeling of cold and the sense of agricultural duty now came into collision. Duty *here* is an inconvenience. In heaven it is not so. Men here are continually crying out for a more convenient season." Thirdly. *That the sacrificing of duty to convenience is an immense evil.* It may look very well to do so. He may be called a prudent man who acts so. He who follows *convenience or expediency* walks a flowery path to hell; he who follows duty walks a thorny and up-hill road to celestial dignities and joys.

Our general position is, *That duty neglected for the sake of convenience is an immense evil:*

I. BECAUSE IT INVOLVES A SACRIFICE OF THE CULTIVATING SEASON. Look at this sluggard! It is spring; the time of

April showers and April sun; the time when the seed is to be put in the earth, which has been prepared for it. Day after day passes away, and the sluggard does not commence his work. Why? Not because he knows that the earth is not worth cultivation, nor because he knows he has not strength to cultivate it. These would be something like good reasons for his neglect. But because it is too "*cold*" for him. The thermometer is too low. He is losing the precious time for cultivation simply because it is a little too "cold."

It is just so with men who are postponing their day of *religious decision.* We would have such to think of three things. First. *That the whole of their earthly life is intended as a season for cultivation.* Why are these days given to you? Why are these years added to your mortal life? That you may pander to your appetites, or that you may amass a little wealth, or that you may get a little speculative knowledge? No! But that you may cultivate a character that will prepare you for endless felicity beyond the grave. This life is your spring-time for eternity. Think, secondly, *That a very large portion of this cultivating season is already gone.* Were every moment of your mortal life devoted to the point it would not be *too much.* The work is so momentous it demands it. But how much have you wasted away? Twenty years some of you have thrown away; some thirty, and some more. Think, thirdly, *That the residue of your time is very short and very uncertain.* What an evil, then, is it to allow the season thus to pass away like the sluggard, simply because of some passing event, or some little inconvenience!

II. Because it involves a disregard of existing facilities. The sluggard had everything else necessary to cultivate his land. The land, perhaps, was in a most arable state; there were, perhaps, the plow and the oxen ready; and he too, perhaps, was full of health and energy; right able to hold the plow and follow the team. But he disregarded all these facilities, merely because it was rather too "cold." Ah! so it is with those who are putting off religion. They have everything else. (1.) They have the Bible with all its quickening truths. (2.) They have their reason and all their powers of thought. (3.) They have Christian agency, ministers, etc. (4.) They have divine influence; the Spirit of God is striving with them, etc.; but they put it off to "a more convenient season."

III. Because it involves the decay of individual qualification for the work. The qualification for any work consists in a *resolute determination* to work and a *sufficiency of executive energy*. All the while this sluggard was waiting, these two things were decreasing. If he stopped at home *one* day because of the cold, the chances were he would stop at home the next day also. The habit of making excuses always destroys the *disposition* to work; and where this is gone, the chief qualification is gone. Who are the men of strong purpose? Not the men who yield to difficulties. These men are everlastingly making excuses; always using their "ifs" and "buts." But the men that brave and conquer inconveniences get new force of will—the highest force—by this. The sluggard would not only lose his *disposition*, but also his *executive energy*. If he had gone out into the field, grasped the plow, upturned the waiting soil, he would have overcome the cold; he would have made the inner fires of his life warm him with their glow, and he would have strengthened his muscles. If he had gone out the first cold day he would have gone the second. The way to conquer difficulties is to master them one by one as they come. The Sandwich Islander has the superstition that the vigor of the enemy he slays in war passes into his own body. In spiritual conflicts this fable becomes fact. Each victorious blow nerves our being for nobler deeds; each conquest gives power for more signal triumphs.

> To overcome at last,
> We must conquer as we go.

IV. Because it involves the loss of great personal enjoyment. What would the man lose day after day by neglecting his duty? First. *He would lose the joy arising from fresh accession of manly power. One of the most pleasurable of sensations arises from the conscious increase of new energy.* See the young cattle gamboling on the sunny hills; hear the newly fledged birds chirping their notes as they test their strength in dancing from branch to branch; behold the children in their homes, how happiness seems to overflow as they perform their little muscular evolutions. A conscious rising of new energy explains the whole. This man lost all this by moping at home, shivering with the cold. "They that wait upon the Lord," etc. Secondly. *He would lose the joy arising from a consciousness that he had done his duty.* How could he be happy in his home when he knew that his land was running to waste? Neither can he be happy who neglects religion. Thirdly. *He would lose the joy arising from a freedom to engage in any other important affair.* So long as he felt he had a duty to do he could engage happily in no other. So in religion; a man cannot throw his being into anything as long as he feels the great question between God and his soul unsettled. He is a slave; he has no liberty heartily to engage in anything else. Fourthly. *He would lose the joy arising from the prospect of a reward of his labors.* How much pleasure the agriculturist must have in seeing the seeds come up and thrive! And so the teacher, the minister. This man lost all this.

V. Because it involves a certainty of ultimate ruin. "He shall beg in harvest, and shall have nothing." Here is, first, *Destitution.* "Have nothing." When other men's fields waved with luxuriant crops, and their granaries were filled with corn, he was destitute. So it will be with those who neglect salvation. What will they lose? Not existence, not powers of reflection, not susceptibility of conscience; but *everything* that is necessary to render existence happy: *self-approbation, friendship, hope.* They will be paupers, *moral paupers;* beings stripped of everything but sheer existence: "Have nothing." Here is, secondly, *Degradation.* "To beg" is degradation; to see one man begging of another is a humiliating sight. A true man will ever say, "To beg I am ashamed;" a man loses a great part of his humanity when he *condescends* to beg. But to beg, and be *refused*, as this man did, is still more degrading. To feel hated by society, cut off, looked upon with the eye of contempt, must be an awful state of existence. In the Scriptures the wicked are referred to as calling, and God refusing. Like the foolish virgins crying out for oil. There are three things that would enhance the misery of this *destitution and degradation:* (1.) *It was self-created.* The man could blame no one but himself. There was the land before him; those fields would have yielded an abundance. (2.) *It was unpitied.* Who could pity him? Neighboring farmers might say to him, Your land is as good as ours, and had you worked as we have, you might have had a crop as good. Such a man would walk the bleak hills of society and have no sympathy. So with the sinner. (3.) *It was irretrievable.* There was no time to sow now; it was *harvest.* He might work now; manure his land, put seed into well-prepared soil, but all would be of no avail. Nature said to him, in effect, I can do nothing for you; I could have helped you in spring; I gave you showers and sunshine. This will be an element of misery in the state of the unsaved. *As nature has a specific time to help the agriculturist, Christianity has a time to help the sinner.*

In conclusion, let me put the question to you, such as are putting off religion from some little idea of inconvenience, Why stand you here all the day idle? Know you not that it is a general law of the universe that indolence brings ruin? Physical indolence brings physical ruin. Commercial indolence brings commercial ruin. Intellectual indolence brings intellectual ruin. Moral indolence brings moral ruin. My brother, what though the temperature be not exactly congenial to thy feeling, still go and work! The field cries for cultivation; nature offers to help thee.

Work! and nature will warm thee with her glowing fires, strengthen thee with her vital energy, and reward thee with her munificent gifts. The soul, like certain plants in the steppes of Siberia, can grow in vigor and stature, and blossom in beauty, though ice imbed its roots, and frosty winds bend its fibers and mantle its foliage in sheets of snow.

HOMILY XLV

THE ONE THING DREADFUL.

It is a fearful thing to fall into the hands of the living God. HEB. x, 31.

A WONDERFULLY suggestive expression is the phrase, "The living God!" When we speak of living men, it is in opposition to dead men; and when God is represented in Scripture as "the living God," it is in opposition to the gods of heathen idolatry. What are idols? Dust. They have no life; but God has life, an infinite fullness of life. There are at least two things which distinguish the life of God from the life of all other living objects. (1.) *God's life was not given to him.* All other life is a gift. He has life *in himself.* His life is underived, independent, absolute. (2.) *God's life had no beginning.* We subscribe to the dictum that *every effect must have a cause;* but we deny that *every being must have a cause.* There is one uncaused Being, and that being we know by the name, "God!" Once there was no universe. Was there ever a period when there was no God? Never. God has existed from eternity, and there never will come a time when the atheistic utterance will be true, "There is no God." As God did not begin to live, so he will not cease to live. He is "the living God!" And what is meant by "*falling into the hands* of the living God?" The hand is the seat and symbol of power, so that to fall into the hands of a man is just to fall into his power; and to fall into the hands of God is to fall into his power for punishment. This is clear from the fact that the apostle pronounces it "a *fearful thing* to fall into the hands of the living God." This brings us to inquire, Wherein consists the fearfulness of falling into the hands of God?

To this inquiry we reply,

First, *Not in the vindictiveness of God.* Although in the preceding verse we have a quotation from Deuteronomy, which runs thus: "Vengeance belongs to me, I will recompense," it must not be imagined that God is of a revengeful temper. The term "vengeance," when affirmed of God, must be taken in the sense of "penal retribution." "*Penal retribution* belongs to me, I will recompense;" that is, I shall punish in the execution of justice. Besides, revenge is defined "the desire of returning an injury." Unless, then, God can really be injured, and we cannot conceive of it, the condition of vindictiveness is absent in his case, and ever must be. We grant that God has threatened to inflict punishment on sinners, but the infliction of punishment is no proof of vindictiveness. Is it vindictiveness that leads a parent to chastise his child?

Secondly. *Not in any inclination in God to overpunish.* The person who is under the influence of vindictive feeling is apt to outrage justice when he meets with the object of his revenge. Indeed, it has often happened that avengers have visited the objects of their vengeance with an undeserved amount of punishment; and were God of a vindictive spirit, it is quite conceivable that he might overpunish. Since he is not, we need not fear that he will treat *cruelly* those who fall into his hands. In his dealings with them he will be guided by this principle of justice, for he loves righteousness, and is by nature averse to its opposite.

Having shown wherein this fearfulness of falling into the hands of God does *not* consist, it next devolves on us to show wherein it *does* consist.

And we remark,

I. That the hands of God are almighty. Earthly kings are no stronger physically than their subjects. Viewed apart from the forces at their command, What are they ?—mere mortals. But God is infinitely stronger than his subjects. What is the combined strength of all God's subjects, and they may be numerous as the rays of the sun, to the strength of God? Less far than a particle of dust is to the solid globe. One man can do many things; men in combination can do a vastly greater number of things. The things, however, which men cannot do exceed numerically the things which they can do. Is there anything to which God is unequal? We do not suppose that the divine power is *perfectly* expressed in creation; but do not the stupendous masses with which the loneliness of space has been invaded impress us with the *greatness* of the Creator's power? The countless worlds that roll in splendor and silence above us may not teach that God is omnipotent. They certainly *justify faith in his omnipotence*, and what cannot omnipotence accomplish? Were the entire universe of rational existences to unite with the intention of overthrowing Deity, would the "I AM" experience difficulty in defeating them? We trow not. God is a stranger to fear. A word, and the universe would instantaneously be as though it never had been. What God has made he can easily unmake. Great, unspeakably, inconceivably great, is the power of God; and hence it must be a fearful thing to fall into his hands.

II. That the existence of God is eternally living. Man's punishment of his fellow may be limited in two ways:

First. *The party undergoing punishment may die.* If the slaveholder applies the lash too freely to the back of his slave, what is the consequence? Body and soul part.

Secondly. *The party inflicting the punishment may die.* It is only during life that man can afflict his fellow. The dead can neither be tortured nor torture. Have not individuals again and again heard with joy of the death of their tormentors? Is it not well for the drunkard's wife that *livingness* is not predicable of her intemperate husband, so far at all events as the marriage union is concerned? Assuredly; but livingness is an attribute of God, and therefore it is a fearful thing to fall into his hands. It does not necessarily follow from God's livingness, or indestructible vitality, that man will live forever.

Nor does it necessarily follow that God will punish forever. But the Bible tells us that man is immortal. It further tells us that the punishment of the incorrigibly wicked will be everlasting; and there is nothing on the part of God to hinder it, for he is the *living God.*

Now, if falling into the hands of God be a thing to be dreaded, yea, "the one thing dreadful," as religion is "the one thing needful," what ought we to do? Manifestly, we should *keep out of his hands:* and how can we manage this momentous business? Christians can, by guarding against the crime of apostasy; and sinners, by reliance on the merits of Christ's mediation. On unbelievers alone is God disposed to lay his hands, and fling them into perdition. Haste, then, O unsaved reader, to Jesus. The hands of God are *nearing* you, and you are not safe until the arms of the world's Redeemer embrace you.

HOMILY XLVI.

MAN IN RELATION TO THE BOUNTIES OF NATURE.

We brought nothing into this world, and it is certain we can carry nothing out. 1 Tim. vi, 7.

The text does not refer, (1.) *To mental constitution.* Every man brings certain brain-power into the world, which is to be developed and applied by education and circumstances. Nor, (2.) *To moral disposition.* Every man is born with a heart opposed to the law of eternal rectitude. The text refers solely to the bounties of nature. So far as these are concerned, we brought nothing to the cradle and shall carry nothing to the coffin. The text teaches:

I. THAT NO MAN HAS ANY ANTECEDENT CLAIM ON THE BOUNTIES OF NATURE. The child of the pauper and the child of the prince came into the world *personally* on equal terms. Yet there *must* be SOCIAL DISTINCTIONS. These will arise,

First, *Through difference of force of character.* Some men could make the *wilderness* bring forth fruit, while others would famish amid the luxury of an Eden.

Secondly. *Through diversity of disposition.* The open-hearted man will be his own executor; he scatters as he goes; whereas the covetous man piles his property that he may boast of his wealth. The text teaches:

II. THAT NO MAN CAN RISE TO ABSOLUTE PROPRIETORSHIP OF THE BOUNTIES OF NATURE. The mightiest monarch cannot touch an atom as *absolutely* HIS OWN. He did not bring it into the world and he cannot carry it out. Amid the clamor of contending monarchs, amid the din of battle for empire, one voice is heard asserting the true proprietorship of the universe: "*The gold and the silver* ARE MINE, *and the cattle upon a thousand hills.*" (1.) Man is not the proprietor, he is merely *a steward.* (2.) Stewardship implies *responsibility.* What a new conception of life is imparted by the thought that *what we have is only borrowed!* The text teaches:

III. THAT MAN SHOULD CONSULT THE ABSOLUTE OWNER IN THE DISPOSAL OF THE BOUNTIES OF NATURE. There *must be* an owner. It is most evident, however, that *man* is not the owner, forasmuch as he "brought nothing into the world and it is certain that he can carry nothing out." The Divine

Being is the owner, and he as such ought to be consulted in the distribution of his own property.

First. *This is reasonable.* Is it reasonable that your servants should dispose of your property without consulting you? "How much more then," etc.

Secondly. *This is profitable.* Does not God know *best* how property should be employed? Can he not reveal the best mode of investment? The text teaches:

IV. THAT MAN MUST EVENTUALLY DISSOLVE HIS CONNECTION WITH THE BOUNTIES OF NATURE. First. *This is inspiring to the Christian.* He has been employing the world merely as so much scaffolding; he is only too glad, therefore, to take it down and enter into the temple of purity and rest. Secondly. *This is heart-crushing to the sinner.* When he parts with the world he parts with his ALL! Having surrendered "things seen and temporal," he stands in God's universe as a penniless pauper! Though we can carry no secular possessions out of this scene of being, there is one thing we *must* take with us, namely, MORAL CHARACTER. We cannot get rid of *that* even in the "dark valley of the shadow of death;" *that* will accompany us into the presence of the dread Judge! Having passed the present life, having known its sorrows and joys, and been disciplined by all its mutations; having been brought into contact with the glorious truths of Christianity; having heard the Gospel in all its fullness and power, it is impossible but that these influences should have produced some effect on our moral nature. What is that effect? Suppose it should be the "savor of death unto death," then there are three inquiries which God may institute: (1.) If you have not honored me in yonder world, what guaranty is there that you would honor me in heaven? (2.) If you have not honored my SON, what guaranty is there that you would honor ME? (3.) If you have morally wasted one world, what guaranty is there that you would not waste another? In hearing these inquiries the sinner must be smitten with confusion and dumbness. On a review of the whole subject, three duties appear plain:

First. *To enjoy the bounties of Providence.* The great Father intended his children to find joy in nature; and the true heaven-born child *will* delight himself according to the dictates of a regenerate heart.

Secondly. *To distribute the bounties of Providence.* There is but little joy in self-appropriation. *Giving* is a means of grace. Have you seen the widow's eye when you have ministered to her need? No artist can reproduce the divine light that shines there!

Thirdly. *To be grateful for the bounties of nature.* A life of gratitude is a life of happiness. If you would be truly grateful, ever look to those who have *less* of this world's goods than you have. A survey of the *palace* may induce discontentment, but a glance at the *work-house* may awaken purest thankfulness!

What are *you* living for? What is the supreme object of your being? Are you not convinced of the folly of expending your energies on the transitory pleasures of the present life? Is there aught in mere material property to meet the requirements of your immortality? Let me charge you to seek the "true riches." Apart from *Christ* there is nothing satisfying: "HE IS ALL IN ALL." You need *pardon*, he can grant it; you are seeking *peace*, he can bestow it. I adjure you to seek him with all your heart! Having found Christ you have found a universe of blessing. You will part with this world as a faded leaf, that you may enter on an unwithering and incorruptible inheritance.

HOMILY XLVII.

GOD'S NOTICE OF LITTLE THINGS.

And whosoever shall give to drink unto one of these little ones a cup of cold water only in the name of a disciple, verily I say unto you, he shall in no wise lose his reward. MATTHEW x, 42.

For whosoever shall give you a cup of water to drink in my name, because ye belong to Christ, verily I say unto you, he shall not lose his reward. MARK ix, 41.

For God is not unrighteous to forget your work and labor of love, which ye have showed toward his name, in that ye have ministered to the saints, and do minister. HEBREWS vi, 10.

"THE cup of cold water" was a more costly gift in eastern countries than it is in our land. It was in many cases more difficult to procure, and more precious to the traveler by reason of the excessive heat with which he was often overpowered. It is evident, however, that Christ regarded it as a *comparatively trifling* gift; he looked upon it as one of the *least* gifts that could be bestowed on a disciple, and yet not too little to attract the notice of an approving Providence. Such being the case, we may naturally consider these passages as teaching GOD'S NOTICE OF LITTLE THINGS.

The word "little" must be understood comparatively. In one sense there is nothing trifling in the estimation of God. When Christ says one of these "little ones," he does not signify the meanness or insignificance of any of his people, but rather their comparative obscurity and feebleness. Understood in this light, the subject suggests:

I. God's intimate acquaintance with every member of his spiritual kingdom. "*One* of these little ones." In order fully to appreciate the *minuteness* of God's knowledge, you must take the *telescope* in one hand and the *microscope* in the other. What wonders are unfolded: unnumbered millions of globes, etc.; system upon system. Microscope: a globe in every water-drop swarming with life; a busy population on every *leaf*, etc.

Then lay down these instruments, and draw aside the vail of the spiritual world, and behold the countless ranks of intelligences, survey the stupendous whole, and then you will appreciate the touching simplicity of the words: "ONE *of these little ones!*" This reflection should, (1.) *Inspire a feeling of profound trust in God.* Am I a little one? He *knows* me. I am not *too little* to be regarded. As he knows me, he will do *right* by me! (2.) *Inspire a feeling of profound reverence for God.* His eye is upon me! upon every passion that swells this heart, every thought that flashes through this *intellect*, every word that escapes these *lips*, and every act done by this *hand.*

II. That God appreciates a gift according to the motive which actuates the giver. This is fully proved by the various expressions in each verse: "In the name of a disciple;" "because ye belong to Christ;" "ye have showed toward his name." It is of vital importance to understand this principle, because, (1.) *It casts light on the subject of good works.* If the gift of a "cup of cold water" is to be rewarded then all the world might be rewarded, because there is hardly a man but would give such a gift to a fellow-creature. Mark, however, the regard which is paid to the subject of motive; it is the *design* which renders value to the gift; it is the *motive* which transforms the cup of water into a cup of blessing! In the case before us a distinction is inferentially drawn between mere *animal kindness* and *Christian generosity.* In the one case the water would be given *without any regard to moral character*, but in the other it would be given out of *love to Christ. Only a Christian can give from this motive;* therefore the reward is limited to the followers of Christ *alone.* "We know that we have passed," etc. Generosity is beautiful wherever it is exhibited; but the generosity which is accepted in heaven must arise, etc. (2.) *It tends to prevent self-deception. Why* was that gift given, that deed done, or that word uttered? "*Because ye belong to Christ*" is the true spring of philanthropy. How prone we are to deceive ourselves on the subject of *motive!*

III. That in the vast economy of the universe there is nothing lost. That "cup of cold water" is not lost. "God is not unrighteous to forget your work and labor of love." In his book the minutest details are made. This thought applies, (1.) *To the sublime processes of physical creation.* In the flight of boundless ages we are taught that not one particle of matter is lost! In the ravages of oceans, the flow of the river, the crumbling of the mountain, there is nothing lost!

"Nothing is lost; the drop of dew
 That trembles on the leaf or flower
Is but exhaled to fall anew
 In summer's thunder-shower."

In the burials of ages, the vanquishment of armies, the moldering dust of innumerable dead, nothing is lost! The least iota cannot be lost.

"The little drift of common dust,
 By the March winds disturbed and tossed,
Though scattered by the fitful gust,
 Is changed, but never lost;

"It yet may bear some sturdy stem,
 Some proud oak battling with the blast,
Or crown with verdurous diadem
 Some ruin of the past."

(2.) *To the moral effects of the Gospel:* "My word shall not return unto me void." It will be a "savor of life unto life, or of death unto death." Poor ungodly hearer, let this momentous announcement fall heavily on thy heart! *A neglected Gospel will be a swift witness against you!* (3.) *To all efforts in the cause of moral regeneration.* The humblest effort in the cause of Christ cannot be lost. It is a seed pregnant with immortal fruit. If that seed does not grow in the heart of the ungodly, still it cannot be lost, for it will grow into a chaplet or a garland to wreathe the brow of the honest laborer.

Sunday-school teachers, hear ye this! Nothing is lost!

"Weary not," etc. *Weeping parents*, hear ye this! All your efforts for the conversion, etc. *Spirits of the just*, hear ye this! All the kind words and earnest entreaties, etc. *What a motive for labor is here presented!* How it should check our murmuring and inspire our courage!

Let us treasure up the holy lessons of the subject!

(1.) *To belong to Christ is the highest of all honors.* Are *you* "one of these little ones?" (2.) *He who belongs to Christ will be a giver as well as a receiver.*

Despisers of the *truth*, oppressors of the *poor*, blasphemers of the sacred name, toiling laborers in Christ's cause, givers of a cup of cold water, hear ye this! Nothing is lost! It will not be lost! That cup of water will be found again! Christ will appear with it in his hand; he will *smile* upon it; that smile will change the water into *wine*, and as you drink it, "lost in wonder, love, and praise," you will exclaim: "Thou hast kept the good wine until now."

HOMILY XLVIII.

THE TWO BROTHERS; OR, EARTHLY RELATIONSHIP THE MEDIUM OF SPIRITUAL INFLUENCE.

Am I my brother's keeper? GEN. iv, 9.
And he brought him to Jesus? JOHN i, 42.

OF the first two brothers who lived on this earth, the one hated and slew the other; and when arraigned before God and his own conscience, denied the obligation of fraternal care and affection.

Of the first two brothers mentioned in the New Testament, the one, having himself found the Messiah and come to some extent beneath his influence, hastened to meet the other and bring him to Jesus too. These brothers we may take as *representative men. Cain* is the embodiment of the spirit of hatred, selfishness, the world. *Andrew* of the spirit of love, self-sacrificing zeal, of Christ.

Let us dwell on a few observations suggested by the above well-known instances. Observe,

I. That earthly relationships involve the duty of spiritual care. Relation, taken in its widest sense, if not, as some hold, the ground of all moral obligation, is certainly very intimately connected therewith. But, however this may be, no man can be a brother, a parent, a son, or even a master or employer, without being specially bound to care for his own.

None doubt for a moment that a man ought to provide for his "own household" in earthly concerns; strange that in spiritual things, which are, indeed, inseparable from earthly good and infinitely more important, the obligation is comparatively so little felt!

If a brother, friend, or master seeks not the soul's good of those connected with them, who else can be expected to do so? As neglect at the hand of a brother is felt to be a double injury, so should care for a brother's eternal interest be felt to be a double duty, the duty of "a man and a brother."

In proportion to the closeness of the relationship is the force of the obligation. We should seek the good of all;

but it is alike the dictate of nature and revelation to "begin at home." Beams of spiritual influence should radiate throughout all the circles of earthly relationship. By example, by act, by speech, by prayer, by every right means should this duty be discharged.

II. THAT EARTHLY RELATIONSHIPS AFFORD PECULIAR OPPORTUNITIES FOR THE DISCHARGE OF THIS DUTY. God has constituted the varied relationships of human life for the purpose of promoting the moral and religious good of man. All the ways in which men are necessarily thrown together in the pursuit of the things of this life may, without interfering with this design, be made opportunities to influence each other for eternal good. Every man is surrounded by an atmosphere of spiritual influence, in the which whosoever breathes, inhales health or poison: so that we cannot, whether we would or not, cease from influencing for good or evil those with whom we come into contact. But opportunity and power should be consciously and voluntarily used for good. If the elder brother "rules over" the younger, he should say, "Let us go into the field" to admire the works of God, to meditate, to pray together; not to tempt, to kill, and destroy. Alas! how many families daily meeting, possessing common interests, extending mutual influence, have little thought of the opportunities thus given to lead one another to Jesus and salvation!

III. THAT ACCORDING AS THE SPIRIT OF CHRIST OR OF SELFISHNESS IS POSSESSED, WILL THIS DUTY BE FULFILLED OR NEGLECTED. Sin, whose essence is *selfishness*, is a severing principle. Hence envy, hatred, divisions. Religious differences even, without Christ's spirit, often sever brotherly sympathies. The first murder was connected with religious rites. "He that hateth his brother is a murderer." But Christ's spirit is a spirit of love and brotherly unity. To come ourselves to Christ, to be imbued with his spirit, is the necessary condition and the all-powerful incentive to this duty. This also shall prevent a "falling out by the way."

IV. That concerning the performance of this duty an account will be required. "And the Lord said unto Cain, Where is Abel thy brother?" Vain will be every excuse for neglect. God will say unto us all, "What hast thou done?" Conscience will speak. "We are verily guilty concerning our brother." On earth, in the judgment, in eternity, what questions will arise on neglected duties and misused opportunities; and how gladly will men evade them if they might!" "To him that knoweth to do good and doeth it not, to him it is sin."

V. That earthly relationships, according to the manner in which they are used, become an eternal blessing or bane. Cain went from the presence of the Lord, a wanderer through the earth; his race followed his footsteps, (Lamech, verse 23,) till the earth was swept away with the besom of destruction. To a man himself, and to all beneath his influence, it is so. On the other hand, Peter was blessed in Christ, united in closer sympathy with Andrew; they lived in the promotion of the same great design, and in death they were not divided. Dives, in hell, dreads the coming of his brethren. In heaven, "friends" are waiting to receive those who "fail" into "everlasting habitations."

HOMILY XLIX.

GOSPEL TRUTH.

Then Agrippa said unto Paul, Almost thou persuadest me to be a Christian. ACTS xxvi, 28.

PAUL was emphatically a great man. He had an intellect that grasped the sublimest truths, a heart that loved his God and bled with compassion for his race. He lived as well as preached Christianity. His conduct confirmed the doctrine that his lips declared. He was a portraiture and a proof of the religion of Jesus. The peculiar estimation which he formed of the world was at once a result and an evidence of his singular greatness. His judgment was not carried away by show. The splendor of the world did not conceal from him its moral deformity. Standing upon an eminence unreached by the mass, he took a view of the world, and with the law of God as his standard, he formed a calm and deliberate judgment of mankind. He deprecated the religion of the religious, pitied the ignorance of the philosophical, and wept over the degradation of the great. He estimated no man according to his birth, office, attire, or wealth; but according to the real amount of Christian truth that lived in his heart and was embodied in his life. These remarks are suggested by the scene in which he appears before us in this chapter. Here the poet, the painter, and the sculptor may find a subject worthy of the highest effort of their genius. He stands before royalty as a criminal undaunted and brave. Neither the anathemas of his own countrymen nor the scowl of the world could crush that spirit of his, which rose in triumph over all. He was in chains, and yet on the face of this globe there was no man more free than he; his spirit exulted in a liberty which no despot could injure, no time destroy. An outcast in the world was *he*, and yet its rulers trembled at the majesty of his looks and the power of his words. Here, with his great mind filled with love to God and man, his cogent, rousing, and eloquent appeals made Felix tremble, and Agrippa exclaim, "Almost thou persuadest me to be a Christian."

Now, we request you to observe that the whole of this scene before us, the boldness and calm of the apostle, the tremor and agitation of Agrippa, are to be referred to one principle; and what was that? Genius? learning? law? No, GOSPEL TRUTH. To a further illustration of the subject I shall invite your attention. The text leads us to notice, the *mighty energy*, the *sublime aim*, the *practical method*, and the *solemn failure* of Gospel truth.

I. THE MIGHTY ENERGY OF GOSPEL TRUTH. Its power is here displayed in two ways: in shaking the religion of the monarch, and strengthening the heart of the apostle.

First. *In shaking the religion of the monarch.* (1.) There is no task more difficult than that of destroying a man's faith in his own religion. Man has a religious nature, a nature made for God, and every opinion that he has entertained on religion he holds with more than an iron grasp. It is easier to argue a man out of anything than out of his religious creed; he has often given up his *home, friends*, and *life* for this. (2.) But while it is thus difficult for men in general to exchange their creeds, it was so especially with a Jew. The attachment of a Jew to his religion is proverbial. No religion, Christianity excepted, ever took such a hold upon the human mind as Judaism. Agrippa was a Jew. (3.) But of all classes of men, no class would find it more difficult to change their religion than *kings*. There are greater obstacles in the way of a sovereign changing his religion than to any one else. He is often a religious slave; the religion of the people must be his. Pride, policy, or fear would bind him to his old creed. (4.) And yet more, add to all this the circumstances of the new religion that was presented to him. It was neither popular nor respectable. The mass was opposed to it, and the high ranks frowned upon it with contempt. Agrippa had just heard his noble friend, Festus, charge the man with madness who was recommending to him this new religion. Notwithstanding all these obstacles, such was the power of Gospel truth, that in a few minutes the creed of the king was shaken to its foundation. He seemed to feel that he was a deluded man, and he felt an inclination to embrace the religion of the apostle. "Almost thou persuadest," etc. Almost! Why, Agrippa, is it possible that thou art dissatisfied with the religion of thy fathers? What strange thing has come over thee? Shall Agrippa stoop so low, run such social and political risks, as to change his religion? Why, the philosophy of Rome will laugh at thee, and every breeze that sweeps over the Seven Hills shall be charged with ridicule for thy folly, shouldst thou assume the degraded name of Christian.

Here is a glorious evidence of the power of our religion! Blessed be God! it is to triumph over all systems; it is to be the conqueror of all religions. We care not what may be their antiquity, their plausibility, their congeniality with depraved tastes. We care not though their principles be inwrought into the moral heart of man. Bring the religion of the cross in fair contact with them, and they, like the mists of the morning in the summer's sun, shall vanish away. Like Aaron's rod, the cross shall swallow up their enchantments. It shall dispel every error that darkens the human judgment, snap every fetter that enthralls the human soul; it shall give to every spirit its right and freedom, the long lost inheritance of man..

Secondly. *Its mighty energy is seen in strengthening the heart of the apostle.* While Agrippa trembles, Paul is calm: there is a moral majesty on his brow. The king must have felt himself a babe in the grasp of this giant, a serf in the presence of this iron-bound freeman. What was it that braced up the soul of the apostle with so much unconquerable energy? The same force that made Agrippa tremble—Gospel truth. The cloudy pillar of old which shone brightly upon the Israelites in the Red Sea, frowned in midnight upon the Egyptians; the former it cheered and guided through the waters, the latter it terrified and overcame with dismay. So here Gospel truth had a very different effect upon these two men. And does it not always act thus? While it overcomes the sinner with the terrors of conviction, does it not fill the Christian with joy and peace in believing? It makes sinners feel their weakness and believers their strength. It shakes the world, but establishes the Church. It is a system to pull down and build up, to uproot and to plant.

II. The sublime aim of Gospel truth. What is its aim? To elevate man from the barbarous to the enjoyment of social life, to stir the human mind to action, to awaken it to a consciousness of its own precious being, and high relation and solemn condition, to dispel its ignorance, correct its errors, remove its opposition? It does all this, but its grand object is to make men *Christians.*

But what is it to be a Christian? This is the important question. Is it to be orthodox in creed? No! there are many wicked spirits profound theologians. Is it to be regular in our attendance on religious ordinances? No! the scribes and Pharisees were so: and our Saviour said, "Except your righteousness exceed the righteousness of the scribes and Pharisees ye shall in no wise enter the kingdom of heaven." Is it to be attached to the person, character, and ministry of God's servants? No! Herod heard John gladly, but the vengeance of God overtook him even in this world. Is it conviction of sin? No! Judas repented, Felix trembled, and Agrippa was *almost* a Christian. What then is it to be a Christian? Paul answers the question: To be as *I am.* But what constituted Paul a Christian? Three things:

First. *He accepted the atonement of Christ as the only hope of salvation.* How numerous and cogent were the arguments he employed to show that by the deeds of the law no flesh could be justified. "For if," said he, "when we were enemies, we were reconciled to God by the death of his Son; much more, being reconciled, we shall be saved by his life." On the sacrificial death of Christ he grounded his hope of heaven and acceptance with God. He disclaimed confidence in everything else. His talents, learning, and morality he thought nothing of: the cross of Christ was his all. "God forbid that I should glory, save in the cross of Christ my Lord."

Secondly. *He made the will of Christ the rule of his conduct.* "What wilt thou have me to do?" was the first question he asked. He regarded Christ as his ruler, his king, as well as his priest. He followed his directions, he obeyed his precepts, he cherished his spirit, he copied his example. Christ's example was the revelation of law; to imitate that example was to obey his will.

Thirdly. *He cherished the love of Christ as the inspiration of his life.* How earnest is Paul! He traversed continents, crossed seas, braved perils, and endured privations, to preach the Gospel. But what was the motive? Love! "The love of Christ constraineth us," etc. He was so deeply impressed with the power of this love that at one time he said, "Though I give my body to be burned," etc. These three things made the apostle what he was; these too are the essential elements of a Christian. Do you ask me what is the worth of this name, what is the value of the object which it is the design of Gospel truth to confer? *We cannot tell.* It is a "name above every human name." A name that suggests matter for everlasting thought, that comprehends within its ample range all the pure, generous, free spirits of men of every age and clime; spirits that shall shine like stars in the kingdom of heaven for ever. A name that shall live in memory when the greatest names of earth shall be forgotten; when every title that emblazons the page of heraldry shall be blotted out by the hand of time. A name with which is connected the sublimest privileges. Are you a Christian? then there is a close, an everlasting, though invisible, oneness between you, Christ and every holy spirit; you live in the sympathies of the good, in the arms of redemptive mercy. Are you a Christian? then the great God is your father, Jesus is your brother, angels are your servants, and heaven at last will be your home. Are you a Christian? then you can look and claim an interest in all. All things are yours. How ardent, benevolent, and pious was that wish of the apostle's: "I would to God," etc. A nobler wish than this never entered a human heart. From it we learn that a Christian in *chains* is *freer*, *happier*, and *nobler* than a king on his throne.

III. The practical method of Gospel truth. How does this powerful truth attain this sublime object? By sentimental rhapsody, bombastic phraseology, dogmatic assertions, noisy declamation? No. These may rouse the passions, but cannot convince the judgment; may beget superstition, but never produce enlightened piety; are more adapted to make infidels than Christians. How then? by baptismal water? This is an outrage on reason. By legislative enactment? There is no way by which coercion can travel to a man's soul, and touch the moral springs of action. Neither of these things separately, nor all conjointly, can effect the object. They who employ them for this purpose betray great ignorance of the laws of mind and the doctrines of the Bible. What then are the means? Moral suasion. "Almost thou persuadest me," etc. This implies two things:

First. *The existence of evidence to convince the judgment.* Persuasion is grounded on previous conviction. Before I could persuade an infidel to love and obey God I must endeavor to convince him, by evidence, of the being, excellency, and claims of the GREAT ONE. Before I can persuade a sinner to seek salvation in Christ he must be convinced of his own immortality, sin, and danger, and of the existence, suitability, and willingness of Christ as a Saviour. Where these things are not believed, and in every congregation there is an immense amount of skepticism in relation to them, the minister has to argue, he has to present evidence to the judgment; and until he can fasten convictions in them as to the reality of these things he cannot *persuade.* He has no ground upon which to stand, no place on which to rest the great lever of the Gospel. That the Gospel has evidence to convince us of its truth is a fact as clear as noon-day. If it can only make Christians by persuasion, and if there can be no persuasion without a conviction of its truth, then it follows that every Christian, whether a saint in heaven or a pilgrim on earth, is a living witness of its truth.

Secondly. *The existence of motives to change the will.* Persuasion consists in the presentation of motives in order to change the will; in bringing all the motives that can be gathered in order to effect a change of heart and conduct. And how tremendous are the motives which the Gospel contains for this purpose! Motives gathered from life and death, time and eternity, the resurrection morning and the judgment day, the heights of heaven and the depths of hell, the scenes of Sinai and the mighty wonders of the cross. O the cross contains a universe of motives in itself! Every page of Gospel truth is charged with infinite motives to bow down the sinner's conscience and to change his will. The presenting of these motives to the mind is persuasion, the means by which men are to be made Christians. This persuasion is a peculiarity of our religion. The religion of heaven needs no persuasion; the spirits there have only to know their duty in order to perform it. Other religions on earth are too false to depend upon it. If the religion of the "false prophet" is to be propagated it must be by the sword; if popery, by mystification; if deism by the construction of fallacies; but our religion can only spread by its own force; it has a self-propelling power. All it wants is to be presented fairly to the mind in humble dependence upon that Spirit that has pledged to crown it with success. Was it not in this way that it spread in the first ages of the Church?

IV. The solemn failure of Gospel truth. "Almost" a Christian; only "almost." What was the reason he did not yield entirely to the divine influence now brought to bear upon him, and become a thorough Christian? Not because the Gospel had not sufficient motive to induce him to advance, but because he did not *think sufficiently and right-*

ly upon it. You are conscious that the power of argument upon your mind depends upon the consideration you give it. An individual may ply me with arguments ever so powerful, yet unless I think upon them they will fall powerless upon my soul. Suppose you had an undutiful son who had left your home; his conduct had often grieved your spirit, his absence had nearly broken your heart; it clothed your days with darkness, it made you sad and restless through the night. Tidings reach you concerning the place whither he has gone, and the gay, foolish, sinful, and ruinous conduct he is still pursuing. Your paternal sympathies are stirred to their very depths, you enter your private room, you resolve to address a letter to your undutiful, though much beloved boy. Into that epistle you throw all the pathos of a parent's heart, and all the arguments that paternal love could form, to induce him to return to your bosom and home. After you have written your letter you show it to the dear partner of your life and the mother of your son. She returns it with a full heart, and says, "If anything will move him this letter will." Now on what does the success of that letter depend? Not on its being sent; not on its being put into the hands of your son, nor even on his reading it; but on his thinking properly upon it, thinking upon it as the expression of a father's heart which his conduct has well-nigh broken.

Just so it is with the Gospel; it is a letter sent down from the Everlasting Father to his undutiful children, containing the most powerful arguments to persuade them to return; and the great reason why it succeeds not is because they do not think. Hence he complains of their thoughtlessness. "O that my people were wise!" Let men but think of these subjects, think of them, etc.

But was this a safe state of mind for Agrippa to be in? Did the Gospel by producing this influence do him any real good? No; if he lived and died in this state the Gospel was an immense evil to him; better he had never seen Paul or heard of Christ. Brethren, are you almost Christians? Allow me affectionately to expostulate with you. Almost a Christian! Why, you are resisting the ministry of the Gospel by striving against the light of your judgment and the conviction of your own conscience. *Almost a Christian!* Has the kingdom of God come so near to you and will you not enter? Have you heard the thunder and seen the flashes of justice, and will you not flee from the wrath to come? *Almost a Christian!* Why the load of responsibility on your shoulders is tremendous; as yet the many privileges you have enjoyed have done you no real good. *Almost a Christian!* you had better die a heathen. The nearer you are elevated to heaven the deeper will be your fall. Methinks if on the judgment day there be one visage more impressed with agony and despair than another it will be that of the "almost Christian;" if there be one shriek more piercing, one wail of anguish more distressing amid the miseries of the lost, it will arise from the bosom of the "almost Christian." I have heard of many awful failures. The failure of your health is sad, the failure of your business is sad, the failure of your country in some terrible campaign is sad; but all is nothing to this failure. If the Gospel fail to save man there is nothing else.

HOMILY L.

THE SPIRITUAL INFIRMITIES OF MAN AND THE AGENCY OF GOD.

Likewise the Spirit also helpeth our infirmities; for we know not what we should pray for as we ought; but the Spirit maketh intercession for us with groanings which cannot be uttered. ROMANS viii, 26.

THERE is something very beautiful as well as instructive in the manner in which Paul describes in this chapter the work of the Spirit, first in operating on the sinner's heart, and subsequently in guiding, developing, and purifying the spiritual life.

The chapter reminds us of the Holy Spirit first *regenerating*, then *leading*, then *furnishing* us with evidence that we are the sons of God, and then *enabling* us to make use of this knowledge by *strengthening* us to call God our Father, and of his *abiding* in the Christian as an all-sufficient helper.

In connection with this verse let us consider,

I. THAT THE GOOD MAN IS SUBJECT TO VARIOUS SPIRITUAL INFIRMITIES. First. *Ignorance is one of the infirmities to which Paul alluded.* We do not mean ignorance in the ordinary use of the word, not the lack of common and requisite knowledge which we generally understand by this term. But a lack of acquaintance with God and the revelation he has given of himself. We sometimes fancy that we have a tolerably complete theoretical knowledge of the word of God. But even on this, the lowest ground of Christian intelligence, how very crude and imperfect is our insight into the merits of the Bible as a written expression of the will and history of the ways of God with respect to man! But if we pass from this merely outward and shell knowledge to the inner and spiritual revelation, we cannot but feel, beyond the power of language to express, the greatness of our ignorance of the *mind* of God. The holiness and power of Christ's precepts and life, the extent to which we may realize the presence and help of the Spirit, and the strength and reach of God's promises, are little thought of and less felt by the vast majority of Christians. We might easily extend the catalogue of points on which believers are grossly and culpably ignorant.

Secondly. *Doubts and fears constitute another infirmity in which the Spirit helpeth us.* We are continually agitated by doubts and fears respecting the Church: as to its peace, if certain circumstances should arise which appear to us possible or probable; as to the maintenance of the outward ordinances, if *the man* should be removed upon whom the chief burden now rests; as to the issue of the struggle through which it has ever and anon to pass with some outward enemy. These and many such questions arise in every earnest Christian heart, and cause anxious but generally unnecessary forebodings. God will take care of his truth as he ever has done. The ark of God must not be touched by profane hands, and those who doubt its security are unmindful of the presence of the Holy Spirit, who will guard from all harm, and more than make up for the absence of any human aid. Under all such circumstances the

Spirit has removed the cause of our infirmity. He will divide the sea, or stay the sun and moon in their course, rather than allow the enemies of the truth to triumph. And the doubts and fears which we have allowed to harass us for a time in seasons of personal affliction have all been removed by the Spirit breathing over our troubled souls, "Peace, be still."

Thirdly. *Inclination to fix our thoughts and affections too much on "things which are seen and temporal."* The objects of sense have more hold on us than those which are unseen and spiritual. Although these spiritual things are infinitely more glorious, and will have to do with our eternal well-being, yet in this world our thoughts and affections are fixed. Living in this world, and dependent upon it in a great measure for our happiness, we cannot but be drawn toward it in thought and affection. There is no harm in thinking of or caring about the things of life. The harm is in allowing these things to keep us continually fastened down to earth; in not seeking the aid of the Spirit, by which we rise to the bright and joy-inspiring feelings and thoughts which are to us foretastes of the rich feast of heaven. We could not of ourselves burst these fetters, or rid our minds of the burdens which press us so to earth. Much less could we attain to that spirituality of mind and enjoyment of divine truth which are earnests of the Spirit and of the inheritance reserved in heaven.

Fourthly. *The reluctance we feel to engage, and the difficulty experienced in continuing in well-doing, are infirmities.* There is great reluctance on the part of many good people to engage in God's work. Feelings of delicacy or a sense of their own unfitness induce them to shrink from what they know to be their duty. It is the Spirit that guides our efforts, preventing us, as he did Paul, from engaging in works that would prove unprofitable, and directing us to spheres where labor is needed, saying, "Come over into Macedonia and help us."

II. THAT AMONG THE SPIRITUAL INFIRMITIES TO WHICH THE GOOD ARE SUBJECT, THERE IS IGNORANCE OF THE NATURE AND MODE OF PRAYER. "For we know not what we should pray for as we ought." The apostle selects this as one instance of the Holy Spirit helping us.

First. *We know not what we should pray for.* We can fancy some one objecting to this proposition, and saying, "Prayer is a very simple and easy duty; surely I know what I need, and am able to ask for what I require." You may know what you *wish for* and what you would like to receive, but this is a very different thing from knowing what is *best* for you to receive. We need not remind you of the instances which are continually furnished of children asking for the bestowment of things which would prove injurious, or the removal of other things which are great blessings. The history of Christ's life will supply us with a sufficient number of cases in which those who had arrived at years of discretion evinced that they did not know what they should pray for. The request of Zebedee's wife and sons is repeated in one form or other every day by those who follow Jesus, and from him they meet with reproof the same. "Ye know not what ye ask." Again, when James and John asked that they might be permitted to call for fire from heaven wherewith to punish the slight done to Christ, he by the rebuke administered shows that they knew not what they asked for. Paul, too, by his own error in prayer (2 Cor. xii, 8, 9) was taught that we know not what to pray for.

Secondly. *We know not how we should pray "as we ought."* We often ask amiss, and as a consequence receive not. We ask *absolutely*, when we should do so conditionally. Our prayers are frequently presented with irreverence. There may be reverential utterances on the lip, but the heart is cold and indifferent as to the character of the Being to whom we present our requests, and with respect to the prayers we utter. We ask amiss because our faith is weak. Earnest and devout Christians go to the throne of grace with a sort of misgiving as to God's power being sufficient to meet their case, or as if his willinghood were limited. If any ask aright, that right asking is the effect of the Spirit striving for us and in us, enabling us to pray, "as we ought." When our heart is enlarged with the earnestness of prayer, when faith is strong, so strong that it raises us far above the world and brings us into close fellowship with God and Christ, it is the effect of the Spirit dwelling in and striving with us."

III. That these various infirmities the Spirit helps us to overcome. The Spirit maketh intercession for us "with groanings that cannot be uttered."

This supplies another view of the Spirit's work from any we had gained from the apostles. In them the verse implies that the Spirit regenerates, instructs, comforts, and guides. Here it is said that the Spirit pleads for us. In this chapter, and 1 John ii, 4, we are taught that Christ intercedes for us in heaven. Here another person in the Holy Trinity is represented as pleading for us. The differences between the advocacy of Christ and that of the Spirit, I take to be the following:

First. *Christ intercedes for us in heaven. The Holy Spirit pleads in us on earth.*

Secondly. *Christ is the believer's advocate with the Father. The Holy Spirit is God's advocate striving in and pleading with men.* Both with the sinner, to convert him to God; and the believer, to bring him nearer in sanctity and fellowship to our heavenly Father.

Thirdly. *Christ is in heaven preparing a place for us. The Holy Spirit is in the hearts of men preparing them for the place.*

IV. The manner in which the Spirit helps us to overcome our infirmities is inexplicable and earnest. "With groanings that cannot be uttered." This may mean,

First. *That the Spirit influences us in a way that is inexplicable.* We cannot understand how he affects and influences us. "The wind bloweth where it listeth, and thou hearest the sound thereof, but canst not tell whence it cometh, and whither it goeth: so is every one that is born of the Spirit." The believer knows, from the teachings of the word of God and his own experience, that the Spirit dwells in his heart and influences his feelings and life; but *how* this power is exerted remains, and ever will remain, a mystery.

Secondly. *The phrase "with groanings that cannot be uttered" may mean that the prayers which the Spirit dictates in us are unutterable.* And does not every Christian find that his desires and feelings (groanings) cannot be uttered? No language can express the intensity of our longings after the presence of God and Christ. There are feelings of sorrow and joy which words cannot reach, much less describe; so there are spiritual agonizings and pantings which the spirit alone excites and allays.

HOMILY LI.

LITTLE PREACHERS AND GREAT SERMONS.

Go to the ant, thou sluggard; consider her ways, and be wise: which having no guide, overseer, or ruler, provideth her meat in the summer, and gathereth her food in the harvest. PROVERBS v, 6.

THE eternal Father has favored his human offspring with a twofold revelation of himself, the Bible and Nature. Looking at men in their relation to this twofold revelation, they divide themselves into three distinct classes: First. *Those who study neither.* There are, alas! millions of men who never attempt to read the lessons God has given them either in nature or the Bible. Their intellects are so submerged in animalism and worldliness, that the great ideas of God are by them unseen and unsought. Secondly. *Those who study one and disparage the other.* There are many that study nature with great earnestness and assiduity, who pay no attention whatever to the Bible. Read the

Cosmos of Humboldt, and observe the entire absence of all reference to God as the builder of this wonderful world. Nay, some of them do worse, and seek to turn the results of their scientific researches against the revelations of the Bible. On the other hand, there are some who study the Bible and disparage the study of nature; they never "look through nature up to nature's God." They labor under the impression that nature is not sufficiently sacred and religious for their investigation. Thirdly. *Those who reverentially study the teachings of both.* Those who regard them as volumes from the same Author, volumes whose contents are in harmony with each other, and adapted mutually to illustrate each other's meaning, and to adorn each other's discoveries. This last class is the only class that is acting worthy of its faculties, and rightly employing the means which kind Heaven has appointed for man's restoration and wellbeing.

The allusion in the text, and which is only one of many, plainly shows us that the Bible encourages the study of nature. It sends us to nature for at least three purposes. First. *The Bible refers us to nature in order to attest its first principles.* That God is all-wise, all-powerful, all-good; that man has a soul and is under moral obligation, are things which the Bible assumes, takes for granted, does not attempt to prove. The man who wants proof it refers to nature's volume. Secondly. *The Bible refers us to nature for illustrations of its great truths.* The sower, the harvest-field, trees, rivers, vineyards, and vales; meads and mountains, skies and seas, it employs as emblems. The old prophets, and our Saviour, especially, used nature for this purpose. Christ gave every part of nature a tongue to speak out the grand principles of his kingdom. Thirdly. *The Bible refers us to nature in order to reprove the sins it denounces.* To reprove us for our ingratitude, it refers us to the ox and the ass. "The ox knoweth its owner, and the ass its master's crib," etc. To reprove us for our want of confidence in the paternal providence of God, it points us to the lilies of the field and the fowls of the air; and to reprove us for our *spiritual indolence* it directs us to the ants: "Go to the ant, thou sluggard," etc.

Now, the sluggard to whom I am going to address myself is the *spiritual* sluggard. Not the man who is neglecting his worldly business, the secularly indolent man, but the man who is neglecting the culture of his own spiritual nature, and the salvation of his own soul. These little ants will teach you four great truths. Here are small preachers but great sermons.

They teach you:

I. That the feebleness of your power is no just reason for your indolence. These little creatures are small, they are feeble; you could crush a thousand beneath your foot; yet see how they work. Naturalists have shown their ingenuity as architects, their industry as miners and builders; they have divided them into mason-ants, and carpenter-ants, and mining-ants, and carving-ants; and have shown that while their ingenuity in these departments of action is remarkable, their industry would put the most indefatigable of human laborers to the blush. If this tiny insect can do so much, do not you, with your bony limbs, strong sinews, robust frame, the engine of a deathless intellect, memory, imagination, conscience, soul, plead your feebleness as an excuse for your indolence. Remember three things: First. *That all power, however feeble, is given for work.* The Infinite Author of our being has not imparted the smallest portion of energy to any creature for which he does not require a certain quantity of work; however humble your power, you can do something; the man of one talent was as much bound to employ that talent as he who had five. Secondly. *That you are not required to do more than you have power to accomplish.* God does not expect the ant to do the work of an elephant, nor does he expect the man of feeble talents to accomplish the works of a Paul or a Luther. Thirdly. *That all power increases by use.* The man who attempts to do something gets power by the attempt. There was once a man with an arm withered, a mere dried stick; but Christ commanded him to stretch it forth: he might have said, "I cannot;" but he resolved to do it, and with the resolution came the power. This is a symbol of the universal truth, that you get power by effort. The man who has one talent can make five by it, and the man of five can make ten. Power increases by use. The naturally strong men who say they cannot do a thing, live and die pigmies. The naturally weak men who say *try* often attain Herculean force.

They teach you,

II. That the activity of others is no just excuse for your indolence. Go to the ant world, penetrate its little mines, its chambers, storehouses, garrets, workshops, for it has all these, and you will see millions of inhabitants, but not *one idler;* all are in action. One does not depend upon the other, and expect another to do his work. The teeming population is busy. This is a lesson to the indolent soul. The Christian world is busy, and there are thousands working; some preaching, some praying, some teaching, some writing; but not one can do *thy* work. Can any one *believe* for thee? *repent* for thee? *think* for thee? *love* for thee? *worship* for thee? Can any one *die* for thee or be *damned* for thee? Like the ant-hill, the Christian world is a scene of action, but not one of the million actors can do *thy* work.

They teach you,

III. THAT THE WANT OF A HELPER IS NO JUST EXCUSE FOR YOUR INDOLENCE. Go to the ant-hill, see them work; each is thrown upon his own resources and powers. "They have no guide, overseer, or ruler." Each works according to his own little nature. Self-reliantly each labors on, not waiting for the instruction or guidance of another. Do you say, I have no minister, no books, no Christian friends, and therefore cannot work? You cannot say this; but if you could, that would be no excuse; you have an intellect that can think, you have a heart that can love, you have a conscience that can guide. You have suggestive nature, you have this wonderful Bible, you have God! You are without excuse. Do not wait and ask for overseers, or guides, or rulers; if they come, and can help you, be thankful. Act out your own powers, use the light you have, and look to God for help. While you are looking for greater advantages, your time is passing; your season for making provision for the future is shortening. Cold, black, bleak winter is approaching.

They teach you,

IV. That the providence of God is no just reason for your indolence. Go to the ant-hill, and see these tiny creatures laying up for the future. The ant "provideth her meat in the summer, and gathereth her food in the harvest." There is a divine providence over these little insects. There is no creature, however small, that comes not within the pale of God's providing agency. But he provides for his creatures by the use of their own powers. *He does not do for any creature what he has given that creature power to do for himself.* He carries provisions to plants and flowers and trees, because they cannot go in search of their food. But the creatures to whom he has given locomotive power must "*seek* their meat from God." The beasts of the field, the birds of the air, the fish of the sea, and even the tiniest insects, must all *seek* their food. God provides for them in connection with their own agency. Let me remind you here of three things: First. *That, like these little creatures, you have a future.* Secondly. *That, like these little creatures, you have to prepare for the future.* Thirdly *That, like these little creatures, you have a specific time to make preparation.* Do not talk of Providence as an excuse for your indolence. Say not, God is good, and he will provide. He has provided for you richly, but he only grants the provision on condition of the right employment of your powers. There is an inheritance for the good, but only on the condition of their working. There is a heaven of knowledge, but only for the student; there is a harvest of blessedness, but only to the diligent husbandman; there are scenes of triumph, but only to the victorious warrior. In conclusion, let me remind you that your harvest time will soon be over. The sun is fading now; the ripened ungathered fruits are falling to the ground; autumn is gradually tinging the scene; nature looks more sterile and somber every day; the air is becoming chilly; the winter is coming; freezing, furious, bleak winter is coming: "How long wilt thou sleep, O sluggard?" etc.

> "To-morrow, and to-morrow, and to-morrow,
> Creeps in this petty pace from day to day,
> To the last syllable of recorded time;
> And all our yesterdays have lighted fools
> The way to dusty death."

HOMILY LII.

THE CONDITION OF MAN AS A WRECK.

O Ephraim, what shall I do unto thee? O Judah, what shall I do unto thee? Hosea vi, 4.

From this book we learn two things which may serve as an introduction to our remarks:

First. *That man is a wreck.* The picture which Hosea gives us of the Jewish people is truly a hideous and lamentable one. Sin rolls its warm, sparkling, but poisonous current through the veins of all. This picture of the Jew, alas! is the picture of the race. Man everywhere is in moral ruin. "From the crown of his head to the sole of his foot, there is no soundness, but wounds, and bruises, and putrifying sores." All our notions of infinite goodness and wisdom urge us to the belief that humanity is not in its normal condition, and that some fearful catastrophe has befallen it. *Physically man is a wreck.* He comes into the world with a puny, shattered frame, the most helpless of all creatures. From the dawn to the close of his brief life he has to struggle against the tyrant death, beneath whose stroke he falls at last. His body, like a fragile bark, no sooner floats on the sea of life than it gives signs of decay, and the first strong billow beats it down and buries it out of sight. "The moment we begin to live we all begin to die." Can it be that this was the original state of the human body! I think not. *Man intellectually is a wreck.* The function of reason is to form and classify true ideas of self, God, and the universe. But such ideas we have not. Our ideas not only clash with those of others, but with our own. We are in perpetual controversy with ourselves as well as with our erring brothers. The light of instinct guides all brutes alike in the true path of life; but our reason has failed to guide us. Instead of being a sun to light up our souls, it is a dim torch flickering amid the gusts of passion, and sometimes clouded by the thick mists of impure desires. The eye of the intellect is diseased, it is subject to optical illusions. *Man morally is a wreck.* He is at war with himself, at war with the universe, at war with God!

Were evidences wanted in support of the position that man is a wreck, I would compare what man is with what our notions of divine wisdom and benevolence would lead us to conclude he would be. I would refer to the universal consciousness of man, and show that man's ideal world ever transcends immeasurably his actual state. I would refer, in one word, to that Oracle whose decisions are ultimate. There we learn that "all have sinned and come short of the glory of God;" that "all like sheep have gone astray;" that "there is none that doeth good, no, not one;" that the whole world "lieth in wickedness." Humanity is in a sad condition. It was a vessel built at first to navigate the sea of life, with truth for its guiding-star and heaven for its destination; but it is now lying in ruins amid rocks and sands. It was once a temple reared for the residence and worship of the Everlasting, but its walls are broken down, its magnificent columns are in ruins.

The other thought suggested by this appeal is:

Secondly. *That God is earnest about man in this condition.* The Almighty, instead of blasting men with the lightning of his righteous displeasure, as might have been expected, appeals to them in the most tender and moving strains of love and mercy. "O Ephraim, what shall I do unto thee? O Judah, what shall I do unto thee?" What wonderful language for the Infinite to employ! It is the utterance of love that tried every means for their restoration, but failed, yet willing to do whatever else is possible. It is the language of love disappointed, yet still on fire! We have other divine utterances analogous to this. In Hosea xi, 8, 9, you have these remarkable words: "How shall I give thee up, Ephraim? how shall I deliver thee, Israel?" etc. And in Isaiah v, 4, you have these words: "What could have been done more to my vineyard, that I have not done in it?"

The divine earnestness displayed in such utterances shows:

I. That man, though a wreck, is an object of importance. There is nothing that impresses me so much with the importance of man as the interest which the great God seems to take in him; the earnestness which he displays for his recovery. A great mind is never earnest about an unimportant object. Little minds grow enthusiastic about small matters. When you see a great soul in earnest about a work, you may be sure that the work is momentous. On this principle how important man's restoration must be, since the Infinite mind is so earnest about it. Christ gives in one chapter three pictures of God's interest in man's recovery. The first is that of a woman who had lost a piece of silver, the second that of a shepherd who had lost one of his sheep, and the third that of the father of the prodigal son.

There is a principle in the practical experience of man which may perhaps throw some light upon the wonderful interest which the great God displays on man's account. It is this: *The power of suffering to heighten our affection.* A father of a numerous family has one little girl, an invalid. While the others are enjoying their sports, she lies from day to day a little sufferer on the couch. Who of all his children occupies most of his manly heart, raises his affection to the highest glow? It is that little suffering girl. When from home he thinks more of her than all the rest;

when he returns he hastens to give her the first salute of paternal love. His ear is keen to catch her feeblest moan. Why does she reign more in his affections? Not because she is more beautiful, for were she ever so deformed it would be the same, perhaps more. Not because he has any selfish idea of her ever being of service to him in the future. No. Though he knows that she will be a source of anxiety and expense to him so long as she lives, it would be the same. Why then? She is a *sufferer*, she is an invalid. This gives her the supremacy in his manly heart. This principle in the human soul I know is an emanation of the Infinite Father, and it may be a reflection of the principle that rules him in his conduct toward his vast family. He is the father of an immense multitude. Man is the moral invalid. While his angelic children are healthful and happy, poor man lies wretched, miserable, blind, and naked. And his heart is set on the suffering child. "There is more joy in heaven over one sinner that repenteth than over ninety and nine just persons," etc. As the cries of the suffering infant travel through all the chambers of the palace to the ear of the royal mother, so the cries of men ascend through the halleluiahs of angels into the ear of the "Lord God of Sabaoth."

The earnestness of God for man's recovery expressed in the text shows:

II. That man, though a wreck, is capable of restoration. This is implied in the question before us. He is not so far ruined as to exclude all hopes of restoration. The ruined temple can be rebuilt, the broken harp can be restrung. There are three things that show this:

First. *The condition of man in this world.* Men in this world are treated neither as innocent beings nor as criminals, neither as saints nor devils. This world to them is neither a prison nor a paradise, but rather an asylum. Men are treated as patients, not in a hopeless but in a recoverable position. Providence acts as a physician rather than a judge; it tries a variety of means for our moral recovery, the depletive and the tonic, the bitter and sweet, pains and pleasures. "Lo, all these things worketh God oftentimes with man to bring him back from the pit, to enlighten his soul with the light of the living."

If there was no intention on God's part to restore man, why is he allowed so many precious years of existence in a world like this? Why is he allowed through numerous ages to multiply his species? Why does not the Infinite make brief his work and treat all according to their deeds, and wind up the affairs of this disordered globe? The very fact that men are permitted to live and multiply in a world like this, intimates to me that there is a design for his restoration.

Secondly. *The deep aspiration of humanity.* Wherever man has been or is, in all places and periods, he is sighing and struggling for a higher conditon. "The earnest expectation of the creature waiteth for the manifestation of the sons of God." The deepest cry of the human heart is for a millennium. What schemes are projected, what efforts of a social, political, and religious character have been put forth to bring the glorious era on! Are these longings and expectations without any foundation? Does not the universality of their existence indicate that they are destined to be realized?

Thirdly. *The extraordinary means that are provided for man's restoration.* "What the law could not do in that it was weak through the flesh." "The Son of man came to seek and to save the lost." What are the means which you have in the Gospel? What does man require? Does he want pardon? "Be it known to you, men and brethren, that through this man," etc. Does he want a cleansing of the soul? "The blood of Jesus Christ, his Son, cleanseth from all sin." Does he want power to conquer his foes? He can become "more than conqueror through Him that loved him." Does he want, in one word, "wisdom" to guide him aright, righteousness to make him acceptable with God, sanctification to prepare him for the fellowship of the holy, redemption from all evils, material and spiritual? "Christ is made unto us wisdom," etc.

Fourthly. *Millions have been restored.* Paul, in writing to the Corinthians, says, "Such were some of you," etc. John saw "a multitude which no man could number, of all nations, kindreds, and languages of people." Who were they? They were those who had "come out of great tribulation, who had washed their robes and made them white in the blood of the Lamb."

I rejoice in the prospect of man's restoration. Man, thou art a temple in ruins, but thou shalt be rebuilt, and the glory of the Lord shall irradiate every chamber of thy being. Thou art bruised and mangled by the fall; but the great Physician will heal thee, and thou shalt be made hale in body and jubilant in soul. Thou art dead; thy dry bones are strewn in the valley of sin and bleached by the winds; but He who "is the resurrection and the life" shall restore thee. At his bidding the breath will come from the four winds, and thou shalt stand up to serve the Lord God of Israel.

This earnestness of God shows:

III. That man, though a wreck, exerts a fearful power. The text implies that God had performed great things for the moral restoration of Israel. "What shall I do?" He had done much. But why did all his operations fail? On account of man's power, even in his wrecked condition, to resist. Look at the antediluvian world. "My Spirit shall not always strive." Look at the Jewish nation. "Ye do always resist the Holy Ghost."

I tremble at man's power, though in ruin. He counteracts the moral influence of nature, the tendency of providence; more, he resists the appeals of the Gospel and the strivings of the Spirit. It is popular to preach man's inability. A guilty conscience is greedy for excuses. Men who are doing nothing toward their salvation are glad to be told that they can do nothing. Shall it be said that man, who has the power to breast the billows of divine influence, to resist the moral operations of God, has no power to yield to the mighty forces against which he battles? Has the besieged city which has triumphantly resisted the most powerful assaults of a mighty foe no power to surrender? Away with the absurdity! The sinner's *cannot* is his *will not*, and his *will not* is his guilt and ruin. "Ye will not come unto me that ye might have life." Hearken then to the question of the text: "What shall I do unto thee?" Eternal Spirit! I know not what more thou canst do for us. Thou hast given us a lovely world, a world teeming with every form of beauty and grandeur, encircled with resplendent skies, and everywhere vocal with thy great thoughts. Thou hast called us into existence in one of the most favored spots under heaven, under a government the most favorable to our full mental and moral development, and in one of the brightest eras of the world's history. Thou hast given us churches and Bibles, sanctuaries and praying friends, and earnest, self-sacrificing ministers; "line upon line, precept upon precept." More, thou hast given us thine only begotten Son, who gave his life a ransom for all, "suffered, the just for the unjust," to bring us unto thee. I know not what more thou canst do in the way of mercy. There is much in the way of judgment that thou canst yet do! Thou canst scathe us with lightning, thou canst crush us with thy thunder! But spare us yet, we beseech thee!

"O thou that would'st not have
  One wretched sinner die;
Who died'st thyself, my soul to save
  From endless misery;
Show me the way to shun
  Thy dreadful wrath severe;
That when thou comest on thy throne,
  I may with joy appear."

HOMILY LIII.

THE MEETING AT APPII FORUM AND THE THREE TAVERNS.

And from thence, when the brethren heard of us, they came to meet us as far as Appii Forum and the Three Taverns, whom when Paul saw, he thanked God, and took courage. ACTS xxviii, 15.

THE text describes a beautiful incident in the journey of Paul from Cesarea to Rome. With the occasion, hardships, perils, and deliverances of that journey we are familiar. And now it is drawing to an end; Appii Forum and the Three Taverns are reached, the former being about fifty and the latter thirty-three miles distant from the imperial city. At these stages Christian brethren from Rome meet and salute the veteran soldier and prisoner of Jesus Christ. No sooner does he recognize them than he experiences a striking elevation of soul. Pausing in his wearying march he offers thanks to God, and, full of hope and confidence, advances with a firm, elastic step to the scene of his final toil and pain. But it is impossible to view the text in its connection without feeling that it requires explanation. The advent of these brethren does not seem to be a cause adequate to the effect produced. Paul found brethren in Puteoli, but it is not said that while there he was the subject of any such happy influences as came upon him at Appii Forum and the Three Taverns. What was there in this incident that it so powerfully and beneficially affected the apostle's mind?

I. That Paul regarded it as expressive of the sympathy of the Christian Church in Rome. Sympathy is solace and help. Like the oil and wine of the good Samaritan, it *heals and strengthens.* It would be thoroughly appreciated by such a man as Paul; he who enjoined upon the Romans this duty: "Rejoice with them that do rejoice, and weep with them that weep." Of this sympathy I observe, (1.) It was *timely.* Think of Paul's circumstances. (2.) It was *practical.* It traveled further than mere sentiment and words, even thirty-three and fifty miles of hard road. (3.) It was *noble.* Paul was a *prisoner*, but they did not despise "his chain;" he was a *Christian*, about to answer for his life, yet they dared to identify themselves with him. And alas! (4.) It was *inconstant:* "At my first answer no man stood with me, but all men forsook me." Now I can well understand how the arrivals of the warm-hearted brethren from Rome would awaken the gratitude and confidence of the jaded and captive apostle.

II. That Paul regarded it as a token of God's providential care. His elation on these occasions implies a previous corresponding depression, produced in part, perhaps, by an imperfect realization of divine paternal care. Once before, during the storm at sea, his heart sank within him, and now as he draws near to Rome it again fails; but as the angel who stood by him in the night season made him of good cheer, so the meeting at Appii Forum and the Three Taverns constrained him "to thank God and take courage." It assured him that he was the object of divine solicitude, and that, perilous as his circumstances were, all was well. But how trivial is the event mentioned! Not in the estimation of faith. It indicated the hand of God. The cloud seen by the servant on Carmel was in itself a little thing, but it was of great moment to Elijah. By no means could Paul be more effectually cheered than by a vivid realization of God's care for him. "If God be for us who can be against us?"

III. That Paul regarded it as prophetic of the universal triumph of Christianity. Doubtless the chief cause of the depression to which I have alluded was the existence in Paul's mind of gloomy apprehensions in reference to the Gospel. The Jews had persecuted him to the uttermost; he was deprived of his liberty; his life was in jeopardy. Alas for the infant Churches he had planted! alas for the progress of the word of life! He had hoped to see the religion of the cross firmly established in the earth before he fell asleep, but now—what? Lo! brethren, genuine Christians arrive from Rome. Rome! the city of the Cæsars; the mistress of the world, whose influence was world-wide; the Gospel has taken firm hold on *Rome*, and from thence it shall diffuse itself to the ends of the earth! Such was the thought which I believe the arrival of these brethren brought vividly before the mind of Paul; and under its influence "he thanked God and took courage." He could not serve the Gospel better than he did during those "two whole years" which he spent in "preaching the kingdom of God and teaching those things which concern the Lord Jesus Christ."

The subject teaches us further,

(1.) That the most eminent of God's servants may be discouraged. (2.) That God will opportunely interfere in their behalf. (3.) That such interpositions should work in them gratitude and confidence.

HOMILY LIV.

THE USE OF CHRISTIANITY.

When thou wast young, thou girdedst thyself, and walkedst whither thou wouldest; but when thou shalt be old, thou shalt stretch forth thy hands, and another shall gird thee, and carry thee whither thou wouldest not. This spake he, signifying by what death he should glorify God. And when he had spoken this, he saith unto him, Follow me, etc. JOHN xxi, 18–23.

THESE words are part of an interesting conversation which Christ had with Peter after his resurrection from the dead. In the fourteenth verse we are told that this was the third time of his appearing to his disciples. He had appeared before to the women, to Cephas, and to James, and to the two disciples on the way to Emmaus. The Sea of Tiberias was the scene where he now displayed himself; a sea whose restless surface and whose silent shores had often felt his presence and witnessed his miracles.

I shall use the incident before us to illustrate the *true service of Christianity to man.* Perhaps there is no question so generally discussed, in such a variety of forms, and for such different purposes, and upon which such a diversity of opinion prevails, as this: "Of what real service is Christianity to man?" There are three classes, I conceive, who are grossly wrong on this question:

First. *Those who maintain that it is a positive injury.* There are many who aver, by significant and plausible insinuations, as well as by broad and bold statements, that Christianity has injured rather than benefited the race. They tell us how it has warped the judgments of men, and nurtured morbid sentimentality; how it has sectionized society, reared the throne of spiritual despotism, and served the ends of superstition, priestcraft, and tyranny. They point us to the inquisitions, prisons, and stakes of past ages, and to the property that, in its holy name, is now wrung from the blood and sinews of the toiling population.

Secondly. *Those who maintain that it is one of the many elevating forces at work in society.* They say it has done some good as well as much evil; that it is generally of service to men in a low stage of civilization, and that, like the theories and superstitions of old times, it has its mission, which it will fulfill, and then, like them, become obsolete and be left behind as the race advances in intelligence and manly virtue.

Thirdly. *Those who maintain that it does everything for man.* These say there is nothing good in the world but Christianity. No good in nature, no good in science, no good in the best feelings of man without Christianity; that if man has Christianity he needs nothing more; it does *everything* for him.

Now these conflicting sentiments suggest the propriety, and urge the necessity, of raising the question: "Of what real use is Christianity to man?" . The incident before us will supply a twofold answer—NEGATIVE AND AFFIRMATIVE:

I. The incident suggests that Christianity does not counteract the natural changes to which man's physical life is subject. "When thou wast young, thou girdedst thyself and walkedst whither thou wouldest; but when thou shalt be old, thou shalt stretch forth thy hands, and another shall gird thee." Peter, notwithstanding his defects, was a genuine disciple of Christ. Christianity had penetrated, fired, and transmuted his nature; yet notwithstanding this Christ foretells that he should experience the natural decay of old age. *The Christianity in Peter's soul would not prevent time wearing out his body.* It is difficult to conceive of a more solemn idea, as to the effect of age, than that which our Saviour here represents. Christ teaches *that age incapacitates man from executing his volitions.* This is slavery. To have a strong desire to do a thing, without the executive power, is the veriest vassalage. If a man is bound in chains and inclosed in a prison, yet has no *desire* to walk abroad, he is no slave. The paralytic that was brought to Jesus is the true picture of a slave. He had the will to ply his members and move his muscles, but he could not. This, Christ here teaches, is the effect of age upon us. "When thou wast young, thou girdedst thyself, and walkedst whither thou wouldest." Thou couldst ply the oar in the water, roam the fields, and scale the hills; there was an energy in thy limbs, a flexibility in the movements of thy young frame, by which thou couldst readily execute thy desires. "But when thou shalt be old," etc. Age leaves the will in vigor, but steals away the executive power. Now, Christianity will not prevent this natural effect of age. It will not prevent the bloom fading from the cheek, the brightness passing from the eye, the strength from dying out of the limb. It allows nature to take its course. Christianity neither offers resistance to the regular course of nature, nor an atonement for her violations.

This fact shows three things:

First. *It shows that physical sufferings are no criteria for individual moral states.* Some of the best of men are the greatest sufferers. Some of the most useful die in the zenith of life, and in the midst of usefulness. A rankling thorn in the flesh is consonant with the piety of an apostle.

Secondly. *It shows that Christianity respects the ordinances of nature.* However deeply you may drink into the spirit of Christianity, however consecrated you may be to its service, if you rebel against nature you must suffer.

Thirdly. *It shows that if the disciples of Christ would be physically happy they must attend like other men to physical laws.* If you are in want of physical comforts it is of no use for you to sing, "The Lord will provide," and sit down in indolence and sloth.

II. The incident suggests that Christianity does not guard a man from the social oppressions of life. "When thou shalt be old," etc. It is here foretold that Peter should die of crucifixion. His hands should be stretched forth, his arms would be extended on a cross, and he would be led to a death of violence at which his nature would revolt. About forty years after this Peter died a martyr. His Christianity did not deliver him from the malice of men, the storm of persecution, and the agonies of a martyr's death. Christianity promises us no escape from the opposition of wicked men; indeed, it teaches us to expect it. It teaches us that they who live righteously "must suffer persecution." "Marvel not if the world hate you," etc. The world has ever persecuted its best men. This fact shows,

First, *That Christianity can do without the favor of the world.* It does not require or authorize its disciples in the slightest degree to compromise their principles in order to gain the patronage of mankind, but to carry them out in all their fullness and force, even though it cause the world to be in arms.

Secondly. *That Christianity can do without the lives of its most devoted disciples rather than without their fidelity.*

III. THE INCIDENT SUGGESTS THAT CHRISTIANITY DOES NOT SOLVE THE SPECULATIVE PROBLEMS OF LIFE. "Peter, seeing him, saith to Jesus, Lord, and what shall this man do?" As if he had said, Why am I thus to be dealt with? What is to become of him (John?) is he to be crucified also, or will he be allowed to live the natural term of life? To this question Jesus replies: "What is that to thee?" There are many questions which the events of life force upon us, to which Christianity offers no response. Why are we in such suffering, while others who contemn our principles and despise our God are exempt from trials? Why are our lives cut short while we have much work to do? Why are we allowed such scope and facilities for working in our world when we have so little time? Why are our principles so tardy in their progress? Why are events allowed to spring up which check their advancement? Such questions as these arise, and to them Christianity makes no reply. The only word she says to the querist is, "What is that to thee?" There are good reasons why Christianity is silent upon such questions:

First. *The encouragement of these questions would strengthen the speculative tendency, rather than improve the heart.* One answer would lead to another question, and so on interminably.

Secondly. *An answer to such questions would create emotions that would paralyze moral action.* Suppose we knew what would happen to us and our children in coming years; where we should spend our eternity; who would go to hell, etc.; would not the feelings that such knowledge would create be likely to check all the free and healthy action of the soul?

Thirdly. *An answer to the questions would multiply the forces that divert us from practical godliness.* They would lead us to the realm of boundless speculation.

IV. THE INCIDENT SUGGESTS THAT CHRISTIANITY DOES NOT INVEST US WITH AN INFALLIBLE JUDGMENT IN THIS LIFE: "Then went this saying abroad among the brethren," etc. The disciples fell into a wrong interpretation of our Saviour's meaning. Christianity does clear and strengthen the human judgment, and furnish it with certain great truths to guide it in its investigation, but it does not render it infallible. The dogma of human infallibility in the Church is a wicked invention and a withering bane. The clergy who claim it grow into heartless tyrants; the laity who bow to it become bondsmen and serfs. The BRETHREN made this mistake.

But while the incident suggests that Christianity DOES NOT these things, it also suggests on the POSITIVE side:

I. THAT IT ENLISTS CHRIST'S INTEREST IN THE HISTORY OF HIS DISCIPLES. What an interest did Christ display in the history of his disciples, both before and after his resurrection! He ever sought to impress upon their minds that there was the closest spiritual relationship subsisting between them and him, that he was vitally identified with them. He calls them his brethren, and teaches that kindness shown to them he regards as shown to him. And what an interest did he show now in foretelling the events of Peter's life, and preparing him to meet them! No truth in the New Testament is more manifest than this, that Christ feels the greatest interest in his disciples. His conversation with them the night on which he was betrayed shows how deeply his heart was with them. *Is not this something?* Is it nothing to enlist the interest of the Governor of the universe in our history?

First. *Having his interest, you have the interest of one who knows the whole of the present, past, and future of your inner and outer life.* He knows everything which is *now* connected with your being and circumstances, all that ever *has* been, and all that ever *will* be. He sees you now as you will be in some other world ten thousand years to come.

Secondly. *Having his interest, you have the interest of*

one who has ample power so to control the events of the outward life, and supply the aspirations of the inward, as to crown your existence with perfect blessedness. "He is able to do exceeding abundantly." If Christianity gives us the interest of such a being as this, is it not an infinite boon? What thought can be more soul-inspiring and uplifting than this, that He "who formed the earth by his power, and garnished the heavens with his understanding," has his heart on me?

II. The incident suggests that it brings glory to God in the death of its disciples: "This spake he, signifying by what death he should glorify God." Ecclesiastical history testifies that Peter suffered martyrdom by crucifixion at Rome in the reign of the Emperor Nero, probably in the year 65. It is added that this death and the torture connected with it were endured by the venerable apostle with marvelous patience and fortitude; and that, deeming himself unworthy to die in precisely the same manner and posture as his Lord, he asked and obtained permission to be crucified with the head downward, a posture which could not fail greatly to aggravate the tortures of the cross.

But how does the death of a true disciple of Christianity glorify God?

First. *It illustrates the mercy of God.* Visit the deathbed of a genuine disciple of Christ; mark the unruffled calmness, the gratitude, the resignation, and sometimes the triumphant rapture which are displayed in the midst of physical anguish the most poignant. What are the attributes in such circumstances but glorious illustrations of divine mercy? It is mercy that thus raises and sustains the spirit amid the mysterious sufferings of dissolution.

Secondly. *It illustrates the fidelity of God.* He has promised to be with his people in the last hour; and when you see all this heavenly composure and triumph you feel that he is as good as his word, for he is there. Now is this nothing? To glorify God, to illustrate his perfections, is the end of creation, the generic duty of all intelligent beings, the supreme aim of the holy in all worlds. Is it nothing for Christianity to enable poor, depraved, guilty man to do this even in the agonies of death, to do in death that which is the highest aim of the highest seraph?

III. THIS INCIDENT SUGGESTS THAT IT GIVES A DEFINITE UNITY AND ATTRACTION TO ALL THE DUTIES OF ITS DISCIPLES. What theories of human duty ethical sages have propounded! How voluminous is the code of human laws! But Christianity reduces all duties to these words: "FOLLOW THOU ME;" "to cherish my spirit, tread in my footsteps, copy my attributes, constitute the totality of human duty and the perfection of the human character." Christianity gives you duty, not in dry propositions, but in fascinating life; not in the life of an angel, but in the life of a man. In Jesus Christ we see it in the most *perfect*, the most *attractive*, and the most *practicable* forms. Is this nothing? Is it nothing to have all our moral problems solved, to be freed from cumbrous codes and endless speculations, to have "the whole duty of man" thus brought to us in the life of a man?

HOMILY LV.

THE CONQUEST OF SELF THE GREATEST VICTORY.

He that ruleth his own spirit is greater than he that taketh a city.
PROVERBS xvi, 32.

THERE is a great disposition among men to *hero*-worship. Not only the history of the past, but the history of modern times indicates that the *ideal* of heroism is military bravery. Men who have returned from the field of battle have been laden with honors and welcomed with the highest ardor and enthusiasm; but those who have for many years been sustaining a deadly struggle with ignorance and vice in the dark retreats of our large towns have been left to pursue their great battle unnoticed and unknown.

Now, while admiring in some respects the heroism that has shed its blood for home and country, we learn from this passage that there is a higher order of heroism than that which is based upon military distinction; there is a nobler courage than that which can encounter physical danger; there is a grander warfare than that of arms.

1. This conquest of self implies that there is a *ruling power* implanted in man, by which he was intended to govern his own spirit. This is reason, conscience, etc. 2. It implies that *the spirit of man is in a state of anarchy*, that it will not be ruled; that there are certain insurrectionary forces which rise up in rebellion against this ruling power. "There is a law in the members warring against the law of

the mind." 3. It implies *that personal religion is self-subjugation.* By the influence of grace bestowed through Jesus Christ man is enabled to rule himself. The passions are subdued, the revolt in man's nature is quelled, reason and conscience are reinstated in their throne, harmony and order are established. The passions, which once governed with an iron sway, now *obey;* reason, which once was a slave, resumes her rightful authority. Thus the Christian is a *king* as well as a priest. He is made "*more* than a *conqueror*."

I. THE CONQUEST OF THE HEART IS GREATER THAN THAT OF A CITY, BECAUSE THE ENEMY IS MORE POWERFUL. (1.) To rule the spirit is to overcome the strongest impulses of our nature, which were intended to be servants, but have usurped the position of *masters.* These are ambition, avarice, pride, the love of distinction, the thirst for power and fame, the desire for sensual indulgence, the spirit of emulation, rivalry, or retaliation, etc. These have usurped the throne of dominion in man's nature. They have ruled the intellect, the conscience, and the life; yea, they have been the sovereigns of the world in every age. (2.) This foe is strengthened by habit. Our perverse tendencies, by repeated indulgence, become deeply rooted habits. Habits are chronic diseases of the *mind.* They can be removed only by a painful kind of moral amputation. The right eye must be plucked out, the right hand cut off. What a foe to conquer is habit! Reason may protest, conscience may reproach and condemn, the spirit may groan beneath its power; but there it sits, bidding defiance to our best energies. (3.) This foe is strengthened by prejudice. When a sinful heart is arraigned before the bar of conscience it calls in great pleaders for its defense. It justifies its sin by appealing to antiquity, to great names, to the custom, fashion, and social usages, etc. (4.) This foe is reinforced by self-interest. The most serious questions are viewed only in the light of the shop window; the most weighty concerns are attended to only as they affect our secular interests. The solemn obligations of religion are considered when there is nothing to do, when it will involve no sacrifice of ease and comfort, when Christianity doffs the garb of the fisherman, is clothed in purple and fine linen, and becomes a mere conventional usage or an element of respectability. "I have bought a piece of ground, and I must needs go and see it. I pray thee have me excused." (5.) This foe is backed by the spirit of the world, by popular opinion, by social usages and customs, and by the agency of Satan. This foe, thus sustained, is like an enemy in ambush, watching its opportunity to betray and ensnare. How very few conquer compared with the hosts that are enslaved!

II. The conquest of the heart is greater than that of a city because the conflict is more difficult. (1.) The city may be taken by *force*. Not so the heart. No array of force can coerce man's *will*, or remove one error. Truth and argument alone can do this. God himself will not coerce the mind to love. He appeals to us by the force of truth and the tenderness of love. "Come now, let us reason together." Force has often been tried; but the history of the rack, the stake, and the dungeon proves that man's spirit is far beyond the reach of such agencies, and can be influenced only by motives. (2.) The city may be taken by skill or science. Not so the heart. Here the profoundest accomplishments and the richest stores of knowledge are of little avail; science may bring the elements of nature into subjection; it may tame the ferocious beasts of the forest; it may harness the winds and make the lightning our messenger; but it cannot subdue the heart. There may be the highest intelligence in the lowest homes of corruption; genius and animalism may coexist in the same breast; the lamp of poetry may sometimes shine in the very *sepulcher* of *spiritual death;* learning has oft rendered a corrupt heart only more deadly and destructive in its influence. (3.) Applause and emulation will impel men in taking a city, but there is neither for the conquest of the heart. In *this* silent struggle there is no admiring multitude looking on. There are no martial strains, no banners floating o'er armed towers, no glittering ranks, no battle shout to inspire the solitary combatant with courage. For him there are no stars and wreaths. No poet's song extols, no ardent voices applaud the bravery of him who has conquered himself. (4.) The prospect of worldly distinction will animate him who takes the city, but not the conqueror of the heart. He can expect no earthly distinction; his name is not enrolled among the world's heroes. No page, no monument records his triumph. Time was when those noble conquerors, who, through faith, subdued kingdoms, stopped the mouths of lions, quenched the violence of fire, waxed valiant in fight, and turned to flight the armies of the aliens, had trial of cruel mockings and scourgings, of bonds and imprisonment. "They were stoned, sawn asunder, tempted, were slain with the sword," etc. Even now the man who conquers himself has sometimes to bear the look of pity and the charge of fanaticism. The pentecostal inspiration was ascribed to "new wine;" Paul was pronounced "mad," and Christ was deemed at one time by his relatives a fanatic.

III. THE CONQUEST OF THE HEART IS GREATER THAN THAT OF A CITY, BECAUSE THE VICTORY IS MORE NOBLE. (1.) The conquest of the city *develops* the worst principles and feelings, that of the heart *subdues* them. In the former there is the lust of power, the pride of victory. There are also the humiliation of defeat, the bitterness of disappointment and subjection, truth suppressed, hatred and revenge. In the latter there are peace and joy; the happiness of having trampled down all unbelief and pride; the ennobling influence of purity, benevolence, and hope. It is the joy of nature, when the tempest passes, leaving a brighter sky, a more balmy air, and a soil refreshed. It is the joy of the bondsman, when just liberated from his chains, tasting the delights of freedom. (2.) The conquest of a city is a scene of sorrow and desolation; the conquest of the heart is a *source of blessedness.* The former is a spectacle of horror. Homes and temples are enveloped in flames; the peaceful streets, where only sounds of industry were heard, are filled with slaughter and blood, with the cries of the wounded, and the groans of the dying; the gorgeous palace is pillaged; the treasures of the great are plundered, and every age, sex, and rank are plunged into indiscriminate massacre and ruin.

But he who conquers his own heart becomes a center of influence for good. He makes the widow's heart to sing for joy. He secures the blessings of them that were ready to perish. He weeps for them that weep. He cheers the disconsolate, counsels the wandering, ministers to the indigent, and lightens the burdens of the oppressed. That heart becomes a well of water, sending forth streams to invigorate the fainting spirits around. (3.) The conquest of the heart introduces a reign of freedom; that of the city may only enthrone a tyrant. Man is in a state of bondage. Christianity comes to set him free! "If the Son make you free, ye shall be free indeed." (4.) The conquest of the heart is associated with the highest dignity; the taking of the city with the deepest brutality and degradation. Ah! how many have taken cities who have never conquered themselves! They could control and discipline armed legions, but were powerless *within*. They gave laws to provinces and states, yet were slaves at home. Beneath that breast, decorated with many stars, was a heart that bade defiance to the voice that made a continent tremble. Conquer yourselves, and you will do more than Washington, Napoleon, and Wellington ever did.

IV. THE CONQUEST OF THE HEART IS GREATER THAN THAT OF A CITY, BECAUSE THE PRIZE IS MORE GLORIOUS. (1.) Their spoil. The one gains a city, the other wins heaven—the soul's immortality—with all the honors and distinctions of the redeemed state. (2.) Their applause. The one secures the fickle applause of the multitude, embittered, too, by much detraction and envy; the other wins the applause of angels and the redeemed Church, with the public approval of the great King. "Well done, good and faithful servant," etc. (3.) The memorial of their conquests. The one will perish. The noble city will crumble away; the bronze of the marble statue will fall; the glory of conquest will die; the proudest exploits of the "brave" shall be forgotten; but he who conquers himself will never want a memorial to record his triumph; for the heart, subdued and won, will by God's Spirit be raised from its ruins into a new creation, more glorious than the old one, over which the morning stars shall sing again, and the sons of God shall shout for joy. That depraved heart, now wrought into a spiritual temple, will be an imperishable monument of the Christian's victory. While the company of warriors bear the palm, and sing the song of victory in heaven, they ascribe all their honors and glories to Him who made them kings and priests unto God, and washed them from their sins in his own blood. (4.) The fame of the one will perish, the influence of the other will live. Piety gives to its possessor a twofold immortality. His spirit inherits the blessedness of heaven. His influence *survives* his dissolution, and may go down to many generations. The Pharaohs have perished, but Moses still lives. Ahab, with his courtly magnificence, is gone; Elijah has survived him, though a poor man. Babylon, with its monarchs, its temples, its palaces, and monuments, has departed. Daniel still remains. Piety thus invests the humblest men with a dignity and power which may survive the downfall of the proudest empires, and the noblest monuments of time! Ah! the time will come when mind will be deemed more important than matter; when holy thought and virtues will be estimated a higher wealth than acres; when the man who conquers a vice, explodes a fashionable error, or demolishes a debasing system, will be deemed a nobler warrior than the man who takes a city.

We learn from this,

First, *That moral courage is higher than physical.* Peter could smite off the ear of the high priest's servant, but he had not the moral courage to confess his Master to the Jewish maiden. Many are there that walk up to the cannon's mouth, who would be afraid to espouse a Gospel truth that was unpopular, or abandon an error that was very fashionable.

Secondly. *This conflict we must all wage.* We cannot reach heaven with hearts unsubdued; and this can be accomplished only by repeated earnest struggles. Our piety will conquer our sin, or our sin will overcome our piety. The spiritual and the animal, the heavenly and the earthly, cannot dwell in our breasts together.

Thirdly. *Defeat in this conflict is as disastrous as victory is glorious.* Though this victory can be achieved only by the help of God's Spirit, this does not supersede any exertion of our own. We are called to work because God worketh within us. Let us gird on the armor as brave soldiers arrayed in the noblest struggle; remembering that we have Omnipotence for our helper, and a crown of righteousness for our prize, which the Lord, the righteous judge, will give us at that day.

HOMILY LVI.

MAN.

And the people served the Lord all the days of Joshua, etc.
JUDGES ii, 6–10.

THIS fragment of ancient history gives us several facts concerning our race:

I. THE MORAL OBLIGATION OF EVERY MEMBER OF OUR RACE. "The people served the Lord all the days of Joshua." The whole obligation of man may be summed up in one sentence: "*Serve the Lord.*" All creatures are the servants of God, but they serve him in different ways. (1.) Some *without* a will. Inanimate matter and insentient life do so. (2.) Some *with* their will. Brutes do this: they act with their instinct. (3.) Some *against* their will. Wicked men and fallen angels. (4.) Some *by* their will. Saints and angels. To serve him in this way is the obligation of the race. But there is one condition indispensable to this, and that is, SUPREME LOVE FOR HIM AS THE SOVEREIGN. This will do two things: First. *Induce man to attain an understanding of his law.* Secondly. *Prompt him cheerfully to obey it.*

II. THE SERVICE OF ONE GOOD MAN TO OUR RACE. "The people served the Lord all the days of Joshua;" but after his death came the degeneracy. The incident before us suggests three things: First. *That a man can induce his race to serve the Lord.* Joshua did so. Secondly. *That a man, to do this, must himself be a servant of the Lord.* Joshua was so. Thirdly. *That however useful a man may be to his race in this respect, he must die.* Joshua died. He "died, being a hundred and ten years old. And they buried him," etc.

III. THE MELANCHOLY SUCCESSION OF OUR RACE. "And also all that generation were gathered unto their fathers: and there arose another generation," etc. The races in the vegetable kingdom have a succession; the races in the brute creation have a succession; but the succession of our race differs from both in two respects: First. *The succession involves no extinction.* When a generation of trees die, they are gone for ever; when a generation of brutes depart, they are gone for ever. Not so with man: he passes from this world to live in another. The mighty generations that are gone live on some other shore. Secondly. *The mode of the succession involves a moral cause.* We say the *mode*, not the *fact.* If the race continue to multiply as now, the limitation of the world's area and provisions would require a succession. This planet was probably intended as a stepping-stone to another. Had there been no sin, however, instead of the succession taking place *through the grave*, it might have been through a "chariot of fire," as in the case of Elijah.

IV. THE DEGENERATING TENDENCY OF OUR RACE. "And there arose another generation after them, which knew not the Lord." History has many examples of this tendency.

David, Peter, etc. Every man's experience proves it. "Our souls cleave to the dust." First. *This degenerating tendency is often found stronger than the most elevating influences of truth.* This generation fell, though the good influence of their ancestors had come down upon them. Peter fell in the very presence of Christ. Secondly. *This degenerating tendency indicates the necessity of a conscious reliance upon the gracious help of God.* "Hold thou us up," etc.

HOMILY LVII.

GOD AND HIS UNIVERSE.

And it shall come to pass in that day, I will hear, saith the Lord, I will hear the heavens, and they shall hear the earth; and the earth shall hear the corn, and the wine, and the oil; and they shall hear Jezreel. And I will sow her unto me in the earth; and I will have mercy upon her that had not obtained mercy; and I will say to them which were not my people, Thou art my people; and they shall say, Thou art my God. HOSEA ii, 21–23.

THE prophecies of this book are so thickly enveloped in figure as to make the interpretation of some passages difficult. We learn, however, that they were addressed to the ten tribes; and under highly figurative representations, they disclose the crimes which Israel had committed, the judgments to which it was exposed, and the mercy which it might still obtain by returning to the one true and living God. The word Jezreel literally means "seed of God;" and taking it in its etymological sense, we shall regard it as designating the children of God, in every age and land.

I. THAT THE OPERATIONS OF THE UNIVERSE ARE UNDER THE INTELLIGENT DIRECTION OF THE GREAT GOD. The universe is here represented as in action: "The heavens," "the earth," "the corn," "the wine," and "Jezreel," all acting. There is nothing stationary; all things are full of labor. Creation is like a flowing river: there is not a particle at rest, and all move simultaneously toward the boundless.

Now, it is our happiness to know that all these operations are presided over by an Infinite Intelligence. The universe is not a self-acting machine, left to work itself out. The great Machinist is ever with it, observing and directing every motion. Read the hundred and fourth psalm. The fact that God presides over all the operations of the universe serves several important purposes. (1.) To account for the unbroken order of nature. Why is it that the ocean does not overflow it boundaries? Why is it that those massive globes above, which move with such terrible celerity, swerve not from their orbits, and come not in collision? etc. Deny the superintendence of an omnipotent Being, and it is unaccountable. (2.) To impress us with the sanctity of nature. He is in all: the brightness of the light, the beauty of the lovely, the majesty of the grand, the support of the feeble, the might of the strong. No temple more holy than nature. (3.) It serves to inspire us with reverence toward his greatness. "How great must he be?" etc.

II. THAT THE OPERATIONS OF THE UNIVERSE ARE GENERALLY CONDUCTED UPON THE MEDIATORY PRINCIPLE. "I will hear the heavens," etc. One part of the universe is here represented as acting upon another, in order to produce, under God, a given result. In the material, as well as in the spiritual world, God works out his plans by *secondary* instrumentalities. Let us look at this mediatory principle in its relation to man. (1.) In relation to him as a *material* being. How did we *receive* these corporeal frames? Not directly. They are the results of instrumentalities that have been at work for six thousand years. How is this corporeal frame *sustained?* Not as the Israelites were sustained in the wilderness, by miracles. There are agencies employed. How are they *broken up?* Not generally by a direct stroke from God. No! There are causes. Look at the principle (2.) in relation to him as a *spiritual* being. How does knowledge come to man? He has teachers. How, as a sinner, is he pardoned? "Be it known unto you, men and brethren, that though this man," etc. How is he converted? God does not call him now as he did Abraham. There are ministers, etc.

III. That the operations of the universe are mercifully subordinated to the interests of the good. "Jezreel," or the children of God, are here spoken of as receiving from God three things: (1.) The blessings they devoutly sought. Jezreel prayed; and all nature is represented as conveying its prayers to God. The universe labors for the man that truly prays. Prayer is answered not by miracle. (2.) The multiplication of their number. "I will say to them which were not my people," etc. The strongest desire of the truly good man is to make others good. This is here promised. The universe is working for this. Why kept up? To multiply the good. (3.) The heightening of the sympathy between them and their God. "I will call them my people," etc. What privilege this! What is the moral end of all the workings of this wonderful universe. To multiply the good, and to heighten the sympathy between them and their Maker.

HOMILY LVIII.

DAVID'S LAMENT OVER ABSALOM; OR, THE TEARS OF PARENTAL LOVE.

And the king was much moved, and went up to the chamber over the gate, and wept: and as he went, thus he said, O my son Absalom! my son, my son Absalom! would God I had died for thee, O Absalom, my son, my son! 2 SAMUEL xviii, 33.

THIS lamentation of David shows two things:

I. THE FORCE OF PARENTAL LOVE. What ever could have induced David to have mourned the death of such a son as this? All might have expected, that day, that the news would have fallen as music on his ears. There are two circumstances which might have induced men to have expected this:

First. *The corrupt character of Absalom.* In the short, strange life of Absalom, we discover several most depraved and morally repulsive attributes of character. There is *revenge* (see chap. xiii, 28, 29); there is *vanity* (see chap. xv, 1); there is *ambition* (chap. xv, 4); there is *meanness* (chap. xv, 5); *hypocrisy* (chap. xv, 7, 8.) There is a tendency in such attributes as these to destroy all love for their possessor. Depravity in a wife is adapted to quench the love of a husband; depravity in a monarch is adapted to quench the love of his people; depravity in a son is adapted to destroy the love of the father.. Yet David's love was too strong for this; it clung to the monster.

Secondly. *The filial rebellion of Absalom.* He was not only corrupt in his character, but he was a malignant opponent to his father, the man whom he ought to have loved and obeyed. He had pledged himself to his father's ruin. His last purpose was a purpose to deprive his sire of his throne, his happiness, his life. David had no greater enemy in Israel than Absalom. One might therefore well have thought that the news of his death would have awakened joy rather than grief. But not so. So strong is parental love.

II. The bitterness of parental love. What bitterness is in this cry: "O Absalom, my son!" etc. Two things would give bitterness to David's feelings now:

First. *The memory of his own domestic sins.* David was a great poet, warrior, and king; but as the head of a family there was much in his conduct to loathe and to deprecate. The carnality, the favoritism, the false tenderness, the want of thorough discipline which he displayed in his own family, were in themselves heinous vices and prolific sources of domestic misery. At this moment, perhaps, the memory of his domestic sins terrified him. He might have thought, O Absalom! had I done my duty by thee in my own family, had I trained thee rightly, had I given thee a good example, such might not have been thine end. I blame myself, etc. Another thing which would give bitterness to David's grief over Absalom now would be,

Secondly, *His fear as to his future state.* O where is my son Absalom? I have no hope that such a character can have entered the holy heavens; and O can it be that he is lost? Can it be that my son is added to the number of the accursed? From this subject we learn: (1.) That good men may have most wicked children. Goodness is not hereditary. (2.) These good men may, nevertheless, be responsible for the wickedness of their children. Home may be neglected, etc. (3.) That good men who neglect their children will one day, most likely, have to repent their conduct, etc.

HOMILY LIX.

THE TWOFOLD FUNCTION OF PERSONAL CHRISTIANITY.

For if we have been planted together in the likeness of his death, we shall be also in the likeness of his resurrection; knowing this, that our old man is crucified with him, that the body of sin might be destroyed, that henceforth we should not serve sin. ROMANS vi, 5, 6.

"FOR if we become kindred with him by death like unto his, then we shall also be kindred with him by a resurrection; for we know this, that our old man is crucified as he was, that the body of sin might be destroyed, in order that we should no longer serve sin." Such is Stuart's rendering, and it certainly makes the apostle's idea more clear than it appears in our own version. The subject of these words is *the twofold function of personal Christianity.* It has a crucifying and a resurrection work.

I. THE CRUCIFYING FUNCTION OF PERSONAL CHRISTIANITY. When Christianity enters a man it crucifies a something in him; and what? (1.) Not any of his native faculties or sensibilities. It energizes, refines, and develops these. (2.) Not any of the ties of his moral obligations. Christianity does not remove man from under the law; it neither annuls nor relaxes his moral obligations. On the contrary it gives a stronger revelation of duty and mightier motives to obey. What then does Christianity *crucify.* "The old man." By "the old man" he means the *corrupt character.* Why does he call this corrupt character "the old man?" Not because it is the original character of *humanity.* This is not true. The first character of humanity was a *holy* one. But because it is the first character of *individual* men. Account for it as you will, the *first* character which every *individual* man possesses is a depraved one. Hence the depraved character is "the old man." It is this "old man," with its "corruptions and lusts," with its perverted views, affections, and principles, that Christianity crucifies. The fact that the apostle compares the process of destroying "this old man" to the crucifixion of Christ, suggests three thoughts: First. *That it is a painful process.* The death of crucifixion was one of the most excruciating that the cruelty of the most malignant spirit could devise. To destroy old habits, gratifications, etc., is a painful work. It is as the cutting off a limb, the plucking out of an eye, etc. Secondly. *It is a protracted process.* No wound was inflicted upon the most vital part, that the agony might be perpetuated. The agonized life gradually, drop by drop, ebbed away. "The old man" cannot be killed at once. There is nothing so hard to die as sin. An atom may kill a giant, a word may break the peace of a nation, a spark burn up a city; but it requires earnest and protracted struggles to destroy sin in the soul. No man grows virtuous in a day. Thirdly. *It is a voluntary process.* The work is likened to the *crucifixion of Christ*, and his crucifixion was voluntary. The other malefactors could not avoid their doom. Christ could. He could have freed himself by a simple volition. He had power to lay down his life, etc. No one could have crucified him contrary to his own will. It is so with the crucifixion of "the old man." No one could do it for us. No one can do it either *without* our consent or *against* it. If "the old man" is to be crucified we must nail him to the cross.

II. THE RESURRECTION FUNCTION OF PERSONAL CHRISTIANITY. "We shall be also in the likeness of his resurrection." Two ideas are here suggested: First. *That the spiritual life of a Christian is a divinely produced life.* "None but God can raise the dead," etc: Secondly. *That the spiritual life of a Christian is glorious.* How glorious was the resurrection body of Christ! Rev. i, 13–18. "We shall be like him," etc.

The subject teaches us (1.) the *value* of evangelical religion, which is to destroy in man the bad, and the bad only, and to revive the good; (2.) the *test* of evangelical religion, which is dying unto sin and living unto holiness.

HOMILY LX.

DAVID AND GOLIATH: A TRUE SPIRIT, THE PLEDGE OF VICTORY IN THE BATTLE OF LIFE.

Then said David to the Philistine, Thou comest to me with a sword, and with a spear, and with a shield; but I come to thee in the name of the Lord of hosts, the God of the armies of Israel, whom thou hast defied. 1 SAMUEL xvii, 45.

WE may look at Goliath and David, as they figure in this strange fragment of history, as illustrating the forms, spirit, weapons, and destiny of the great moral antagonists of our world, *good* and *evil.*

First. *These two men give us a picture of the forms of good and evil.* Evil in our world is like Goliath, of gigantic stature, immense energy, and imposing aspect. It is a Colossus. Good in our world is like David in its appearance, small, weak, and insignificant; possessing nothing to which the world attaches the idea of strength or glory. So it appeared in Christ: "He was as a root out of a dry ground."

Secondly. *These two men give us a picture of the spirit of good and evil.* The spirit of evil, like that of Goliath, is proud, contemptuous, malignant. The spirit of good, like that of David, is that of humble trust and dependence upon God.

Thirdly. *These two men give us a picture of the weapons of good and evil.* Evil, like Goliath, has many and powerful weapons to fight its battles. Like Goliath it is full-armored. Armies and navies are on its side. The weapons of good are of the simplest kind; the sling and stone of David would symbolize them. "The weapons of our warfare," etc.

Fourthly. *These two men give us a picture of the ultimate destinies of good and evil.* Goliath, notwithstanding his great strength, proud vauntings, and mighty weapons, was slain, and his body given to the fowls of heaven and the beasts of the earth. So it will be with evil. Like the image in the monarch's vision, the little stone of truth shall shiver it into atoms. The end of truth will be like that of David, triumphant and progressive in honor and influence in the empire of God.

But the subject on which at present we would fasten attention is: *A true spirit the pledge of victory in the battle of life.* Life is a battle. Physical life is a battle against danger and disease; intellectual life is a battle against ignorance and error; moral life is a battle against selfishness and wrong. He who has not felt life to be a battle has not woke up as yet to the reality of existence. Now a true spirit alone will make us victorious in this battle.

From the passage we infer,

I. That a true spirit is superior to the greatest material strength of our foes. Goliath was perhaps a second Samson, endowed with almost supernatural physical energy. "He arose," says Matthew Henry, "and came and drew nigh, like a stalking mountain overlaid with brass and iron, to meet David." David was a stripling, possessing not a tithe of the energy that belonged to his antagonist;

and yet Goliath fell prostrate beneath the blow of this stripling. What was the cause of the victory? It was to be found in the spirit that animated the breast of David—the spirit of dependence upon God. "Thou comest to me with a sword, and with a spear," etc. Difficulties and oppositions are nothing to a man who has the true spirit in him. "He that hath faith as a grain of mustard seed," etc.

II. A TRUE SPIRIT IS SUPERIOR TO THE GREATEST SOCIAL PRESTIGE OF OUR FOES. Goliath had obtained great fame as a warrior. He was renowned not only through Philistia, but also through all Judea. The sound of his name, everywhere, would strike terror into the heart of his enemies and awaken courage in the bosom of his friends. *Prestige is a wonderful thing, a mighty power.* Give a man or an institution a prestige, and, however feeble and worthless it may be, people will be disposed to yield to its influence. Many institutions, governments, books, live not on the ground of their merits, but because of the prestige they have obtained. *But the true spirit will overcome this.* Goliath, with all his prestige, fell. Whatever may be the prestige of evil, the true spirit will overcome it. Idolatry, war, etc., have prestige, but they shall fall.

III. A TRUE SPIRIT IS SUPERIOR TO THE COMPLETEST ACCOUTERMENTS OF OUR FOES. Goliath was well armored, panoplied with all the accouterments of ancient warfare. His robust frame, with bones like granite and sinews like iron, was in every point thoroughly protected. David had no such armor, but only his simple sling and stone; yet

Goliath fell. Huge evil, in our world, is well armored, defended by armies, navies, governments, customs, learning, wealth; but a man with the true spirit will overcome it. "This is the victory that overcometh the world," etc.

IV. A TRUE SPIRIT IS SUPERIOR TO THE PROUDEST VAUNTINGS OF OUR FOES. How Goliath vaunted! "And when the Philistine looked about and saw David, he disdained him: for he was but a youth, and ruddy, and of a fair countenance," etc. Evil has ever been full of its vauntings. Its language to the good is, "Let us break their cords asunder." The world has the same spirit of disdain for the Church that Goliath developed toward David. It virtually says: "Who art thou that comest to us with such simple instrumentality as the preaching of the cross? Insignificant creature! What art thou in our presence? Dost thou vainly hope to put an end to our pleasures, our amusements, our engagements, our habits? to animate our literature, and control our government by thy spirit? Dost thou vainly expect to put down our idolatries, which long ages have rooted in the heart of humanity? our infidelities, which many of the most thoughtful of the race have philosophically defended? our pastimes and our gratifications, so dear to the heart of mankind? But the Church, inspired with the true spirit may reply to all this vaunting: "Thou comest to me with a sword, and with a spear," etc.

But *how* does this true spirit insure victory in the battles of life?

First. *It enables man to employ the best means.* It is

fanaticism that makes man regardless of means. Enlightened devotion is ever anxious to select the most fitting. Though it feels that all success is from God, it presumes on no supernatural help. It is devoutly self-reliant, that is, it relies upon its own energies, under the blessing of God. The means which David employed now, though very simple, were the *most adapted.* He evidently had his method of attack definitely settled. He knew that the only unprotected part of his antagonist was his forehead. That was the point to be attacked; and what so adapted as the sling and the stone! David could stand at a distance from his huge antagonist, could calmly take his aim, and make his calculations with that expertness which, as a shepherd, he had acquired in the use of the sling and the stone. He could hurl the pebble at the vulnerable spot. The whole instrumentality seems well adapted. No miracle was used, for no miracle was wanted. God's method of helping man is through the wise and right use of his own faculties; and the man of the true spirit learns this and acts accordingly.

Secondly. *It enables man to use the best means in the best way.* (1.) With undaunted courage. While under the well-armored breast of his giant foe there pulsated the emotions of fear, in the unprotected bosom of David there was nothing but a fearless daring. He could sing, "Because the Lord is on my side, I shall not fear what man can do unto me." Paul had this feeling: "None of these things move me," etc. Luther too. Confidence in God is evermore the foundation of true courage. (2.) It inspires the possessor with invincible determination. The man says, It *shall* be done. You may as well try to turn a planet from its course as to turn a true man from his purpose. Hence martyrdom, etc.

Thirdly. *It insures the aid of God in the best use of the best means.* Felt dependence upon God is the settled condition and guarantee of divine assistance in every work. The more we feel our need of him, the more he will help. "I come to thee," says David, "in the name of the Lord of hosts, the God of the armies of Israel, whom thou hast defied." This is the spirit, the spirit that takes hold upon the energy of God. Brothers, get this spirit! Great intellectual endowments, vast and varied attainments, material strength, wealth, fame, social influence: all are worthless in comparison with this spirit. They are a curse in the absence of this. The man who has this spirit feels himself superior to all outward difficulties. Mountains may be piled in his way, but they depress him not. He looks calmly at them, challenges them to impede his progress, and bids them to be gone. "Who art thou, O great mountain?" etc.

HOMILY LXI.

MAN'S NEED OF SEASONS OF DEVOUT SOLITUDE.

Arise, go forth into the plain, and I will there talk with thee.
EZEKIEL iii, 22.

UTTER abandonment of society, perpetual hermitage, this is far enough from our doctrine. We recognize man's need of society as well as solitude. Perpetual retirement might perhaps exclude much evil, but would exclude also much that might be turned to our advantage. Had we no force within us to modify, counteract, and even resist, the forces from without; were we like lumps of clay in the plastic hand of society, perpetual solitude would be our only safety. But this is not the case. We have faculties within, by which we can make the billowing tide of social forces a pathway to conduct us to our self-elected destination.

In truth, we cannot do without society. Shut us up from others, and our powers will remain dormant and undeveloped. Society is to our souls what soil and air, showers and sunbeams, are to the grain: the conditions of quickening and of growth. But even could we do without, we ought not to attempt it. The better a man is, the more public he should be. He should be out in the open fields, scattering the seeds of the kingdom; up the mountain height, catching the rays that stream from above, and throwing them upon the benighted millions below.

But while I hold not the principle of perpetual, I do that of periodical solitude. Never, perhaps, was there an age requiring the religious teacher both to practice and enforce the obligation and necessity of *seasons of devout solitude* with greater earnestness and constancy than the present. We live in exciting times. Voices from without are hourly calling us forth from our retirements, and urging us to take our part in the passing scene.

God's voice to Ezekiel is especially applicable to us: "Go forth into the plain;" retire a while from the din of the world, and in the impressive eloquence of silence "I will there talk with thee." The prophet did so, and he tells us that he had there the same manifestations as he had by the river Chebar. He says: "The heavens were opened, and I saw the visions of God."

I shall submit three arguments for *seasons of devout solitude:* I say with emphasis, *devout* solitude, for there is much undevout solitude, solitude for secular study, mere intellectual improvement and self-indulgence. The solitude I now advocate is a solitude to "talk" with God.

I. SEASONS OF DEVOUT SOLITUDE ARE NECESSARY IN ORDER TO FREE US FROM THE CORRUPTING INFLUENCE OF SOCIETY. There are many elements and powers in the social atmosphere most pernicious in their operations upon our moral sensibilities and character. We may specify a few of the baneful tendencies of society upon the soul:

First. *Society has a tendency to stir and strengthen the impulses of our animal nature.* Without referring to the *institutions* which abound among us for the purpose of giving edge to animal appetites and fire to animal passions, it must be admitted that the whole spirit and style of society in this age have this tendency. Society dresses and acts, even in its everyday walk and life, as if it had no higher mission than to please the senses and to wake the passions. Just so far as it succeeds in this we are injured. The rise of passion is the fall of principle; the energizing of appetite is the enervating of intellect; the indulgence of the senses is the bane of the soul.

Secondly. *Society has a tendency to produce habits of superficial thought.* Your man of society, who is ever out in social scenes, and has no hours of thoughtful retirement, may become a clever talker, but never a thoughtfully earnest man. The things that float on the surface will float through him. Society ever likes the echo of its own voice, and he who would become its favorite must sound, as much as possible, its own notes. Even in its religious assemblies it can scarcely tolerate the deeply thoughtful. The spicy anecdote, the volatile language, the feathery and the flippant, these are the popular wares. All this is bad. Nothing can benefit us but truth; and truth, to bless, must be looked upon in its broader and deeper aspects.

Thirdly. *Society has a tendency to destroy the sense of individual responsibleness.* The man who is ever out in society is likely to become so fused into the common mass of metal, that he will lose even the feeling of individuality. He will flow with the stream, and become a mere bubble, that will rise, glitter, and burst, according to the state of the general current. All this is an evil. A deep and ever-living sense of our personal responsibility, a vivid and practical realization that we stand *alone* before God, having duties which no other can discharge, sins for which no other can answer, interests which no other can promote, are essential to the origination and growth of virtue in the soul.

Fourthly. *Society has a tendency to promote a forgetfulness of God.* Men in the multitude forget God. His voice is lost in their chatterings, his claims are overlooked in their own projects and interests. In but few circles is he acknowledged, and in fewer still is he loved and regarded as the sweetest theme of conversation, and the greatest charm of fellowship.

Such are a few of the many baneful influences which impregnate the social atmosphere of this age. How are they to be counteracted? How are the impressions they make on us every day to be neutralized? I know of nothing that can do it, apart from *seasons of devout solitude.* Would you cool down into a healthy temperature the animal feeling which society may inflame? Withdraw to devout solitude. Alone with God, all the streams of thought that will well up from the depths of our spiritual nature about the interests of the soul, the solemnities of eternity, the glory of the Infinite, will put out the animal fires. Would you exercise all the empty and frivolous thoughts that society is powerful in evoking within you? Withdraw to devout solitude. Alone with God, such thoughts will pass away from the firmament of your soul like the mountain mists of morning at the approach of the sun. Would you rally and invigorate that sense of individual responsibility which society has a tendency to destroy? Withdraw to devout solitude. Alone with God, you will feel isolated, like a little island detached from all, and encompassed by the boundless. Would you strengthen that practical conviction of God's being and presence which society tends to obliterate? Withdraw to devout solitude, and you will feel that he is the all-in-all, "the Alpha and Omega, the first and the last."

Brother! acts of devout isolation, like those which Jesus wrought when he sent the multitude away in order to be alone with God on the mountain, we *must* attend to as the necessity of our spiritual existence. We must often bid the multitude to depart, or we shall be ruined. The lamp of piety will soon flicker and expire in the gusts of social influences, unless we retire to devout solitude for fresh oil to feed its waning fires. The social air is full of noise and thick with fog. Wouldst thou hear His voice thou must go, like Ezekiel, into the "plain" of solitude, and he will there talk to thee. His voice is only heard in silence. Wouldst thou see his moral beauty and be enchanted with it, thou must leave the foggy scenes of social life, retire into the sunny plain of devout solitude, and thou shalt, like Ezekiel, see "the visions of God."

II. Seasons of devout solitude are necessary in order personally to appropriate the good there is in society. There are good things in society as well as bad. There are good institutions, good books, good men. Great truths are pronounced, and noble deeds are wrought every day in this false and selfish world. We gratefully acknowledge the good we discover, we devoutly pray that it may grow on until, like the mountain in Belshazzar's vision, it fills this mundane sphere. But however much good there may be in society, you cannot make it good to *you* without devout solitude. The conversations of the noblest circles, the most renovating principles of the most Christlike discourses, the suggestions awakened by the most sacred and solemn scenes or services, will all prove worse than useless if their good effect is allowed to terminate with their first impressions. First impressions of a holy kind, if they are not cultured by devout reflection, will not only pass away as the early dew goes off in the sun, but will carry off with them something of the freshness and the sensibility of the heart—something that will render the spirit less susceptible to other good impressions.

There is a large class of persons who seem to act under the idea that by going to certain scenes of a religious character, now entering one place of worship and now another; now listening to this preacher and now to that, and always giving the preference to the most exciting, they will become in some mystic way moulded into a character that will obtain the approval of their Maker. Great delusion this. All the more pernicious because popular.

Souls are often represented as gardens for cultivation; but strange to say, they are gardens that must cultivate themselves. They must break up their own fallow ground and uproot their own weeds. We cannot be made good independently of ourselves. Put a human spirit into angelic circles, where it should see only virtue and hear only truth, all would be useless without its own devout reflection. A holy character is not a manufacture. No Church can make a saint. The Creator, I may suppose, put into the earth, at first, the seed of all the life that should ever grow or move on its surface. The germs of all the forests, gardens, and landscapes of all times were embedded, mayhap, in its soil. But there they would have remained dormant for ever unless the earth had periodically turned its face to the sun. It is so with the soul. There are seeds of truth in the mind; some, perhaps, inbred, and more imparted; but these germs will remain dead forever unless the soul is brought periodically into conscious contact with God, the central sun of truth.

In devout solitude, and nowhere else, can the faculty of discrimination rightly do its work. Here the mind has its "senses exercised to discern good and evil." The two opposite elements, alas! are so mixed together here, so compounded, that a rigid and searching discrimination is required to separate the chaff from the wheat, the dross from the gold. In the presence of God evil and good dissolve their connection, and appear in their own distinct essences. The night is divided from the day. Now without this discrimination there can be no true appropriation. In devout solitude, therefore, I can turn the universe to my service; aye, even make enemies serve my purpose. As the bee turns the bitterest herb to sweetness, so the soul in devout solitude can turn the worst things to the best account. The pious man can summon his greatest foes into his presence in his chamber, and make them minister to his spiritual service. From them he can draw lessons that shall enlighten his intellect and strengthen his heart. He can turn the insult that wounded him into a power to weaken his confidence in man, and confirm his faith in God.

III. Seasons of devout solitude are necessary in order to qualify us to benefit society. We cannot live to ourselves if we would. By a necessity of our nature we must influence others for good or ill. We are fountains that send out streams that flow in all directions, and that will never be dried up. Nature and the Bible teach that our bounden duty is to "serve our generation," to endeavor to improve the condition of the race.

How shall we become qualified to do so? This is the

question now. Three things seem indispensable, and these are dependent upon devout solitude.

First. *Self-formed conviction of Gospel truth.* Gospel truth is our great instrument of social usefulness; that without which nothing else will be of any service. It is "the power of God unto salvation." But how is this to be wielded? By circulating copies of the Scriptures, or by a mere recitation of their contents, or by repeating what other people have said or written concerning those truths? All these may be, and are useful in their way. But there is one thing indispensable even to do these things effectively, and that is, *self-formed convictions.* Heaven has so far honored our nature, that the Gospel, in order to obtain its grand victories, must pass as living beliefs through the soul of him that employs it. If we would effectually use the Gospel to help society we must see, taste, and handle it with our *own* souls. The men who speak the Gospel without such convictions can never enrich the world. But he who speaks *what* he believes, and *because* he believes, speaks in some sense a new thing to the race. The doctrine comes from him instinct and warm with life. His individuality is impressed upon it. The world never had it in that exact form before, and never would have had it so had he not believed and spoken.

Now, devout solitude is necessary to turn the Gospel that is in the Bible into this power of living conviction; you can never get it elsewhere. Alone with God you can search the Gospel to its foundation, and feel the congruity of its doctrines with your reason, its claims with your conscience, its provisions with your wants.

Secondly. *Unconquerable love for Gospel truth.* There is an immense practical opposition to Gospel truth in society. Men's pride, prejudices, pleasures, pursuits, and temporal interests are now, as ever, against it. It follows, therefore, that those who think more of the favor and applause of society than of the claims of truth, will not deal with it honestly, earnestly, and therefore successfully. The man only who loves truth more than popularity, fortune, or even life, can so use it as really and lastingly to benefit mankind. In devout solitude you can cultivate this invincible attachment to truth, and be made to feel with Paul, who said, "I count all things but loss for the excellency of the knowledge of Christ."

Thirdly. *A living expression of Gospel truth.* We must be "living epistles." Our conduct must confirm and illumine the doctrines which our lips declare. Gospel sermons which are the expressions of life, are life-giving. Gospel truth must be embodied; the word must become flesh; it must be drawn out "in living characters" in all the phases of our every-day existence; its spirit must be our inspiration if we would make it instrumental for good. Sermons which are the expressions of a Gospel life, a life of Christlike philanthropy and devotion, are the only sermons of any service to the universe. Verbal sermons, expressions of a little invention and sentiment, are common enough among us; what we want is life sermons, expressions of a whole Christianized existence. "The intelligence," says Carlyle somewhere, "that can with full satisfaction to itself come out in eloquent speaking, in musical singing, is after all a small intelligence. He that works and does some poem, not he that *says* one, is worthy of the name of poet." Even so. He that works and does some sermon, not he that *says* one, is worthy of the name of preacher. Now for the production of such sermons I am convinced there must be seasons of devout solitude; hours when, under the silent sunbeams of eternity, ideas run into emotions, circulate as a vital torrent through every vein of the soul, and form the very *stamina* of our being. It is said of Moses "that the skin of his face shone while he talked with God." But in seasons of devout solitude our whole nature may grow luminous, and every phase of our character coruscate with "the deep things of the Spirit."

Brothers, let us imitate Christ in his isolating acts; let us often "send the multitude away," and climb the mountains of solitude, there in the depths of silence to commune with the spiritual and infinite. Thus we shall get strong for our work. John the Baptist gained his invincible energy in the lonely wilderness. Paul grew to an apostle in the quiet of Arabia, and it was in the awful midnight solitude of Gethsemane that an angel from heaven came to strengthen Jesus for his work. It is beneath the earth's green mantle, in secret and silence among the roots, that the trees of the forest turn the elements of nature to their own advantage. And it is down in the quiet deeps of spiritual realities, alone with God, that the soul only can turn this world to its use.

HOMILY LXII.

THE IMPOSSIBLE SERVICE A MOTIVE TO RELIGIOUS DECISION.

Ye cannot serve God and mammon. MATTHEW vi, 24.

LIGHT and darkness, holiness and sin, God and mammon, these are *eternal opposites.* Such is the plain meaning of our Saviour's words. "*Ye cannot.*" This implies the fact that many attempt to do so.

Naturally man does *not* attempt to "serve God and mammon." He makes no effort in the matter. He yields simply to his own inclination. He serves mammon. "God is not in all his thoughts." He is of one mind, and seeks one object, the gratification of self. Sin is sweet, the world is sweet, self is sweet. He has not a wish, nor will he make an effort to change masters.

Awful spectacle! A man contented to serve the prince of this world; a man contented to live without loving, fearing, or serving God; a man contented to live without prayer, without any communion with God, without any hope beyond the grave! Poverty is an evil; sickness we shrink from; but the *soul* without God, without any desire after God, is a *lost* soul. And who shall estimate the terrible meaning of that word *lost?* Jesus Christ, who came to seek and to save "the lost;" Jesus Christ, who came to redeem the ungodly and make them godly; Jesus Christ, who "bore our sins in his own body on the tree," must tell us what it *cost* to redeem our souls before we can estimate their value. He has left us this question to ponder: "What shall it profit a man if he gain the whole world and lose his own soul?"

Such a question, *thoughtfully* pondered, may, under God's blessing, excite within the minds of some careless ones the resolution to renounce the service of mammon in order henceforth to serve God. It is a movement God's Spirit prompts, when the lost soul anxiously asks, "Who will show me any good?" This is the preparation of heart indispensable to the right and profitable understanding of our Lord's words: "Ye cannot serve God and mammon."

The faithful warning was designed to act as a *powerful motive to religious decision*—to the avowal of discipleship, real, not nominal—experimental, not professional.

To every one who is *anxious* after God, to every man whose conscience is at work, to every man who is hesitating, really hesitating between the service of God and the slavery of Satan, sin, and self, Jesus Christ saith, "Ye cannot serve God and mammon."

Observe:

I. The necessity of religious decision. There are many persons who have been deeply concerned who have never *decided* for God. A decision is final. We *act* upon our decisions. To be undecided even in earthly matters, is most injurious to our interests and our comfort. "Unstable as water, thou shalt not excel." "A double-minded man is unstable in all his ways." Indecision is a foe to all peace of mind. An undecided state cannot be a happy state.

Peace and joy *are* the Christian's portion; but he must be a *decided* Christian to possess the portion. Where Satan cannot lull anxiety to repose, he strives to prevent decision. He urges a partial sacrifice, a half-hearted compact. He urges that it is needless to renounce either the world or religion. You may enjoy both. And he even misquotes Scripture for his purpose. "Godliness hath the promise of the life that now is, and of that which is to come." Quite true in one sense, quite false in another. The religious man *does* make "the best of both worlds," but it is not by serving God and mammon. Mark the word "*serve;*" it is the key which will open and expose the hollow sophistry of Satan. "Thou shalt worship the Lord thy God, and him *only* shalt thou *serve*." God claims the heart; a divided heart he cannot accept. There is a moral *impossibility* about it. God and Mammon are in direct opposition. You cannot yield at once to two forces that pull you different ways. You cannot give free scope to the affections and impulses of two natures which are contrary to one another, the "flesh" lusting against the "spirit." You cannot "crucify the flesh with its affections and lusts," and live for self, and pleasure, ambition, vanity, pride, and sensuality; you cannot "*set* your affections on things above" and on things on the earth, things that are only earthly. You cannot vibrate between God and mammon. You cannot faithfully serve both. "Halting between two opinions" God cannot approve: you hinder him from bestowing the full blessing. Even the *world* cannot approve. The trifling professor, the hesitating man, who is now seeking God and now seeking the good things of this world, (so called by those who "call evil good,") is the subject of ridicule not unmingled with contempt. The world admires consistency. Satan only is opposed to it. He and he only would persuade you that decision is unnecessary, that you *may* serve God and mammon! *Jesus Christ* saith, "Ye *cannot* serve God and mammon."

II. Religion is a reality and a service. It does not consist in forms and ceremonies. The lips do not proclaim the state of the heart. We may be in God's house serving Satan. "Solemn words on thoughtless tongues" are not the service of "our Father which seeth in secret!" It does not consist in opinions however orthodox, or zeal however fervent. Zeal may have many motives. Knowledge may be without charity. The service of God must be in spirit and in truth, the service of love! And love makes no reserve; love sacrifices everything, and counts it a happiness to do so.

Christ ever taught thus. On no occasion did he tamper with his hearers. He sought no nominal followers. His miracles, the novelty and authority of his teaching, often attracted many, but he would not retain them for the sake of numbers. "Ye seek me," he said once, "because ye did eat of the loaves and were filled:" "Ye would make religion subserve your worldly interests:" "Ye cannot serve God and mammon."

A master of Israel, a man of influence and learning, sought him by night. Human prudence might have induced a reservation of truth likely to offend; but Jesus Christ utters the faithful saying: "Except a man be born again he cannot see the kingdom of God." "Ye cannot serve God and mammon."

A young ruler, with true, though unenlightened zeal, professes discipleship. He is "not far from the kingdom of heaven." His amiability is lovely in the Saviour's eyes. He asks, "What lack I yet?" But instead of the approbation he looked for, the direction to persevere in his course of supposed righteousness, how stern, how unexpected is the warning! "One thing thou lackest; if thou wilt be perfect, go and sell that thou hast and give to the poor, and thou shalt have treasure in heaven." "Thou canst not serve God and mammon."

A candidate for discipleship professes, "Master, I will follow thee whithersoever thou goest." The answer from Him who could read the heart applied a test that detected the flaw in his decision. "The foxes have holes, and the birds of the air have nests, but the Son of man hath not where to lay his head." "Thou canst not serve God and mammon."

In all these cases Jesus seems to say: "If you decide to serve God you must remember it is to be a *real* service. Do not be deceived. Count well the cost. Lukewarmness will not do. 'If any man draw back, my soul hath no pleasure in him.' Let there be no misapprehension. Are you prepared to serve the Lord? *Why* will you serve him? Is it because you are constrained by the overwhelming force of his claims who has bought you? Are you truly convinced the advantages of his service outweigh those of mammon? Do the purity of heart, the poverty of spirit, the deadness to the world, the cross-bearing involved in the service of God, charm and win you? Are the terms not too austere? 'Take up your cross daily, forsake all and follow me?' Will you take God on his own terms? Is his service really your inclination? Can you honestly prefer God to mammon?"

Happy would it be for us if we all thus counted the cost before we undertook the service of God. Alas! how often, when a temptation comes, the professing Christian yields; when a cross is in his path he steps aside or murmurs at it. A worldly sacrifice is demanded by religious principle: it is refused, or unwillingly made. Much obedience, much profession, when it "costs us nothing;" but when Christ is "despised and rejected of men," when "the reproach of Christ" falls upon us, how prone to forsake him and flee!

"Wounded in the house of his friends," Jesus Christ would faithfully warn us against a half-hearted decision, a decision made without remembering that the way of God's service is a strait path, a cross, a denial of self, a "crucifixion of the flesh with its affections and lusts." "Ye cannot serve God and mammon." And now how does all this bear upon the case of the man who is earnestly concerned about his soul, the man who is "feeling after God if haply he may find him?" How is the *impossible service a motive to religious decision?*

Some might conceive *encouraging*, *approving words* more adapted to win anxious seekers. But Jesus Christ "knew what was in man," and he is not mistaken here. Those who are *not* anxious may not see the value of this faithful dealing with conscience; but those who *are* anxious will feel that it just meets their case. To them the warning will have a gracious aspect. They feel it is their *temptation* to try and serve God and mammon. And they wish to regard it *as a temptation*, in order that they may be delivered from it; and hence it is they can perceive the *close connection* between the warning and the precept which immediately follows: "Ye cannot serve God and mammon." "*Therefore*," giving up the vain attempt, place your unreserved trust and dependence upon God, and renounce not only the service of mammon, the covetous desires of the world, but the *anxieties and the fears* which must ever *attend* the service of mammon, which may even be a *delusive form of that service.* "*Therefore* take no thought," no disquieting, distrusting thought; "seek first the kingdom of God, and his righteousness, and all these things shall be added unto you." Matt. vi, 24. Thus Christ would guard his disciples, who feel their *inclination* to attempt to serve God and mammon is a *temptation*, against the *most dangerous form* this temptation can assume. Many who overcome the temptation of worldly pleasure yield to the temptation of worldly *care*. The Christian should yield to neither. He "cannot serve God and mammon."

Let there be then A CONSISTENT DECISION. Let there be a counting of the cost while forming that decision. Then the service of God will bring its own reward.

Those who serve mammon are serving a master whose wages is death; they are toiling in a field where they must reap corruption. Those who are *trying* to serve God and mammon are miserably deceiving themselves. They *cannot* make religion *easy to the flesh.* Christ's religion is "a crucifixion of the flesh." But those who in the faith of Christ yield themselves to the service of God, live in and through Christ a "new life," a new life of spiritual privilege. They bear uncomplainingly Christ's "easy yoke" and "light burden." The yoke is "easy" and the burden "light," because they bear them willingly, because they bear them "after Christ," and know that if they "suffer with him" they shall be also "glorified together."

"Ye cannot serve God and mammon." May the *impossible service* prove an effectual motive to *religious decision!* Happy is the man who does not *wish* to serve God and mammon, who is ever praying in the Spirit: "Quicken me, O Lord my God, and I will run the way of thy commandments."

HOMILY LXIII.

JOHN'S BURIAL, OR THE TRIALS OF HUMANITY.

And his disciples came, and took up the body, and buried it, and went and told Jesus. MATTHEW xiv, 12.

THERE are two things which strike us about the trial of the martyred Baptist and reformer which the disciples of John were now called upon to endure:

I. THAT IT MUST HAVE BEEN A VERY PAINFUL ONE. It must have been painful,

First, *To their affections as social beings.* Tender, numerous, and strong are the ties by which a thoroughly honest and enlightened religious teacher binds the hearts of his loving and docile disciples to himself. Such a teacher in fact, from his access to the arcana of the soul, and the constant influence of his spirit and ideas upon its most vital parts, roots to a great extent the mind of his pupils in himself. They live in him, they draw their spiritual nutriment from his great thoughts. Such pre-eminently, we presume, was the connection between the Baptist and his disciples. The fact that they followed him shows that they loved him; and if they loved *such a man* at all, their love must have been decided and strong. For John, like all great men, had those salient, bold, marked attributes of character which would evoke in the minds of those he affected at all no half-and-half emotions. For such men there are no apathetic or sentimental friends or foes; they are sure to have from society either intense hate or intense love; out and out censure and opposition, or out and out approval and co-operation. A moral reformer of John's type, intrepid in purpose, inflexible in principle, defiant but unostentatious in bearing, fiery in zeal, must ever reveal the hearts of men, and make society positive and intense in their feelings toward him. John therefore must, we conclude, have been ardently loved by his followers. Though one greater than their master came, even Jesus, of whom their master was but the harbinger, they still adhered to John. They fasted when he was in prison, and no doubt often prayed with many tears for his deliverance. What therefore must have been their grief now, as they looked upon, handled, bore to the grave the mutilated remains of their most beloved teacher and friend? They "took up the body, and buried it." But this trial,

Secondly, Was not only painful to their affections as social beings, but *to their faith as religious beings.* What questions concerning God and his government would this murder of John be likely to start in the minds of his bereaved disciples! Questions tending to shake the very foundation of their religious faith. Even John's imprisonment seems to have shaken his own faith! Though on the banks of the Jordan he had borne such a noble testimony to Christ when he said, "Behold the Lamb of God," etc., yet his incarceration led him to doubt as to whether he was the true Messiah or not. "When John heard in the prison the works of Christ, he sent two of his disciples and said unto him, Art thou he that should come, or do we look for another?" If John by his mere imprisonment was thus tried, it is natural to suppose that much more must have been the trial of the faith of his disciples at his cruel martyrdom. I can imagine them looking at the mutilated body of their beloved teacher, and asking themselves in utmost agony of heart, Can it be that there is a God who judgeth in the earth? If so, why does he allow the perpetration of such enormities? Is he ignorant of what is going on among mortals? Has he withdrawn all providence from this planet? If not, why does he permit such terribly iniquitous and bloody scenes to be enacted? Has he no controlling power over the purposes and doings of men? If so, why does he not thwart the designs of the wicked, and frustrate their infernal plans? Has he any interest in the progress of right and truth on this earth? Is it his desire that the true and the righteous shall triumph over the false and the wrong? If so, why does he allow the vilest to sit on thrones, and thus oppress and murder the good? Such questions would be natural, and such questions would tend to shake the foundations of that old religion which was the loved home and the glorious temple of their hearts.

The other point which strikes us about their trial is,

II. That although it was very painful, it was morally useful. After they had buried the body of John, laid him in some quiet grave, they "went and told Jesus." With hearts full of sorrow and anxiety they wisely and rightly went to "the Consolation of Israel." "They told Jesus." What? Not merely, we think, the painful incidents connected with John's martyrdom, but unbosomed to him their own sad feelings. They told him, we presume, what they thought and what they felt. This is a sight I should like to have witnessed; I should like to have seen those poor disconsolate men standing around the blessed Comforter, and unfolding their tale of woe. I should like also to have seen his sympathizing looks as he listened, and to have heard the soothing and balmy words that fell from his lips. Perhaps he wept with them. We may be certain that he pointed them to comforting truths, and to the ever-pitying Father of souls. We may suppose that he assured them of three things: (1.) That that mutilated body was not John; that their master was living in higher realms. (2.) That even that mutilated body should not be lost; that he would raise it up at "the last day;" and (3.) If they truly followed the teaching they had received they would meet their master again.

Inasmuch as this trial led them to Christ it was morally

useful. Whatever trials lead poor humanity to him are blessings in disguise. He is the center and Eden of the soul. If the destruction of property, the loss of health, the death of friends, lead us to him, all will be well. Would that little child, whose heart is full of glowing sorrow on account of having done something contrary to its mother's wish, obtain relief? let it go and tell its mother, unbosom its little heart, and confess its offense, and in the responsive love of the mother's genial look a calm sunshine will overspread its being. This is the divine principle of relief under trial. Weeping soul, go and tell Jesus.

HOMILY LXIV.

EMMAUS; OR, FELLOWSHIP WITH CHRIST.

And they drew nigh unto the village whither they went; and he made as though he would have gone further," etc. LUKE xxiv, 28–35.

CHRIST appeared no less than *ten* different times to his disciples after his resurrection. There are incidents and utterances connected with each appearance which would form interesting and profitable themes for discourse. Here we have his second appearance after his resurrection. We have selected just this one part of the incident that occurred, and the words uttered on the occasion, in order to illustrate some truths in relation to an ever important subject, namely, that of fellowship with Christ.

The fact that Christ has left the world, and is, perhaps, countless leagues distant from our planet, does not render our fellowship with him impossible. *Fellowship of souls does not consist in the proximity of persons.* There are millions who live in close personal contact, dwell under the same roof, board at the same table, and work in the same shop, between whose minds there is scarcely a point of contact, whose souls are as far asunder as the poles; while, contrariwise, there are those separated by oceans and continents, aye, by the mysterious gulf that divides time from eternity, between whom there is a constant intercourse, a delightful fellowship. In truth, we have often more communion with the distant than the near. There are four ways through which we can now hold fellowship with Christ: *Through his works, his ordinances, his word, his Spirit.* "If any man," says he, "hear my voice I will come in and sup with him."

Having made these remarks, we proceed to notice a few points of analogy between the fellowship which the disciples on their way to Emmaus had with Christ, and the fellowship which good men of every age have with him.

I. Their fellowship with Christ was secured by earnest seeking. "And they drew nigh unto the village whither they went; and he made as though he would have gone further; but they constrained him, saying, Abide with us; for it is toward evening, and the day is far spent. And he went in to tarry with them." The expression, "He made as though he would have gone further," must not be taken, of course, to imply anything like pretense on his part. It means that he intended to go further, and would have gone further had they not constrained him to enter their homes. The words teach us that he turned in that night to their home and tarried with them, because they "constrained" him to do so. This is one of many other instances in which *Christ showed his susceptibility of being influenced by human entreaty.* Bartimeus, the Syrophenician woman, the disciples in a storm, are further examples. The doctrine here brought forth is, that Christ will do for us by seeking what he will not do without it. Would you have Christ turn into your hearts to abide with you, you must earnestly seek him, seek him by a devout study of his word and by importunate prayer and supplication.

II. Their fellowship with Christ was the means of their knowing him. "And their eyes were opened, and they knew him." The expression "their eyes were open," means that they discovered who he was. Up to this time they regarded him as a stranger who possessed singular intelligence, unearthly virtues, and a sublime dignity of character, one who charmed them with his conversation. But they knew not who he was. Now, however, by a closer intercourse, after he had entered their house, broke the bread and blessed it, they discovered him. "They knew him." It was close intercourse that discovered him to them. So it ever is. If you would know Christ you must constrain him to enter your hearts and abide with you. It is one thing to know something *about* him, and another thing to know *him* with the heart. "This is life eternal to know thee," etc.

III. Their fellowship with Christ was subject to painful interruption. "And he vanished out of their sight;" that is, he suddenly disappeared. Whither he went, or how, is not stated, but all at once they missed him. What a change must have come over their feelings! It was as if the summer sun fell at once from its zenith, and left the world in *darkness and dismay*.

Fellowship with Christ here is often subject to interruption. The bright clouds pass from Tabor, and the mountains are covered with sackcloth. There are several things that serve to interrupt our fellowship with Christ: *Secular concerns, physical infirmities, material tendencies, and evil suggestions.* These, however, will not continue forever. The hour hastens on when the true disciple shall enjoy uninterrupted communion with his Lord.

IV. Their fellowship with Christ was exquisitely delightful. "Did not our hearts burn within us," etc. They left Jerusalem that morning with very heavy hearts; their hopes concerning Jesus seemed to have been frustrated; they were victims of disappointment. "We trusted," said they, "that it would have been he who should have redeemed Israel. Though that day was one of the brightest days that ever dawned upon this depraved world, the day when death was conquered and its scepter broken, yet to them it was dark. Perhaps the outward sun shone brightly, and the scenery around was beautiful; but *they* were heavy-hearted until Jesus met them on the road. As he talked a new sun rose on the firmament of their souls. "Did not our hearts burn within us?" Christ's communications to the soul will make the heart burn, burn with *gratitude, adoration, hope.*

V. THEIR FELLOWSHIP WITH CHRIST QUALIFIED THEM FOR USEFULNESS. "And they rose up the same hour and returned to Jerusalem and found the eleven gathered together, and them that were with them, saying, The Lord has risen indeed and appeared unto Simon." *They were enabled to proclaim to society something worth knowing:* "The Lord is risen indeed."

> "Hear, O ye nations! hear it, O ye dead!
> He rose! he rose! he burst the bars of death!"

If so, *the truth of revelation is incontrovertible.* If so, *a general resurrection may be anticipated.* If so, *Jesus may be boundlessly trusted.* Fellowship with Christ qualifies us for usefulness, and nothing else. *Learning, argument, eloquence, influence,* these are worthless, as far as preparing us for usefulness is concerned, unless we have fellowship with the Son of God.

We are, my friends, like these two disciples on the road from Jerusalem to Emmaus, burdened with questions and filled with anxieties. There is but one being that can help us, and that is Christ. Let us constrain him to abide with us. We may throw the words of these poor disciples into a prayer, and address that prayer to him: "Abide with us, for it is toward evening, and the day is far spent." Yes, with some, the day is literally far spent; the sun of life is going down, and the shadows of evening are falling. Let not the night come without Christ. Constrain him to abide with thee, and though he appears to be going further, moving on in his grand redemptive career, still he will enter thy poor heart and thy humble home, and thou shalt know him " whom to know is life eternal."

HOMILY LXV.

THE WAY OF THE TEMPTER.

Now there dwelt an old prophet in Bethel; and his sons came and told him all the works that the man of God had done that day in Bethel: the words which he had spoken unto the king, them they told also to their father. And their father said unto them, What way went he? etc. 1 Kings xiii, 11–32.

Somewhere about one thousand years before Christ the old Hebrew kingdom was riven into two great divisions. The ten tribes revolted and organized themselves into an independent power. Jeroboam became their first monarch. He was a man of great native ability, and had risen to considerable influence in the kingdom prior to the disruption, under the illustrious reign of Solomon. Not having his ambitious views realized, he became inspired with the most malignant hatred toward the king of Judah. From this feeling of opposition, it would seem, he gave himself to the promotion of idolatry in its most hideous forms. He established shrines at Dan and Bethel, the extremities of the kingdom, where he set up golden calves for the people to worship. To the kingly office he united that of an idolatrous priest, and acted as the great pontiff of that nation.

While thus officiating at the altar of Bethel, at the very outset of his idolatrous career, the great God in mercy sent to him "a prophet from Judah" to warn him of his impiety and to predict his doom. The prophet walks up to the altar, confronts the king as he is officiating, flashes his burning looks of inspiration upon him, and exclaims: "O altar, altar, thus saith the Lord; Behold, a child shall be born unto the house of David, Josiah by name; and upon thee shall he offer the priests of the high places that burn incense upon thee, and men's bones shall be burned upon thee." After these mysterious utterances he stated the sign that should indicate the event, whereupon the king, enraged at the conduct of the stranger, put forth his hand from the altar, saying: "Lay hold of him." The monarch's hand at once became so withered and paralyzed that he could not use it. The altar, according to the prediction, is shivered to pieces. The king relents, and entreats the prophet to pray to the God of heaven that his hand may be healed. The prophet generously accedes to the request, the prayer is answered, and the royal hand is healed. Touched with gratitude, Jeroboam invites the prophet to his house to partake of his hospitality, but the invitation is declined with emphatic energy and decision: "If thou wilt give me half thine house I will not go in with thee, neither will I eat bread nor drink water in this place: for so was it charged me by the word of the Lord."

The prophet departs for his home; tidings of the strange events that had just occurred at the altar quickly spread through the neighborhood; all minds are astir with curiosity, and one theme rules the talk of the district for the time.

Two sons of an "old prophet" living in Bethel, having personally witnessed, perhaps, the strange occurrence, hastened to their home and told their aged father. The old man's curiosity is excited; he inquires the way the "prophet of Judah" went; he is told; he pursues him; his ass is saddled, and he departs. At length he overtakes him, per haps well nigh exhausted, sitting down under the cool shadow of an old tree. He addresses him: "Art thou the man of God that camest from Judah?" The answer is, "I am." Then said the old man from Bethel: "Come home with me, and eat bread." The invitation is declined. Again he is urged, and urged by a falsehood in the name of God. This gives it the effect upon the pious heart of Judah's prophet. He returns, partakes of the proffered hospitality, and thus disobeys his God. The very man who tempted him to this act of disobedience, now, at his own table, is made the instrument to denounce his conduct and to predict his doom: "He cried unto the man of God that came from Judah, saying, Thus saith the Lord," etc. The prophet, after refreshment, leaves the house of his tempter and his guest, and proceeds homeward on his ass. He soon meets with the fate predicted. A lion attacks him, kills him, but instead of devouring him stands by his carcass, as if to protect it. The tempter, hearing of the catastrophe, hastens to the scene, brings back the body to Bethel, buries it in his own grave, and mourns over him, saying, "Alas, my brother!" And then he commanded his sons, saying: "When I am dead, then bury me in the sepulcher wherein the man of God is buried; lay my bones beside his bones."

Now this little piece of strange Hebrew history, thus briefly sketched, I shall employ in order to illustrate some important facts in connection with the mighty system of TEMPTATION to which we are every moment subject while in this world. I shall infer from the history,

I. THAT THE TEMPTER OF OUR RACE ASSAILS THE BEST OF MEN. The man who now became the victim of temptation was no other than a prophet of the Lord. He was Heaven's appointed delegate. From the multitudes of good men in Judah he was singled out as God's messenger to Jeroboam to denounce that monarch's impiety, and to predict his fate. In the prosecution of this high mission, too, he displays many noble attributes of character. Mark his *courage.* See him walk along with a firm step up to the altar, where the monarch of a great people was, in stately pomp, officiating as pontiff or high priest on behalf of the nation. He approaches the spot; he meets the eye of the king, and feels no trepidation; he speaks, but not in the language of a flattering courtier; no compliment escapes his lips; he does not even address a single word to his majesty; on the contrary, as if to show his utter contempt for the man who was thus outraging the reason of humanity, and insulting the God of heaven, he cries to the *altar*, as if the dead stone was more worthy his notice and more likely to be impressed by his appeals. Noble courage this! There is more true heroism in a man, thus single-handed, and in the face of royalty, conscientiously fulfilling his individual mission, than you could find perhaps in all the parade or military companies of the country. Mark his *magnanimity.*

The monarch had stretched forth his hand over the altar, probably in order to deal a fatal stroke upon the head of this prophet, but just Heaven struck it with paralysis. It was "dried up, so that he could not pull it in again to him." When, in this terrible condition, he entreated the prophet to supplicate Heaven for his restoration, what was the result? Did the seer, with the spirit of revenge, rejoice in the king's affliction and refuse? No; but with solemn earnestness he "besought the Lord," and thus removed the affliction. I see more greatness of soul in an act like this, an act of mercy to an enemy, than I see in all the vaunted victories of revenge. He is the truly great man, not who strikes a nation dead with a retaliating blow, but who overcometh evil by good, and, like this old prophet, prays for those who despitefully use him. Mark his *fidelity to God.* When the king, struck with a momentary gratitude, invited him to his house, and said, "Come home with me, and refresh thyself, and I will give thee a reward," did he accept the request? Who would refuse the invitation of a monarch? Why the mere bow of recognition from a king some would feel to be a sufficient honor for the talk of their life; but to go home to eat with a king, who would refuse? Yet our prophet did so. And why? Not from bashfulness, nor from a bravado of independence, but from respect to the command of God. Hear his noble words: "If thou wilt give me half thine house, I will not go in with thee, neither will I eat bread nor drink water in this place: for so was it charged me by the word of the Lord."

Loyalty to heaven was at this time a sentiment in him stronger than physical hunger, self-esteem, or respect for royalties. Among a race of sycophants, it is truly inspiring to see a man like this prophet, who, from an inviolable attachment to duty, refuses the monarch's invitation.

Now it is noteworthy that this man, who, in the special communion of Heaven, displays all these noble attributes of character, was assailed by temptation and fell a victim to its seductive influence. What the king failed to accomplish in turning him from the commandment of God, another within a few minutes (the old prophet of Bethel) achieved. Here is a lesson to us all. While in this world we are on the tempter's ground. His agencies thickly play around us, and try us in every point of our character. Satan transforms himself into an angel of light, and by the manners of a courtier, the beauty of a seraph, or the artifice of a veteran general, leads us on, step by step, little by little, to degrees of sin which would have shocked us if we had seen their full enormity from the beginning. If invulnerable in one part he tries us in another.

"O what a goodly outside falsehood hath!"

In that sad night, before the crucifixion, while the Son of man was with his disciples on the Mount of Olives, he said, "All ye shall be offended because of me this night, for it is written, I will smite the Shepherd, and the sheep shall be scattered;" to which, with impulsive earnestness, Peter replied: "Though all men shall be offended because of thee, *yet will I never be offended.*" Again Jesus spoke, and this time in direct reply to Peter: "This night, before the cock-crowing announces another day, thou shalt deny me thrice." To which Peter, with a warmer and intenser affirmation, replied: "Though I should die with thee, yet will I not deny thee."

We all know the result. To the denial of Christ, Peter, before six hours had passed, added bitter cursings and swearings. Moses once, by temptation, was turned from his meekness to a creature of stormy wrath, and the spiritually-minded David into a hideous adulterer. "Let him that thinketh he standeth take heed lest he fall."

We infer from the narrative,

II. That the tempter of our race acts through the agency of man. How did the tempting spirit appear to this prophet of Judea now? Not in the form of a serpent, as he appeared of old in Eden, nor in the form of an angel, but in the form of a man. The devil comes to man through man; acts on man by man. Do not suppose that the great enemy of souls is somewhere in the clouds. He is incarnate; he dwells among men; "he worketh in the children of disobedience." He is in the craft of the false priest, who officiates at the altar, and in the superstitious services of his deluded votaries; he inspires the mercenary merchant in business, and works in the countless tricks of trade. He is in the overbearing arrogancies of one class, and the cringing civilities of another. He fills the haunts of pleasure. He plays seductively in the smiles of beauty, and breathes in the song that warms the passions. He is in the man who, with polished manner, approaches the boy, far from his father's home, and whispers in his ear that the Bible and the domestic altar are only for weak women and imbecile young men. He speaks in the words that shake faith in virtue, and guides the pen of the thousand sciolists who minister to the wishes of the skeptic, the tastes of the depraved, and the cravings of the sensual. Look for the devil in man.

You who sit from Sabbath to Sabbath in God's temple listening to his ministers, where are your temptations? There are no signs of peril without, no sound of the enemy's approach. Your temptations, where are they? "Not marching down your streets, a bannered host, with trumpets to proclaim their siege, and with warlike notes of preparation. Virtue's victories would then be comparatively easy. But your temptations hover about you in wary ambush. They lurk in the common labor, where the world gambles for your soul; in the social fellowship, where criminality corrupts under the name of cordiality; in the flatteries of your beauty, or your talents, or your disposition, which borrow the silver tones of friendship, and sound so like them that you listen; in the familiar pleasures that make the feet of the hours so swift, and the earth so satisfying, that you feel no need of heaven. Here are your tempters. They are disguised; they take circuitous paths; they carry gifts in their hands, and place crowns on your heads; they are clothed like angels of light."*

The fact that man is the tempter of man shows:

First. *The moral degradation of human nature.* Man has become the tool of Satan. The false religionists, the hypocrites, the infidels, the blasphemers, the carnal, what are they? The instruments of the devil, to seduce and corrupt their fellow men. "Demoniacal possessions" were not confined to Judea, nor limited to the theocratic age and

* T. D. Huntington, D.D.

people; they, in a moral sense, pervade all lands, and run through all times. "The works of the devil" are everywhere around you. Alas for human nature! Who shall deliver us? Who shall cast out the evil spirit from the world? Who shall destroy his works? There is ONE who can, and to him we look, and in his all-conquering strength we trust. "Gird thy sword upon thy thigh, O most mighty," etc.

The fact that man is the tempter of man shows,

Secondly, *The necessity of constant watchfulness.* In social circles be ever on your guard; be cautious as to the companionship you form, as to the books you read, as to the guides you follow. The evil spirit, as of old, is going to and fro through the earth; beware of "his devices;" arm yourselves against his "fiery darts." Failing in one way, he is more than ever active in side-works and in "tract oblique." When the Russian troops were retreating across a frozen lake before Napoleon's army, Bonaparte stationed his artillery on a neighboring elevation, and ordered them to fire on the ice and break it up, and thus engulf the enemy's regiments. The guns were leveled and discharged, but the balls glanced and rolled on the ice without breaking it. Suddenly one of his colonels thought to elevate his howitzers and fire into the air. The momentum of the descending projectiles, a falling shower of iron and lead, shattered the ice, and sent down the host into the waters of the lake. It is not the only instance in which the arts of war have followed precisely the arts of the devil. It is by the oblique shot of our tempters that

'The meanest foe of all the train
Has thousands and ten thousands slain.'"

Satan never plays a bold game. He wins in ways and places we dream not, and he is sinking mines and laying powder trains where few or none of us expect.

We infer from the narrative,

III. That the tempter of our race always assumes the garb of goodness. The temptation came to this "old prophet" not only through a man, but under the *garb of piety*. Listen to the tempter's argument: "I am a prophet also as thou art; and an angel spoke unto me by the word of the Lord, saying, Bring him back with thee into thine house, that he may eat bread and drink water. But he lied unto him." Yes, it was a lie. No angel in the universe ever made such a communication to him; it was a fabrication of his own in order to deceive. What could have induced him, the prophet of Bethel, to have invented this falsehood to deceive? "I cannot," says Matthew Henry, "but call him a false prophet and a bad man; it being much easier to believe that from one of such a bad character should be extorted a confirmation of what the man of God said, (as we find, verse 32,) than that a true prophet and a good man should tell such a deliberate lie as he did, and father it upon God. 'A good tree could never bring forth such corrupt fruit.' Perhaps he was trained up among the sons of the prophets in one of Samuel's colleges; but growing worldly and profane, the spirit of prophecy had departed from him. If he had been a good prophet he would have reproved Jeroboam's idolatry, and not have suffered his sons to attend his altars, as it should seem they did." What could have been his ruling motive? Was it *kindness?* Did compassion for the hunger and thirst of the traveler stimulate him to this? Were it so, kindness cannot justify falsehood. Was it *pride?* Did he wish the honor of entertaining the man who had refused the pressing hospitality of the king? Was it *envy?* Did he desire the ruin of the man who had thus by a prophetic act won the good-will and respect of Israel's mighty monarch? Was it *contrition?* Having heard of the faithfulness of this prophet from Judah, did conscience smite him with a sense of his own prophetic infidelity, and did he seek this interview in order to make himself morally right? Even this would be no proof of his goodness, and no justification of his falsehood. Whatever was the motive, it worked under the garb of truth and religion. He spoke in the name of humanity and of God, and it was this that gave effect to his utterance. This is our point. Temptation ever comes in this form. It is only as the devil arrays himself in the costume of virtue that he becomes seductive; it is only as he speaks the language of truth that his blasphemous errors take effect. Gross depravity is repulsive; error fully expressed is weak; sheer selfishness disgusts; Satan, represented as he has been sometimes with cloven feet and all concentrated malignities on his countenance, is so ugly that men fly as by instinct from him. But adorn depravity, put error into the language of truth, robe selfishness in the attire of love and generosity, and these evils become the mighty mouldering forces of society. In our age and country the devil puts on all the beauteous forms that genius can invent, or that art can produce. Truly exclaims England's famed dramatist:

> "O! that deceit should steal such gentle shapes,
> And with a virtuous visage hide deep vice."

We infer from this narrative,

IV. That the tempter of our race generally becomes the tormentor of his victim. The prophet of Judah has yielded to the invitation; in disobedience to the command of God, he is now sitting at the table and partaking of the hospitality of his tempter; his conscience, most likely, is by no means satisfied with the position in which he has placed himself. It may be that he is morally uncomfortable, and expresses to his host his painful misgivings. But what comfort does the man offer who has turned him from the right? None. On the contrary, he makes a declaration which must have struck agony into his heart. In the name of heaven he denounces the conduct of the man whom he had seduced. Hear his taunting: "Forasmuch as thou hast disobeyed the mouth of the Lord, and hast not kept the commandment which the Lord thy God commanded thee, but camest back, and hast eaten bread and drunk water in the place of the which the Lord did say to thee, Eat no bread, and drink no water; thy carcass shall not come unto the sepulcher of thy fathers." This conduct reminds us of the conduct of those chief priests and elders who had tempted Judas to betray his master for thirty pieces of silver. When the conscience of the miserable betrayer of his Master was roused to anguish at the enormity of his sin, he hurried to his tempters, with the silver burning in his hands, crying vehemently in their ears, saying, "I have sinned in that I have betrayed innocent blood." What did they say? Did they offer any consolation? or made they any attempt to soothe the distracted heart of their victim? No! but they said: "*What is that to us? See thou to that.*" When some subtle infidel has enticed the young man of prayer from the right path, and has filled his heart with doubts, and the day of death comes on, what ray of light for him has he as the dark valley is being entered? "They have made me curse my old mother," said a dying backslider; "they have filled my heart with cursings and bitterness, they have blown out the last starlight, and now *I am making my way* alone to the land of unending night. May God have mercy on my young companions, who have been misled by the leaders of that infidel club."

This tormenting conduct of tempters is,

First, *A matter of necessity.* A tempter is a sinner, and no sinner has any consolation to offer a sinner. All hell, peopled, as it may be, with intellects of gigantic order, is too weak to conceive one consolatory thought or utter one soothing word. Sin has no balm for a guilty conscience.

This tormenting conduct of tempters is,

Secondly, *Prophetic.* It shows what must be the case for ever. The response of every appeal in the future world of misery, of the infidel to his agonized disciple, of the seducer to his tormented victim, will be, "What is that to us? See *thou* to that." We infer from the narrative,

V. THAT THE TEMPTER OF OUR RACE, ONCE YIELDED TO, MAY ACCOMPLISH OUR RUIN. The prophet of Judah leaves the house of the tempter, mounts the ass, and recommences his homeward journey with feelings, we should imagine, of no happy description. He had done the wrong thing; he had brought guilt upon his conscience; the menace of the tempter rang in his heart; there was a boding darkness over his whole soul. In every step, perhaps, he felt he was approaching something mysteriously terrible. How different are his feelings now to those he had when he commenced his journey the first time from the temple of Bethel and from the presence of the king! He was strong then in the consciousness of having fulfilled his sacred mission; he moved then with a firm step on his homeward way. Consciousness of having done the right thing energizes the whole system, body and soul, and suns the whole scene of life with a warmer glow and a brighter radiance. Kind nature smiles the sunshine of her approbation on him who has the well-done of his conscience.

Not far did this man proceed on his way before the denunciation of his tempter took effect: "A lion met him by the way, and slew him: and his carcass was cast in the way, and the ass stood by it, and the lion also stood by the carcass."

In the physical fate of this prophet we are reminded of two things:

First. *The course of justice.* That dead carcass lying in the wayside is an eloquent homily against sin. In it the voice of justice declares, with telling emphasis, that compliance even with the most plausible temptation is a sin, and that sin, even in a good man and a true prophet must be punished.

In the physical fate of this prophet we are reminded of,

Secondly, *The interposition of mercy.* The ravenous lion, contrary to his instincts, instead of *devouring* his victim, stands over it as a kind guardian. Justice made that lion do so much, but mercy restrained him from doing more. Mercy triumphs over judgment. The philosophy of all human history is symbolized here. Justice goes with nature. It was the nature of the lion to destroy. Mercy interrupts the course of justice. It was contrary to the nature of the lion to guard rather than devour its victim. Verily this dead carcass, with the lion standing over it, constituted one of the most full and forcible sermons on God's government ever delivered on this earth. More truth comes from this dead carcass than from the living lips of many a modern preacher.

VI. That the tempter of our race is compelled to do homage to the virtue he has assailed. The old prophet of Bethel having heard of the sad fate that had befallen the man he had tempted, struck perhaps with contrition, had his ass "saddled" and hastened to the spot. He finds "the carcass cast in the way, and the ass and the lion standing by the carcass; the lion had not eaten the carcass nor torn the ass." He placed the dead body on the ass, brought it back to Bethel, laid it in his grave, wept over it, exclaiming: "Alas, my brother!" and then commanded his sons, saying: "When I am dead, then bury me in the sepulcher wherein the man of God is buried; lay my bones beside his bones." Such is the homage which the tempter pays to the virtue of his victim.

Such homage vice must ever pay to virtue. There is not a being in the universe, even the prince of tempters, that is not bound by the laws of conscience to respect the virtue he seeks to destroy. Ye young men and women, whose hearts throb in warm sympathy with "the true, the beautiful, and the good," and whose aim it is to embody in your life the high moral aspirations of your soul, let me assure you that those who may endeavor, from time to time, to shame you out of your virtue by ridicule, or to win you from it by blandishments, have an inward reverence for all the good they discover in your character. It must be so. Universal conscience approves the right. Every groan in hell is an impressive tribute to virtue. The tempter

"Wails those whom he strikes down."

To the young specially, in conclusion, let me say, I have endeavored to use this strange fragment of old Hebrew history in order to unmask the tempter, and to show you his devious ways, and thus put you on your guard. Remember, however exalted the mission to which you are called, and high the virtues that distinguish your character, you are still within the sphere of the tempter. Remember that the tempter comes not to you in any black, Tartarean form, with cloven foot, and hollow, sepulchral voice, but that he approaches in the guise too often of an angel of light, thinks with the brain, feels with the heart, and talks with the tones of a silvery sweetness. "Satan does not march his victims up to face perdition point blank. He leads men to it by easy stages, and through a labyrinth that shows no danger. Round and round go these circling currents of the Northern

Sea that swallow the ship; and by the same winding coil goes the spiritual decline that ends in spiritual death." A mile above the Falls of Niagara the water is limpid and glassy; none unacquainted with the river would say that a terrible cataract was at so short a distance away. You launch your boat, and your oar flashes in sunlight and beauty. From the shore the tempter cries "All is safe," and down you glide; but soon the current shows itself in a strength that cannot be mistaken. On if you go death certain and most terrible will befall you. Listen to the syren voice of the tempter, be guided by his counsel, and you are lost. There is ruin in every wave of his hand. Remember that ruin lurks underneath the most winsome or sanctimonious smiles. Remember that the tempter, after he has won you to his wish, and brought the fire of remorse into your conscience, instead of breathing to you a word of comfort, will taunt and torment you. Remember that yielding even to one suggestion of the tempter is sin; and that even one sin must be punished either here or in the great hereafter. Remember that those who seek to rob you of your virtues by the sneers of malice, or by the promises of love, will, if they are not made virtuous here, find an everlasting hell in rendering the homage of their nature to that virtue of which they have robbed you, but which they have not, and to which they can never attain.

Trust in Him who is the great conqueror of Satan and the Captain of human salvation. Quit you like men. "Put on the whole armor of God, that ye may be able to stand against the wiles of the devil." Unbounded trust and vital faith in Christ are our defense and our victory. I know of nothing else on which to depend.

> "If this fail,
> The pillared firmament is rottenness,
> And earth's base built on stubble."

HOMILY LXVI.

AN EVER-GROWING ARGUMENT FOR EVANGELISM.

Many shall run to and fro, and knowledge shall be increased.
DANIEL xii, 4.

OUR age realizes the scene here predicted. This generation is pre-eminently migratory; men are everywhere on the move; a restless impulse has seized the world, and the fixed habits which bound our ancestors to their hearths are giving way. Our countrymen are now found in every part of the world, and are mingling with all the varied tribes of mankind. By the invention of steam, and the improvements of navigation, distance is almost annihilated. Thoroughfares are open up through every part of the globe, and distant nations are brought into close and frequent intercourse. Men are here in the morning and three to six hundred miles distant at night; here this week, and treading the continent of Europe next. Different principles stimulate men in this incessant migration. The emigrant moves for bread, the merchant for wealth, the hero for conquest, the traveler for pleasure, the philosopher for truth, the Christian for souls.

Now the intellectual results of all these intermigrations is *knowledge!* "Knowledge," says the prophet, "shall be increased." There are other creatures which migrate as well as man. "The crane and the swallow" migrate, yet they get no knowledge: their bodies are active but their souls are stationary. Their journeying during sixty centuries has not yielded them one new idea. In their mental world there is no accession of light. Not so with men. Knowledge increases as they journey to distances and mingle with foreigners. Their knowledge of the physical world increases: of its geological formations, political divisions, its productions, extent, climates, and tenantry. Their knowledge of man increases: of his antiquity, identity, and spiritual condition. What a wonderful increase in knowledge has taken place in modern times! Indeed, the great discoverers of science have only just departed from our midst. Bacon, who freed the mind from scholastic bondage; Newton, who gave us a true theory of the universe; Harvey, who discovered the circulation of blood; Locke, who explored the world of mind; Watt, who gave us a steam engine; these great men that have given the modern world such an impulse to knowledge, are scarcely cold in their graves. The tide of human knowledge is set in; it is flowing, and destined to flow higher and higher. Mind is roused from the slumber of ages, the floodgates of thought are broken up, and knowledge must go on increasing.

Now I shall use this necessary *augmentation of knowledge as an argument for the necessity of propagating the Gospel.*

I. THE MORE SECULAR KNOWLEDGE THE WORLD HAS THE MORE NEED IT HAS OF THE GOSPEL. Some deny this, others doubt it, and but few, perhaps, believe it. The following thoughts, however, would make it evident:

First: *That mere knowledge effects no radical change in the great principles of human character.* The sources of all action are in the heart. Our likes and dislikes are our controlling impulses. Philosophy, consciousness, and the Bible show that "out of the heart are the issues of life." Now does secular knowledge change the heart? Does it make a dishonest man honest, a selfish man generous, and a sensual man spiritual? Let the history of intelligent nations answer. Greece was philosophic, but what was its moral character? Consult Paul's Epistles to the Corinthians. Rome was philosophic, but what was its moral condition? Read the first chapter to the Romans. Why, Socrates himself was accused of sensuality. Plato's republic was constructed on the principle of a community of wives; Cicero contended for fornication; Zeno considered unnatural sins as indifferent. China and India are learned in their way, but where are their virtues? I grant, indeed, that knowledge may induce and qualify a man to act out the evil principles of his heart in a more refined and less offensive manner. The intelligent man, instead of committing some petty deed of larceny, will rob on a large scale; and under the protection of the law will form and execute schemes of legal fraud. It is fashionable now for statesmen, orators, and journalists to trace crimes to ignorance, and to represent education as the effective purifier of public morals. My impression is that you may multiply schools on every hand, fill the nation with secular knowledge, and still the springs of morals may remain as polluted as ever. Some of the most illustrious chiefs in English literature figure as the most despicable characters in English morals. Bacon, Dryden, Churchill, Burns, Pope, and many other literary peers were certainly not eminent for virtue. Nothing but the Gospel can act upon the heart.

Secondly. *The more knowledge the greater will be the power for evil.* "Knowledge is power." A few intelligent men in a village or a town will exert far greater influence than hundreds of the ignorant. As the world grows in knowledge it grows in power to trample upon the laws of God, to poison the fountains of influence, and to rebel against the interest of the universe. The power of the devil is the power of knowledge.

Thirdly. *The more knowledge the larger the amount of responsibility.* Christ taught this. "He that knoweth his master's will," etc. Here then is my argument: If secular knowledge is destined to increase, if this knowledge has not the power to change the heart, while it increases man's power to do evil and enhances his responsibility, then ought not our earnestness in the propagation of the Gospel to rise with the increase of general intelligence?

II. The more knowledge the world has the more likely it is to receive the Gospel. It seems to me a common impression that a state of rude savage heathenism is more favorable to the reception of the Gospel than a state of enlightened civilization. We think that this impression is contrary to fact and injurious in influence. We would rejoice indeed in the fact that the Gospel is suited to man in the lowest stage of development; that no spirit is so sensualized, so deeply sunk that the Gospel cannot reach it. But we contend that the more intelligent a man is the more favorable his condition for Gospel influence.

First. *The more intelligent a man is the more evidence he will have to convince him of the truth of the Gospel.* The more information a man gets, either from testimony, observation, or research, concerning the facts, scenes, and customs referred to in the Bible, the more evidence he will have to convince him of its truth. If the function of evidence is to convince, the intelligent man is in a far better condition than the ignorant.

Secondly. *The more intelligent a man is the more illustrations he will have of the power of the Gospel.* What illustrations of the power of the Gospel has an intelligent man which are hid entirely from the ignorant! He can trace its conquests on the page of history from the day of Pentecost to this hour. From the little room of Jerusalem, spreading over the east, flowing to the west, and sending back its streams eastward again, he can follow it.

Thirdly. *The more intelligent a man is the more indications he will see for the necessity of the Gospel.* The more a man understands his own nature the more he will be prepared to feel that laws, education, and science are not sufficient to meet the spiritual wants of his nature and condition.

Fourthly. *The more intelligent a man is the more fitted he will be to appreciate the discoveries of the Gospel.* The more knowledge he has the better will he be able to appreciate the wisdom of the scheme, the righteousness of the claims, and the adaptation of the provisions of the Gospel. (1.) The character of the Gospel encourages this impression. What a sublime system is Christianity! It has aspects of grandeur, relations and bearings which an ignorant man is incompetent to discover. (2.) The effects of missionary labor encourage the impression. Where does the missionary succeed most? among the barbarous or the civilized classes? Compare the reports of our home missions with those of foreign. (3.) The example of the first ministers of Christianity. Where did the apostles go to preach? Did they search out the darkest parts of the world? Did they go among barbarous and savage hordes? No; they selected the most enlightened and influential parts of the world for their spheres of labor. To Philippi, and Ephesus, and Antioch, and Corinth; to Egypt, the fountain of learning; to Athens, the seat of science, "the eye of Greece;" to Rome, the enlightened empress of the world, they went! These men knew that the more enlightened the population were the more likely they would be to appreciate the message, and the more qualified afterward to propagate it.

From this subject we learn,

(1.) The glory of the Gospel. Let the intellect of the world advance! it can never outgrow the Gospel; the Gospel will never become obsolete. As the sunny vault above us widens to the advanced step of the traveler scaling the hills, so the Gospel expands to the intellectual progress of the ages. (2.) Our encouragement to diffuse it. Were I assured that the Gospel would succeed better among the ignorant than the learned, and that as men advanced in intelligence, the farther they passed from the reach of the Gospel, I should lose hope in the final triumph of Christianity; for knowledge, secular knowledge, is destined to advance. The tide of human intelligence must rise. But such is not the fact. More knowledge the better. Let knowledge increase; let schools multiply; let the streams of literature deepen and widen; let men run to and fro; let nations mingle together; let the thoughts of men, the world over, flow and reflow, and the sea of knowledge cover the world. Both the world's *need* of the Gospel and its *capacity* for receiving it are heightened by all this.

HOMILY LXVII.

THE BRIGHT LIGHT IN THE CLOUD.

And now men see not the bright light which is in the clouds.
JOB xxxvii, 21.

THIS chapter is the conclusion of Elihu's fourth and last speech to Job. The design of the whole of his argument is to indicate the character of God in his dealings with mankind. This he does by showing that such is the wisdom he has displayed in the creation and management of the world, that men ought to repose the utmost confidence in him.

The moral of the whole is, that as we cannot "find him out" we should reverence and trust him as the all-wise and just.

I shall take the text to illustrate *the disposition of men to look upon the dark side of things.*

I. The text will apply to the skeptic in relation to the dark things of revelation. These men in looking at the Bible "see not the bright light that is in the clouds." They see the clouds, and through the unbelief of their heart these clouds blacken and spread until they cover the whole firmament of revelation. No star breaks through their impervious mass, no ray brightens the fringe of their sable robes. That there are clouds hanging over this book it is far more Christian to admit than to deny. Not a few of the historical discrepancies, and recorded utterances and doings of God, are clouds to me. Notwithstanding the explanations of talented critics and able theologians they still continue; no breeze of argument has yet borne them off. There are men, of course, to whom this book has no mystery; they can explain everything—it is "reading-made-easy;" and they would brand as dolts or infidels those who thus frankly acknowledge their ignorance. Albeit we must be candid, and confess that the Bible to us contains "things hard to be understood." We feel with Paul, when he said, "How unsearchable are his judgments, and his ways past finding out!"

But, thank God, though we see the clouds, the clouds which the skeptic sees, we do not see them like him. We see a bright light upon them. Every one is silvered with celestial beams.

There are several things which give the darkest of them a bright light:

First. *There is the love of the infinite Father.* This shines through all its pages. Even his denunciations and judgments are but modifications of his love. They are but his breath cleansing the moral atmosphere of the world. His love lights up every sentence and sparkles through every cloud.

Secondly. *The unspotted holiness of our great Example.* The Bible records sad deeds of enormous wickedness and defects even in those it represents as the saints of God. This is a cloud. But the character of him it represents as our great Exemplar is without a spot. His excellences radiate through all. They are a bright light upon the cloud.

Thirdly. *The provision he has made for our spiritual recovery.* Whatever else you may doubt by, there is no room to doubt the freeness, the abundance, and the efficacy of redeeming grace. This is a bright light upon the cloud.

Fourthly. *The existence of a blessed immortality.* Whatever difficulties you may have, you can have no difficulty with this. "I am the resurrection and the life," etc. "Brethren, I would not have you ignorant," etc. "It doth not appear what we shall be," etc. Immortality is a bright light upon all the clouds of revelation. So long as I see these bright beams upon the clouds of revelation, I am not anxious about them. I could not live under a firmament of clear burning azure. The clouds give variety and interest to the scene; they soften and cool the brilliant and burning rays.

II. THE TEXT WILL APPLY TO THE FACTIOUS FAULT-FINDERS OF GOD'S PROVIDENCE. Some people are everlastingly musing on the difficulties of providence. (1.) The permission of moral evil is a cloud. (2.) The apparent disregard of God to the moral distinctions of society is a cloud. "All things come alike to all," etc. (3.) The power which wickedness is often allowed to exercise over virtue is a cloud: chains, dungeons, stakes. (4.) The premature deaths of the good and useful are a cloud. We feel these clouds; we feel that "clouds and darkness are round about him," that "his way is in the sea and his path in the great waters, and his footsteps are not known."

But there is a bright light upon these clouds. The belief that they are *local*, *temporary*, *transitional*, is a bright light upon all the clouds. I look up on them as they roll over me, and feel that they are not universal, that they are mere vapor-spots on the great sky of being; that they are not eternal, they are only of the other day; and that they are only introductory to a higher state of things. Out of their darkness and confusion will one day come a beautiful system. "Our light afflictions which are but for a moment," etc.

III. THE TEXT WILL APPLY TO THE MISANTHROPIC IN RELATION TO THE CHARACTER OF THE RACE. There are men who have gloomy and uncharitable views of the character of mankind. All men are as corrupt as they can be; virtue is but vice in a pleasing garb; benevolence is but selfishness in disguise; chastity is but lust refined, and pure religion is but superstition and hypocrisy. Every man has his price —increase your offer, and he who is most famed for virtue and godliness will fall. All men "are worldly, sensual, and devilish." Very dark indeed are the clouds which these men see hanging over society ; there is no ray to relieve their darkness.

Now, our view of society is anything but cheering. The longer one lives, the deeper he enters into the inner circles of life, the more he feels its hollow-heartedness, its miserable selfishness. Still we see bright light upon the clouds; there is not unmitigated, unrelieved corruption. There is the light of *social love* which streams through all the ramifications of life. It is seen in the unwearied attention and ministries of the mother; in the anxious toils and labors of the father; the tenderness of the sister, the attachment of the brother, the oneness of the husband and wife, and the sympathy of the neighbor. There are countless acts of quiet and self-denying philanthropy in every circle, especially, perhaps, among the poor, where they pass unobserved and find no account. It is seen in the showers of tears that fall every day on the graves of departed friends. All this shows that, bad as the world is, there is a fountain of love in its heart whose streams are everywhere. This love gives a bright light to the clouds of depravity that hang over the moral world.

There is a light of *moral justice* which flames forth when the right and the true are outraged. There is the light of *true religion.* Though there is an immense amount of hypocrisy, formality, superstition, and cant, associated with the Church of God, there are nevertheless multitudes of true and genuine disciples of the great Christ. There are men who are throwing on society the right thoughts, putting forth the right efforts, and breathing to heaven the right prayers. These men are destined to multiply ; their influence is destined to grow, their principles are destined to triumph. As these men increase, the light upon the cloud will brighten, until at length the whole shall melt into sunshine.

IV. THE TEXT WILL APPLY TO THE DESPONDING CHRISTIAN IN RELATION TO HIS EXPERIENCE. There are hours in the experience of many of the good when all within is cloudy. The proneness to fall into sin, the coldness of our devotional feeling, the consciousness of our defects, the felt distance between our ideal and ourselves, sometimes bring a sad gloom over the heart. "We walk in darkness and have no light."

But there are bright lights, however, upon this cloudy experience. In the first place, the very feeling of imperfection indicates something good. Unless there was light on the background you could not see the clouds. "Blessed are the poor in spirit," etc. "Blessed are they that mourn," etc. The more we feel the dangers of our road, the more earnestly should we grasp the hand of our guide. In the second place, most of those who are now in heaven once felt this: Jacob, David, Job, Paul. In the third place, Christ is ready to help such as you. "He shall feed his flock like a shepherd," etc. "Come unto me all ye that are weary," etc.

From this subject we learn,

First, *To cultivate the habit of looking upon the bright side of things.* There is a light upon all the clouds connected with our mortal history. There is a world upon whose dark, stormy, battling clouds no ray of light descends. Not so with us. Let us cherish that faith in the improvability of our nature, the purpose and the power of Christ to help our world, and the future perfection of the race, which will cheer and give us heart in all our efforts. Let the clouds roll and thicken over us, I know that there is sunshine in the sky of human life; let me believe in it.

Secondly. *To anticipate the world of future light.* Yet a little while and the clouds of ignorance and error shall pass away. "What we know not now we shall know hereafter." "Now we see through a glass darkly, then shall we see face to face." Yet a little while and the clouds of doubts and fears which roll over our spirits and depress our hearts, shall be dispelled by the glory that shall be revealed within us. Yet a little while and the clouds of sorrow and suffering shall melt into the sunshine of infinite love.

Ye skeptics! I see the dark shadows that rest upon many portions of this Book, of which you complain, and often have I shivered under their frowning forms and chilly breath; but I look up and see a bright light on the clouds; the darkest is silvered round with eternal truth and infinite love. Ye factious fault-finders with the providence of God! who, like your prototypes in the wilderness, are everlastingly murmuring at the ways of heaven, the sky of the divine government is not as dark as you suppose; there is a bright light on every passing cloud. Ye gloomy misanthropes who have lost all faith in your species, and can see no good in human character, but evil in all! the heart of humanity is not so hellishly dark as ye imagine. Human thoughts and human feelings, though clouded with error and wrong, have still their rays: there is a bright light in the clouds. Ye desponding Christians, who, amid the dark memories of past sins, and the depressing consciousness of present imperfections, often weep beneath the dark shadows of self-criminating and self-suspicious thoughts, take heart! there is a bright light in the clouds:

> "The clouds ye so much dread
> Are big with mercy, and shall break
> With blessings on your head."

HOMILY LXVIII.

THE PRODIGAL AND HIS BROTHER.

And he said unto him, Son, thou art ever with me; and all I have is thine. It was meet that we should make merry, and be glad: for this thy brother was dead, and is alive again; and was lost, and is found. Luke xv, 31, 32.

There are two classes of sins. There are some sins by which man crushes, wounds, malevolently injures his brother man; those sins which speak of a bad, tyrannical, and selfish heart. Christ met those with denunciation. There are other sins by which a man injures himself. There is a life of reckless indulgence; there is a career of yielding to ungovernable propensities, which most surely conducts to wretchedness and ruin, but makes a man an object of compassion rather than of condemnation. The reception which sinners of this class met from Christ was marked by strange and pitying mercy. There was no maudlin sentiment on his lips. He called sin sin, and guilt guilt. But yet there were sins which his lips scourged, and others over which, containing in themselves their own scourge, his heart bled. That which was melancholy, and marred, and miserable in this world, was more congenial to the heart of Christ than that which was proudly happy. It was in the midst of a triumph, and all the pride of a procession, that he paused to weep over ruined Jerusalem. And if we ask the reason why the character of Christ was marked by this melancholy condescension, it is that he was in the midst of a world of ruins, and there was nothing there to gladden, but very much to touch with grief. He was here to restore that which was broken down and crumbling into decay. An enthusiastic antiquarian, standing amid the fragments of an ancient temple, surrounded by dust and moss, broken pillar and defaced architrave, with magnificent projects in his mind of restoring all this former majesty, to draw out to light from mere rubbish the ruined glories, and therefore stooping down among the dark ivy and the rank nettles; such was Christ amid the wreck of human nature. He was striving to lift it out of its degradation. He was searching out in revolting places that which had fallen down, that he might build it up again in fair proportions a holy temple to the Lord. Therefore, he labored among the guilty; therefore, he was the companion of outcasts; therefore, he spoke tenderly and lovingly to those whom society counted undone; therefore, he loved to bind up the bruised and broken-hearted; therefore, his breath fanned the spark which seemed dying out in the wick of the expiring taper, when men thought that it was too late, and that the hour of *hopeless* profligacy was come. It was that feature in his character, that tender, hoping, encouraging spirit of his, which the prophet Isaiah fixed upon as characteristic. "A bruised reed will he not break."

It was an illustration of this spirit which he gave in the parable which forms the subject of present consideration. We find the occasion which drew it from him in the commencement of this chapter: "Then drew near unto him all the publicans and sinners for to hear him. And the Pharisees and scribes murmured, saying, This man receiveth sinners and eateth with them." It was then that Christ condescended to offer an excuse or an explanation of his conduct. And his excuse was this: It is natural, humanly natural, to rejoice more over that which has been recovered than over that which has never been lost. He proved that by three illustrations taken from human life. The first illustration, intended to show the feelings of Christ in winning back a sinner, was the joy which the shepherd feels in the recovery of a sheep from the mountain wilderness. The second was the satisfaction which a person feels for a recovered coin. The last was the gladness which attends the restoration of an erring son.

Now, the three parables are alike in this, that they all describe more or less vividly the feelings of the Redeemer on the recovery of the lost. But the third parable differs from the other two in this, that besides the feelings of the Saviour, it gives us a multitude of particulars respecting the feelings, the steps, and the motives of the penitent who is reclaimed back to goodness. In the first two the thing lost is a coin or a sheep. It would not be possible to find any picture of remorse or gladness there. But in the third parable the thing lost is not a lifeless thing, nor a mute thing, but a being, the workings of whose human heart are all described. So that the subject opened out to us is a more extensive one, not merely the feelings of the finder, God in Christ, but, besides that, the sensations of the wanderer himself.

In dealing with this parable, this is the line which we shall adopt.

We shall look at the picture which it draws of,

I. God's treatment of the penitent.

II. The conduct of a technical or formal professor.

I. God's treatment of the penitent divides itself in this parable into three distinct epochs: *The period of alienation, the period of repentance, and the circumstances of a penitent reception.* We shall consider all these in turn.

The first truth exhibited in this parable is the ALIENATION *of man's heart from God.* Homelessness, distance from our Father, that is man's state by nature in this world. The youngest son gathered all together and took his journey into a *far* country. Brethren, this is the history of worldliness. It is a state far from God; in other words, it is a state of homelessness. And now let us ask what that means. To American hearts it is not necessary to expound elaborately the infinite meanings which cluster round that blessed expression, "home." Home is the one place in all this world where hearts are sure of each other. It is the place of confidence. It is the place where we tear off that mask of guarded and suspicious coolness which the world forces us to wear in self-defense, and where we pour out the unreserved communications of full and confiding hearts. It is the spot where expressions of tenderness gush out without any sensation of awkwardness and without any dread of ridicule. Let a man travel where he will, home is the place to which "his heart untraveled fondly turns." He is to double all pleasure there. He is to divide all pain. A *happy home* is the single spot of rest which a man has upon this earth for the cultivation of his noblest sensibilities. And now, my brethren, if that be the description of home, is God's place of rest your home? Walk abroad and alone by night. That awful other world in the stillness and the solemn deep of the eternities above, is it your home? Those graves that lie beneath you, holding in them the infinite secret, and stamping upon all earthly loveliness the mark of frailty, and change, and fleetingness; are those graves the prospect to which in bright days and dark days you can turn without dismay? God in his splendors; dare you feel with him affectionate and familiar, so that trial comes softened by this feeling: it is my Father, and enjoyment can be taken with a frank feeling—my Father has given it me without grudging, to make me happy? Do you feel, as the world's waves buffet you, as the sky drops blackness on your path, as all earth's pleasures are being sacrificed, that you have peace in believing, in trusting, in looking up to God through his Son your Redeemer? Do you feel as you go out from one resting place to another that you are no exile from joy, but that as the old roof drops away the Almighty arms will still close around you, and that, lo! another house, not built with hands, is revealing its spiritual symmetry, its fairer form and eternal strength, in the heavens? Can you sing and adopt as your own,

"There is my house and portion fair;
My treasure and my heart are there,
And my abiding home;
For me my elder brethren stay,
And angels beckon me away,
And Jesus bids me come?"

All this *is having a home in God.* Are we, are *you*, at home there? Why, there is demonstration in our very childhood that we are not at home with that other world of God's. An infant fears to be alone, because he feels he is not alone. He trembles in the dark, because he is conscious of the presence of the world of spirits. Long before he has been told tales of terror, there is an instinctive dread of the supernatural in the infant mind. It is the instinct which we have from childhood that gives us the feeling of another world. And mark, brethren, if the child is not at home in the thought of that world of God's, the deep of darkness and eternity is around him—God's home, but not his home, for his flesh creeps; and that feeling grows through life; not the fear—when the child becomes a man he gets over fear—but the dislike. The man feels as much aversion as the child for the world of spirits.

Sunday comes. It breaks across the current of his worldliness; it suggests thoughts of death and judgment, and everlasting existence. Is that home? Can the worldly man feel Sunday like a foretaste of his Father's mansion? If we could but know how many go to church, not to have their souls lifted up heavenward, but from curiosity, or idleness, or criticism, it would give us an appalling estimate of the number who are living in a far country, "having no hope and without God in the world."

The second truth conveyed to us in this parable is *the unsatisfying nature of worldly happiness.* The outcast son tried to satiate his appetite with husks, literally with the pods of the *carob* tree. A husk is an empty thing; it is a thing which looks extremely like food, and promises as much as food; but it is not food. It is a thing which, when chewed, will stay the appetite, but leaves the emaciated body without nourishment. Earthly happiness is a husk. We say not that there is no satisfaction in the pleasures of a worldly life; that would be an overstatement of the truth. Something there is, or else why should men persist in living for them? The cravings of man's appetite may be stayed by things which cannot satisfy him. Every new pursuit contains in it a new hope; and it is long before hope is bankrupt. But it is strange if a man has not found out long before he has reached the age of thirty that everything here is empty and disappointing. The nobler his heart, and the more unquenchable his hunger for the high and the good, the sooner will he find that out. Bubble after bubble burst, each bubble tinted with the celestial colors of the rainbow, and each leaving in the hand which crushes it a cold, damp drop of disappointment. All that is described in Scripture by the emphatic words of "sowing the wind and reaping the whirlwind;" the whirlwind of blighted hopes and unreturned feelings and crushed expectations, that is the harvest which the world gives you to reap.

And now is the question asked, Why is the world unsatisfying? Brethren, it is the grandeur of the soul which God has given us which makes it unsatiable in its desires; an infinite void which cannot be filled up. A soul which was made for God, how can the world fill it? If the ocean can be still with miles of unstable waters beneath, then the soul of man, rocking itself upon its own deep longings, with the infinite beneath it, may rest. We were created once in majesty, to find enjoyment in God, and if our hearts are empty now, there is nothing for it but to fill up the hollowness of the soul with God. Let not that expression, *filling the soul with God*, pass away without a distinct meaning. God is love and goodness. Fill the soul with goodness, and fill the soul with love; that is, the filling it with God. If we love one another, God dwelleth in us. There is nothing else that can satisfy. So that when we hear men of this world acknowledge (as they sometimes will do when they are wearied with this phantom chase of life, sick of gayeties and tired of toil) that it is not in their pursuits that they can drink at the fount of blessedness; and when we see them, instead of turning aside either broken-hearted or else made wise, still persisting to trust to expectations—at fifty, sixty, or seventy years still feverish about some new plan of ambition—what we see is this: we see a soul formed with a capacity for high and noble things, fit for the banquet-table of God himself, trying to fill its infinite hollowness with husks.

Once more, *there is degradation in the life of irreligion.* The things which the wanderer tried to live on were not husks only; they were husks which the swine did eat. Degradation means the application of a thing to purposes lower than that for which it was intended. It is degradation to a man to live on husks, because these are not his true food. We call it degradation when a man is living for purposes lower than those for which God intended him. We were sent into this world to love God and to love man, to do good, to fill up life with deeds of generosity and usefulness. And he that refuses to work out that high destiny is a degraded man. He may turn away revolted from everything that is gross. His sensuous indulgences may all be marked by refinement and taste. His house may be filled with elegance. His library may be adorned with books. There may be the sounds in his mansion which can regale the ear, the delicacies which can stimulate the palate, and the forms of beauty which can please the eye. There may be nothing in his whole life to offend the most chastened and fastidious delicacy; and yet, if the history of all this be powers frittered upon time which were meant for eternity, the man is degraded; if the spirit which was created to find its enjoyment in the love God has settled down satisfied with the love of the world, then, just as surely as the sensualist of this parable, that man has turned aside from a celestial feast to prey on garbage.

We pass on to the second period of the history of God's treatment of a sinner. It is the period *of his coming to himself*, or what we call repentance. The first fact of religious experience which this parable suggests to us is that common truth, men desert the world when the world deserts them. The renegade came to himself when there were no more husks to eat. He would have remained away if he could have got them; but it is written, "no man gave unto him." And this, brethren, is the record of our shame. Invitation is not enough; we must be driven to God. And the famine comes not by chance; God sends the famine into the soul, the hunger and thirst and the disappointment, to bring back his erring child again. Now, the world fastens upon that truth, and gets out of it a triumphant sarcasm against religion. They tell us that just as a caterpillar passes into the chrysalis, and the chrysalis into the butterfly, so profligacy passes into disgust, and disgust passes into religion. To use their own phraseology, when people become disappointed with the world, it is the last resource, say they, to turn saint. So the men of the world speak, and they think they are profoundly philosophical and concise in the account they give. The world is welcome to its very small sneer. It is the glory of our Master's Gospel that it *is* the refuge of the broken-hearted. It is the strange mercy of our God that he does not reject the writhings of a jaded heart. Let the world curl its lip if it will when it sees through the causes of the prodigal's return, and if the sinner does not come to God, taught by this disappointment, what then? If affections crushed in early life have driven one man to God; if wrecked and ruined hopes have made another man religious; if want of success in a profession has broken the spirit; if the human life, lived out too passionately, has left a surfeit and a craving behind which end in seriousness; if one is brought by the sadness of widowed life, and another by the forced desolation of involuntary single life; if, when the mighty famine comes into the heart, and not a husk is left, not a pleasure untried, then, and not till then, the remorseless resolve is made, "I will arise and go to my Father:" well, brethren, what then? Why this: that the history of penitence, produced as it so often is by mere disappointment, sheds only a brighter luster round the love of Christ, who rejoices to receive such wanderers, worthless as they are, back into his bosom. Thank God, the world's sneer is true! It *is* the last resource to turn saint. Thanks to our God, that when this gaudy world has ceased to charm, when the heart begins to feel its hollowness, and the world has lost its satisfying power, still all is not yet lost if penitence and Christ remain to still, to humble, and to soothe a heart which sin has fevered.

There is another truth contained in this section of the parable. After a life of wild sinfulness religion is servitude at first, not freedom. Observe, he went back to duty with the feelings of a slave: "I am no more worthy to be called thy son, make me as one of thy hired servants." The first steps of the religious life, very often, are constrained and difficult. If I speak to any one who is trying to be religious, and heavy in heart because his duty is done too formally, my Christian brother, fear not. You are returning, like the prodigal, with the feelings of a servant. Still it is a real return. The spirit of adoption will come afterward. You will often have to do duties which you cannot relish, and in which you see no meaning. So it was with Naaman at the prophet's command. He bathed, not knowing why he was bidden to bathe in Jordan. When you bend to prayer, often and often you will have to kneel with wandering thoughts and constraining lips, to repeat words into which your heart scarcely enters. You will have to perform duties when the heart is cold and without a spark of enthusiasm to warm you. But, my Christian brother, onward still. Struggle to the cross, even though it be struggling as in chains. Just as on a day of clouds, when you have watched the distant hills, dark and gray with mist, suddenly a gleam of sunshine passing over reveals to you in that flat surface valleys, and dells, and spots of sunny happiness, which slept before unsuspected in the fog; so in the gloom of penitential life there will be times when God's deep peace and love will be felt shining into the soul with supernatural refreshment. Let the penitent be content with the servant's lot at first. Liberty and peace and the bounding sensations of a father's arms around you come afterward.

The last circumstance in this division of our subject is the reception which a sinner meets with on his return to God. "Bring forth the best robe and put it on him, and put a ring on his hand, and shoes on his feet, and bring hither the fatted calf and kill it, and let us eat and be merry."

This banquet represents to us two things: It tells of the father's gladness on his son's return; that represents God's joy on the reformation of a sinner. It tells of a banquet and a dance given to the long lost son; that represents the sinner's gladness when he first understands that God is reconciled to him in Christ. There is a strange, almost wild rapture, a strong gush of love and happiness in those days which are called the days of first conversion. When a man who has sinned much, a profligate, turns to God, and it becomes first clear to his apprehension that there is love instead of spurning for him, there is a luxury of emotion, a banquet of tumultuous blessedness in the moment of first love to God, which stands alone in life, nothing before and nothing after like it. And, brethren, let us observe this forgiveness is a thing granted while a man is yet afar off. We are not to wait for the right of being happy till we are good: we might wait forever. Joy is not delayed till we deserve it. Just so soon as a sinful man trusts that the mercy of God in Christ has done away with his transgression, the ring and the robe, and the shoes are his, the banquet and the light of a father's countenance.

II. We have now very briefly to consider the CONDUCT OF A TECHNICAL SAINT—A FORMAL PROFESSOR OF RELIGION. There is another brother mentioned in this parable, who, with considerable of an outside character that was not positively discreditable, had yet very little of heart enjoyment or practical religion. There are commentators who have imagined that this personage represents a real Christian, but a Christian very strangely perplexed with God's mysterious dealings. But this is a position that is scarcely tenable. Very clearly this elder brother represented in Christ's time the proud and self-righteous Pharisee, who looked with envy and contempt upon the publicans who, under the ministry of the Saviour, pressed into his kingdom. The elder brother is a type of a large class of characters that have existed in connection with the Church in all ages: men who have the form of godliness, but not the power; who are alive to the letter, but dead to the spirit. There are three things which this elder brother develops which ever mark the history of all formal religionists:

First. *A heartless indifference to the moral reclamation of a brother.* He "would not go in," and more, he felt anger and indulged in censure. There is a class of men who belong more or less to all Churches; men who, whatever their professions, are manifestly indifferent to the conversion of souls. They do nothing. They sit at home and read the daily newspaper, or they go when opportunity offers and spend half the night dancing at a neighbor's, when they ought to be at the prayer-meeting. Feeling that their conduct is anomalous, they, when forced to an explanation, urge a defense on a variety of grounds: 1. Some urge a defense on *doctrinal grounds.* They say that conversion is the work of God, and we ought not by our instrumentality to endeavor to take it out of his hands. We do not deny its being the work of God. The Bible refers it to three agencies: the agency of the sinner himself, the agency of God, and the agency of the Christian. There is no contradiction here: the harvest is both the work of the husbandman and the work of God; and the work of conversion is the work of the sinner, of God, and the Church together. 2. Some urge a defense on *ecclesiastical and business grounds.* They say it is the work of the preachers, not of the laymen. "We have no time," is their language, "to talk to men about heaven or hell, the soul and its destiny. We believe there is a hell, a heaven, a soul; we believe more, that one soul is of more value than the entire world; but we have no time to help save it." Observe, these men cannot give one hour in seven days for the purposes of religion; observe, they believe in an eternity that has no limits of duration, but at the same time they are not willing to do anything toward preparing themselves or others for it; and observe farther yet, that these men will work by gas and lamplight to the middle of the night in drawing up deeds, sketching mortgages, measuring out cloths, selling sugars, and the like, and all not for the sake of procuring the comforts or necessaries of life, but simply to obtain a superabundance of its luxuries and artificialities. Could hypocrisy in any being be greater than this ?

Another feature which the elder son developed was,

Secondly, *An exaggerated estimate of his own excellence:* "Lo, these many years do I serve thee." Here is the real Pharisean spirit, which always extols its own virtues, and "rates its morals high." "I am not as other men. I give tithes of all I possess," etc. A mere professor of religion, a technical saint, always overestimates his goodness. Indeed, it is *imaginary* merit that reconciles his conscience to his heartless life; and this spiritual *conceit* frequently develops states of mind similar to those which now came out in this elder son. Here is, First, *Displeasure at the happy reception of a brother.* Instead of rejoicing at the return and happy reception of a brother, he was "angry." *Envy*, the indwelling demon of selfish natures, kindled its hell-fires of anger in that breast of his, which should have glowed with blithe and heartsome love. Your technical saint, instead of rejoicing in the interest felt in a fresh convert, feels often a suppressed dislike, especially if it be in connection with any other branch of the Church than his own. Here is, Secondly, *An irreverent discontent with the doings of a father:* "And he answering, said to his father, Lo, these many years," etc. What a heartless and irreverent way to address a father, especially at a period when his heart was so full of inexpressible delight! Your technical saint has no profound reverence. He has devotion on his lip, but murmurousness in his soul. Here we have, Thirdly, *A censorious reflection upon the faults of others:* "But as soon as this thy son was come, which hath devoured thy living with harlots," etc. A reference to the faults of an erring brother, in this hour of his penitence, was not only bad taste but bad feeling. It was the hateful captiousness of a callous, hateful heart; it indicated a deadness to all true sentiment. Observe how invidiously he compares the father's conduct to his brother: "*This thy son*," he says, not my brother, "*which hath devoured thy living*," again invidiously, for in a sense it was *his own*, "*with harlots*," very probably, yet only a presumption on his part, "*as soon as he was come*," he says not, *was returned*, as of one who had now at length resumed his own place, but speaks of him as a stranger; upon the first moment of his arrival, and after years not of duty, but disobedience, "*thou hast killed for him*," not a kid merely, but the choicest calf in the stall.* Observe the bitter censoriousness, and remember that the technical saint is always of this temper, possessing great mercy on himself and none or little mercy on the sins of others. Perhaps the critical tendency is always the strongest in the weakest brain. Certainly the censorious is always the strongest in the basest heart. The greatest sinner is frequently the greatest censor. The Jeffreys are always the most merciless judges. The men in the Church who complain the most are the men who give least to the support of the ministry, least to the Bible, the missionary, and the Sabbath-school cause. More than this, they are men who are very sensitive to touch in the pocket

* Trench.

nerves, and cry out against the abilities and do-nothing qualities of the preacher when the word quarterage is mentioned.

Another thing which is here suggested in relation to a technical sainthood, a whitewashed religious life, is,

Thirdly, *A voluntary exclusion from the true circle of joy:* He "would not go in." All were happy within. The father and the reclaimed son were happy, though their happiness flowed from different sources. All the domestics shared the joy. "There was music and dancing" in the house. All were joyous but this "elder son." And why was not he happy? 1. Not because the scene was not adapted to yield it. The rich banquet is spread. There is the long lost brother, whose heart, freed from the bitter sorrows and dread forebodings of years, bounds with inexpressible emotions of joy; there is the father, whose soul is too full for speech. Attentions, looks, and tears take the place of words, and declare that his happiness is too great for utterance. Servants and neighbors catch the inspiration of the scene, and feel the ecstasy of joy. There was everything to make the elder brother happy, everything to cause the chords of his heart to vibrate the sweetest music. 2. Not because he was not invited to participate in the scene: "Therefore came his father out, and entreated him." How could he have refused the entreaties of such a father at such an hour! Why then was he excluded? "He was angry and would not go in." His own cold, selfish heart shut him out from all this joy. He was self-excluded from the joyous circle.

Thus it ever is with technical saints, with formal professors of religion; they are a murmuring and a discontented class. They have nothing but trials in the world. They have no comfort in the Church; religion to them is a burden on the back, beneath which they bow and groan; not a new life in the heart, causing them to look sunward and mount up as on eagle's wings. There is happiness around them. Nature spreads out her banquet under the sunny banner of love, the great Father is happy, and his servants rejoice, and the house is filled with "music and dancing;" but the earth is a plain of misery to them, and their song is:

> "Lord, what a wretched land is this,
> That yields us no supplies!"

The Church spreads out her banquet, a feast of fat things, of wines on the lees, well-refined. Returned prodigals are there, the happy Father is there, delighted servants are there, and the house is full of all things to exhilarate and delight; but their cry is: "The ways of Zion do mourn." *Happiness ever depends upon the state of the heart.* It cannot stream as a river into a man's heart from some extraneous or far-off source; it must well up from his own soul.

What greater evil than this *technical sainthood?* Bold infidelity is bad, open profligacy is bad; but this technical sainthood, for many reasons, is worse. It is infidelity repeating creeds and saying prayers; it is Belial in the dress of virtue; it is Judas in the character of an apostle; it is the devil transformed into an angel of light. It is the greatest *living* lie in the world. It is an Achan in the camp; not in one camp, but in every camp in Christendom.

"There is an accursed thing in the midst of thee, O Israel: thou canst not stand before thine enemies until ye take away the accursed thing from among you."

And now in conclusion, as a remark of application derived from the consideration of the case of the first brother, let me say one word to those who are living the life he did, thinking to become religious as he did when they have got tired of the world. I speak to those who are leading what, in the world's softened language of concealment, is called a gay life. Young friends, let two motives be urged earnestly upon your attention. The first is the motive of mere honorable feeling. We will say nothing about the uncertainty of life. We will not dwell upon this fact, that impressions resisted now may never come back again. We will not appeal to terror. That is not the weapon which a Christian minister loves to use. If our lips were clothed with thunder, it is not denunciation which makes men Christians; let the appeal be made to every high and generous feeling in a young man's bosom. Deliberately and calmly you are going to do *this:* to spend the best and most vigorous portion of your days in idleness, in uselessness, in the gratification of self, in the contamination of others. And then weakness, the relics, and the miserable dregs of life; you are going to give *that* sorry offering to God because *his mercy endureth forever!* Shame, shame upon the heart which can let such a plan rest in it one moment. If it be there crush it like a man. It is a degrading thing to enjoy husks till there is no man to give them. It is a base thing to resolve to give to God as little as possible, and not to serve him till you must.

Young friends, I speak principally to you. You have health for God now. You have strength of mind and body. You have powers which may fit you for real usefulness. You have appetites for enjoyment which can be consecrated to God. You acknowledge the law of honor. Well, then, by every feeling of manliness and generosity, remember this: now, and not later, is your time to learn what religion means.

There is another motive, and a very solemn one, to be urged upon those who are delaying. Every moment of delay adds bitterness to after struggles; the moment of a feeling of hired servitude must come. If a man will not obey God with a warm heart he may hereafter have to do it with a cold one. To be holy is the work of a long life. The experience of ten thousand lessons teaches only a little of it; and all this, the work of becoming like God, the man who delays is crowding into the space of a few years or a few months. When we have lived a long life of sin, do we think that repentance and forgiveness will obliterate all the traces of sin upon the character? Be sure that every sin pays its price: "Whatsoever a man soweth that shall he also reap." O there are recollections of past sin which come crowding up to the brain with temptation in them. There are old habits which refuse to be mastered by a few enthusiastic sensations. There is so much of the old man clinging to the penitent who has waited long, he is so much as a religious man like what he was when he was a worldly man, that it is doubtful whether he ever reaches in this world the full stature of Christian manhood. Much warm earnestness, but strange inconsistencies, that is the character of one who is an old man and a young Christian. My young friends, do you wish to risk all this? Do you want to learn holiness with terrible struggles, and sore affliction, and the plague of much remaining evil? Then *wait* before you turn to God.

HOMILY LXIX.

THE STARTING POINT OF CHRISTIANITY.

Beginning at Jerusalem. LUKE xxiv, 47.

THE verse of which this is a part contains four facts:

First. *That "repentance and remission" are the two greatest blessings humanity requires.* This is evidently implied in the fact which Jesus here expresses, namely, that he suffered and rose from the dead on the "third day," according to the Scriptures, in order that these blessings might be offered to the human race. Man is inwardly *depraved*, and consequently *divinely condemned;* he needs "repentance" to remove his depravity, and "remission" to remove his condemnation.

Secondly. *That these great blessings are both supplied in the "name of Christ."* They are to "be preached in his name." Christ's history is at once the only *moral power* that can produce this "repentance," and the only *governmental ground* which can secure this "remission."

Thirdly. *That the offering of these blessings to humanity, through the name of Christ, is the great work of the Gospel ministry.* They "should be preached in his name." The work of the ministry, as such, is not theological disquisition, nor polemic controversy, nor priestly fulmination, but the generous, earnest, and faithful offering of these blessings to humanity through the name of Jesus Christ.

Fourthly. *That it was the plan of God that the Gospel ministry should commence the offer of these blessings in Jerusalem.* "Beginning at Jerusalem." Why begin at Jerusalem? Why not begin in Egypt, or Greece, or Persia, or in some other city of Judea? Why begin at Jerusalem? Antecedently we should have thought that Jerusalem would have been one of the last places in which "repentance and remission" would have been preached, rather than the first. There are, especially, three reasons which would have led to this conclusion: (1.) *The abundant opportunities which it had long possessed of becoming fully acquainted with the Gospel.* Jerusalem had been for ages the scene of that splendid ritualism which Infinite Wisdom instituted to symbolize the Gospel; for ages, too, it had been the home of prophets and of priests; and many times, moreover, had Jesus, to whom all these ceremonies referred and predictions pointed, walked its streets and appealed to its population. As this city had opportunities of knowing the Gospel that no other city ever had, and as there were other numerous Jewish cities which had not these advantages, and many Gentile cities which had no opportunities at all, we might have thought that Jerusalem would have been among the last to have had the offer. (2.) *Its abuse of all the opportunities with which it had been so highly favored.* Its very privileges had become means of formality, hypocrisy, and crime. Under all its religious means it had become one of the most corrupt and wicked cities under neaven—the city that had martyred the prophets of every age. Would it not, therefore, have been natural to suppose that a city which had thus abused such unparalleled religious privileges would rather have been destroyed than have been chosen as the first to be offered the great blessings of the last dispensation? (3.) *Its heartless, wicked, and impious treatment of Christ.* He addressed doctrines to it, but those doctrines it proclaimed blasphemy; he wrought miracles for it, but those miracles they referred to Satanic power; he wept tears of compassion over it, but those tears it spurned. Jerusalem was the scene of his insults and the home of his murderers. Would it not, therefore, have been natural to conclude that if Jesus offered mercy to this city at all, it would not have been until others had received this overture.

But although, antecedently, we might have concluded thus, we discover good reasons for the plan adopted in offering salvation *first* to Jerusalem. What are those reasons?

I. "BEGINNING AT JERUSALEM" SERVES TO STRENGTHEN THE EVIDENCES OF CHRISTIANITY. That the starting of Christianity from Jerusalem serves to augment the force of evidence in favor of its truth, will appear if you consider three things:

First. *Jerusalem was the most proximate city to the scene of the principal facts of the Gospel.* Paul tells us (2 Cor. xv, 1–4) that the facts which *constitute* the Gospel are that "Christ died," that he was "buried," and that he "rose again." These facts all happened in the immediate vicinity of Jerusalem, under the public eye of the population. But how does the fact of its being the most proximate city strengthen the evidence in favor of the truth of Christianity? In two ways: (1.) *It would show that those of the number who believed the apostles were intelligent believers.* If the apostles had gone *first* to a distance and got a large number to believe, it might fairly have been said by the opponents, the believers had no way of testing the truth of the facts for themselves, and their credulity was imposed upon by the apostles. But the possibility of such an objection is precluded by "beginning at Jerusalem." Each man had the opportunity of testing the facts for himself. The people to whom the apostles spoke had seen Him suffer in the streets —they had seen him upon the cross—they had seen him buried on the Friday, and witnessed the empty grave on the first day of the week. Peter, in his first sermon to them, appeals to their *knowledge* of these facts: "As ye yourselves also know." If these men therefore believed, *their faith*, being *intelligent*, would have an argumentative force everywhere to convince. "Three thousand" of them did believe under the first discourse; and who but God can tell the *force* of that fact in commending Christianity to the credence of men of remoter places and later times? (2.) *It shows that the first preachers were no impostors, but had full confidence in the truth of what they affirmed.* Had they gone first to a distance, skeptics might have charged them with imposture; they might have said, These men went to remote places to proclaim extraordinary things which they knew their hearers had no opportunity of testing, etc. But the fact of their stating them to the eye-witnesses of Christ's history shows, at any rate, that they had no intention to deceive; deceivers would have gone to a distance. "Beginning at Jerusalem" shows that the apostles were *genuine men*, worthy of confidence.

Secondly. *Jerusalem was the most antagonistic city to the moral purport and purpose of these facts.* The men of Jerusalem profoundly and passionately hated the character, doctrines, and aim of Christ. Going *first*, therefore, to this city, (1.) Showed the daring strength of the apostles' faith. (2.) Precluded the possibility of the objection that the first believers were prejudiced in its favor. (3.) Demonstrated the mighty power of the Gospel in triumphing over opposition.

Thirdly. *Jerusalem was the city predicted as the starting point of Christianity.* Isaiah, Joel, Zachariah, David, and others, predicted this.

II. Beginning at Jerusalem serves to display the benignity of Christianity. The men of Jerusalem were the greatest personal enemies of Christ, and the greatest sinners against him. In commanding the Gospel, therefore, to be preached to them, there was an astonishing display of benignity. This benignity may be looked upon in two aspects:

First. *As an expression of human duty.* Christ has "left us an example that we should follow in his steps." How did he treat his enemies? The men of Jerusalem treated him with the greatest indignity; they plucked off his hair; they made long furrows on his cheeks; they crowned him with thorns; they crucified him. But how did he treat them? Did he commission, now all power was given to him, some messenger of justice to hurl thunderbolts of vengeance at them? No! he commissioned his apostles to offer them the choicest blessings he had to bestow—blessings, the procuring of which cost him his life—"repentance and remission." Learn a lesson from this, ye men who in the name of Christianity stand up for war.

Secondly. *As an expression of a divine doctrine.* What is the doctrine? *That there is mercy for the chief of sinners.* What city under heaven contained greater sinners than Jerusalem? What privileges they had abused! What holy men they had persecuted! What innocent blood they had shed! What saints and prophets they had martyred! And now in the crucifixion of Christ they filled up the measure of their crime. "Begin at Jerusalem;" go to Caiaphas, go to Pilate, go to the chief priests, go to the Roman soldiers, etc., tell the worst man that through my name there is mercy for him. If there is mercy for the men of Jerusalem, who need despair?

III. Beginning at Jerusalem serves to indicate the method of propagating Christianity. The method is, to begin at home—*home first.* This method Jesus acted upon in his own ministry; this method he enjoined on his apostles, and this method they strictly followed in all their endeavors to propagate the Gospel.

First. *This method harmonizes with the dictates of a genuine heart.* The heart says, *Home first.*

> "Friends, parents, neighbors, first, it doth embrace;
> My country next, and next the human race."

We say *genuine* heart, for the heart of a morbid, sentimental philanthropy crosses seas and traverses continents to convey blessings to the most distant, which the nearest urgently require.

Secondly. *This method harmonizes with the dictates of an enlightened judgment. If our obligation to propagate the Gospel to the largest possible extent* was given to us in order to find out the most *effective* way, we think we should soon reach the conclusion that we ought to concentrate our *chief* efforts upon that section of our race that would (1.) be most susceptible of evangelical impressions; (2.) on whom we could bring to bear the largest amount of our influence; and (3.) who would, after their evangelization, become the most effective auxiliaries in speeding on the glorious work.

Now Jerusalem, *to the apostles*, presented these three conditions. Who would be so likely to be evangelically impressed as the men of Jerusalem? Under the very first discourse three thousand were converted! On whom could they bring so much force effectively to bear as upon the men of Jerusalem? The apostles understood their language, their prejudices, their habits of thought and life. And what class, when converted, could become such useful agents in helping forward the new faith?

HOMILY LXX.

THE NEEDLESSNESS OF MAN'S RUIN.

Why will ye die? EZEKIEL xviii, 31.

THE needlessness of man's ruin is the subject which we deduce from this question. There are, however, other important ideas manifestly implied in this divine utterance, which may be usefully set forth as a suitable preface to the general theme.

The question implies,

First, *That man is made to act from reason.* His Maker here appeals to his reasoning faculty, and demands a reason for his ruinous conduct. He has made some creatures to act from instinct, but man from reason. It is true that man has, in common with all irrational existences, certain corporeal impulses which prompt him to action. These, in natures of certain temperaments, and under certain circumstances, become exceedingly potent, tend to overbear intellect and break down the boundaries of reason. But as in no case is their power necessarily resistless, in no case is their reign justifiable. The engine may be full of steam; but reason, as the regulator, should make it serve the use of the intelligent moral man. Strong gales and billows of impulse may rise, but reason, as the helmsman, should so adjust the bark as to make these blind forces do its work. The steed may be full of Arabian fire, but reason, as the rider, should hold the reins and direct its lightning speed.

Some men plead the power of their impulses as a justification for their wicked and reckless deeds. Such pleas are inadmissible; for wisely and kindly has our blessed Maker proportioned in our constitution the measure of reason to impulse. The man of strongest impulse has generally the strongest intellect. Men of weak impulses are generally weak in everything; weak tradesmen, weak mechanics, weak thinkers, weak writers, weak speakers, weak saints. Complain not, therefore, of your strong *natural* impulses; thank God for them, for he has given you a sufficient amount of reason to manage and master all their operations. When they become too dormant, let reason muse until their fires kindle; and when they grow too furiously hot, let reason muse until the flames expire. Never act from them, but always by them; let them be your servant, not your sovereign.

The question implies,

Secondly, *That man is amenable to his Maker for the reasons that influence him.* "Why will ye die?" He demands a reason, and he has an unquestionable right to do so. The reason or motive of an act is in his view the act. The muscular effort is not the act; it is but its contingent form. The theater of human actions is the soul, and that is hidden from all but God. Man's deeds before his Maker are completed before a limb or muscle moves. Thefts, adulteries, and murders are committed when the body has never performed one dishonest, lascivious, or cruel act. We shall "have to give an account of all the deeds done *in* the body," as well as the deeds done *by* the body. The latter are nothing in their nature or number as compared with the former. When these are revealed, as revealed they must be, "the hidden things of darkness will be brought to light."

The question implies,

Thirdly, *That notwithstanding man's rational and responsible nature he is pursuing a course of self-destruction.* "Why will ye die?" "The wages of sin is death." What is this death? We can more readily tell you what it is not than what it is. *It is not the death of the body.* Men do not generally *will* this; on the contrary, they are supremely anxious to avoid it. But this is impossible. No ingenuity, influence, or power can ward off the stroke of death. "There is no man that hath power over the spirit to retain the spirit, neither hath he power in the day of death; and there is no discharge in that warfare." Nor does it mean *the extinction of the spirit.* Man may kill his body; he has done so; but he cannot kill his spirit. The soul is an inextinguishable spark from the Eternal Source of life; it must flame on forever. No power but the power of Omnipotence can put it out. "It smiles at the drawn dagger, and defies the point." Nor does it mean the *destruction of personal consciousness.* We can conceive of the spirit existing, and yet its personality destroyed. Like a branch, it may be so engrafted on some other existence as to lose its own individual attributes in the connection; like a drop, it may fall into the ocean, and though it still exists, its individuality is lost. But this will never be the case with the soul. Souls, unlike material elements, can never amalgamate. Each must remain a distinct existent forever. Personality is essential to soul. Still more, we can conceive of personality existing, and yet consciousness be dormant. The butterfly exists in the chrysalis. May not spirits pass into such a state; exist, but exist without consciousness? We do not pronounce such a state impossible; but we say, instead of there being any reason to believe that it will ever be the case with man, there is every reason to believe the contrary. Man can no more kill the personality and consciousness of his spirit than he can kill itself. What does it mean then? *Dissolution of the ties of moral obligation?* The chain that binds us to moral government is one that cannot be broken. To be honest, truthful, generous, devout, godly—what can possibly terminate our obligation to be all this? Nothing. To be all this is as much the duty of fallen angels now, as it was when they sang and served in heaven.

What is this death then to which the wicked expose themselves? Or, in other words, Why is the ruin to which they expose themselves represented as "death?" There is some analogy. For example, in corporeal death there is utter *deprivation*. You see the dead body laid out. The material organization appears complete; but the principle which warmed that frame, moved those limbs, looked out through those eyes, heard through those ears, and beautified that form, is gone. The house is there, but the tenant has left. There is utter *hideousness*. How soon after life has gone does that lovely form, which we once pressed to our bosom, become loathsome, and, like Abraham, we seek for a place to bury our dead out of our sight! There is in death, moreover, utter *slavery*. The body which once used the elements of the world, drank in its light, breathed its air, appropriated the various gases, becomes the creature of all. All serve to break it up and sport with its dissolving atoms. In all these respects the ruin which sin brings upon the soul is like unto death. There is the greatest *deprivation*—truth, honesty, love, piety—the animating principle of the soul departs. It loses its beauty and its life. There is *hideousness*. By sin the soul becomes odious to all moral minds. A corrupt character is loathed by all consciences. There is *slavery*. Instead of the spirit using all things for its own ends, it becomes the creature of all, tossed about by every force. This *deprivation*, *hideousness*, and *slavery* constitute the death of the soul. And this is going on where sin is. It is not something in the future. "To be carnally-minded *is* death." The spirit of the sinner is dying every day; every day deprived of something, every day becoming more hideous in the universe, every day becoming more the powerless creature of things.

Now the point is that man need not meet with this ruin; he need not die; there is no necessity for it.

I. THE DECREES OF GOD DO NOT RENDER YOUR RUIN NECESSARY. That the infinitely wise Maker and monarch of the universe has a decree, purpose, or plan by which his operations are determined cannot but be admitted. But that he has any decree or plan against any man's salvation, or for any man's ruin, is an idea repugnant alike to our reason, our intuitions, and our Bible. God is good to all, and "his tender mercies are over all the works of his hand." The Bible teaches that "he has no pleasure in the death of the sinner, but rather that he should return unto him and live." But you inquire, Does not Paul teach that

God makes vessels for dishonor as well as vessels for honor? No. All that he avers is, that he *could* do so. And it is to the glory of God's benevolence to assert that while he could make and organize creatures for misery, he has *never* done so. Let the naturalist search through all the endless species of animal life, let him take the microscope, and let him find one single creature among the smallest, and say, this little creature was evidently made to suffer, was organized for misery, is a vessel built for dishonor. No; God could, but he does not. There is no divine decree which requires your ruin; you are not predestinated to damnation. If you are lost it is because you act against, not with the divine plan.

II. Your sinful condition does not render your ruin necessary. You are sinners. Conscience, society, and the Bible unite in the declaration of the dark fact in your history. You sometimes feel your sins as a millstone on your heart, as a dark thunder cloud in your sky. Your sins deserve your ruin, demand your ruin, and if you continue in them will realize your ruin; but as yet they do not render your ruin necessary. Why is this? Because the Gospel makes provision for you in your present state. There lies a man on the bed of suffering. A malignant and painful disease has done its work on his constitution; in a few hours unless some remedy come he must breathe his last. A skillful physician enters the room; he has in his hand a little medicine, which if taken will inevitably restore him. It is offered to him, pressed on him, and he has yet power to take it. Need that man die? If he refuse the remedy he must die; but since the remedy is offered, and he has the power to take it, his death is needless. It is thus with the sinner. He is infected with the malady of sin, he is on the margin of death; but here is the remedy, the great physician of souls is at his side offering an infallible antidote. Had not this physician appeared in our midst our death would have been unavoidable. But now he is at our side pressing on us the remedy; we need not die. Though the malady has assumed the most malignant form, though the spiritual grave yawns at our feet, we need not die.

III. The external circumstances in which you are placed do not render your ruin necessary. These are often pleaded as an excuse for indifference, indecision, and sometimes profligacy. It is said, It is impossible for me to become religious. I live among the gay, the worldly, the profane, the skeptical. My worldly engagements too are all-absorbing. I live in the bustle of the crowd, I am lost in the din of business. Were I in other circumstances I would become a religious man; I would discipline my soul, and prepare for eternity. Would that I had a home in some rural spot away from all connection with the thoughtless multitudes, whose corrupt sentiments are ever falling on my ear, and surging through my soul. Some quiet spot in nature where I should hear nothing but the rustling of the trees and the murmuring of the brooks, the warbling of the birds and the other voices of nature, see little but the ever-changing, but ever-lovely face of nature. Were I in such circumstances as these I would be a religious man; I would train my heart and worship my Maker. My brother, this is all sentiment. Remember that the God who requires you to become religious placed you in the circumstances in which you are found, and if you trust in him, "as your day, so your strength shall be." Remember that it is the glory of a rational being to bend circumstances to its own purpose rather than to be mastered by them. "It is not that which goeth into a man that defileth him." Bad thoughts may be conveyed to your mind, bad impressions made on your hearts, but they need not harm you; you have a power to transmute them into spiritual nourishment. Remember that some of the most eminent saints that ever lived have been among the most trying and tempting circumstances. Remember that the more trying your circumstances may be, the more corrupt the society in which you live, the more need there is for you to carry out noble principles. The deeper the gloom the more need of light; the more parched the soil the more need of the shower. Hold forth the word of life in the midst of the crooked and perverse. Your circumstances therefore do not render your ruin necessary.

IV. THE CONDITION ON WHICH SALVATION IS OFFERED DOES NOT RENDER YOUR RUIN NECESSARY. What is the great condition? The New Testament teaches us that it is *faith*. "He that *believeth* shall be saved;" "He that *believeth* hath everlasting life." Now belief as an act is one of the most simple. It is as natural to believe an evident truth as it is to see. Moreover, man has a strong *propensity* to believe, especially the things that tend to his injury. His credulity is his curse. It is this that hath given to the world those monstrous systems of error under which it has been groaning for ages. But what must we believe in order to be saved? If it be responded, "The facts of the Gospel," I ask, Are there any facts attested by clearer or more potent evidence? Or if it be said, "The principles of the Gospel," then we declare that those principles are moral axioms, and recommend themselves to the intuitions and felt necessities of the human soul. Or, should it be replied, "It is faith in the Author of the Gospel, the living, loving, personal Christ," then we ask, What character is so adapted to enlist your faith and inspire your confidence? He is honest, loving, truthful, religious, and transparent in all! "Believe on the Lord Jesus Christ, and thou shalt be saved." Where is your difficulty in this? No! if you are ruined it is not because you cannot comply with the conditions. "Why then will ye die?" I beseech you, endeavor to make some reply. The very effort to make some reply perhaps may startle you. Can you assign a single reason? Can you tell me of anything that renders it necessary that you should die? Anything in nature? Anything in the Bible? Anything in Christ? Anything in God? Why, O why will you turn that soul of yours into a demon, which is capable of rising into a seraph? Why will you become a curse to yourself and the universe rather than a blessing? Why will you spurn a destiny ever brightening in splendor, ever heightening in joy, and select a doom terrible in woe and wickedness?

HOMILY LXXI.

THE TREASURE AND THE PEARL; OR, CHRISTIANITY THE HIGHEST GOOD.

The kingdom of heaven is like unto treasure hid in a field; the which when a man hath found, he hideth, and for joy thereof goeth and selleth all that he hath, and buyeth that field. Again, the kingdom of heaven is like unto a merchantman, seeking goodly pearls; who, when he had found one pearl of great price, went and sold all that he had, and bought it. MATTHEW xiii, 44–46.

WE have Christianity here in two aspects:

I. AS A TRANSCENDENT GOOD IN ITSELF APART FROM MAN. It is here represented as a treasure and a pearl. "A pearl of great price." Looking at it apart from man it is "a treasure," a good in itself: it has *intrinsic* worth. But it is "a hid" treasure, hid in the field of revelation. It is "a pearl" in the sea of divine events. There are material treasures in those hills around us, and pearls beneath the waters that roll at our feet, sufficient, could we obtain them, to invest us with the wealth of a Crœsus. It is so with spiritual things. There are elements of good in the Scriptures, and in religious literature, and in the Church of God, which, if men could only discover and possess, would enrich and ennoble them forever. "The unsearchable riches of Christ," like treasures concealed by the earth, or pearls buried in the waters, are in our world; but they are unseen and unowned by the millions.

There are four criteria by which we determine the value of an object: *Rarity*, *Verdict of competent authorities*, *Durability*, *Usefulness*. First. *Rarity*. This makes gold more valuable than brass or iron, pearls and diamonds more valuable than ordinary stones. In this sense Christianity is valuable. It is perfectly unique. There is nothing like it. Among all the systems of the world there is but one Gospel; among all the books but one Bible. "There is no other name given," etc. Secondly. *The verdict of competent authorities*. Whatever article in the markets of the world is pronounced valuable by men whose judgment is considered most correct on such subjects, derives at once a value from the fact. The opinions of such authorities will invest almost any article, however intrinsically worthless, with a commercial value. Intrinsically worthless books, if praised by those who are considered judges of literature, will pass as the most precious productions of genius. Apply this to Christianity. The greatest sages, the sublimest poets, the purest saints, have all pronounced Christianity to be of incomparable value. They have felt with Paul, who said, "I count all things but loss," etc. Thirdly. *Durability*. The duration of an object often gives it value. The thing if of ephemeral existence is not esteemed of much worth. The Gospel is durable. It is the incorruptible seed. "It is the word of God that endureth for ever." Fourthly. *Usefulness*. We value an object according to the service it is capable of rendering. Metals and plants, animals and men, are estimated by this rule. What has rendered such service to humanity as Christianity? We need not speak of its intellectual benefits, and show how it has broken the monotony of thought and set the mind of the world in action. We need not speak of its political benefits, and show how it has flashed and frowned upon injustice and tyranny, and moulded governments according to the principles of rectitude. We need not speak of its social benefits, and show how it has evoked and refined the best sympathies of our nature, given man a kindly interest in his fellow, and laid the foundation of social order and progress. We speak of its spiritual blessings. How it purifies the fountains of life, how it pacifies the guilty conscience, how it fills the soul with the sunshine of divine love, how it raises our nature above the fear of death, and enchants it with glowing visions of an ever expanding and brightening futurity.

Blessed Gospel! It is indeed "a pearl of great price." Take it from us, and you will freeze up the fountains of our spiritual energy and blight the springing germs of our hopes; you will turn our landscapes into deserts, and our hemispheres into midnight. Take it from us and what are we? Frail barks struggling with the heaving billows of life, without a chart to direct us, or a star to break the darkness that enshrouds us on the surging wave.

II. As a transcendent good in the process of appropriation by man. It is interesting to look upon Christianity as an infinite good in itself; but it is more interesting to look upon it as a good appropriated by ourselves. Such is the view we now pass to. The appropriation includes two things: *Discovery, and joyous surrender of all for it.* First. *Discovery.* The pearl and treasure were "found" in two very different ways: one by an *apparent accident*, and the other by an *intelligent purpose.* (1.) There is apparent accident in the discovery of the treasure. It is not said that the man was in search of it. Perhaps the man as he was digging, or driving his plowshare through his land in the process of its cultivation, turned up the treasure unexpectedly.

"The circumstance," says Trench, "which supplies the groundwork of this parable, namely, the finding of a con cealed treasure, must have been of much more frequent occurrence in an insecure state of society, such as in almost all ages has been that of the East, than happily it can be with us. A writer on Oriental literature and customs mentions that in the East, on account of the frequent changes of dynasties and the revolutions which accompany them, many rich men divide their goods into three parts: one they employ in commerce, or for their necessary support; one they turn into jewels, which, should it prove needful to fly, could be easily carried with them; a third part they bury. But while they trust no one with the place where the treasure is buried, so is the same, should they not return to the spot before their death, as good as lost to the living, until by chance a lucky peasant, while he is digging his field, lights upon it. And thus when we read in Eastern tales how a man has found a buried treasure and in a moment risen from poverty to great riches, this is, in fact, an occurrence that not unfrequently happens, and is a natural consequence of the customs of these people. Modern books of travels continually bear witness to the universal belief in the existence of such hid treasures; so that the traveler often finds great difficulty in obtaining information about antiquities.

and is sometimes seriously inconvenienced, or even endangered, in his researches among ancient ruins, by the jealousy of the neighboring inhabitants, who fear lest he is coming to carry away concealed hoards of wealth from among them, of which, by some means or other, he has got notice. And so also the skill of an Eastern magician in great part consists in being able to detect the places where these secreted treasures will successfully be looked for. Often, too, a man abandoning the regular pursuits of industry will devote himself to treasure-seeking in the hope of growing, through some happy chance, rich of a sudden."

This man represents those who meet with the saving power of the Gospel at a time when they had no intention of so doing. These are the men who are found of Christ though they ask not for him. Such was the woman of Samaria at Jacob's Well; such were Peter and Andrew "casting a net into the sea;" such was Nathaniel "under the fig tree." How many have been converted in a seemingly casual way! Christ has come to them in a tract, or a conversation, or a sermon, or in some other event in an unexpected manner. The inestimable treasure has been found in a most casual way—casual to the finder, but prearranged by Heaven. (2.) There is *intelligent purpose.* The merchant was engaged in "seeking goodly pearls." This man believed in the existence of "goodly pearls," he strongly desired them, and visited all the markets within his reach in quest of the same.

This appears to indicate the antiquity of a still Oriental profession, that of a traveling jeweler, a person who deals in precious stones and pearls, and goes about seeking for opportunities of making advantageous purchases or exchanges, and taking journeys to remote countries for this purpose, and again in another direction to find the best market for the valuables he has secured. In the course of their operations it frequently happens that they meet with some rich and costly gem, for the sake of obtaining which they sell off all their existing stock, and every article of valuable property they may possess, in order to raise the purchase money. Something similar may sometimes occur in the transactions of stationary jewelers, but not so often as among those who travel; indeed, the jewelers of the East, as a body, are perhaps the greatest travelers in the world.

This represents the men who believe in a higher good than they have reached, anxiously search for it in science, in literature, in worship, and at last find it a rich prize. "We have, perhaps," says Trench, "no such a picture of a noble nature seeking for the pearl of price, and not resting till he had found it, as that which Augustine gives of himself in his '*Confessions;*' though we, also, have many more, such as Justin Martyr's account of his own conversion, given in his dialogue with Trypho, in which he tells how he had traveled through the whole circle of Greek philosophy, seeking everywhere for that which would satisfy the deepest needs of his soul, and ever seeking in vain, till he found it at length in the Gospel of Christ."

Though, however, the chief good is often found casually, no one has a right to expect it without acting as the merchant did. Nay, every man incurs guilt who acts not thus. A man must go into the field and not merely upturn its soil with the plowshare of cursory thought, but he must dig and delve as a miner. He must not merely look into the face of the waters for the pearl, he must dive to the sandy bed on which it rests. He must prosecute an earnest quest for it. "Yea, if thou criest after knowledge, and liftest up thy voice for understanding; if thou seekest her as silver, and searchest for her as for hid treasures; then shalt thou understand the fear of the LORD, and find the knowledge of God. For the LORD giveth wisdom: out of his mouth cometh knowledge and understanding. He layeth up sound wisdom for the righteous: he is a buckler to them that walk uprightly."

Secondly. *A joyous surrender of all for it.* "He selleth all that he hath and buyeth the field." The merchant did the same and bought the pearl. The only condition on which you can obtain this transcendent good is by selling all you have; your preconceived notions, old habits, and selfishness, pride, time, talents, your all. It must be regarded of more worth than all other things put together. We say a *joyous* surrender of all for it. "With joy," etc. The purchase must be made, not mechanically, reluctantly, but joyously, with an exultant heart. "What things were gain to me," said Paul, "I counted loss," etc.

HOMILY LXXII.

THE DISCIPLES IN THE TEMPEST; OR, MENTAL DISTRESS.

And when he was entered into a ship, his disciples followed him. And behold, there arose a great tempest in the sea, insomuch that the ship was covered with the waves: but he was asleep. MATT. viii, 23, 24.

THE extraordinary cures which Christ had effected at Capernaum had, it would seem, attracted to him throngs of people from all parts of the neighborhood. In his personal ministry there was a fulfillment of a prediction which had been uttered some twenty centuries before. Jacob, on his death-bed, wrapt in prophetic vision, had said that unto "Shiloh shall the gathering of the people be." During the brief period of Christ's public life, "great multitudes gathered about him." Wherever he went, whether to the quiet mountain, the secluded village, or the solitary shore, he attracted crowds. His life was a magnet, drawing to itself all that came within the sweep of its influence. All the attraction, however, of his personal ministry on earth is but a faint representation and pledge of that more spiritual and higher influence which he is destined one day to exert upon all the nations under heaven. He will "draw all men unto him." The day will come when the whole population of the globe will have their thoughts, sympathies, and souls centered in his person and guided by his will.

It is remarkable that Christ, at various times, seemed anxious to avoid popularity. The incident before us is an example. In the eighteenth verse we are distinctly told that when "Jesus saw great multitudes about him, he gave commandment to depart unto the other side." And forthwith he enters into a ship in order to cross to "the other side." This desire to escape notoriety which he on several occasions manifested, is a subject which, though it may lead to interesting speculation, is, we consider, of not much practical importance. Whether it arose from that instinct to shun rather than to seek popularity which has ever characterized all truly great men, or from some prudential reason, we stay not to inquire.

The scene before us needs no description from us. In a few sentences of exquisite simplicity the evangelist presents an event of most stirring sublimity and suggestive significance. Had a modern biographer of the popular stamp to represent some such a scene as this in the life of his hero, how much labor and time would he expend in order to work it into effect! How many fine words he would employ! How many allusions to other scenes which would serve to show off the superior character and extent of his reading! How many pages would he fill, and how much of the precious time of the reader would he waste with his tawdry pencilings! But the evangelist sketches this magnificent scene with a few simple strokes, in such a way as to prevent all wise expositors from making any effort to heighten its effect. The men who wrote this book were not book-makers. They had too much to communicate to be such. The writers and speakers who have the most thoughts have always the fewest words. Verbosity is always the offspring either of vagueness or vacuity.

We take this incident of Christ and his disciples in the tempest to illustrate *the mental distress of the good:*

I. Mental distress frequently comes unexpectedly. The distress of the disciples, now in the tempest, came upon them by surprise. When they embarked that night and moved off from the shore there was, perhaps, every prospect of a safe and happy voyage. The stars, it may be, shone upon them from a peaceful sky, and their bright images seemed to sleep upon the calm bosom of the azure wave. But this serenity was temporary. A storm was brooding. The scene soon changes. Matthew tells us "there arose a great tempest in the sea, insomuch that the ship was covered with the waves." Mark describes it as a "great storm of wind;" and Luke says, "there came down a storm of wind on the lake." There is no need of supposing that this storm was miraculous. The Galilean sea, being surrounded by mountains and hills, was naturally subject to sudden storms. It was evidently a most terrific scene. The billows dashed over the vessel, threatening every moment to fill and engulf her. Thus their distress came *unexpectedly.*

Is not this frequently so in the history of man? How often men enter on some new enterprise, period, or relation of life with every prospect of much enjoyment and prosperity; all things seem to smile on them with promises of an auspicious future, when suddenly some storm obscures the lights of their sky, lashes their sea into commotion, and threatens them with ruin! Abraham, Job, and David are striking examples of this on the side of the good; and on the other side such names as Belshazzar and Judas may stand. How strikingly does this fact show *that our destiny is ever in the hands of another.* "We know not what a day may bring forth." In imagination our to-morrow may be a period redolent with bright joys; but let it come, and we may find it a day of thick darkness and sorrow. The path of our history is filled with the vestiges of frustrated plans and blighted hopes. "Our times are in His hands." "The lot is cast into the lap; but the whole disposing thereof is with the Lord." "The horse is prepared against the day of battle, but safety is of the Lord." As there was an invisible power beyond the hills that bounded the Galilean sea, working up a storm at the moment everything seemed bright and calm to the disciples, so there is always a mighty spirit beyond our sensuous horizon who can at any moment lash the calmest sea on which we glide along into the wildest fury of the tempest.

II. Mental distress oftentimes induces earnest prayer. How earnestly now do the disciples cry to Christ for help! Jesus was asleep. The benevolent toils of the day had fatigued him; and participating in our natural infirmities, he retires to the hinder part of the ship, lays his weary head on some wooden pillow, and sinks to repose. The storm disturbs him not; its most furious blast bore no alarm to him. Innocence can calmly sleep in storms. There is no room for fear in that heart whose sympathies and aims are ever in concert with the Infinite will. But while Jesus sleeps the disciples are in an agony of fear; they hasten to him, rouse him from his slumbers, and exclaim: "Lord save us, or we perish." "Carest thou not for us?" "Master, master, we perish!" Here is earnest prayer.

We may look at this appeal to Christ, under these circumstances, in two aspects:

First. *As a tendency in human nature to call upon God, when exposed to imminent peril.* History abounds with examples of this. The heathen crew of the ship in which Jonah embarked for Tarshish, cried every man to his God in the midst of that terrible storm which threatened their destruction. The Psalmist states, as a general truth, that those that go down to the sea in ships, and do business in the great waters, "cry unto the Lord in their trouble." Now, the fact that men do this, whether they be theists or atheists, their character depraved or holy, is very significant. It shows, (1.) *An instinctive belief in the divine existence.* There is such a belief in man, and no infidel logic can argue it away. (2.) *It shows a belief in God's connection with individual history.* If man did not feel him near, he would not pray. It shows, (3.) *A belief in his power to help; else why invoke his aid?* And, (4.) *A belief in the efficacy of prayer.* These beliefs seem to me involved in the fact that men do *involuntarily* cry to God for help in danger. And do not these beliefs lie at the foundation of Biblical truth?

Look at the case in another aspect:

Secondly. *As an indication that these disciples had an impression of Christ's superhuman power.* Had they regarded him to be what he appeared, a poor man worn out with the fatigues of the day, and glad to rest his weary frame in some secluded spot of that humble ship, would they have appealed so earnestly to him now? Would they have called him "Lord," and "Master," and thus humbly and importunately implored his help? We trow not. The supernatural energy of Christ was not a mere article in their creed; it was a deep and practical conviction of the heart; a something that had become more powerful than any native impulse of the soul. They had heard such divine things flow from his lips, and seen such stupendous deeds effected by his power, that they could see in that tried, sleeping frame of his, the might and majesty of a God.

III. MENTAL DISTRESS GENERALLY ORIGINATES IN UNBELIEF. Jesus arose and saith unto them, "Why are ye so fearful, O ye of little faith?" Mark expresses the idea, that the want of faith was the cause of their fear, more forcibly still. "Why are ye so fearful? how is it that ye have no faith?" As if he had said: Had you faith, you would not be in all this trepidation; but you would be calm, brave, self-possessed. The fact that they approached Christ with the prayer, "Lord save us, or we perish," indicates, as we have already said, that they had some measure of faith in his supernatural energy; but their faith was still defective and weak. What is the faith that is wanted? The faith that will make one calm and truly brave in difficulties; that will save us. Not a mere belief in the doctrines of Christ's teaching, or the facts of his life. This is common. But an *all-confiding trust in the love of his heart, in the might of his arm, in the truth of his word, in the rectitude of his administration, and in the benevolence of his aims.* This is the ennobling faith, the faith that will give us heroism of soul. What examples we have in the Bible of its power! See Abraham, with knife in hand, offering up his son Isaac. See Moses at the margin of the sea. See Job bereft of all—property, friends, children, health; yet hear him say, "The Lord gave," etc. What is the cause of this calmness? Here it is: "Though he slay me, yet will I trust in him." See Paul at Ephesus—how dark his prospects! but how calm is he! "None of these things move me," etc. What is the cause? Here it is: "I know in whom I have believed," etc.

How true, then, is the idea which is here implied in the words of Christ, that distress arises from unbelief! History tells us that Julius Cesar was at sea in a little boat when a terrible storm came on. He sought to inspire the courage of the men who plied the oars, by telling them that their little boat bore Cesar and his fortunes. Let us be encouraged by feeling that if we are *genuine* disciples, Jesus is on board the bark of our being, voyaging with us on the mighty sea of existence. He holds the helm in his hand, and winds and waves obey his voice.

IV. Mental distress can be easily allayed by the interposition of Christ. "And he arose and rebuked the winds and the sea." There are two ways of doing it:

First. *By removing the external causes of distress.* This he did. Now he hushed the outward storm. He has all power over our external circumstances, and if we trust in him, he will one day remove from them all that has a tendency to pain or agitate the heart.

Secondly. *By removing the internal susceptibilities.* What are these? *Selfishness, guilt, dread* of death. Christ removes these; and where these are not, mental distress cannot exist. No storm can make an angel fear.

Friend! thou art on the sea of life. A sea, not like the sea of Galilee, lying within small limits; thy sea stretches into the infinite; new billows are ever rising up from the great eternity. There are rocks, quicksands, shoals, and other dangers in thy way. Who can pilot thee safely? who is able to steer thy bark? It must be some one that *knows* that sea, knows its soundings, its boundaries, and all its perilous points; and has, at the same time, power to guide thy fragile and complicated ship, and control the mighty elements that play around thee.

HOMILY LXXIII.

PAUL "DRIVEN UP AND DOWN IN ADRIA;" OR, THE VOYAGE OF LIFE.

And there the centurion found a ship of Alexandria sailing into Italy; and he put us therein, etc. ACTS xxvii, 6–44.

MAN'S life is a book; a book "in the right hand" of the ever-blessed One, and "written within and without." It is full. The spirit and type of all man's future history are inscribed upon its mystic page. "In thy book all my members were written, which in continuance were fashioned when as yet there was none of them." Life is its own interpreter. It proclaims its own facts and writes its own comments. In the light of life only can life be understood. My past experience is a commentary on my being; it is in the light reflected from my by gone days that I see my present self. So of my race. I see the world in the rays that beam from the ages that are gone. Its historic events are "ensamples," and "are written for our admonition."

There are some events in history that throw much more light on human life than others. Some only throw a glimmering ray upon some one phase and sphere; others seem to light up the whole realm and radiate on all sides. Such is Paul's stormy and perilous voyage over the Adriatic billows, as graphically portrayed in the chapter before us. Far indeed am I from a taste for or a belief in what is called the "spiritualizing" method of treating God's book. I deprecate such a method as a sad and impious perversion; but to look upon its historic records in order to interpret life is, I think, both legitimate and wise. When I look upon Paul, with two hundred and seventy-five other men of various tribes, social grades, and religious sects on board a frail bark, struggling through many cloudy days and starless nights in the fierce tempest, I discover much which throws light upon a whole generation of men. This globe is a ship crowded with passengers; all are battling with the fierce storms of time as the ship bears them through seas of ether on their way to a destiny eternal.

Thus using the narrative before us, I observe:

I. That in the voyage of life we have a great variety in our cotemporaries. On board this vessel that was "now driven up and down in Adria, exceedingly tossed with a tempest," there were no less than two hundred and seventy-five souls with Paul, and they were of a very mixed character. There were the rough, weather-beaten sailors, with might and main endeavoring to guide the bark which bounded on the swelling billows like a maddened steed amid moving mountains; there were merchants on their way from Egypt to Italy, some to buy, others to sell, and all in quest of gain; there were "prisoners," in the custody of the stern officers of Roman law, who had either been convicted of crime or were on their way to Rome to be tried at the tribunal of the emperor himself. There were soldiers, men trained for murder on a gigantic scale, and taught to regard a bloody crime as the most illustrious virtue. Luke, the physician, the evangelist, and historian, was there, and so was Aristarchus, one of Paul's most faithful friends. Indeed, on board this storm-tossed bark you have a whole age, a whole generation in miniature. Almost all the social forces of an age are in that vessel. There is labor represented in the sailors, there is war in the soldiers, there is commerce in the merchants, there is law in the men who hold the prisoners in custody, there are literature and science in Luke, there is religion in Paul and Aristarchus as well as Luke. So varied, indeed, were the companions of Paul in their tendencies, tastes, habits, and aims, that amid the numbers there could, I think, be but little society. Though in close material contact they lived in spiritual worlds remote from each other, worlds lighted, warmed, and ruled by different centers.

In all this you have a mirror of the human world at the present moment. In our voyage through time we are thrown, in the district in which our lot is cast, among cotemporaries between whom there are such immense *accidental* differences that, instead of souls meeting and mingling together in sweet and harmonious intercourse, there are but few instances, comparatively, in which you have any spiritual contact. Each has his own little world and interests. Like Paul, we are thrown among numerous cotemporaries; but there are only a few Lukes or Aristarchuses among them with whom we can have much intercourse. If we are of the Christianly true, "the world knoweth us not." Our sphere of being as far transcends the ken of worldlings as planets that roll beyond telescopic vision. A man morally must *be* what he would understand. He must be a saint to understand a saint, a devil to understand a devil. The tyrant, the pope, the philanthropist, the Christian, are little else than sounds to men who have not the elements that form these characters in their own hearts. Morally no man *can* be judged but by his own peers.

Now this immense spiritual variety among our fellow-voyagers, or, without trope, among our cotemporaries in this life, is to a reflective mind suggestive of certain important considerations:

First. *It suggests a characteristic of human nature as distinguished from all other terrestrial life.* Natural history shows that there is a perfect correspondence in the tastes, impulses, and habits among all the members of any species of non-rational life. To understand one of the individuals is to understand the entire species. The same external influences produce on all the same results. Their *conscious* life is the same. They move within the same circle; not one has power to take one step beyond the boundary line. Not so with man. Each individual has the power of striking out an orbit for himself; an orbit in some respects different from that in which any one had ever moved before or will ever move again. Wonderful in this respect is the power of a moral creature. A self-determining, self-transfiguring power is his. All modes of life are possible to man. He can transmigrate into the grub, the seraph, or the fiend. That living soul which is breathed into our material frames at first may through this sensuous body work itself into a beast, like Nebuchadnezzar, a devil, like Herod, or an apostle, like Paul.

Secondly. *It suggests that mankind are not now in their original condition.* The power to form different modes and spheres of life is confessedly a distinguishing gift of our being; but to use that power inconsistently with the royal law of benevolence is the essence of sin and the source of ruin. Power is the gift of God and is a blessing; the employment of it is the prerogative of man, and may be either a virtue and a blessing or a sin and a curse. It can never be that the God of love and order intended that our innate moral energy should be so employed as to create such an immense variety in the tastes, tendencies, and aims of our cotemporaries as to render social intercourse and harmony impossible. The divine idea of humanity seems to me this: that all souls should have a common center, and that in all their revolutions their social radiations, borrowed from a common source, should genially and harmoniously blend, intermingle, and combine. Some great catastrophe has befallen man's social system, a catastrophe which has hurled souls from the normal center into regions of darkness and confusion.

The Bible explains this.

Thirdly. *It suggests the probability of a future social classification.* Will such men as Paul, Luke, Aristarchus, be doomed forever to live with mercenary merchants, besotted seamen, and bloody soldiers? Shall good men, whose deepest prayer is, "Gather not my soul with sinners, nor my life with bloody men," dwell forever with such companions? Is the world to go on forever thus? Are the Herods to continue kings and the Johns prisoners. Are the Pauls ever to be at the mercy of centurions? Are the Jeffries to be on the bench and the Baxters at the bar forever? It cannot be. Man's deepest intuitions say it cannot be; the prayers of the good say it cannot be; and the Bible says it shall not be. The tares and the wheat will one day be separated, the good and the bad one day divided. We are only mixed while on board this earth; as soon as we touch the shores of the retributive and everlasting we separate on the principles of moral character and spiritual affinities. Blessed be God! there is a world in which the "nations of them that are saved shall walk in the light of it, and the kings of the earth do bring their glory and honor into it," and into which there shall "in no wise enter anything that defileth, neither whatsoever worketh abomination or maketh a lie; but they which are written in the Lamb's book of life," a world outside of which will be "dogs, and sorcerers, and whoremongers, and murderers, and idolaters, and whosoever loveth and maketh a lie."

From this narrative I observe:

II. THAT IN THE VOYAGE OF LIFE THE SEVEREST TRIALS ARE COMMON TO ALL. The one trial common to all on board that bark was the danger of losing life. Luke's description of their common trial is very graphic. "And when neither sun nor stars in many days appeared, and no small tempest lay on us, all hope that we should be saved was then taken away." They tried every expedient, but all failed; the lamp of hope for a time went out. Their souls were in despair; as dark were they as those heavens that had not seen "sun nor stars for many days." Danger of life is universally felt to be the severest of trials. Death is "the king of terrors." It is that which gives terror to every other terror. And to this trial all are exposed in a thousand different ways every day. All the individuals, families, tribes, nations of the earth, at the present moment, are like Paul and his companions on an ever-surging sea, battling for life. The clouds of death darken every sky; its gales breathe about all. Some, it is true, are in more immediate and conscious contact with death than others, and their struggles are more severe. But all, every hour, are in danger, and all must one day, like Paul and his companions, feel "all hope" of being saved from death taken away. For a short time, in healthy youth and vigorous manhood, you may flow on propitiously like this vessel in the first stage of its voyage, when "the south wind blew softly;" gentle gales awhile, my brother, may fill thy sails, and flattering seas may smile; but further on the sea will rise to mountians and marshal its billows against thee; the winds will grow wild with fury, the sun will set, the moon go down, and every star disappear, and thou shalt feel thyself only as a bubble on the breakers.

> "Sure a time will come
> For storms to try thee and strong blasts to rend
> Thy painted sails, and spread thy gold like chaff
> O'er the wild wave; and what a wreck,
> If judgment find thee unsustained by God!"

There are two thoughts suggested by the common trials of men:

First. *That they develop different dispositions.* How different were the feelings of Paul, Luke, and Aristarchus from the others. This storm blew open as it were the doors of their hearts, and disclosed the moral stuff they were made of. In all, perhaps, on board, save Paul and his two spiritual brothers, there was a wild tempest of terrific emotion, of which the outward storm was not merely the occasion, but the material type. Fear had unmanned them all; so that for fourteen days they could eat nothing: they "continued fasting." Even the brave sailors were at their wits' end; they sought to "flee out of the ship." None of them thought of anything but their own safety. Selfishness, the source of all fear, and indeed evermore the source of all painful feeling, had in them risen to a passion. What cared the sailors now who perished, so long as they were saved? The soldiers too displayed their base and heartless selfishness; for they proposed to "kill the prisoners" rather than they should have the slightest chance of escape. In sublime contrast with all this was the spirit of Paul, and we presume of his two companions in the faith. None of these things seemed to have moved him. The whole of his conduct, as here recorded, during these fourteen eventful days, was characterized by a magnanimity which can only take its rise in a vital alliance with the Infinite, and a benevolent sympathy for mankind. His every word shows an unfaltering faith in Him to whom he had committed himself. His bearing too was calm and hope-inspiring. His great nature was taken up with the sufferings of his companions; he seemed to have no care for himself. "I pray you," said he, "take some meat, for this is for your health." Severe trials, especially those which powerfully threaten life, are sure to develop the moral dispositions of men. Never did the faithless, ungenerous, selfish, dastardly nature of the Jews, as a whole people, show itself so fully as when they stood in front of the Red Sea, with unscalable heights on both sides, and the avenging Pharaoh and his host swiftly advancing in the rear. They said to Moses, their friend and temporal deliverer, "Because there were no graves in Egypt hast thou taken us away to die in the wilderness?" In this one utterance their base natures leap into daylight. So it ever is. The trials of life reveal the dispositions of the heart; they take off the mask, they strip off all shams, and show us to ourselves and the universe. Trials test our principles as fire tries the minerals.

Secondly. *That they develop the indifference of nature to social distinctions.* Nature cares nothing for any of the distinctions among men. The centurion and his subordinates, the prisoners and the officers, the Christians and heathens, were all treated alike on board this vessel. Old ocean cares no more for the boats with which Xerxes bridged the Hellespont than for any worthless log of timber. It heeds no more the voice of Canute than the cries of a pauper's babe. Nature knows nothing of your lords and kings. The ocean in her majesty of wrath cares nothing for your Cesars. "Napoleon," says Mr. Lowe in his eloquent little work, "The Pilot of the Galilean Lake," "was once made to feel his littleness and impotence, when at the height of his power and glory, in a storm at sea, off Boulogne. His mighty fleet lay before him, proudly riding at anchor. Wishing to review it in the open sea, he desired Admiral Bruyes to change the position of the ships. Foreseeing that a fearful storm was gathering, the admiral respectfully declined obedience to the emperor's commands. The ominous stillness of the atmosphere, the darkening sky, the lowering clouds, the rumbling of distant thunder, fully justified the fears entertained by the admiral. But Napoleon in a rage peremptorily demanded obedience to his iron will. Vice-admiral Magon obeyed the order. The threatening storm burst with terrible fury. Several gun sloops were wrecked, and above two hundred poor soldiers and sailors were plunged in the raging waves, very few of whom escaped. The emperor instantly ordered the boats out to the rescue of the perishing crews. He was told no boat could live in such a sea. He then ordered a company of his grenadiers to man the boats, and as he sprang the first into a large boat, exclaimed, 'Follow me, my brave fellows.' They had scarcely entered the boat before a huge wave dashed over the emperor, as he stood erect near the helmsman. 'Onward, onward!' he cried; his voice swelling above the tempest's roar. But the daring effort was vain, progress in such a sea was impossible. 'Push on! push on!' cried Napoleon; 'do you not hear those cries? O this sea! this sea!' he exclaimed, clenching his hands; 'it rebels against our power, but it may be conquered!' At this moment a mighty billow struck the boat with tremendous force, and drove it back, quivering, to the shore. It seemed as though this were the ocean's answer; or rather the answer of the God of the ocean to the proud monarch's boast! Napoleon was cast ashore by the spurning billows of the stormy sea, like a drifting fragment of dripping sea-weed."

Nature's indifference, however, to mere *secular* distinction is not so strange as her want of respect to the *moral*. She paid no deference to the good men now on board; she looked down as indignantly on Paul and his two Christian friends as on the rest. She hid her stars, and made her winds and waves dash with the same wild fury around the heads of all. Nature treats apostles and apostates alike. The sun shines alike, and the showers descend alike upon the just and the unjust. Nature knows nothing here of moral retributions. Her fires will burn, her waters will drown, and her poisons destroy the good as well as the bad. Our character and moral position in the universe are not to be estimated by nature's aspect toward us. "The tower of Siloam" may fall on the good as well as on the bad; children may be "born blind" of righteous parents as well as of wicked. The ground of wicked men may bring forth plenteously while the soil of the good man may be struck with barrenness. As far as the system of nature is concerned, "all things come alike to all: there is one end to the righteous and to the sinner, to the clean and the unclean, to him that sacrificeth and to him that sacrificeth not." She has her own system of laws; he who attends to them most loyally, let him be vile as hell can make him, shall enjoy most of her bounties and smiles. In this respect she is an emblem of the moral system. Both are impartial. Both treat their subjects according to their conduct toward them, not according to their conduct toward anything else. Neither shows respect to any man's person: the great cardinal dictum of each is, "He that doeth the wrong shall suffer for the wrong."

From this narrative I observe,

III. That in the voyage of life special communications from God are mercifully vouchsafed. "And now I exhort you to be of good cheer; for there shall be no loss of any man's life among you, but of the ship. For there stood by me this night the angel of God, whose I am, and whom I serve, saying, Fear not Paul, thou must be brought before Cesar; and lo, God hath given thee all them that sail with thee." The great God knew the fearful situation of the vessel, the dire perils to which Paul and his companions were exposed, and mercifully interposed. It is even so with our world. He knows the moral difficulties and dangers to which we are subjected through sin in our voyage to eternity, and he has graciously vouchsafed the necessary communications for our relief. Between the divine communication vouchsafed to the men on board this vessel and that which in the Bible God hath given this world, there are certain points of instructive resemblance:

First. *The divine communication to the men on board this vessel came through the best of men.* Paul was the selected medium of communication. It was not one of the influential merchants, not the commander and owner of the ship, nor even the Roman centurion; but Paul the prisoner, the heretic, the outcast. There was no man on board the ship, probably, in a more abject condition than he. Notwithstanding his secular abjectness he was a *good* man. There was no one on board of such high spiritual excellence. He was God's. "Whose I am and whom I serve." This was the reason for his selection as an organ of divine communication. God has ever spoke to the world through the best men. It matters not how poor they are if good. He speaks to them and makes them his messengers. "The secret of the Lord is with them that fear him, and he will show them his covenant." What is the Bible but communications which God addresses to the world through holy men "who spoke as they were moved by the Holy Ghost?" Moral goodness alone can qualify a man for this. The divine voice can only be heard by the holy; the carnal mind "discerneth not the things of the Spirit, neither can he know them, for they are spiritually discerned." "Blessed are the pure in heart, for they shall see God."

Secondly. *The divine communications which came to the men on board this vessel were the final and effective means of meeting the emergency.* The maritime genius and energy of all on board had been taxed to the utmost, and all in vain. Finding at the outset of the tempest that they could not direct the vessel through the full fury of the storm, they "let her drive," gave her as much sea-room as possible, and yielded her up to the mercy of the elements; then having ran under "a certain island," they used their best efforts to bind up the shattered ship. "When they had taken up the boat they used helps, undergirding the ship; and fearing lest they should fall into the quicksands, they strake sail, and so were driven." They took down the sails, and perhaps the masts and yards, and bound the vessel round with ropes and cables. Still she was "exceedingly tossed." They then lightened her, committing to the waves part of her precious cargo. Still the tempest continued. Next and last they threw "the tacklings" overboard. "And when neither sun nor stars appeared for many days, and no small tempest lay on us, all hope that we should be saved was taken away." Now it was while in this hopeless state that the communication came. After human effort had exhausted its powers then God interposed. It is so with the Gospel. It was after human reason had tried every effort to solve the stormy problems of the conscience, and guide the soul into the haven of spiritual peace that Christ came. "You may see," says Culverwell, a writer whose thoughts are ever fresh because always real and earnest, "Socrates in the twilight lamenting his obscure and benighted condition, and telling you that his lamp will show him nothing but his own darkness. You may see Plato sitting down by the water of Lethe, and weeping because he could not remember his former notions. You may hear Aristotle bewailing himself thus, that his 'potential reason' will so seldom come into act, that his 'blank sheet' has so few and such imperfect impressions upon it, that his intellectuals are at so low an ebb, as that the motions of Euripus will pose them. You may hear Zeno say that his 'porch' is dark; and Epictetus confessing and complaining that he had not the right 'handle,' the true apprehension of things."

Thirdly. *The efficacy of these communications depended upon a practical attention to the directions.* "There shall be no loss of any man's life among you, but of the ship;" yet, though this is the purpose, "unless these"—the sailors, who understand how to manage the ship—"abide in the ship, ye cannot be saved."

The practical lesson I learn from this is, *that every promise which God makes to man should be regarded as conditional, unless a most unequivocal assurance is given to the contrary.* Paul regarded the promise that all on board should be saved, as depending upon the right employment of the suitable means. Hence he captured by his orders the affrighted seamen as they were attempting to abandon the wrecking vessel. "Unless these"—these men, who alone among us understand nautical matters—"abide in the ship, ye cannot be saved." But what reason had Paul to regard the promise as *conditional?* There was no *if* in it; it is most positive and unqualified: "There shall be no loss of any man's life among you, but of the ship." It does not contain, does not suggest a hint about means. What reason had he, therefore, to understand the promise as conditional? Every reason. His natural instincts, his experience and observation, and all analogy, satisfied him that the divine ends are always reached by means; that God carries on his universe by an inviolable principle of connection between means and ends.

Unless, therefore, the great God who worketh all things makes to man a promise of good with the most unequivocal and emphatic assurance that it will come without means, he sins against his own reason and against the established system of the universe in so interpreting it. Thus understanding his promises, they afford no pretext for a Calvinistic carelessness. Has God promised knowledge? It implies study. Has he promised salvation? It implies "repentance toward God and faith in our Lord Jesus Christ."

From this narrative I observe,

IV. That in the voyage of life one morally great man, however poor, is of immense service to his contemporaries. Let us notice two things:

First. *The characteristics of a truly great man as illustrated in Paul's history on board the vessel.* Observe his *forecast.* At the very outset he had a presentiment of the danger which awaited them. "Sirs," said he to the officers, "I perceive that this voyage will be with hurt and much damage, not only of the lading and ship but also of our lives." But these men, "dressed in a little brief authority," paid of course no attention to the statement of a poor prisoner. "The centurion believed the master and the owner of the ship more than those things which Paul spoke." One can imagine the old captain looking with proud contempt at Paul, and saying, What does he know about nautical matters? he is one of those poor timid landsmen that we brave sailors often have to deal with on board. They see danger in every approaching wave; in every turn of the vessel they fancy they are going down. Poor cowards! I wish those timid landsmen would mind their own business. I know how to manage my gallant ship; I have steered her through fiercer storms and more perilous waves than these! Hush! captain, that poor prisoner, Paul, has a *sensibility* which enables him to see nature and interpret her as thou canst never do.

An *intense sympathy* with a man's principles and aims will enable me to foresee and predict much of his future conduct. *Godliness*, the soul of all moral greatness, is this sympathy. It is such a close and vital alliance with the Eternal Spirit as enables the soul to feel the very pulsations of the Divine Being, and to anticipate his doings. This sympathy with God is the prophetic eye. Give me this, and, like Isaiah, in some humble measure, I shall foretell the ages. This sympathy is a new faculty, a new eye to the soul. Because of this, Paul saw what the captain could not. His heart was in such a contact with that Spirit which controls the winds and the waves that he felt that something terrible was about to transpire. The first motion as it were of the great Spirit of nature in waking this tempest vibrated through his heart. Moral greatness, because it is godliness, has always forecast: it "foreseeth the evil." Never let us disregard the warnings of a great and godly man.

Observe his *magnanimous calmness*. We have already referred to this. Paul displays no perturbation; his spirit seems as unruffled by the storms as those stars that roll in placid brightness beyond the black tempestuous clouds; stars, whose peaceful faces he had not seen "for many days." Indeed, he had such an exuberance of calm courage, that when the storm was at its height, he breathed a cheerful spirit into the agitated hearts of all, and got them to feast with him in the tempest: "they were all of good cheer, and they also took some meat." A man must be sublimely calm to breathe calmness into the agitated hearts of all these men in the fury of the tempest. Trust in God was the philosophy of his remarkable calmness. He could sing with David, "God is our refuge and strength, a very present help in trouble. Therefore will we not fear, though the earth be removed, and though the mountains be carried into the midst of the sea: though the waters roar with the swelling thereof."

Observe his *self-obliviousness.* While all others were struggling for themselves, he seemed only concerned for them; though, for the most part, they stood in an antagonistic position toward him. He was a prisoner in the custody of Roman officers. The vessel was bearing him not to his home, not to a scene of friendship, but to that of punishment and death. He did not seem to think of this. His own trying circumstances did not appear to affect him; he was careful for others; he had the "charity that seeketh not her own."

Observe, moreover, his *religiousness.* "He took bread and gave thanks to God in the presence of them all." This explains his greatness. He felt that God was with him. He saw God in the tempest and in the bread. He bowed in resignation to the one, he thanked him for the other. While his piety would not allow him to complain of the greatest trial, it prompted him gratefully and devoutly to acknowledge the smallest favor.

Secondly. *The service which he rendered was both direct and indirect.* The spirit of confidence which he breathed, the efforts he put forth, the directions he gave, were all direct. Then the *indirect* service was great. For the sake of Paul the prisoners were not killed. "And the soldiers' counsel was to kill the prisoners, lest any of them should swim out and escape. But the centurion, willing to save Paul, kept them from their purpose, and commanded that they which could swim should cast themselves first into the sea and get to land." One might have thought that the common trials which they had endured would have softened in some measure their brutal natures into genial sympathy. But as soldiers they had been trained to a reckless disregard of life, and to deeds of cruelty. By habits of carnage the spirit of humanity had been expelled from their breasts, and the tiger-nature had become theirs. The particular reason, however, for this bloodthirsty suggestion was, probably, the fear that, should they escape, they themselves would be charged either with unfaithfulness or negligence by the military authorities at Rome, their masters. The poor prisoners, however, were saved from this fate for the sake of Paul. "The centurion, willing to save Paul, kept them from their purpose." The signal service which Paul had rendered conciliated the centurion. For Paul's sake the prisoners were saved. None but the great One can tell the benefits, not only directly but indirectly, that a *good* man confers upon his cotemporaries. On the great day of account it will be found that many an obscure saint has conferred far greater service on the age in which he lived, and the race to which he belonged, than those illustrious generals, statesmen, poets, and sages who have won the acclamations of posterity. The world has yet to learn who are its true benefactors.

The service of a *good man is appreciated as trials increase.* In the first stage of the voyage, when "the south winds blew softly," Paul was nothing. When he uttered his impression of danger he was treated probably, if not with insolence, yet with indifference. "The centurion believed the master and the owner of the ship more than those things which were spoken by Paul." But as the storm advanced Paul's influence increased. Like all truly great men, he rose into more majestic attitude as difficulties thickened. The merchants, the soldiers, and the centurion, who were very great men, no doubt, in their way, and were conventionally regarded as great in their own departments on land; and who, perhaps, in their own circle would not condescend to speak to Paul, grew less and less as the tempest rose. Your conventionally great men are only great in fair weather. But the truly great become greater in storms. Paul who, at the outset, when "the south winds blew softly," was nothing in that vessel, became the moral commander during the tempest. Amid the wild roaring of the elements, the cries of his fellow-voyagers, the crashes of the plunging ship, the awful howl of death in all, he walked upon the cracking deck with a moral majesty before which captain, merchant, soldier, and centurion bowed with loyal awe. So it has ever been; so it must ever be. The good show their greatness in trials; and in trials the evil, however exalted their worldly position, are compelled to appreciate them. How often do the world's great men, on death-beds, seek the attendance, sympathies, counsel, and prayers of those godly ones whom they despised in health!

Brothers! we are on a voyage. Thank God! that while various worthless classes are sailing with us, and we are destined to meet with storms in which they can render us no help, yet in the Bible "the Angel of God" hath appeared unto us, and hath given us a *conditional* promise that "there shall be no loss of any man's life." Let the fiercest tempest arise, let winds and waves dash about us with utmost fury, yet if we follow the counsels of this Angel Book, and rightly employ the skill and energy we possess, we shall, though "on boards and broken pieces of the ship," escape "all safe to the land."

> "Give thy mind sea-room, keep it wide of earth,
> That rock of souls immortal: let loose thy cord,
> Weigh anchor; spread thy sails; call every wind;
> Eye the great polestar; make the land of life."

> "Land ahead! its fruits are waving
> On the hills of fadeless green,
> And the living waters laving
> Shores where heavenly forms are seen."

HOMILY LXXIV.

MAN'S MORAL MISSION IN THE WORLD.

I will stand upon my watch, and set me upon the tower, and will watch to see what he will say unto me, and what I shall answer when I am reproved. And the Lord answered me, and said, Write the vision, and make it plain upon tables, that he may run that readeth it. For the vision is for an appointed time, but at the end it shall speak and not lie: though it tarry, wait for it; because it will surely come, it will not tarry. HABAKKUK ii, 1–3.*

WHEREFORE are we in this world? Here we are the tenants of a magnificent, beautifully furnished, and well-supplied district of God's glorious creation. We came not here by choice; we had no voice in the matter, no voice in determining whether we should be or not be, be here or elsewhere. Manifestly we are not here by chance. There

* The life of Habakkuk is wrapt in obscurity. All that we can gather concerning him is, that he lived and prophesied about the time of the Chaldean invasion; that he was a cotemporary with Jeremiah; that most probably he prophesied in Judah during the reign of Jehoiahaz and Jehoiakim; that this book is his production; and that the apostle, in his letters to the Hebrews, the Romans, and the Galatians, quotes from his writings, and thereby demonstrates their inspiration.

Amid the terrible and thickening perils to which the prophet and his country were now exposed by the incursion of the Chaldeans, he turns for safety and protection to Him who had ever been the refuge of his people, "a present help in time of trouble." "I will stand," he says, "upon my watch," like "as a sentinel on the walls of a besieged city;" not to mark the approaches of the enemy, nor to look out for deliverance from man; but to consult the INFINITE ONE, to seek counsel from him, "to see what he will say unto me, and what I shall answer when I am reproved."

is an obvious purpose in our existence on this planet. The exquisite fitness of our organization to the scenery and circumstances in which we are placed shows this. But for what purpose did infinite wisdom send us here? What is the great work given us to do? This is the problem. We eat and drink, we use our senses and our limbs, as do the lower creatures around us; we buy and sell and get gain; we observe and reason and get knowledge; and yet we have a profound and constant impression, an impression we cannot shake off, that these operations form but a very subordinate part of our mission. The involuntary conclusion of our reason and the dictates of our conscience assure us that we have something far higher and nobler to accomplish. But what? The answer of the Assembly's Catechism is, "To glorify God and to enjoy him forever." But this answer involves two questions which admit of much debate: What is it to glorify God? and, What is it to enjoy him?

Perhaps the whole of man's mission as a moral being may be defined as consisting in three things: *The receiving of communications from the Eternal Mind, the imparting of communications from the Eternal Mind, and the practical realization of communications from the Eternal Mind.*

We shall use the passage before us to illustrate these three things:

I. MAN'S MORAL MISSION IN THIS WORLD CONSISTS IN RECEIVING COMMUNICATIONS FROM THE ETERNAL MIND. That is, in doing that which the prophet now resolved to do: "To watch, and see what he will say," etc. That man is constituted for, and required to receive communications from the Infinite Mind, and that he cannot realize his destiny without this, will appear evident from the following considerations:

First. *From his nature as a spiritual being.* (1.) Man has a native *instinct* for it. His being naturally cries out for the "living God." "O that I knew where I might find him!" Is not this the prayer of the human heart under all religions, in all ages and climes? It is only the logic of infidelity that makes a revelation from God appear impossible; the moral sentiment, instead of believing in its impossibility, so deeply yearns for it that it accepts the forgeries of impostors in its stead. Like Saul at Endor, the moral heart will resort to the darkest haunts of superstition and imposture for a revelation from the Eternal. The heart expects the Almighty to speak. The soul is as truly made to receive into it, as its breath and life, thoughts from God, as the eye is made to receive the light, as the earth is made to receive the sunshine and the shower. There is a craving in it for divine utterances. (2.) Man has a native *capacity* for it. The human mind can take in ideas from God; ideas of his power, his wisdom, his independence, his truthfulness, his goodness, and his love. You will find ideas about him, either true or false, in every human soul. This is one of the distinguishing features of our being. Unlike the low creatures around us, we can rise to a conception of the great First Cause. On the wing of thought we can pass beyond the remotest boundaries of the material universe into the presence of the very "Fountain of life." (3.) Man has a native *necessity* for it. There are germs of power and susceptibility within us that can never be quickened and developed without communications from God. The soul without thoughts from the Infinite will be as an eye without light, having the power of receiving wonderful impressions of beauty and grandeur, but dark withal. The earth is filled with germs of every species of life, but they will remain dormant forever without the solar beam. An intelligent spirit apart from communication with God is a globe without a sun; dark, cold, chaotic, dead. You may as soon think of cultivating the earth without rays from the central orb, as to think of educating the human soul without ideas from the EVERLASTING.

That man requires communications from God will appear,

Secondly, *From his condition as a fallen being.* His spiritual constitution shows that had he continued in a state of innocence he would have required communications from God. The highest seraphs in glory require such. But as a *sinner* man has a deeper and a more special need. As fallen creatures, we want answers to various questions. A deep haze has settled on our path of duty. We want to know the way wherein we should walk. The conflicting ethical theories proposed by the world's great sages show that philosophy cannot answer this question. As a sinner, man is oppressed with guilt; he feels that he has offended the Creator, and justly deserves misery without mitigation and without end, and he asks for the way of reconciliation and pardon. "Wherewithal shall I come before the Lord?" Neither priests nor sages have been able to solve the problem. As a sinner man is mortal. He ascertains from history that numerous generations lived on the earth before he appeared, and are gone; he follows to the grave friends and relations, he feels the sentence of death in himself, and he looks at the grave with an anxious heart, and asks, "If a man die shall he live again?" No satisfactory answer can be given to the question; the reply must come from Him on whose sovereign will all life depends. As a sinner, therefore, communications from God are of infinite moment to man.

Man's need of communications from God will appear,

Thirdly, *From the purpose of Christ's mediation.* Why did the Son of God descend to this guilty world to suffer poverty, obloquy, degradation, and death? In one word, it was to bring man to God. His cross is the meeting-point between man and his Maker. It is the great and moral magnet by which those who are "afar off" are to be "brought nigh." Ask me why he did this or why he suffered that? and the answer is, That the Lord God may "dwell among men." He is a mediator between God and man; his blessed work is to bring the holy mind of God and the depraved mind of man together in sweet intercourse and intimate friendship. Man's spirit apart from God is a star that has lost its center, and, wandering from its orbit, is going every moment into deeper darkness, and hasting to ultimate destruction. The work of Christ is to arrest that wandering star, bring it back to its orbit, link it to its divine center, and cause it through all its future to catch and reflect the influences of eternal truth, rectitude, and bliss.

Man's need of communications from God will appear,

Fourthly. *From the special manifestations of God for the purpose.* I say special; for nature, history, reason, heart, and conscience, are the original and regular organs of communication between the human and divine. But we have something more than these. We have in this book, the Bible, extraordinary communications which the great God made to different men in different ages. What is this volume but a history of God's communications to some men, in order that all men may communicate with him? Here we find him in olden times "speaking to the fathers by the prophets, and in these last days speaking to us by his Son."

Man's need of communications with God will appear,

Fifthly, *From the general teaching of the Bible.* In this book men are called to an audience with God. "Come now, and let us reason together," etc. "Behold, I stand at the door and knock; if any man hear my voice," etc. In this book communion with God is not only inculcated as a duty, but exhibited as the highest privilege. "In thy presence there is fullness of joy," etc. "Truly our fellowship is with the Father," etc. This book represents all its good men, the men who are held forth as having most faithfully fulfilled their mission, as men in the habit of intercourse with heaven.

Sufficient, we think, has been advanced to show that man's moral mission involves receiving communications from God. But how are divine communications to be received? Two things are at least necessary, and these things are in the text:

First. *That we resort to the right scene.* The prophet

ascended "his tower." It is not necessary to suppose that the prophet had any particular locality in view; the language is metaphorical. He withdrew from his usual avocations and associations, and retired to some quiet spot in order "to see what he would say." God is everywhere, and everywhere is he speaking; but you cannot hear him unless you resort to silence and solitude. Amid the shouts of worldly pleasure, the din of passions, and the stir and bustle of business, we cannot hear his voice. Moses heard him in Midian, Ezekiel in the field, Daniel on the banks of the Ulai, and John in Patmos.

Secondly. *That we resort to the right scene in the right spirit.* "I will watch and see," etc. It is of no service to resort to the most favorable scene, unless you take with you the right spirit, the spirit of devout attention and inquiry. If you will go with your spiritual ear open to listen to him you will hear his voice, not otherwise. I believe that God makes communications to man *immediately* as well as by means; but in neither way can we receive from him without the devout spirit of attention. There is a general impression that God has no communication with the soul now but through means; that since the canon of Scripture has been completed all direct communications are ended. I cannot believe this. He is in ever-living contact with souls. This age is as near to him as those ages in which the patriarchs, prophets, and apostles lived. The Great Father does not desert his children. How often have good men received thoughts, felt emotions, and been thrown into moods of a holy character apart altogether from the ordinary means! God speaks to us now in "visions of the night, when deep sleep falleth upon man," etc.; but we hear him not for the want of a right attitude of soul. Love gives new senses to the soul, new ears and eyes. What is it that makes that mother's head so restless on the pillow, and renders her sleepless during the silent watches of the night? All the other residents in the house are still and calm in the soft arms of repose. It is the faint moaning of an afflicted child that lies in a distant room. No one else hears those faint notes of disease; they are too weak to reach any other ear. Even the nurse on whose arm the dear child is resting its little feverish head hears them not. But the feeblest of them travels into the chamber of the mother, enters not merely her ear, but her heart, and heaves her spirit into surges of anxious thought. Amid the loudest peals of thunder peradventure she might sleep, but not amid those faint moans which are inaudible to all besides. What is it that makes that woman's ear so exquisitely quick? It is love. It is so with man and God. Fill man's soul with divine love and you will fill his universe with divine voices.

II. MAN'S MORAL MISSION IN THIS WORLD CONSISTS IN IMPARTING COMMUNICATIONS FROM THE ETERNAL MIND. The communication which the prophet received he was commanded to make known: "Write the vision and make it plain upon the tables, that he may run that readeth it." From this we may conclude that writing is both an ancient and a divinely sanctioned art. For it we cannot be too thankful. Through writing the past is handed down to us. It gives an imperishable power, a ubiquitous influence to thought. It reflects the institutions and deeds of men and nations long since departed. A true book is a second incarnation of man's self; in it, as in a second body, he lives and works long after his mortal frame has crumbled to ashes. The press is the most effective organ through which we can reach the past, and one of the mightiest instruments by which we can influence the present and help the future. Writing is as divine an ordinance as preaching: the prophet was commanded to "write the vision, and to make it plain." Let the characters be bold, let the language be simple, so "that he that runneth may read;" that men in bustle and haste may decipher the meaning.

That we have to impart as well as receive is evident:

First. *From the tendency of divine thoughts to express themselves.* Ideas of a religious kind always struggle for utterance; they cannot well be suppressed. The divine things which "we have seen and heard" "we cannot but speak." There are certain thoughts which a man may keep secret; they have no connection with his conscience and social nature; but not so with divine thoughts; he who has them will feel "a necessity laid upon him" to *proclaim* them. Like beams of light, their very nature is diffusive.

Secondly. *From the universal adaptation of divine thoughts.* The thoughts we receive from God are not for a class; they are "for all generations." The communications, for example, which David received and wrote are as suited to us as they were to himself and the generation to which he belonged. Men have thoughts which are only for the initiated; but God's are for the race.

Thirdly. *From the spiritual dependence of man upon man.*

Man is as dependent upon his fellow for spiritual blessings as he is for material. He is dependent upon him for his education, his knowledge, and his religious impressions. It is God's plan that man should be the spiritual teacher of man. The world wants the religious thoughts we get from God. They are the only forces that can break its fetters, chase away its darkness, and lift it into true freedom and light.

Fourthly. *From the general teaching of the Bible.* What the prophets and apostles received they taught, what they heard they communicated. What the apostles received from Christ they were commanded to go and preach unto all the world. When "it pleased God, said Paul, to reveal his Son in me, immediately," etc.

Men are giving their thoughts and impressions every day to others; and these exert an influence upon the character and destinies of men that will be fully known only in eternity. None of us can live unto ourselves. In every act we produce a ripple upon the great sea of existence that shall go on in ever-widening circles. Every moment we touch chords that shall vibrate through the ages. Let us then get from God the true thoughts and give them out; let us catch the divine rays and reflect them, and we shall help to light up the world with the "true light."

III. Man's moral mission consists in the practical realization of communications from the eternal mind. "Though it tarry, wait for it, because it will surely come; it will not tarry." "For the vision is yet for an appointed time, but at the end it shall speak, and not lie." Rest assured, that all he has said shall be accomplished. There is a time afforded for the fulfillment of all God's promissory communications to man. The vision of the prophecy is "yet for an appointed time." In the divine purpose there is a period fixed for the realization of every divine promise. That time may seem very remote to us; but "one day with the Lord is as a thousand years, and a thousand years as one day." However distant it may seem, our duty is to wait in earnest practical faith for it. "It will surely come; it will not tarry." Has he promised that the world shall be reduced to the genial and merciful sovereignty of Christ? It may seem far off to us: "wait for it." "As the rain cometh down from heaven," etc. "Heaven and earth shall pass away," etc. To live under the practical influence of the truth of all the communications which God makes to us, to embody his word in our life, to work out his doctrines in living characters, to furnish the world with a living exposition of this book, to become "living epistles of Christ," known and read of all men, this is our mission. O to be ruled in everything, to be moulded in every part, by his communications! to have his word dwelling in us as the nucleus around which all our thoughts gather, as a light through which we look at the universe, and in which we pursue our way!

From the whole we learn then who it is that fulfills his moral mission in this world. Who is it? Not the man who amasses the most wealth and becomes the most secularly influential; not the man who revels most in material luxuries and animal gratifications; not even the man who has risen to the most clear and comprehensive knowledge of the universe and God. No, but the man whose spiritual eye and ear are open to receive communications from the Eternal; whose soul is ever in a waiting attitude, receiving thoughts from him, and saying, "How precious are thy thoughts unto me, O God!" the man who not only receives but communicates what he receives, either by pen or tongue, or both. For it is the thoughts we get directly from communion with him, which are full of freshness and life, and not the thoughts we excogitate from our own poor brain, or borrow from other men, that give value to our written or our oral discourses. The man, moreover, who not only receives and communicates, but practically realizes and carries out in the spirit and habits of his life God's revelation, is the man that fulfills his moral mission.

We are here then, brothers, for these three purposes, not for *one*, but for *all*. God is to be everything to us; he is to fill up the whole sphere of our being, our "all in all." We are to be his *auditors*, hearing his voice in everything; we are to be his *organ*, conveying to others what he has conveyed to us; we are to be his *representatives*, manifesting him in every act of our life. All we say and do, our looks and mein are to be rays reflected from the "Father of lights."

In conclusion we remark,

First, *The reasonableness of religion.* What is religion? It is rightly to *receive*, *propagate*, and *develop* communications from the Infinite Mind. Is there anything unreasonable in this? Is it not in keeping with the analogy of nature? If there be a great Parent Spirit of the universe, and if "we are his offspring," can anything be more reasonable than that we should seek a living fellowship with his mind?

Secondly. *The grandeur of a religious life.* What is sometimes called religion is indeed a despicable thing. The adoption without individual reflection of some narrow creed which leads its votaries to damn all who will not believe the same, often passes, alas! for religion. The narrowness, the intolerance, the bigotry, the selfishness of many professors and many sects, are hideous and hellish misrepresentations of the true thing. O ye skeptics, remember that the conventional religion you denounce is not the religion of God. We loathe it as you. To be religious is to be a *disciple* of the all-knowing God. To be truly religious is to be a *minister* of the all-ruling God. To be religious is to be a *representative* of the all-glorious God. Is there anything more grand in conception than this. A religious life is a transcendentally glorious life.

Thirdly. *The function of Christianity.* What is the specific design of the Gospel? To qualify man to fulfill his mission on earth. It does this and nothing else can. The greatest of ancient sages felt the need of such help as Christianity offers. "We must," says Socrates, "of necessity wait till some one from Him who careth for us shall come and instruct us how we ought to behave toward God and man." "We cannot," says the illustrious Plato, "know of ourselves what petitions will be pleasing to God, or what worship we should pay to him; but it is necessary that a lawgiver should be sent from heaven to instruct us. . . . O how greatly do I desire to see that man and who he is!" That SOME ONE for whom Socrates waited, that LAWGIVER whom Plato so devoutly desired to see, has, thank God! come into our world, and we have "seen his glory, as the only begotten of the Father, full of grace and truth." He does all, and more than these renowned sages in the vastness of their aspirations ventured to expect. He transcends their IDEAL TEACHER. In Christianity he supplies all we require to enable us to perform our mission. He provides a medium of intercourse between man and his God. He has furnished a moral "ladder" by which men in the lowest degradation of sin can ascend to God. Human depravity, which has created a mighty chasm between man and his Maker, he has bridged over by his sacrifice, and now a free intercourse can be carried on. "THROUGH HIM WE HAVE ACCESS BY ONE SPIRIT UNTO THE FATHER."

THE END.

www.ingramcontent.com/pod-product-compliance
Lightning Source LLC
LaVergne TN
LVHW020916110826
845150LV00004B/690